The Yoga of Siddha Tirumūlar

(Essays on the Tirumandiram)

T.N. Ganapathy
KR. Arumugam
Dr. Geetha Anand

The Yoga Siddha Research Center
Publication Series No. 6

Babaji's Kriya Yoga and Publications, Inc.
St. Etienne de Bolton, Quebec, Canada

THE YOGA OF SIDDHA TIRUMULAR **Rs. 675/-**
by T.N. Ganapathy, KR. Arumugam

First published in January 2006 by
Babaji's Kriya Yoga Publications, Inc.,
196 Mountain Road, P.O. Box 90
Eastman, Quebec, Canada J0E 1P0
Tel: 450-297-0258; 1-888-252-9642
email: info@babaji.ca web: www.babaji.ca

Book design: Vinod Kumar R.C.
Printed and bound in India

Distributed by: Babaji's Kriya Yoga Trust
P.O. Box 5608, Malleswaram West, Bangalore, India 560 055
Tel: (91) (080) 23560252, 9845661221 email: india@babajiskriyayoga.in

Library and Archives Canada Cataloguing in Publication
The Yoga of Tirumular: essays on the Tirumandiram / by T.N. Ganapathy, KR. Arumugam.

(Yoga Siddha Research Series; No. 6)
Includes bibliographical references and index.
ISBN 1-895383-21-8

1. Yoga. 2. Tantrism. 3. Saivism. 4. Philosophy, Hindu.
I. Arumugam, K.R., 1971- II. Title. III.Series

BL1281.845.G35.2005 294.5'436 C2005-903597-8

CONTENTS

FOREWORD

I

Thanks to the tireless efforts of M. Govindan of Babaji's Kriya Yoga and Publications, the Ramakrishna Mission and the late Swami Subramanya of Hawaii, Tirumūlar is now well known in the West. The present work by T.N. Ganapathy and KR. Arumugam, *The Yoga of Siddha Tirumūlar*, ventures to present an in-depth study of Tirumūlar's monumental work, the *Tirumandiram.*

Tradition cherishes it as one of the important Śaivite scriptures. Tirumūlar who can be considered to belong to the 5th Century A.D. believed that the Śaivism of his times was not only a religion with a convincing philosophy and Yoga system but that it formed an integral part of our mundane life also.

The Philosophy of the Tirumandiram

After surveying various *pramāṇas* or *aḷavais* (processes of acquiring valid knowledge), the author of this chapter states that Śaiva Siddhānta accepts only three processes *(aḷavais)*—perception, inference, and testimony. He has considered in depth the views of Tirumūlar about God, soul and the world (Pati, paśu and pāśa). He explains both the accidental nature and the essential nature of God as delineated in Śaiva Siddhānta in the times of Tirumūlar. He has often quoted the *Tirumandiram* to explain the following concepts of Śaiva Siddhānta:

1. Māyā
    a. śuddha-māyā
    b. aśuddha-māyā
2. Karma

3. Āṇava
4. Nature of the soul
5. States of the soul (stages of consciousness)
6. The soul's liberation and
7. The nature of the soul in the state of release.

Śaivism as Conceived in the Tirumandiram

Tirumūlar's philosophy was based on the religious concepts of Śaivism, which spoke of the four steps *sāloka, sāmīpa, sārūpa* and *sāyujya* in order to reach Śiva. The popular myths about it are re-interpreted by Tirumūlar to explain the metaphysical truths behind them.

The Yoga of the Tirumandiram

The author interprets Yoga as a means by which the basic features of the individual, namely, the physical body, the vital current, mind, consciousness and energy get mobilized and harmonized.

Tirumūlar has founded a new tradition in Tamil which goes beyond Patañjali's concept of Yoga. To Tirumūlar, Siddhas are yogins who practice Śiva-Yoga and have attained Śiva-jñāna. These yogins are called *jīvan-muktas; jīvan-mukti* (liberation while living) is a state of embodied wisdom in which the yogin's attainment transforms all aspects of human life.

The author reveals similarities between the Tāntric school of Yoga and the Yoga of Tirumūlar by analyzing Laya-Yoga. Laya-Yoga is concerned with the functioning of the kuṇḍalinī, the cosmic power that is inherent in the human body. He considers Laya-Yoga as the highest form of Haṭha-Yoga, though its lower stages are now claimed to be Yoga in the Western countries.

The cakra system extolled by Tirumūlar is an important component of the Laya-Yoga. The author of this chapter has viewed it in the right perspective and appreciates it as one of the subtle operative powers. The cakras are believed to be awakened by the kuṇḍalinī—the form of the great cosmic power in the individual body. The awakening corresponds to the predominant psychological states and the levels of spiritual consciousness, the aspirant has attained. Kuṇḍalinī-Yoga is a technique for transforming ordinary consciousness into supreme consciousness.

The function of prāṇāyāma (the control of breath and prāṇā) is to awaken the cakras and thus facilitate the rising kuṇḍalinī through them.

An important element of Tantra-Yoga is the use of mantras and *maṇḍalas*. The *Tirumandiram* is a repository of many mantras. The author has given the right explanation to these mantras, the focus being on *bīja-mantras* (the syllable seeds). He defines the *bīja-mantras* as the concentration of the vital force at a point where its sound emitting power gets exhibited.

According to Tirumūlar, the sphere of the six ādhāras is classified into three *maṇḍalas, agni* (fire), *sūrya* (sun) and *candra* (moon). Tirumūlar devotes a separate chapter to describe in detail the powers of these *maṇḍalas*. There is an exclusive discussion in this book on Pariyaṅga-Yoga of Tirumūlar. It is called Maithuna-Yoga in which the semen instead of getting ejected is sublimated upwards.

The author considers Pariyaṅga-Yoga as a type of Yoga in which the heroic yogin and his consort participate in the great banquet, a secret sex ritual, which culminates in their act of intercourse. It is an expression to show that the yogin's sensory tumult is stilled, paving way for an ever-increasing identity with the cosmic consciousness.

The Mysticism of the Tirumandiram

According to Tirumūlar, mystical experience is a state of transcendental awareness or a state of oneness. The author analyzes the various levels of consciousness which pertain to Tirumūlar's concept of mysticism and mystic experience. Here, the Tamil terms, *yōga-samādhi, corugi-k-kiḍakkum-tuṟai, veṭṭaveḷi, tūṅgi-k-kaṇḍēṉ*, etc., are well explained. The five divisions of consciousness according to Tirumūlar are *jāgrat, svapna, suṣupti, turiya* and *turiyātīta*. Tirumūlar considers them as being experienced at five levels—*kevala, madhya-jāgrat, śuddha, para* and a still higher level.

The Twilight Language of the Tirumandiram

The Siddhas usually employ a paradoxical language to describe mystical experiences. The meaning of their poems has to be understood at two levels:

1. The exoteric and the linguistic and
2. The esoteric and the symbolic.

Tirumūlar too follows the same pattern. The author of this chapter analyzes and classifies the language adopted by Tirumūlar and identifies more than ten kinds, which are characterized by various kinds of symbols. In one chapter Tirumūlar has composed all the verses in this twilight language. The author has taken great pains to bring out their hidden meaning.

The Concept of the Human Body in the Tirumandiram

Metamorphosing of the *sthūla-deha* (the ordinary physical body) into *divya-deha* is called *kāya-sādhana*. The *Tirumandiram* specifically assures us that the jīva moves from one body to the other in reincarnation. *Kāya-sādhana* implies a change of perspective where physical existence is not denied but replaced by a permanent spiritual existence.

When a body is tempered by yogic techniques, one attains the *yoga-deha*. The ordinary physical body is "burnt out" through continual exposure to the fire of Yoga. For this purpose, the Siddhas have used the following techniques, *cāgā-t-talai, vēgā-k-kāl, pōgā-p-puṉal.* Saint Rāmaliṅgar too has referred to *śuddha-deha, praṇava-deha* and *jñāna-deha.*

The Concept of Guru in the Tirumandiram

A guru (spiritual preceptor) to Tirumūlar is an illuminator who imparts knowledge and helps the disciple glow with spiritual knowledge. A guru is a person who has realized the self (self-realization is the state of the guru becoming Śiva Himself). It is a state of unitive experience where there is no distinction between the guru and Śiva.

The Social Concern of the Tirumandiram

The Indian thought does not demand of a yogin the renunciation of the world itself. True saṁnyāsa (renunciation) means only the renouncement of desires. Being kind towards other beings (love thy neighbor as thy self) is an important tenet in Tirumūlar's spiritual work. Tirumūlar's message is:

One the caste
One the God
Thus intense hold
No more death will be.

These lines hint at the highest goal of life, i.e., attainment of the love of God. It is possible only through our loving attitudes towards other beings without any discrimination.

The author classifies the ethical principles of Tirumūlar into two classes:

1. The ethics which is prior to realization and
2. The ethics which is the result of realization.

Though Tirumūlar accepted the transitoriness of the body, he knew well its value as an excellent instrument to succeed in one's spiritual endeavors. Hence, he gives suggestions to enrich the instrument (the body) through observance of medical and ethical principles. He even shows the way for the delivery of defectless birth of progenies. The scope of the *Tirumandiram* is not only the advancement of the individual, but the welfare of the whole society.

II

It appears from the epic Maṇi-mēgalai that Śaivism did not have a great following in Tamil Nadu before the times of Tirumūlar. Buddhism and Jainism enjoyed greater respect then. Besides Śaivism there also existed the Vedic faith, which considered Vedas to be the only object of worship. The scholars were aware of the darśanas —Būta-vāta, Sāṁkhya, Nyāya and Upaniṣads.

Vedāntic thoughts could have evolved only after Maṇi-mēgalai, which belongs to the third century A.D. The Āgamas of Śaivism could have been composed in Sanskrit only then. The works in Sanskrit were only based on those in Tamil. These works incorporated *yāgas* and mantras in a way that suited them. (Refer: P.T. Srinivasa Iyengar, *History of the Tamils*, chapter on "The Rise of the Agamas." Also refer: V. Ponniah, *The Saiva Siddhanta Theory of Knowledge*, p. 7).

Śaivism which had the four divisions of *carya*, *kriya*, *yoga* and *jñāna* and included temple worship, rituals, *homas* (oblations in fire), methods of initiation into religion, spiritual practices and the search for ultimate truth could have developed only during this period.

Tirumūlar's reference to the concept that Vedas and Āgamas were different appears to suggest that the Āgamas in Sanskrit did not follow the Vedic faith.

There had been many attempts to blend the Vedic faith and the faith of the Tamil people. While Vedas came to be considered the basic and common scriptures, the Āgamas were viewed as specific works. The Śaivites began equating Lord Śiva with the ultimate power spoken about in the Upaniṣads called Brahman. It was believed that the chief God referred to by the Āgamas was none other than Śiva.

As Tirumūlar lived during the formative stage of Śaivism, his attempts had been chiefly to compile all that had been said about Śaivism; explanations are only very brief. The four steps beginning with *carya*, the four ways beginning with *dāśa-mārga*, the two types of liberation—*pada-mukti* and *para-mukti*, *śakti-nipādam* (God's grace) types of experience etc., have been mentioned as facts and not discussed as the different aspects of Śaivite philosophy.

Though Vedic faith and the Tamil people's faith were coming together in Tirumūlar's times, Tirumūlar categorically points to the separate identity of Tamil faith.

The Lord, however, gave me a good birth,
So that I may sing His glory in sweet Tamil.

The lines of Tirumūlar clearly show his faith in the Tamil religious heritage as well as his aim in life to compose Āgamas in Tamil. In fact, the *Tirumandiram* is the first Āgama in Tamil. The stress by Tirumūlar on the path of love to be the basis of Śaivism reinforces the immemorial faith of the Tamil people. Tirumūlar's insistence on love can be well inferred from the invocatory verses of the *Tirumandiram*.

Tirumūlar states firmly that Yoga cannot be beneficial without love. Combining the Vedic concept of one God and the belief of the Tamil religion that all men are born of the same, Tirumūlar coins a new concept—One caste and one God.

Yoga is being one with God. A devotee being one with Śiva is called Śiva-Yoga. In the ascent of the ten steps in spiritual growth (daśa-kārya), Śiva-Yoga is the ninth step.

To the questions,

1. Who is Śiva?
2. Who are we?
3. Are we not different from Śiva?
4. Is it possible to be one with Him? etc.,

Tirumūlar affirms that being one with Him is certainly possible. The means to attain Śiva is to be conscious of the significance of "One caste and one God." To know how it is attainable we need to reflect on the following verse:

One the caste; One the God
Thus intense hold,
No more death will be
None other is Refuge, with confidence you can seek
Think of Him and be redeemed,
In your thoughts, holding Him steadfast.

Before analyzing the verse it would be helpful to consider the following:

1. Love and Śivam are not different; Śiva is Love. According to Tirumūlar this is a fundamental concept of Yoga. How are we to reconcile this with the concept that Śiva is grace-personified and that human soul is love-personified?

2. We need to remind ourselves that Śiva, who is manifest in all, is manifest in our minds also.

He is the One within, He is the light within
He moves not a wee bit from within
He and your heart are thus together
But the heart His Form knows not.

How are we to identify the hidden Śiva in us? There are quite a few ways. An inkling of Śiva is possible in nature's beauty, in music, in sounds of mantras and in mystic experiences.

Tirumūlar feels that the ability to consider others as oneself, service to society and being charitable can also facilitate our efforts to be one with Śiva. This is suggested by the above reference that there is only one caste and one God.

Living beings are innumerable and men have been classified into many castes. However, there is no real difference among them. Their intelligence, talents and qualifications may vary; in aliveness and love, there is no place for difference. Further, there is ground to unite all the beings for it is the same God who manifests in all. God being One, there can be only one caste, according to Tirumūlar.

Tirumūlar has well blended his knowledge obtained by yogic practice, the knowledge of other Śiva-yogins as well as the facts from the Upaniṣads and Āgamas to offer us what he calls Vedānta-Siddhānta faith. His work *Sadaśiva Āgama* is only a book on the faith of wisdom, as wisdom is the consequence of reflections about feelings and experiences, the stages of it (wisdom) get stated first.

Yogic practice causes vibrations all over the body. It enables us to experience the vibration from the waist (mūlādhāra) to the scalp (sahasrāra). It is averred that this vibration goes twelve inches above the scalp. During the course of such experience, visualizing a light in between the brows and at the top of the head are considered the best. The spirit (jīva) in us is supposed to grow by such experiences.

This (same) spirit is called jīva, when it resides within the body and called soul (ātman), once it is out of it. The significance of Śiva-Yoga is that it helps life (the spirit within) attain wisdom, joy and oneness with Śiva even while alive.

III

I was really elated to write a Foreword to this important work. This is the first work to present a comprehensive and clear explanation of the contents of the *Tirumandiram* for the reader of the English language.

Suba. Annamalai

11th May 2005.
98, Arignar Anna Nagar,
Madurai – 625 020

PREFACE

The *Tirumandiram* is known as the refined Tamil Agama *(centamiḻ Āgamam)*. According to the Śaiva tradition of Tamil Nadu, there are twelve *Tirumuṟais*, i.e., sacred Tamil Saiva scriptures. They are:

1. Tiru-jñāṉa-cambandar - *Tēvāram*—constituting the first three *Tirumuṟais*.
2. Tiru-nāvukkaracar - *Tēvāram*—constituting the 4th, 5th and 6th *Tirumuṟais*
3. Cundara-mūrti - *Tēvāram*—constituting the 7th *Tirumuṟai*
4. Māṇikka-vācagar - *Tiru-vācagam*—constituting the 8th *Tirumuṟai*
5. Nine Śaiva Saints - *Tiru-v-icai-p-pā* and *Tiru-p-pallāṇḍu* (a collection of poems)—constituting the 9th *Tirumuṟai*
6. Tirumūlar - *Tirumandiram*—constituting the 10th *Tirumuṟai*
7. Twelve Śaiva Saints - A collection of works—constituting the 11th *Tirumuṟai*
8. Cēkkiḻār - *Periya-purāṇam*—constituting the 12th *Tirumuṟai*

All the above *Tirumuṟais* are called *tōttirams* (*stotras*—devotional literature), which constitute the bhakti literature of Tamil Śaivism. The philosophical literature of Tamil Śaivism is called *cāttirams* (śāstras—philosophical treatises). The *Tirumandiram* is the only *Tirumuṟai*, which is both a *cāttiram* and a *tōttiram* in Tamil Śaiva tradition.

The *Tirumandiram* is a work with a little more than three thousand stanzas written in *kali-viruttam* metre. It consists of nine sections called *tantirams* of different length with varying subject-matter. Calling the different sections of a work as *tantiram* is not to be found in any other classical Tamil work except in the *Tirumandiram*. *Tantiram*, following the Sanskrit meaning, stands for elaborate statement. It means Āgama or scripture, what has come down from tradition. Each *tantiram* contains several *adhikārams* (sections) showing the method of attaining the blissful state. There are totally 232 *adhikārams*. The whole work has been classified into three parts—namely, *tantra*, *mantra*, and *upadeśa*. *Tantiram (tantirams* 1, 2, and 3 of the *Tirumandiram)* deals with karma, mantra (*tantirams* 4, 5, and 6) deals with *upāsana* or worship and *upadēśa* or spiritual teachings (*tantirams* 7, 8, and 9) deals with jñāna.

In verse 62 of the *Tirumandiram*, Tirumūlar says that he got the nine Āgamas from God. Hence the Śaiva tradition as delineated by Tirumūlar is called the Āgamāntam or the Siddhānta Śaivam.

Though the *Tirumandiram* is treated basically as a Śaiva Siddhānta classic, i.e., a classic of Tamil Śaiva philosophical tradition, it has the unique privilege of being called a pioneer work on the Tamil Siddha tradition as well. While the four great *camayācāriyas*, i.e., the four Śaivite saints, Appar, Cambandar, Cundarar and Māṇikka-vācagar may be called religious men, Tirumūlar may be called the man of spirituality (and philosophy as well). These religious men worshipped God as Śivaṉ in the various temples situated in Tamil Nadu. According to Na. Subramanian, Tiru-jñāṉa-cambandar worshipped the deities in 262 temples, Tiru-nāvukkaracar (Appar) worshipped in 191 temples and

Cundarar in 83 temples (*Tirumūlar Tiru-neṟi*, p. 20). But in the case of Tirumūlar one does not find any reference in the *Tirumandiram* that he worshipped the individual deities in any particular temple. According to Tirumūlar the best form of worship is not flower worship, but it is non-killing even an atom of life and the best place of worship is the heart where the soul resides (verse 197). He does not seem to have sung poems in praise of gods and goddesses of local temples as done by the Nāyaṉmārs and the Āḻvārs. This is a significant feature that distinguishes Tirumūlar from the other Śaiva saints. This feature is one of the characteristic features of a Siddha. A Siddha believes in a Supreme Being but not a God of this or that religion. Tirumūlar feels that rigid theism has been responsible for a good deal of unnecessary controversy and hostility among the followers of different religions (verses 1568 and 1533). Even though Tirumūlar speaks of the religious aspect of God, he believed in a Supreme abstraction "Śivam" without any limitation or attributes. Śivam is grammatically and philosophically an impersonal conception. As the Siddhas say, the ideal name for Śivam is "It" or "Adu" or "Thatness" or "Suchness" or "Parāparam." From the perspective of the Tamil Śaiva tradition one may view *Tirumandiram* as a *purely* philosophic, Śaiva Siddhānta treatise calling it as Āgamāntam. Yet one can view *Tirumandiram* as a Siddha work as well. To borrow Shelly's phrase, the *Tirumandiram* is a precious diamond stone, which has a spectrum of many colors. A deeper study of the concept of Śiva would reveal that it took two channels in Indian thought, one theistic with a personal or devotional relationship to God based on the method of bhakti, and the other Tāntric, i.e., absolutist, based on Kuṇḍalinī-Yoga and jñāna. Kailāsapathy has made a distinction between the use of the terms "civaṉ" and "civam." He writes:

> ... the Siddhas were not devotees in the sense of idol-worshippers... They believed in a Supreme Abstraction. The recurrent use by the Siddhas of the word *civam* (an abstract noun meaning 'goodness,' auspiciousness' and the highest state of God, in which He exists as pure intelligence) in preference to the common term *civaṉ* (meaning Śiva), makes this point very clear. In other words, they believed in an abstract idea of Godhead rather than a personal God ("The Writings of the Siddhas," p. 313).

In this connection it is worthwhile to note the observations of Na. Subramanian. He says that in *Tolkāppiyam* it is said that the ancient Tamils worshipped a nameless, formless God as *kandaḻi*. He also says that Ka. Subramania Pillai interpreted the term *kandaḻi* as the name of fire (*Tirumūlar Tiru-neṟi*, p. 15). Both these interpretations can be applied to the *Tirumandiram* since it speaks of the formless Śiva as well as the inner fire in one's self. The section on *Nava-kuṇḍam* in *tantra* four speaks of the inner fire, which may be termed as Kuṇḍalinī fire.

Tirumūlar refers to Śivam as love. His basic philosophy is love—an unadulterated, pure, spiritual love—that expects no bargain nor results. His burden of the song is love, which is reflected in many of his verses (270, 272-274, 276, 279, 280-282, 286, 287, 416, 1005, 1456 and 2980). The three great statements of Tirumūlar are: (i) Love is God (*aṉbē civam*, verse 270); (ii) Let the whole world attain the bliss that I have received (*yāṉ peṟṟa iṉbam peṟuga i-v-vaiyam*, verse 85), and (iii) Mankind is one family and God is one (*oṉṟē kulamum oruvaṉē tēvaṉum*, verse 2104). All these mahā-vākyas of the *Tirumandiram* are the different ways of expressing that the Supreme Thing is love and love only. Love is bliss which can be attained by anyone and hence mankind, nay, the world, is one family with love (God) as the basis. To prevent the eruption of egoism, which is the anti-thesis of love, Tirumūlar has bestowed to the world the śāstra (treatise) of the *Tirumandiram* (verse 87).

The basis of Yoga or union is love. Only through love one is merged with Śivam. *Śiva-aikya* or Yoga is possible only through love. Tirumūlar says,

> Like the sweet-love in sex-act experienced,
> So in the Great love, let yourself to Him succumb. (verse 283)

Tirumūlar calls Yoga as Śiva-Yoga (verse 122). It is the method by which the jīva identifies itself with Śiva. He calls Śiva-Yoga as the new type of Yoga *(nava-yōga)*. By calling it as *nava-yōga* Tirumūlar indicated that this new type of Yoga was not in vogue before him in the Tamil country. It is for the first time that this Yoga is *explicitly explained and discussed* in the *Tirumandiram*. Though Tirumūlar does not use the expression Kuṇḍalinī-Yoga in any place in the *Tirumandiram*, what is discussed as Śiva-Yoga by him is Kuṇḍalinī-Yoga, since he speaks of cakras, prāṇāyāma, Pariyaṅga-Yoga, twilight language, etc. Tirumūlar develops Aṣṭāṅga-Yoga as Śiva-Yoga. But its message is wider than Patañjali's *Yoga-Sūtras*. Therefore, we may safely say that the *Tirumandiram* is a seminal work in Tamil, and is the first treatise, which deals with the different aspects of the Kuṇḍalinī-Yoga, under the name Śiva-Yoga. Thus this great work began a new tradition in Tamil.

In the *Tirumandiram*, Tirumūlar explains six types of "ends" of philosophical discussions. The expression *anta* stands for the term "end." *Anta* is the sum and substance of any system of thought.

The six types of *antas* (ends) are *Vedānta, Siddhānta, Yogānta, Kālānta, Nadānta* and *Bhogānta*. In the *Tirumandiram* one finds far more concepts and explanation of Yoga *(Yogānta)* and *Siddhānta*, than of the other four *antas.*

Tirumūlar refers to his method as *tiru-neṟi* or the Supreme Path or the divine path (verse 54). He refers to his work as an Āgama (verse 73). He expresses how happy he feels that the Lord has given him a good birth so that he may sing His glory in sweet Tamil (verse 81). He says that God has bestowed him with His grace to write the Tamil work the *Tirumandiram* in order to prevent the eruption of egoism among the human beings. He says that God has made him to include all aspects of the Tamil śāstras in it (verse 87), and states that he has explained all the categories of philosophy in his work (verse 90). Tirumūlar says that he belongs to the Kailāya-tradition (verse 91) and expresses his modesty by saying that he has very poor qualifications to sing the praise of the Lord (verse 96). Yet he says that he has rendered this work after the Lord thoroughly tested him and his ability. He states: "After interrogation holy, testing me entire He revealed to me the real, the unreal and the real-unreal" (verse 1573). This testing and interrogation by the Lord is a form of *dīkṣā* (empowerment) by the guru, which may be termed as *satya-nirvāṇa-dīkṣā* (in Tamil *cutta-urai*), an empowerment bestowing true liberation from the bonds of the carnal body.

Though there are different views regarding the *Tirumandiram*, it is to be treated without any doubt, as a major work in Tamil on Tantra-śāstra. A clue to this can be found in verse 2422, wherein Tirumūlar says that the purity of the jīva can be attained through pāśa or attachment itself. He says that just as the cloth's dirt is removed by earth-dirt (saline-earth), pāśa is removed by pāśa. This is a basic Tantra concept; just as a washer man makes a very dirty cloth clean with some water which itself is dirty or as some water which accidentally goes into one's ears is taken out by the help of some additional water itself, Tirumūlar says that one can get rid of pāśa by pāśa itself. The *Kulārṇava Tantra* says that man should learn to raise himself by that which carries his fall (John Woodroffe and M.P. Pandit, ed., *Kulārṇava Tantra*, "...success is achieved by these very things which lead to fall." p. 8). The same idea is reflected in a Buddhist Tāntric work, *Advaya Siddhi*, which says:

> By those self same terrific deeds which create bondage for beings, one can be liberated from the bondage of this world, if these are accompanied by the upāya. (7, p. 26).

Tirumūlar expresses the same idea by calling it the wisdom's way (verse 2033). His Pariyaṅga-Yoga is an expression of this basic concept of the Tantra.

One finds a lot of interpretations and commentaries on the *Tirumandiram* in Tamil. We have the commentary by Sivaprakasa Desigar, by Dandapani Desigar, by G. Varadharajan, by P. Ramanatha Pillai, and a critical edition and explanation of the *Tirumandiram* in three volumes by Suba. Annamalai, not to speak of the critical essays and monographs on the *Tirumandiram* by Tudisai Kilar A. Chidambaranar, P. Varadharajan, Sathiyavel Muruganar, N. Subramanian and others. There is a commentary on the *Tirumandiram* by Kailaya-c-cittar, which is treated as a non-Siddhanta interpretation. Apart from these critical commentaries and monographs there is a multitude of popular books on the *Tirumandiram*, big and small, and one may mention here the books by Yogi Suddhananda Bharati, Rajaji-Somu, Dr. P. Arunachalam, Tiru. Sambandham, etc. There is a small Tamil book exclusively dealing with the *yantras* in the *Tirumandiram* by C.S. Murugesan. One book dealing with the technical terms of Śaiva Religion as used in the *Tirumandiram* has been written by A.M. Parimanam. Though there is only one English translation of the *Tirumandiram* by B. Natarajan, Sathiyavel Muruganar (in his Tamil book on *Tirumandiram – An Introduction*) states that an English translation of the *Tirumandiram* has been undertaken by one Sankar, a Government Auditor in South Africa. More information is yet to be collected on this translation.

In this connection it may be noted that the Yoga Siddha Research Center, Chennai has undertaken (from April 15th 2005, i.e., Tamil New Year's day) a mammoth project of translating all the verses of the *Tirumandiram* in English with the Tamil verse, its transliteration, its word by word meaning, its translation and its commentary. This work has been undertaken by a team of scholars consisting of Dr. T.N. Ramachandran, Sri. T.V. Venkataraman, Dr. S.N. Kandaswamy, Dr. KR. Arumugam and Dr. T.N. Ganapathy who will also be the editor, and the coordinator of this work.

To sum up, in short, the *Tirumandiram* is a work, which deals with how one may live a divine life in the midst of the worldly one. It fulfils the meaning of the word "Tantra" a "web" which joins the spiritual and the material dimensions of life. It expresses the thread of unity, which exists behind the many differences of time, country, language, caste, religion, higher and lower, happiness and misery, wealth and poverty. It deals with all the aspects of life, which makes life worth-living by dealing with dharma, *artha*, *kāma*, *mokṣa*, *tapas*, Yoga, jñāna, siddhi, *buddhi*, *mukti*, planets, days, the art of breathing, mantra, *tantra*, *yantra*, cakras, meditation, medicine, etc. In short, it is a Tamil encyclopedia of philosophical and spiritual wisdom rendered in verse form.

This book which is named as *The Yoga of Siddha Tirumūlar* does not purport to cover all the ideas, concepts and topics discussed in the *Tirumandiram*. The aim of the work is to provide a critical understanding of the basic ideas in the *Tirumandiram* so that it may stimulate readers to make a detailed study of the work. With this idea in mind the authors have written the chapters, which bring out the salient features of the *Tirumandiram*.

In this task the authors acknowledge their indebtedness to the sponsors, the Babaji's Kriya Yoga Order of Acharyas, USA, Inc., and its President Sri Govindan Satchidananda and his wife Smt. Durga Ahlund Govindan and Sri Neelakantan, the Secretary of the Babaji's Kriya Yoga Order of Acharyas Trust, Bangalore and for their constant and consistent encouragement to bring out this volume as "a curtain raiser" to the forthcoming translation of the poems of the *Tirumandiram* by a team of scholars. Sri Govindan and Smt. Durga have made their significant contributions by going through the chapters carefully and making suggestions for a better understanding of the chapters. Our grateful thanks are due to Dr. M. Tamizhchelvaṉ, Librarian, Sri Krishna College of Engineering and Technology, Coimbatore, in preparing the index for this work and to Professor T.B. Siddhalingaiah for patiently putting the diacritical marks.

We are immensely grateful to Professor Suba. Annamalai for having favored us with a thoughtful foreword.

Through out this work the authors have followed the numbering of verses of the *Tirumandiram* as found in the Śaiva Siddhānta Mahā Samājam edition (1940) of it and for English translation, they have followed Sri B. Natarajan's translation, published by Sri Ramakrishna Math (1991) and by Babaji's Kriya Yoga and Publications, 1992.

Our salutations to Tirumūlar who has been constantly guiding us by his spiritual vision and love in our attempt to understand him. As Kamban̲ speaks of his work on Rāmāyaṇa, we, the authors, try to drink the grand ocean of the milk called the *Tirumandiram* by licking it like small kitten.

T.N. Ganapathy

11th May 2005.

The Yoga Siddha Research Centre,
"Rajkamal," 45 (21), 4th Avenue, Ashok Nagar,
Chennai – 600 083
Phone: (044) 4202 9150 / 2489 7396
Email: tngana@yahoo.com

Guide to Pronunciation in Tamil

Transliteration Table

Vowels

Short		Long	
அ	a	ஆ	ā
இ	i	ஈ	ī
உ	u	ஊ	ū
எ	e	ஏ	ē
ஒ	o	ஓ	ō

ஐ – ai

ஔ – au

ஃ – k̲, ḥ

Consonants

Hard		Soft		Medial	
க்	k/g	ங்	ṅ	ய்	y
ச்	c, j	ஞ்	ñ (jñ)	ர்	r
ட்	ṭ/ḍ	ண்	ṇ	ல்	l
த்	t/d	ந்	n	வ்	v
ப்	p/b	ம்	m	ழ்	ḻ
ற்	ṟ	ன்	ṉ	ள்	ḷ

Grantha Letters

ஸ் – s ஷ் – ṣ ஹ் – h ஜ் – j

க்ஷ – kṣ, ksh

Note:

All Tamil and Sanskrit words are transliterated and italicized. The following popular words are not italicized:

Āgama, āṇava, Aum, cakra, cit-śakti, dharma, guru, iḍa, jñāna, jñāni, jīva, karma, kuṇḍalinī, kuṇḍalinī-śakti, liṅga, māyā, mahāvākya, mala, mantra, mutt, nāḍi, names of the six ādhāras, nirvāṇa, pañcākṣara, pāśa, paśu, Pati, piṅgala, prāṇa, Praṇava, prāṇāyāma, sahasrāra, śakti, śāstra, sādhaka, sādhana, samādhi, Siddha, siddhi, Śivāyanama/Namaśivāya, śūnya, suṣumna, Tantra, tattva, Veda, Yoga, yogin, etc.

Chapter 1

Introduction

KR. Arumugam

tirumūla dēvaṉaiyē cindai ceyvārkku-k
karumūlam illaiyē kāṇ.

For those who meditate on Tirumūlar,
Their birthroot is uprooted.

–Anonymous

1. INTRODUCTION

KR. Arumugam

The *Tirumandiram* is a Tamil classic. It is a spiritual treasure trove. This book, *The Yoga of Siddha Tirumūlar,* is an attempt to throw light on the *Tirumandiram.* An effort is made in this book to give an overall view of the *Tirumandiram.*

The Tamil Śaiva religious literature is classified into two types: *tōttirams* and *cāttirams* (*stotras* and śāstras). *Tōttirams* are the works that praise the Lord. They constitute the *bhakti* literature of Tamil Śaivism. *Cāttirams* are the works that philosophize Śaivism, that is, they constitute the philosophical literature of Tamil Śaivism. Normally the *tōttirams* and the *cāttirams* are mutually exclusive. But the *Tirumandiram,* though it is traditionally included in the *tōttiram,* that is, in the *bhakti* literature, it enjoys the status of *cāttiram* also, that is, the philosophical literature. It is a rare privilege that no other Śaiva literature enjoys.

1. The author

The author of the *Tirumandiram* is Tirumūlar. The primary source of the biographical details of Tirumūlar is the Tamil work known as the *Periya-purāṇam,* authored by Cēkkiḻār. The *Periya-purāṇam* is a work which gives the life stories of all the sixty-three saints *(Nāyaṉmārs)* of Śaivism. Though Tirumūlar is a Siddha, he is popularly known as a Śaiva saint of the Siddhānta tradition and hence his biography is included in the *Periya-purāṇam.* The other sources are Nambiyāṇḍār Nambi's *Tiru-t-toṇḍar Tiru-v-andādi,* Umāpaty Śivacāriyār's *Tiru-t-toṇḍar-purāṇa-cāram,* Swaminatha Tambiran's *Tiru-v-āvaḍu-tuṟai-p-purāṇam,* Dandapani Swamigal's *Pulavar-purāṇam,* and the *Agastiyar Vaittiya-rattiṉa-c-curukkam-300.* We may also find some accounts in A. Cidambaranar's article on Tirumūlar's biography.[1]

The *Periya-purāṇam* speaks of the life story of Tirumūlar in detail under the title "Tirumūla-dēva Nayāṉar Purāṇam." The life sketch runs as follows:

After getting initiated by the graceful Nandi (Śiva) at Mount Kailāsh and attaining the *aṣṭa-mā-siddhis* (the eight supernatural powers) one yogin (who's original name is not given in the *Periya-purāṇam*) started for the southern hill called Podigai to meet and to spend some days in the company of his long time friend Agastya.

On his way to Podigai, the yogin visited Kedār-nāth, Paśupati-nāth (in Nepal), bathed in the Ganges, worshipped in Kāsi, and visited Vindhya and Parvata mountains. He then proceeded to Śrī Kāḷahasti, Tiru-v-ālaṅgāḍu, Kānchipuram, Tiru-v-adigai and to Chidambaram. After worshipping Lord Naṭarāja at Chidambaram he reached Tiru-v-āvaḍu-tuṟai, paid obeisance there and began to go towards Podigai.

On the way, on the banks of the river Kāvēri, he saw a herds of cows grieving over the death of their herdsman whose name was Mūlaṉ. Mūlaṉ was a resident of the nearby village Cāttaṉūr. Pitying the cows, the yogin, using his power of transmigrating into another's body, which is one of the eight siddhis, hiding his original body somewhere in safety, entered into the dead body of Mūlaṉ, the cowherd. The cows were happy over the return of their master. The yogin led the cows and drove them into the village and without entering stood outside the village.

The wife of Mūlaṉ was anxious about her husband, who still had not returned even after sunset, which was unusual. She came in search of her beloved husband and found him standing outside the village strangely. She rushed towards him and touched him. At her touch Mūlaṉ jerked and told her disinterestedly that there was no relationship existing between them and sat in meditation in the nearby mutt meant for the public. The surprised wife was dumbstruck and remained sleepless the whole night. She was afraid that her husband had gone mad. The next day she told the happenings to the villagers. All of them came to the spot. Seeing Mūlaṉ in meditation, his body glowing, the villagers understood that the strangeness in Mūlaṉ is not caused by madness, but by Śiva-Yoga. They pacified the wife of Mūlaṉ and asked her to leave the yogin alone to pursue the spiritual path in peace.

After spending some time in meditation the yogin came to the riverbank in search of his original body. It was not there where it was hidden by the yogin. Thinking that it was a play of Lord Śiva to make him live in the newly acquired body, the yogin left for Tiru-v-āvaḍu-tuṟai. (Tiru-v-āvaḍu-tuṟai was the name of the temple while Cāttaṉūr was the name of the village. Later the name of the temple became the name of the village). The yogin's name became Tirumūlar. (*Tiru* is a prefix in Tamil meaning "holy"). One should take note of this that the names and the worldly possessions are meant only for the mortal body and not for the immortal self. When the body changes, the name also changes, like in the episode of the yogin from Kailāsh, whose name is now changed to Mūlaṉ. The moral of the story is that one should let go all of one's attachments, worldly possessions, including body and one's name, which are impermanent. Why should one strive for fame while one's name itself is impermanent?

Tirumūlar sat there in Śiva-Yoga under an *araca-maram* (the king of trees), i.e., a pipal tree *(Ficus Religiosa)* situated west of the temple Tiru-v-āvaḍu-tuṟai. Once in a year he woke up from his meditative slumber and wrote one verse. Thus he wrote three thousand verses (which means he lived at least three thousand years in Śiva-Yoga). The three thousand verses he wrote are compiled as the *Tirumandiram.* Then he traveled to Mount Kailāsh and attained mahā-samādhi.

There is not much difference between the version of the *Periya-purāṇam* and the versions given in other sources, because the other sources are only secondary to the *Periya-purāṇam* except Nambi- yāṇḍār Nambi's *Tiru-t-toṇḍar Tiru-v-andādi,* which precedes the *Periya-purāṇam.* Only in the *Agattiyar Vaittiya-rattiṉa-c-curukkam-300* one finds a difference. We find it with a few more additions in the *Caturagiri-t-tala-purāṇam.*[2] This version is:

In the *Śveta-varāha-kalpa,* there was a king by name Śveta Mahā-rājaṉ, ruling over the country of Rājendra-pura of Pāṇḍiya kingdom. He was married to Cundara-vadaṉi and Candra-vadaṉi, the daughters of King Āditya, who was ruling another country with Aṉanta-nagar as its capital. The son born to Cundara-vadaṉi was named Vīra-ceṉaṉ and the three sons of Candra-vadaṉi were called Dharmārttaṉ, Cūra-ceṉaṉ and Vajraṅgadaṉ. Years rolled by and at the proper age Vīra-ceṉaṉ was married to Guṇa-vati, the daughter of the king of Mahara-pura. As Dharmārttaṉ happened to be the eldest, the king wanted to crown him as his successor. But, showing the legal and moral issues, Dharmārttaṉ refused to be crowned and insisted that the fittest son to be the successor was only Vīra-ceṉaṉ, his half-brother. The king was pleased and crowned Vīra-ceṉaṉ as the king of the country.

One day, when the king Vīra-ceṉaṉ was returning to the palace after completing his royal procession through the city, he saw a fascinating flower in the palace garden. Charmed by the flower, he plucked and smelt it, then fell to the ground dead. The royal physician was sent for, and he, after examining the body declared the king was dead. An uproar of weeping and crying arose through out the kingdom. Guṇa-vati 's grief was inconsolable.

Tirumūlar heard the outcries from the palace and understood what had happened. In order to help the grieving people, Tirumūlar decided to occupy the body of Vīra-ce<u>n</u>a<u>n</u>. He went to his hermitage, and instructed his disciple Guru-rāja-ṛṣi to protect the safety of the body, which he would leave in a cave. He, then, left his own body and transmigrated into the body of Vīra-ce<u>n</u>a<u>n</u>.

To the astonishment of all, Vīra-ce<u>n</u>a<u>n</u>, animated by Tirumūlar, rose up and he explained to Guṇa-vati and others that the drop of poison deposited on the flower petal by a venomous snake indeed had killed him, but he was brought back to life through the grace of a Siddha.

In due course, Guṇa-vati noticed that his way of moving with her, his mode of speech and other activities were different. Realizing that she was experiencing greater joy than before, one day Guṇa-vati requested him to explain the reason. Tirumūlar (now Vīra-ce<u>n</u>a<u>n</u>), revealed who he was and told her that only for the sake of the people he migrated into the body of Vīra-ce<u>n</u>a<u>n</u> and he would return to his hermitage within a short period. When Guṇa-vati asked what he would do if his original body had already been burnt or destroyed, he told that his original body was an immortalized one and it could be burnt only by certain process known only to him. He revealed to her the secret process of incinerating the immortalized body.

Guṇa-vati feared that once he left the palace, she would lose not only his company, but all her royal fortunes. So she conceived a plan of burning his original body. She secretly sent for some forest folks, gave them a lot of money, instructed them the process of burning the immortalized body which was in the cave and asked them to fulfill the deed. Meanwhile, very much concerned over the long absence of his guru, the disciple Guru-rāja had left the hermitage in search of his master. Finding the cave empty, the forest folks entered its inner chambers searching for the body and found and burnt it, as Guṇa-vati had directed.

Tirumūlar (i.e., Vīra-ceṉaṉ), deciding that it was time for him to go back to his hermitage, left the palace. He happened to meet along the way, Guru-rāja, who was in search of his master. Feeling full of apprehension, he reached the cave and he found that his original body had been burnt to ashes. Dismayed, he returned to the palace and led a disinterested life with Guṇa-vati. One day he finally relinquished the palace comforts and traveled towards the eastern side of Catura-giri. There on a riverbank, he saw the dead body of Jambukeśvara, a learned Brahmin of Tiru-v-āṉai-k-kā (Tiruchirappalli district of Tamil Nadu). Tirumūlar made a quick decision. He left the body of Vīra-ceṉaṉ, and placed it inside the hollow of a tree, which henceforth came to be known as *araca-maram* (king of trees, because it held a king's body within its hollow). He then transmigrated into the body of Jambukeśvara, revived that body and retired to the forest known as Kāḷi-vana, and soon lost himself in deep samādhi. When he came out of samādhi, literally thousands of verses with the highest principles of *Siddha-vidyā* poured out from him. Tirumūlar thereafter came to be known as Jambu-muni and Jambukeśa-muni. It is also stated that Tirumūlar belonged to the Kaikkōḷar (weaver) community.

One may find it hard to accept this story of Tirumūlar as narrated in the *Caturagiri-t-tala-purāṇam* and it seems to be mythical.

According to A. Cidambaranar's version, Tirumūlar was born in Tamil Nadu. He was named by his parents as Cundaraṉ. At a young age he joined the *Tamil-c-caṅgam* (The Tamil Academy – assembly of the learned) of Agastya, gained the friendship of Agastya, and he studied books of knowledge and excelled in learning. After completing his studies there, and wanting to know more, he traveled north to Mount Kailāsh. He learnt the Vedas and the Āgamas from Nandidevar and received the suffix *Nātha.* Cundaraṉ was in company with his co-disciples, Sanaka, Sanantana, Sanātana, Sanatkumāra, Śivayoga Māmuṉi, Patañjali, and Vyākrama.

While he was doing penance in Kailāsh, Patañjali and Vyākrama wanting to see the blissful dance of Lord Naṭarāja invited Cundara-nādar (Tirumūlar) to accompany them. Patañjali and Vyākrama stayed on in Chidambaram, however Cundara-nādar returned to Kailāsh to continue his penance. After some time he had traveled to the south again to meet his old friend Agastya. The remaining story is the same as in the *Periya-purāṇam.*

In the second canto of the *Agattiyar-12000,* Siddha Agastya states that Tirumūlar stayed on the northern side of Mount Meru and he initiated and instructed Lord Kṛṣṇa in the *dvāpara-yuga.* Mārkaṇḍeya also received initiation and instruction from Tirumūlar.

The *Bōgar-7000* says that Tirumūlar's father was a *ṛṣi* (a sage) and his mother was a lower caste woman (paḷḷar caste).[3]

Some of the data given in the *Periya-purāṇam* are found in the *Tirumandiram.* In one place Tirumūlar says that he lived for seven crore (seventy million) *yugas* (an age/aeon).[4] One should not take it literally at its face value. This should be interpreted in the sense that Tirumūlar had a prolonged life enough to accomplish his mission.

Everyone comes into this world with a mission and one's body is an instrument to fulfil the mission. When this mission is fulfilled, the job is over and one can be rid of one's instrument. Tirumūlar says singing the glory of the Lord in sweet Tamil,[5] rendering accessible the holy feet of the Lord to the worldly people[6] and guiding people to the utter bliss which he has attained are his life mission.[7] When this was done he discarded his body. Tirumūlar neither had a yearning to live long nor did he want to show off his abilities of living long. He lived to that extent his mission demanded and he shrugged off his mortal coil when things were over.

If it be so, is the statement of Tirumūlar that he remained for seventy million aeons a lie? Certainly not! In the state of samādhi time is transcended. Samādhi is transcending space and time and entering into *veṭṭa-veḷi* or *śūnya* or emptiness. We see people say after a short, sound sleep 'I slept well,' feeling as if they have slept for a long time, which is not the case. Sometimes even after a long, disturbed sleep people say 'I did not sleep well,' sounding as if they slept only for a short time. So it is not the time factor that determines sound sleep but the physical/mental condition. It is better to understand that in the state of samādhi, Tirumūlar was utterly indifferent about the category called time. It is difficult to calculate his longevity with no conclusive evidence.

In the *Tirumandiram,* Tirumūlar says that he was taught by Nandidēvar[8] and gives the names of his co-disciples, as stated in the *Periya-purāṇam.* (Most of A. Cidambaranar's version was drawn only from the *Tirumandiram.* But in no place Tirumūlar says that his original name was Cundaraṉ as Cidambaranar says. It was a possible misreading of the manuscript).

There are so many works that claim the authorship of Tirumūlar (see Appendix-A). It is worth noting here that Cēkkiḻār, who drafted the popularly accepted biography of Tirumūlar in his *Periya-purāṇam,* did not mention any other work written by Tirumūlar other than the *Tirumandiram.* Tirumūlar does not claim authorship of any work other than the *Tirumandiram.*

2. A Prologue to the Tirumandiram

In modern days the details of a work such as the name of the work, the name of the author, the name and address of the publisher, the year of publication, the price of the work, copyright details, cataloguing data, etc., are given in the reverse of the title page. A small introduction to the readers by the author, which invites the readers inside the work, is given in the preface. The efforts exerted by the author to write the work are mentioned in the foreword, which is written by someone else, who is considered to be a scholar in the area that the work deals with. The foreword also points out the features of the work, sometimes critical, generally appreciative.

All these details put together is called *pāyiram* in Tamil grammar. The term *pāyiram* may be translated as preface, introduction, preamble, prologue, synopsis, epitome, etc. This *pāyiram* is very much essential to take the reader to the heart of the work, without which his reading will be a clueless one. The Tamil grammar work the *Naṉṉūl* says, though a work may be extensive dealing with a thousand titles, if it does not have an introduction *(pāyiram)* it will not be considered as a work at all.[9]

This introduction is divided into two: general and special (in Tamil *podu* and *ciṟappu*). The general introduction is written by the author himself. The special introduction is written by others. Generally it is written by the teacher of the author or the student of the author or some other eminent scholar in that field. A work without a special introduction will resemble a city without towers and a woman without ornaments, says so a Tamil verse.

There is a story about Kambar the great poet, who re-created the epic *Rāmāyaṇa* in Tamil. Kambar, after completing the writing of his monumental work *Rāma-Kādai (Kamba-Rāmāyaṇa)*, went to present it in a platform of scholars.[10] Kambar was not allowed to present his work since it did not have a special introduction, i.e., *ciṟappu-p-pāyiram*. He was asked to get a special introduction for his work from Ambigā-pati, who was the only son of Kambar, and a renowned poet himself. Kambar approached Ambigā-pati and got a special introduction, so goes the story. This shows the importance given to the special introduction.[11]

It is defined that an introduction must have the following details:

1. The author's name
2. Source of the work
3. Territory of the work
4. Name of the work
5. The structure of the work
6. Subject-matter
7. People who can read the work
8. The end-result.[12]

The *Tirumandiram*, following the grammatical convention, starts with a *pāyiram*, that is, introduction. It has a general introduction, which is the rendering of the author Tirumūlar and it surely has a special introduction. But it is unknown who gave the special introduction to Tirumūlar. May be it was authored not by a single person but by many. May be after Tirumūlar some of his disciples might have done it. May be some of the inspired readers of the *Tirumandiram* might have done it. One does not know.

It is to be kept in mind that the present editions of the *Tirumandiram* do not carry the author's original arrangement. In the process of survival several verses were misplaced, interpolated and manipulated. This disarrangement starts right from the beginning and through out the work. Hence it becomes difficult

1) to differentiate between the original verses and the interpolations; and
2) to differentiate between the general introduction and the special introduction.

Anyhow it is better to start the process of introducing the *Tirumandiram* with the details given in the *pāyiram* (introduction) – without making any attempt to differentiate between the general and the special introductions, a task about which this book is not concerned with.

2. 1. The author's name

The name of the author is Tirumūlar. It is a combination of two terms *Tiru* and *Mūlar*. *Tiru* is an honorific prefix given to all saintly beings and *Mūlar* is the name of the physical body into which the adept from Mount Kailāsh entered. The name Mūlaṉ (the 'r' in *Mūlar* is a reverential ending of the name *Mūlaṉ*) can be found in many of the verses of the *Tirumandiram*.[13]

But there is a strong contention that the author's original name was Cundara-nādar. A. Cidambaraṉār and Sathiyavēl Muruganār claim so. They quote a verse from the *Tirumandiram* to support their view. The verse is:

vanda maḍamēḻum maṉṉumcaṉ mārkkattiṉ
mundi udikkiṉṟa mūlaṉ maḍavarai
tandiram oṉbadu cārvumū vāyiram
cundaraṉ āgama-c colmoḻin dāṉē.[14]

It is better to explain here one more difficulty in reading texts like the *Tirumandiram*, that is, the textual difference, known as *pāḍa-bēdam* in Tamil. Texts like the *Tirumandiram* were originally written in palm-leaves. In those days whoever wanted a copy of a work, which is in the form of palm-leaf manuscript, had to copy it himself. This process involves two– the reader and the copier. The one who is already having a copy (usually a teacher) will read it out and the one who wanted to copy it (usually a student) will write it down. It is a process of dictation. In this process there is every possibility of making mistakes either by the dictator or by the copier. "I said ear, he repeated year" says so a Tamil proverb. The reader or the teacher will be one and the copiers or students may be many. In a one-time reading many copies are created. Out of the copies thus created some may be exact copies of the original (that is the copy that had been read out by the teacher, which itself may have mistakes) and some may have some mistakes added here and there. This leaves us in confusion as to which version is correct and which version is corrupt, and to which version we have to subscribe, because even the corrupt versions pose some meaning.

When a version, which has so many mistakes, was copied, the already existing mistakes were multiplied in the new copies. In this way many of the verses became corrupt and these corruptions were not allowed to be corrected by the believers of the infallibility of their teachers and the corruptions were carried on and on. Fearing still more corruptions no body dare to make corrections to what had been handed over to them. Yogi S.A.A. Ramaiah– who had done enormous service to the cause of the Siddhas– advises:

> Do not alter even a single letter of the Siddha even if you happen to be a great Tamil Scholar. Stick on to every letter of

> the Siddha as long as it makes sense which may be different from scholarly misinterpretation. Do comment upon the verses separately and make a show of your scholarship and interpretation but spare the verses of the Siddhas from distortion. We, humans, with a pigeon intellect, cannot sit in judgement over the cosmic consciousness of the Siddhas.[15]

This is the typical mentality of the copy-writers, editors, compilers of the Siddha texts. The only way out is to collect all the available versions of a particular Siddha work, compare them, and to subscribe to the suitable version, which sounds more sensible. The difficulty is that the versions of the Siddha manuscripts are very limited in number, to facilitate comparison. Thinking that the Siddha works are inferior, people have not copied or collected them carefully. Even if one overcomes this difficulty and collects a sizeable number of versions to compare and correct the mistakes, the Siddha scholars would not accept the corrections. Their field of research demands them to read between the lines of the Siddha poetry, but often they cross the lines and read too many things beyond the lines. Minding the infallibility of the Siddhas they tend to read many things even in the corrupt versions. The Siddhas may not be fallible but the copiers are.

The task of fixing the mistakes in the other works of Tamil literature is easier because they do not have obscure meanings and a number of copies are available to compare and fix. But it is not the case with the Siddha literature and fixing the mistakes becomes a Herculean task. Dr. Suba. Annamalai is one who has made a brave and successful attempt in achieving the task by way of bringing out an edition with textual criticism for the *Tirumandiram* in three volumes by comparing several available texts and manuscripts.[16]

Keeping this difficulty in mind we will return to the problem concerning the name of Tirumūlar. Cidambaranar and Sathiyavel Muruganar argue that the original name of Tirumūlar– before his entering into the body of Mūlaṉ, the shepherd– was Cundaranādar. It is their contention that only after entering into the body of Mūlaṉ, Tirumūlar came to be known by that name. To support their view they quote a verse from the *Tirumandiram* mentioned earlier.

The verse can be translated freely thus:

Of the Seven monasteries emerged in the lineage of Kailāya
The first one is that of Mūlaṉ and all the seven preach *sanmārga*
In nine sections, three thousand verses,
Cundaraṉ has rendered the message of the Āgama.

The problem lies in the first word of the fourth line of the verse– as to whether it is *cundaraṉ* or *cundara*. *Cundaraṉ* is the text found in the Tiru-p-paṉandāḷ Kāsi Mutt edition. *Cundara* is the text found in the Śaiva Siddhanta Maha Samajam edition. A small difference makes a lot. If it is *cundaraṉ*, then it is a name and in that case the above translation holds good. If it is *cundara*, then it is an adjective, which means beautiful. In that case the translation of the fourth line will be,

He has rendered the message of the beautiful Āgama.

Sathiyavel Muruganar argues that it is not suitable to give an adjective to the Āgama as 'beautiful Āgama.' He further argues that nobody has given such an adjective to Āgama and hence it is not appropriate to take the term *cundara*, an adjective, as the textual variant. On this ground he suggests that the term *cundaraṉ*, which is a proper noun should be considered as the correct textual variant.[17] The argument of Sathiyavel Muruganar is less convincing. One may legitimately ask: is it wrong to give an adjective to the Āgamas and the Vedas? Or is there any rule disapproving such a thing? Is it not that one gives adjectives even to the Lord who is beyond everything? In another verse Tirumūlar himself gives the same adjective (using another word *eḻil* meaning beautiful) to the Vedas. It is as follows:

irukkuruvām eḻil vēdatti ṉuḷḷē,[18]

which means "inside the beautiful Vedas in the form of poetry *(ṛk).*" So it is not unconventional to give an adjective to works like Vedas and Āgamas and Tirumūlar had done it in so many verses using different adjectives– *divya-āgamam* – divine Āgama; *nal-āgamam* – good Āgama, and so on. So Sathiyavēl Muruganār's view does not carry conviction.

Further Sathiyavel Muruganar says that if the word *cundara* is an adjective given to the Āgama, whom does the word 'he' stands for? The simple answer is that it stands for the one who renders the message of the beautiful Āgama, Mūlaṉ.

Cidambaranar and Sathiyavel Muruganar further quote a verse from the *Tirumandira-mālai-300* to support their claim that the original name of Tirumūlar is Cundara-nādar. This verse is:

mandiram koṇḍu vaḻipaḍu vōrkku-c
cundara nādaṉ colliya mandiram
nandiyeṉ nādaṉ nāvāra ōdiṉēṉ
paintoḍi mēṉi-p payaṉidu tāṉē.

For those who worship with the mantras
Cundara-nādaṉ has imparted the mantra
I uttered with the grace of my guru
This is for what the body is meant for.

In the second line of the verse the name Cundara-nādaṉ occurs, and this feeds oil to the fire kindled by Cidambaranar and Sathiyavel Muruganar. But this verse is a corrupt form, which is referred only by Cidambaranar in his essay on the biography of Tirumūlar. In the *Tirumandira-mālai-300*, from which the above verse is quoted, the entire verse completely differs from what is given by Cidambaranar, save the last line. The editor and commentator of the *Tirumandira-mālai-300*, Na. Sivapiragasa Desigar gives all the available variants of the text and in none the name Cundara-nādaṉ occurs. He also writes a note that "Cundara-nādaṉ is the textual variant taken by A. Cidambaranar. This variant is not found in the available palm-leaf manuscripts."[19] To conclude the discussion, it is contended that the work the *Tirumandira-mālai-300* is not a work written by Tirumūlar, the author of the *Tirumandiram* which we are considering here, and the discussion of Sathiyavel Muruganar is off the mark.

We can safely conclude this dispute regarding the name of the author of the *Tirumandiram* by saying that it is Tirumūlar. Is this his original name or had he some other name before entering into the body of Mūlaṉ, the shepherd? One does not know. It may be an acquired name. Even the authentic biographer Cēkkiḻār refers to the author of the *Tirumandiram* only by the name Tirumūlar. Cēkkiḻār refers to Tirumūlar before his entering into the body of Mūlaṉ, the shepherd, as the adept of Kailāsh (*Kayilai*-yogin). It is true that he is referred to by names such as Mūlar, Mā-mūlar, Śri Mūlar, Śri Mula-nādar, Tirumūla-nādar, Tirumūla-dēvar,

Tirumūla-nāyaṉār, Sadāśivaṉ etc., in the texts and commentaries of works other than the *Tirumandiram* and it is to be noted that nowhere he is referred to as Cundara-nādar. In all the names given above only the prefixes or the suffixes differ; the name Mūlar remains the same except that of Sadāśivaṉ. Sadāśivaṉ is not a name but a title conferred on Tirumūlar by his guru, which is recorded by Tirumūlar in the second line of verse 92.

nandi aruḷālē cadācivaṉ āyinēṉ

By the grace of Nandi I became Sadāśivaṉ.

2. 2. Source of the work

There are three types of works as classified in the Tamil grammar: original or primary *(mudal-nūl)*, secondary *(vaḻi-nūl)*, and supportive *(cārbu-nūl* or *puḍai-nūl)*. Of these three, the original works are written out of the author's own reflections and hence they are called primary. Secondary works are those, which elaborate the primary ones without making any distortions. The supportive works are those, which alter the original a little in necessary places to suit the needs of the time, keeping the central theme of the original intact.

Under which category the *Tirumandiram* falls is the question to be answered. It is for sure that the *Tirumandiram* is not a supportive work. It is the view of some scholars that the *Tirumandiram* is a secondary work and it is an attempt to write or translate the Āgamas, which are in Sanskrit, into Tamil. They also quote some verses from the *Tirumandiram* to support their view. But the verses quoted in support of the claim are established by scholars as interpolations.[20] Scholars have also established after comparing the *Tirumandiram* with the available editions of the Āgamas, which are referred to in the *Tirumandiram*, that the *Tirumandiram* is not a translation or a remake of the Āgamas.[21]

Hence it is an original/primary work only. Yet it is accepted that Tirumūlar was very much influenced by the Āgamas.

V.V. Ramana Sastry had the view that the *Tirumandiram* is a translation of a Sanskrit work called *Śrī-mantra-mālika*.[22] It was the argument of V.V.R. Sastry that when Tirumūlar came to Tamil Nadu from Mount Kailāsh, he brought the Sanskrit work with him and later translated it into Tamil. But Vellaivarananar had disproved Sastry's claim in his *Pan̲n̲iru-Tirumur̲ai-Varalār̲u* with ample evidences and established that the *Tirumandiram* is an original work rendered in Tamil.[23]

2. 3. Territory of the work

The word "territory" here stands for the people who live in a certain geographical boundary as a society. When one says that the territory of this work is such and such then it is to be understood that the work is meant only for the people living in that particular area. Each territory will have its own social conditions and cultural contexts and a work written for the people of a particular territory will certainly reflect the territorial characteristics, which may not be understandable to the others who live beyond the territory. Even the insiders of the territory cannot understand the work without awareness about their territorial traits, social conditions, and cultural contexts. At the same time it is possible for the outsiders of the territory well-versed with the territorial characteristics to understand a work meant for the particular territory. Hence it is expected of the author to define the territory of his work to help the reader prepare himself before entering into the work.

A territory may be a linguistic territory, a racial territory, a national territory and so on. Here, in the case of the *Tirumandiram*, the territory is a linguistic territory. That is, the Tamil speaking land is the territory of the *Tirumandiram*. In one of the verses Tirumūlar specifically says that he has been awarded this birth to sing the glory of the Lord in sweet Tamil.[24] In another verse he indicates the territory consisting of five Tamil speaking regions, Cēra, Cōḻa, Pāṇḍiya, Toṇḍai and Koṅgu.[25] These regions include the present day Kerala, Tamil Nadu, and some parts of Andhra and Karnataka. So knowledge of Tamil Nadu and its characteristics will form the back-drop to follow and understand the *Tirumandiram*.

2. 4. The name of the work

The name of the work is the *Tirumandiram*. But we do not know whether the name was given by the author Tirumūlar, or by somebody else. The name *Tirumandiram* is mentioned only in the following verse:

tiruman diramē cidambaram dāṉum
tiruman diramē ciṟanda ubāṅgam
tiruman diramē tirukkūttiṉ ceygai
tiruman diramē tirumēṉi dāṉē.[26]

This verse may be translated as

It is *Tirumandiram*, the Chidambaram
It is *Tirumandiram*, the best *upāṅga*
It is *Tirumandiram*, the meaning of the divine dance
It is *Tirumandiram*, the divine form.

(Chidambaram - name of a holy place where the Divine Dancer Lord Naṭarāja is worshipped; this can also be interpreted as the space created of wisdom; *upāṅga* - an appendage which remains near to Lord always; *upa* - near, *aṅga* - appendage; e.g.: dress, garland, ornaments, etc.; divine dance - performed by Lord Naṭarāja, symbolizes all the five acts of Lord– *aintoḻil-naḍaṉam*– creation, sustenance, destruction, concealment, benediction).

This verse cannot be taken as one rendered by the author Tirumūlar for the following reasons:

1) This verse falls out of the three thousand verses of the *Tirumandiram* and included in the appendix with some more verses under the title Extra-verses.
2) The tone of this verse boasts that the *Tirumandiram* is everything. The author, who is so humble in all his appeals, would have never written in such a tone.
3) Though the authenticity of the above verse is cloudy, one can say that this verse forms a part of the *ciṟappu-p pāyiram,* the special introduction.

Even if one accepts the authenticity of the above verse, it can be interpreted that the word *Tirumandiram,* which occurs in all the four lines of the verse, stands not for the name of the work but for the sacred mantra, viz., namaśivāya. Replacing the word *Tirumandiram* with the mantra namaśivāya makes sense.

Treating this verse as not authentic, accepting it under the category of *ciṟappu-p-pāyiram,* the special introduction, let us move on to another verse in which the word *mandira-mālai* occurs. *Mandira-mālai* means a garland of mantras. One should bear it in mind that the *Tirumandiram* is also known as the *Tirumandira-mālai.*

piṟappili nādaṉai-p pērnandi taṉṉai-c
ciṟappoḍu vāṉavar ceṉṟukai kūppi
maṟappilar neñjiṉul mandira mālai
uṟaippoḍuṅ kūḍiniṉ ṟōdalu māmē.[27]

This verse may be translated thus:

The heavenly beings with folded hands approach Nandi,
The Lord above and free of the bonds of birth;

Deep in their hearts the *mandira-mālai* revolve
Forget not to chant it.

No doubt that this is an authentic verse. Can we, then, say that the *mandira-mālai* referred to in this verse as the name suggested by Tirumūlar to his work? No. If we say so, then it would amount to saying that Tirumūlar is singing the praises of his own work, the *Tirumandiram*. Tirumūlar is not that sort of a man who blows his own trumpet.

Here *mandira-mālai* stands for a garland of mantra or mantras, which revolve in the hearts of the heavenly beings, who do not forget chanting it. A garland may be made of only one flower or several. Here, this *mālai*, i.e., garland, is made of only one flower– i.e., mantra– namaśivāya.

There is a custom to count the number of mantras chanted, with the term *māla*. *Māla*, here, denotes a garland made of one hundred and eight rosary beads. It is customary to chant a mantra at least one hundred and eight times, i.e., one *māla* of rosary beads. If one says that "I have chanted the mantra once" that means he had chanted one *māla*, i.e., one hundred and eight times. It suits here to interpret this verse that the heavenly beings chant the mantra namaśivāya counting it in terms of *mālas*.

This makes us to conclude that Tirumūlar has never mentioned the name *Tirumandiram* in his work. But he mentioned a lot about the mantras. So it is better to hold that the name *Tirumandiram* was given to it by somebody else, after examining the nature and contents of the *Tirumandiram* later.

Cēkkiḻār, the author of the *Periya-purāṇam*, calls it as the *Tirumandira-mālai*, the sacred garland of mantras. This garland is composed of four flowers as per the account of Cēkkiḻār. The four flowers are: 1. *jñāna*, 2. *yoga*, 3. *kriyā*, 4. *caryā*. These four will be dealt with in the following chapters.

Is there any significance in naming the work as *Tirumandira-mālai?*

Na. Sivapiragasa Desigar tries to bring out the significance of the name *Tirumandira-mālai:*

> In the Sanskrit work called *Nitya-tantra*, it is stated that, the ones (māntric word/s) made of ten to twenty letters are named mantras and the ones made of letters more than twenty are named *māla-mantra.* Accordingly all the verses contained in this work *(Tirumandiram)* are made of four lines, each line having mostly twelve letters, the verse taken as a whole exceeds twenty letters. Hence it is known as mantra and *mantra-māla* or *māla-mantra*, as called by Sanskrit scholars. (That is, taken as a single line it is a mantra; the verse taken as a whole it is *māla-mantra* or *mantra-māla. Mandira-mālai* is the Tamil version of *mantra-māla*).[28]

Desigar further continues to give reasons for naming the work as *Tirumandira-mālai:*

> Order, regularity and so on are the meanings of the term *mālai* (garland). Gold, flower, gems, words, anything that is strung together in an order is called *mālai.* Since the verses in this work *(Tirumandiram)* are made of the same poetic metre *(yāppu)*, are made of *andādi-t-toḍai* (that is, the ending– word or letter– of the previous verse constituting the beginning of the following verse), are made in such a way that the first verse is connected to the last verse making a circle *(maṇḍalittal)*,

this work is called *Tirumandira-mālai*. This is also called *Tirumūlar-mālai*.[29]

The first interpretation may be questioned but not the second. The first one cares for the letters only. Further, not all the verses are dealing with mantras. Ethics, definitions of various Śaivisms, descriptions about the saints and other things are also dealt with in the *Tirumandiram*. So the Sanskritised version of explaining the name *Tirumandira-mālai* is far-fetched. The second interpretation is based on structural grammar and it is acceptable.

Desigar also quotes a number of verses from other works which mention the *Tirumandira-mālai*. So the *Tirumandira-mālai* seems to be the name and later it was shortened as the *Tirumandiram*.

Suba. Annamalai in his edition of the *Tirumandiram* says that it can be inferred from the verses that Tirumūlar has named his work as *Sadāśiva-Āgamam*.[30] We have seen that Tirumūlar was conferred with the title Sadāśivaṉ by his *guru*. It is nothing new in the Tamil tradition to name the work after the author. The work of Tol-kāppiyar was named as *Tol-kāppiyam*; the commentary written to *Tol-kāppiyam* by Iḷam-pūraṇar is known as *Iḷam-pūraṇam*; the work by Muttu-vīrar is known as *Muttu-vīriyam*. In the same vein there is nothing wrong in naming the work written by Sadāśivaṉ which is an Āgama as *Sadāśiva-Āgamam*. But this name suggested by Suba. Annamalai is not referred to either in the *Tirumandiram* or in the *Periya-purāṇam*.

2. 5. Structure of the work

The structure of a work is referred to by the Tamil term *yāppu*, which means the graduated serial order of treatises to be studied. That is, in order to understand a work one must have a background knowledge for which he must have studied certain other treatises. It becomes the duty of the author to indicate the serial order in which his work comes under and thus guide the reader about the works to be studied before the reader starts studying the work of the author.

It is indicated in one of the verses of the *Tirumandiram* that it is the final treatise to be studied by those who want to attain liberation. This verse may be included under the special introduction. The verse is:

In the Holy Three Thousand is the Salvation fine
Of the diverse works, true and good;
In the Divine Three Thousand, original and wise
All knowledge is, special and general.[31]

After reading works on liberation, reading the *Tirumandiram* will be beneficial.

2. 6. Subject-matter of the work

An author should briefly state the subject-matter dealt with in the treatise. Tirumūlar brings out the gist of the *Tirumandiram* in one single verse:

I have completely established
The jñeya, the jñāna, the jñātṛ
The māyā, the parai-āyam that comes out of the mā-māyā,
The Śiva and the agōcara-vīya.[32]

Tirumūlar claims that he has explained in full in his text all the categories named in this verse. These are the core essentials of Śaiva Siddhānta philosophy. It is better to give the meanings of the terms used in this verse: *jñeya* – that which is to be known; *jñāna* – knowledge; *jñātṛ* – knower; *māyā* – impurity *(mala)*; *parai-*

āyam – the evolutes of māyā; Śiva – the Lord; *agōcara-vīyam* – the bliss of experiencing Śiva.

So, the subject-matter of the *Tirumandiram* is to instruct one about the categories mentioned above.

2. 7. People who can read the work

Some works openly rule out a section of people as not eligible to read them and say that they should be punished severely if they make an attempt to read. But no such discriminations are made in the *Tirumandiram*. It addresses one and all. This is clearly communicated in the verse "The entire world may well attain the bliss I have attained... "[33] "Lord has opened His treasure trove for distribution; people of the world! Come and join to get your share" is the clarion call given by Appar and Tāyumāṉavar, two great saints of Tamil Nadu following the footsteps of Tirumūlar. Anybody who is interested in spiritual liberation can read or listen to the *Tirumandiram*, which is open to all irrespective of caste, sex and creed.

2. 8. The end-result of the work

The statement made by Tirumūlar in verse 85, "The entire world may well attain the bliss I have attained... " may be taken as the end-result intended in the *Tirumandiram*. A verse from the special introduction claims that those who wake up early at the dawn and sing the *Tirumandiram*, understanding its meaning will surely attain liberation.[34]

3. The Period of the work

There is a view that when one is so convinced about the contents of the *Tirumandiram*, why should one discuss and ponder over the period of the *Tirumandiram* instead of concentrating on the teachings of it. But this view is a mistaken one for it is always better to read and understand a work against its socio-cultural milieu to get an in-depth understanding of it. To have a glimpse of the milieu one needs to have an idea of the period in which the work was produced. As far as the *Tirumandiram* is concerned the task of fixing its period is a difficult one.

Sundaramūrti-Nāyaṉār– who was one of the four leaders of Tamil Śaivism and who has listed the Śaiva saints called *Nāyaṉmārs* – mentions the name of Tirumūlar in his list. It is an agreed view that Sundaramūrti-Nāyaṉār (hereafter Sundarar) lived in the period of 840-865 A.D.[35] So it may be taken that Tirumūlar lived before 840 A.D.

It is stated in Cēkkiḻār's *Periya-purāṇam* that Tirumūlar had lived for three thousand years in Śiva-Yoga and wrote one verse every year, thus completing the *Tirumandiram* comprising of three thousand verses. If this be the case, it leads one to conclude that Tirumūlar lived at least in 2160 B.C. But nowhere in the *Tirumandiram* Tirumūlar says that he lived for three thousand years and wrote one verse a year.

Scholars like Sathiyavel Muruganar say that the period of Tirumūlar is 5,500 B.C. Sathiyavel Muruganar's argument is based on the mention of the names of Vyākrama and Patañjali in the *Tirumandiram.* Vyākrama and Patañjali were co-disciples of Tirumūlar. Vyākrama was a cousin of Vaśiṣṭa. Vaśiṣṭa belonged to the Rāmāyaṇa period. So do Vyākrama and his co-disciple Tirumūlar. The Rāmāyaṇa period is fixed to be 5000 B.C. by the Russians using the carbon method of dating. This helps to conclude that the period of Tirumūlar is 5000 B.C.[36] This argument of Sathiyavel Muruganar was taken from A. Cidambaranar.[37]

Palur Kannappa Mudaliar, a Śaiva scholar, says that Tirumūlar belonged to the Saṅgam age (2nd century A.D.).[38] His argument is that the metre that Tirumūlar used to compose the verses (known as *kali-viruttam*) was mostly used in the Saṅgam period and hence Tirumūlar might have belonged to the Saṅgam Period. M.S. Puranalingam Pillai holds the same view but does not reason it out.[39]

Ka. Vellaivaranar tries to fix the date of Tirumūlar on the basis of an internal evidence found in the *Tirumandiram.* In one of the verses Tirumūlar makes a reference about the five *maṇḍalas* (regions) of Tamil land. In a certain period there was only three regions namely Pāṇḍiya, Cēra, and Cōḻā regions. Later a part of the Cēra country became a separate region called Koṅgu region and a part of the Cōḻā country went separate to become the Toṇḍai region, thus making the five regions of Tamil Nadu. This split of regions into five happened around the third century A.D. Since Tirumūlar makes a reference about the five Tamil regions, the period of Tirumūlar may be fixed after the third century A.D. In another verse Tirumūlar makes a reference about the *poṉ-ambalam,* the golden-hall of Chidambaram. It is called the golden-hall because the roof of the hall was thatched with gold by the kings of the different regions of Tamil Nadu. It was the Pallava king Cimma-varmaṉ-I who thatched the roof with gold for the first time. The period of Cimma-varmaṉ-I was fixed as fifth century A.D.[40] Since Tirumūlar makes a reference to the golden-hall he should have lived only after that. Based on this Vellaivaranar concludes that Tirumūlar should have lived in the end of the fifth century A.D. or in the beginning of the sixth century A.D.[41]

For the same reason regarding the five regions, C.V. Narayana Ayyar fixes the period of Tirumūlar between fourth and sixth centuries A.D.[42]

T.V. Sadasiva Pandarattar relies on the verse, which refers to the golden-hall, and fixes the period of Tirumūlar as either the end of the fifth century A.D. or the beginning of the sixth century A.D.[43]

Suba. Annamalai, who is an authority on the *Tirumandiram*, also shares the same view.[44]

Maraimalai Adigal, one of the torch-bearers of Tamil revivalism of the twentieth century, fixes the period as the middle of sixth century A.D.[45]

Now let us consider the strengths and weaknesses of these claims.

1) Cidambaranar and Sathiyavel Muruganar say that Tirumūlar lived around 5,500 B.C. Their argument is based on the verse in which Tirumūlar mentions about his co-disciples Vyākrama and Patañjali; Vyākrama lived in the Rāmāyaṇa age and it was calculated as 5,000 B.C. It is customary in India to name oneself after the elders. There are more than two Avvaiyārs, Paṭṭiṉattārs, Tirumūlars, Agastyas and so on. So the Vyākrama mentioned in the *Tirumandiram* need not necessarily be the Vyākrama of the Rāmāyaṇa age. The same argument holds good for the case of Patañjali also.

   Though M. Govindan holds the view that Patañjali, the compiler of the *Yoga-Sūtra*, and Tirumūlar belonged to the same period,[46] there is no conclusive evidence to say so. Govindan argues that Tirumūlar and Patañjali share "more than" thirty common philosophical ideas and this coincidence is highly improbable unless they were contemporaries or that they influenced one another or had a common guru or lineage.

While referring to the name of Patañjali, Tirumūlar refers to it as *manṟu toḻuda patañjali* which means "the Patañjali who worshipped the hall" at Chidambaram. It is the opinion of scholars that just to differentiate his co-disciple Patañjali from Patañjali, the compiler of *Yoga-Sūtra* and Patañjali the grammarian, and from other Patañjalis, Tirumūlar refers to his co-disciple as Patañjali who worshipped in the hall at Chidambaram. Moreover the fact that Tirumūlar and Patañjali share "more than" thirty common philosophic ideas is not enough to vouchsafe that they were contemporaries. We can only say that one was influenced by the other.

So it will be only over enthusiasm on the part of Cidambaranar and Sathiyavel Muruganar to fix the period of Tirumūlar at 5,500 B.C.

2) It is the view of Palur Kannappa Mudaliar that Tirumūlar belonged to the Caṅgam age. He bases his argument on the poetic meter that Tirumūlar used to compose the verses of the *Tirumandiram.* One cannot just decide such matters on the basis of the usage of the meter only. Even in the present age a poet can write in the meter used by Tirumūlar. One cannot conclude that since he has used the meter used by Tirumūlar that he must be a contemporary of Tirumūlar.

3) The argument of Vellaivaranar and others who fix the period of Tirumūlar around fifth to sixth century A.D. is on the right track. Further Vellaivaranar also shows how freely the phrases, words, and ideas of the *Tirumandiram* are used in the *Tēvāram,* a compilation of the verses of the Śaiva-trio– Appar, Sambandar and Sundarar. Of these three

the first two, Appar and Sambandar, were contemporaries, and they lived around the sixth and seventh centuries A.D. and one can arrive at the conclusion that Tirumūlar lived before them, that is, between the fifth and sixth centuries A.D.

4. The socio-cultural milieu of the work

The motive behind the process of identifying the period of a work/author is to know the socio-cultural back-drop of the work, which makes the intentions of the author clear, and helps in understanding the work. Let us now peep into the backdrop of the *Tirumandiram*.

Tamil Nadu, during the period of the *Tirumandiram*, was swinging from a secular phase to a religious phase. The governments were stable and the rulers were concentrating on propagating the ideals they were fond of. It was a turbulent time for the indigenous religions of Tamil Nadu, namely Śaivism and Vaiṣṇavism, which were striving hard to secure a firm foothold in their homeland. The Tamil country was, at that time, under the rule of outsiders like Kaḷa-p-piras and Pallavas who have marginalized the native Pāṇḍiyas and Cōḻās.

The Kaḷa-p-piras were not Śaivas. They were in support of Jainism and Buddhism. Under their rule, the monks of Jainism and Buddhism were freely propagating their religions, through an organization that was supported by the rulers. The Jains and the Buddhists provided education and medical assistance to the poor, which remained a privilege of the upper class people. The new religions were well received by the people, for they saw them as a welcome relief helping the people to get rid of the suffocating social hierarchical practices.

The major religions existed at that time were Jainism, Buddhism, Śaivism, Vaiṣṇavism, and the Vedic religion. In an existential crisis the religions were opposed ideologically. In this background, Tirumūlar played the historical role of philosophizing Śaivism, thus fully enabling it to meet the ideological clash. Later on, this ideological clash slowly transformed into a physical clash of which this book is not concerned with.

5. Tirumandiram as an Āgama

In his effort to expound Śaivism Tirumūlar had drawn ideas from Āgamas. In fact he claims the *Tirumandiram* itself as an Āgama.[47] Here it is better to understand what an Āgama is. Āgama is a word which came from the root *gam*, which means "to draw near," "to approach."[48] According to *Piṅgaḷa-mata*, Āgama is that by which the objects around are known. The name is also explained as that class of Tantra which is addressed to Pārvati (the consort of Śiva) by Śiva. It is said that the word is formed by the first letters of *āgata* (that which comes from Śiva), *gata* (that which goes to Pārvati) and *mata* (that which is established).[49]

Āgama is also called as Śāstra, Jñāna and Tantra. It is called Āgama because from it knowledge proceeds, Śāstra because everything is controlled and protected by it, Jñāna because everything can be known through it and Tantra because everything is preserved and perpetuated by it.[50]

The Āgamas are divided into three main branches according to the deity that is worshipped therein. Pāñcarātra and Vaikhānasa Āgamas are the Vaiṣṇava scriptures which extol Viṣṇu. The Śaiva Āgamas extol Śiva. And the Śakta Āgamas extol Śakti. An Āgama deals with four topics: temple construction, making idols, etc.; philosophical doctrines; meditative practices; and methods of worship *(kriyā, jñāna, yoga,* and *caryā)*. These four topics are divided into three divisions: *tantra* which teaches rituals; *mantra* which teaches the *yoga* stage of worship; and *upadeśa* which expounds the existence and nature of the three eternal entities– Pati, paśu and pāśa.[51] This is vouchsafed in the *Śiva-jñāṉa-siddhiyār.*[52] All these three, i.e., *tantra, mantra,* and *upadeśa* are found in the *Tiruman- diram,* the Tamil Āgama.

The basic Śaiva Āgamas are 18 in number according to one tradition, and 28 according to another.[53] According to tradition Śiva has five faces– Īśāna (facing upward), Tatpuruṣa (facing east), Sadyojāta (facing west), Vāmadeva (facing north) and Aghora (facing south). The five mouths had produced initially ten Āgamas: *Kāmika, Yogaja, Cintya, Makuṭa, Amsumān, Dīpta, Ajita, Sūkṣma, Sahaśra* and *Suprabheda.* These were the precursors of the eighteen Raudra Āgamas: *Vijaya, Niśvāsa, Madgita, Pārameśvara, Mukhāvimba, Siddha, Santāna, Nārasimha, Candrāmśu, Vīrabhadra, Agñeya, Svāyambhū, Visāra, Raurava, Vimala, Kiraṇa, Lalita* and *Saumeya.* All these constitute the twenty-eight Śaiva Āgamas.[54] Tirumūlar also endorses that the Āgamas are twenty-eight in number and they are uttered by the five mouths of Śiva.[55] According to Tirumūlar it is not the number that is important, but the essence. If one starts counting the Śivāgamas it will grow innumerable. Tirumūlar raises a pertinent question: what is there in the number if one could not grasp the essence of the Āgamas?[56]

It should be remembered that these traditional twenty-eight Śaiva Āgamas are regarded as authoritative by all the Śaiva sects, even by the later social reformative Vīra-Śaivas, because the Āgamas are the utterances of Śiva.

Though it is generally considered that Āgama and Tantra are identical, some scholars try to differentiate them. According to

Manoranjan Basu the scope of Tantra is wider than that of Āgama, as the former deals with as many as about twenty-five subjects, whereas the term "Āgama" covers only seven of the said twenty-five subjects.[57] He also observes that the term "Tantra" is also used in the sense of a system having predominance of Śāktaika character, while "Āgama" bears an overtone of Śiva in terms of knowledge.[58]

Like the Vedas, it is believed, the Āgamas are designated as the *śrauta-śāstras* (that which are heard), brought down to us from time immemorial through spiritual tradition. But the Āgamas and the Vedas stand separately. Here again Tirumūlar plays a historical role of bridging the gap between the Vedas and the Āgamas and it is remarkable that Tirumūlar was a forerunner of Tamil Saivism in many respects. In one of his verses he says,

Veda and Āgama alike
Are revelations of God,
That is Truth;
The one is general
The other special;
Their goals two, they say;
Search them both,
For the truly learned,
There is difference none.[59]

Though Tirumūlar says that there is no difference between the Āgamas and the Vedas, Tirumūlar draws his sources from the Āgamas only. No doubt that he praises the Vedas, but all his thoughts are strongly influenced by the Āgamas.

Scholars like Maraimalai Adigal and Ka. Subramania Pillai claim that the Āgamas are firmly rooted in the Tamil tradition and only later, when the process of sanskritisation was taking place, they were written in Sanskrit.[60] This shows the stand-off between the palanquin-bearers of Tamil and Sanskrit. This confrontation between the supporters of these two equally footed languages was there even at the time of Tirumūlar, and he tries to cool it off by saying that Śiva made his utterances in both the languages.

> ... Then did He in Sanskrit and in Tamil at once,
> Reveal the rich treasure of His compassion to our Mother Great.[61]

> ... The Lord who in Tamil sweet and northern tongue
> Life's mystery revealed.[62]

From the verses of the *Tirumandiram* we can infer that Lord Śiva instructed the nine Āgamas to Śakti, Śakti in turn instructed to Sadāśiva, Sadāśiva instructed to Maheśvara, Maheśvara instructed to Rudra, Rudra instructed to Viṣṇu and Viṣṇu instructed to Brahma and all the nine Āgamas were instructed to Nandi.[63] Nandi instructed to Tirumūlar.[64] This made Tirumūlar to become an important link in the Kailāya lineage,[65] and it became his mission to reveal the Lord in Tamil in a defined way.[66] Taking protection from the holy feet of his guru by keeping them on his head mentally, thinking of the Lord daily, Tirumūlar rendered this Āgama, the *Tirumandiram*.[67]

6. The Structure of the Tirumandiram

The *Tirumandiram* has been classified into nine *tantras* and into various sub-titles. Scholars say that this classification was not done by the author; it was done by somebody else later.[68] Anyhow, we will go by the *tantra* classification for the sake of convenience.

The first part of the *Tirumandiram* is the *pāyiram*. The term *pāyiram* has been explained already. In this part the author introduces the subject the work is dealing with. *Pāyiram* is followed by the *tantras*. Of the nine *tantras* it is the fifth *tantra* which is considered by the scholars as the central one; the preceding four *tantras* serve as instrumental to what is emphasized in the fifth *tantra* and the succeeding four indicate the results of Śiva-jñāna.

6. 1. The first tantra

The first *tantra* prepares the aspirant both internally and externally. There are twenty-three titles in this *tantra*. They include the transitoriness of body, transitoriness of wealth, transitoriness of youth, etc. In dealing with this subject, Tirumūlar draws tremendously from the ethical treatises like the *Tiru-k-kuṟaḷ* and the *Nālaḍiyār*, but adds his personal touch. The first part of the first *tantra* is *upadēcam*. This part contains some important verses, which put the philosophy of Śaiva Siddhānta in a nutshell, and define who is a Siddha.

6. 2. The second tantra

The second *tantra* speaks of the Purāṇic stories and gives philosophical interpretations to them. It reasons out the five gracious acts of Lord Śiva for the benefit of the jīvas. Creation is explained. The souls are classified into three, namely *vijñāna-kala*, *praḷayā-kala* and *sakala*. The second *tantra* advises the *sakalas*, who are destined to live in this world, that they should know the eligibility and non-eligibility of the other jīvas and should conduct themselves accordingly; should know the nature of temple and other rituals; should not abuse Śiva, guru and maheśvara (those who are in the service of Śiva).

6. 3. The third tantra

While the second *tantra* prepares the sādhaka, the third involves him in the sādhana. The content of the third *tantra* is the technique of sublimating the body *(śarīra-siddhi-upāya)*. The other subjects dealt with in this *tantra* are Aṣṭāṅga-Yoga, Amuri-dhāraṉai, etc. All are related to the *śarīra-siddhi.* This *tantra* also elaborates some special types of Yoga, like Kechari-Yoga, Pariyaṅga-Yoga, etc.

6. 4. The fourth tantra

The next step for the sādhaka to attain the results of Śiva-Yoga is mantra-siddhi, i.e., the fruition of the mantras. To make this easy Tirumūlar elaborates the various cakras *(yantras)*, their forms, sizes, the letters *(akṣaras)* to be written in them, the appropriate mantras, the presiding deities, their strengths, the way of worshipping the cakras, and the fruits of worshipping.

6. 5. The fifth tantra

The fifth *tantra* brings out the central theme of the *Tirumandiram.* The four methodologies to reach Godhead– *caryā, kriyā, yoga* and *jñāna*; the four respective *mārgas* or ways for attainment – *dāsa-mārga, sat-putra-mārga, saha-mārga* and *sanmārga*; and the four respective stages of liberation attained– *sāloka, sāmīpya, sārūpya* and *sāyujya* are explained in this *tantra.*

Those who grow in maturity by attaching themselves to one of the four *mārgas* will be blessed with the grace of the Lord. In this *tantra* the *Tirumandiram* divides the descent of divine grace *(catti-nipādam)* into four grades– *mandam, manda-taram, tīviram* and *tīvira-taram.* This *tantra* also explains the three realities of Śaivism – Pati, paśu and pāśa. Following the foot-steps of Tirumūlar and taking a cue from this *tantra,* Aruḷ-Nandi-Śivācāriyār– disciple of Mey-kaṇḍār, the systematizer of Śaiva Siddhānta philosophy– elaborates his findings.[69]

6. 6. The sixth tantra

In continuation with the fifth *tantra*, the sixth *tantra* explains the sādhanas (instruments) to attain jñāna. This *tantra* has eleven titles starting with *Śiva-guru-daricaṉam* to *pakkuvaṉ*.

6. 7. The seventh tantra

The important features of the seventh *tantra* are the explanation of the six-ādhāras, worshipping the guru, liṅga (the symbol) and *jaṅgama* (the moving gods), controlling the five senses, explaining the features of a true *guru* and controlling the semen. Under the last title of this *tantra*, *hitha-upadeśam*, it is explained how the Śaivites should conduct themselves.

6. 8. The eighth tantra

It is generally held that the aim of the eighth *tantra* is imparting the nuances of Śiva-Yoga. In this *tantra* the *avasthas* (the states of experience) of the *jīva* are explained.

6. 9. The ninth tantra

The ninth *tantra* explains the *Śiva-bhoga* (experiencing Śiva). Tirumūlar tries to bring out the state of mystical experience in language; such verses are compiled under the title *sūnya-sambhāṣaṇai*. This *tantra* also explains the nature of the liberated souls.

7. The nine tantras of the Tirumandiram and the nine Āgamas

Some scholars are of the view that the nine *tantras* of the *Tirumandiram* are mere elaborations of the nine Āgamas. Their equation is as follows:

First *tantra* - *Kāraṇa-Āgama*
Second *tantra* - *Kāmika-Āgama*
Third *tantra* - *Vīra-Āgama*

Fourth *tantra* - *Cinta-Āgama*
Fifth *tantra* - *Vātula-Āgama*
Sixth *tantra* - *Vyāmala-Āgama*
Seventh *tantra* - *Kālottara-Āgama*
Eighth *tantra* - *Supra-Āgama*
Ninth *tantra* - *Makuṭa-Āgama*

For this the scholars quote one of the verses of the *Tirumandiram*, in which the above-mentioned nine names are referred to. The verse is:

The Āgamas so received are Karanam, Kamigam,
The Veeram good, the Sindham high and Vadulam,
Yamalam the other, and Kalottaram,
The Subram pure and Makutam to crown.[70]

This verse is discussed in detail by V.V. Ramana Sastri.[71] According to him,

1) the Āgamas mentioned in this verse are only eight and not nine. The third line of the verse is translated here as 'Yāmaḷam the other, and Kālōttaram.' But actually it should be translated as 'the Yāmaḷam known as Kālōttaram.' Because there is no primary Āgama called Yāmaḷam.

2) More than that the Kālōttaram is not a primary Āgama; it is only an upa-Āgama.

For the above two reasons, this verse is viewed as interpolation, rightly. This view is also endorsed by Suba. Annamalai.[72]

Notes on Chapter One

1. Preface of A. Cidambaranar in the *Tirumandiram* (Chennai: Saiva Siddhanta Nul Patippu-k-kalagam, Reprint, 1996), pp. 63-86.
2. S.P. Ramachandran (Ed.), *Caturagiri-t-tala-Purāṇam*, pp. 51-62.
3. Yogi S.A.A. Ramaiah (Ed.), *Bogar Kanda Yogam*, Vol. III, pp. 1536-1537, verse 881.
4. Four *yugas* are mentioned in the Hindu mythology. They are: *Kṛta* or *Satya-yuga*, *Treta-yuga*, *Dvāpara-yuga*, and *Kali-yuga*. Of these *Kṛta* is 1,728,000 years; *Treta* is 1,296,000 years; *Dvāpara* is 864,000 years; *Kali* is 432,000 years. Their total is one *Mahā-yuga* – 4,320,000 years. 100 *Mahā-yugas*, i.e., 432 million years are one *kalpa*. One *kalpa* forms one day of Brahma, the God of creation. There are seven *kalpas* and we are in the sixth one – Refer: M. Govindan, *Babaji and the 18 Siddha Kriya Yoga Tradition*, p. 192.
5. *Tirumandiram*, 81.
6. *Ibid.*, 108.
7. *Ibid.*, 85.
8. *Ibid.*, 67, 68.
9. *Nannul*, 54.
10. It was customary in those days to present one's work in a platform of scholars. After due examination, the scholars assembled there will acknowledge the work on its merits or reject it on its demerits. This can be compared with the modern *viva-voce* conducted for the Ph.D. scholars, where a number of scholars will drill the presenter/defender with a number of questions.
11. Attavadanam Veerachamy Chettiyar, *Vinōdha Raca Mañjari*, M. Sanmugam Pillai and N. Chandrasekaran (Eds.), pp. 76-79.

12. *Nannul*, 47.
13. *Tirumandiram*, 68, 92, 99, 101, 102, 3046.
14. *Ibid.*, 101.
15. S.A.A. Ramaiah, *op.cit.*, Vol. II, Preface, no page numbers.
16. Suba. Annamalai (Ed.), *Tirumandiram.*
17. Sathiyavel Muruganar, *Tirumandiram– Ōr Aṟimugam (Pāyiram)*, pp. 18-19. B. Natarajan is also of the view that the original name of Tirumūlar is Cundarar. Refer: B. Natarajan (Trans.), *Tirumantiram*, p. vii.
18. *Tirumandiram*, 53.
19. Na. Sivapiragasa Desigar (Ed.), *Tirumandira-mālai-300*, verse 363, pp. 976-967.
20. The commentator of *Jñāṉāvaraṇa-viḷakkam*, Velliambala Swamigal had established this with ample reasons. Also refer the Preface of V.V. Ramana Sastry in M.V. Viswanatha Pillai (Ed.), *Tirumandiram.*
21. Pa. Arunachalam, *Tirumandira-k-kōṭpāḍu*, p. 19.
22. M.V. Viswanatha Pillai, *op.cit.*
23. Ka. Vellaivaranan, *Paṉṉiru Tirumuṟai Varalāṟu*, Vol. II, p. 435.
24. *Tirumandiram*, 81.
25. *Ibid.*, 1646.
26. *Ibid.*, 3101. Author's Translation.
27. *Ibid.*, 86. With little modifications in the translation of B. Natarajan.
28. Na. Sivapiragasa Desigar, *op.cit.*, p. 13.
29. *Ibid.*, p. 13.
30. Suba. Annamalai, *op.cit.*, Vol. I, p. XLII.
31. *Tirumandiram*, 100. Translation of B. Natarajan.
32. *Ibid.*, 90. Author's translation.

33. *Tirumandiram*, 85.
34. *Ibid.*, 99.
35. Ma. Racamanikkanar, *Periya-purāṇa Ārāycci*, p. 2.
36. Sathiyavel Muruganar, *op.cit.*, pp. 59-60.
37. Preface of A. Cidambaranar in *Tirumandiram*, *op.cit.*, pp. 67-82.
38. Palur Kannappa Mudaliar, *Tamiḻ Mandiram*, p.38.
39. M.S. Puranalingam Pillai, *Tamil Literature*, p. 96.
40. Suba. Annamalai, *op.cit.*, Vol. I, p. XXXV.
41. Ka. Vellaivaranan, *op.cit.*, p. 417.
42. C.V. Narayana Ayyar, *Origin and Early History of Saivism in South India*, pp. 223-224.
43. T.V. Sadasiva Pandarattar, *Tamiḻ Ilakkiya Varalāṟu*, (250-600 B.C.), p. 83.
44. Suba. Annamalai, *op.cit.*, Vol. I, p. XXXV.
45. Maraimalai Adigal, *Māṇikka-vācagar Varalāṟum Kālamum*, p. 334.
46. M. Govindan, *Kriya Yoga Sutras of Patanjali and the Siddhas*, p. xvii.
47. *Tirumandiram*, 73.
48. Vishva Nath Drabu, *Sivagamas*, p. 23.
49. N.N. Bhattacharyya, *History of the Tantric Religion*, p. 38.
50. *Ibid.*, pp. 38-39.
51. John Grimes, *A Concise Dictionary of Indian Philosophy*, p. 14.
52. Mu. Tiruvilangam (Comm.), *Śiva-jñāṉa-siddhiyār Cubakkam*, "Aḷavai ilakkaṇam," 13.
53. N.N. Bhattacharyya, *op.cit.*, p. 39.
54. *Ibid.*, p. 66.
55. *Tirumandiram*, 57.

56. *Ibid.*, 64.
57. Manoranjan Basu, *Tantras: A General Study*, p. 1.
58. *Ibid.*, p. 2.
59. *Tirumandiram*, 2397. Translation of B. Natarajan. Also refer 2403, 2404.
60. Ki. Lakshmanan, *India-t-tattuva Jñāṉam*, pp. 356-357.
    Also refer Suba. Annamalai, *op.cit.*, Vol. I, p. XXXVI; Sathiyavel Muruganar, *op.cit.*, pp. 38-42.
61. *Tirumandiram*, 65. Translation of B. Natarajan.
62. *Ibid.*, 66. Translation of B. Natarajan.
63. *Ibid.*, 62. Suba. Annamalai interprets this verse as follows: The Āgamas are numbered as nine because they are instructed through nine gods– Para-Śiva, Para-Śakti, Śakti, Śivam, Sadaśiva, Maheśvara, Rudra, Viṣṇu and Brahma. The number nine stands for nine types of Āgamas. Tirumūlar himself says in one of his verses (1429) that the Āgamas are nine, from these nine came the twenty-eight. It is the contention of Suba. Annamalai that Āgamas are twenty-eight in number and that they are classified into nine types, because they are instructed through nine gods. Refer: Suba. Annamalai, *op.cit.*, Vol. I, p.52.
64. *Tirumandiram*, 67, 73 & 74.
65. *Ibid.*, 91.
66. *Ibid.*, 81.
67. *Ibid.*, 73.
68. Suba. Annamalai, *op.cit.*, p. XLII
69. Ka. Vellaivarananar, *Śaiva Siddhānta Cāttira Varalāṟu*, p. 597.
70. *Tirumandiram*, 63. Translation of B. Natarajan.
71. M.V. Viswanatha Pillai, *op.cit.*
72. Suba. Annamalai, *op.cit.*, p. 52.

Chapter 2
The Philosophy of the Tirumandiram

KR. Arumugam

padi pacu pācam e̲na-p pagar mūn̲r̲il
padiyin̲ai-p pōl pacu pācam an̲ādi
padiyin̲ai-c cen̲r̲aṇugā-p pacu pācam
padiyaṇugil pacu pācam nillāvē.

Of the so-called three, the Pati, the paśu and the pāśa,
Like the Pati, the paśu and pāśa are eternal;
The paśu and the pāśa do not reach the Pati;
If the Pati reaches the paśu, the pāśa will wane away.

–*Tirumandiram, 115.*

2. The Philosophy of the Tirumandiram

KR. Arumugam

1. Introduction

To know a system of philosophy is to understand its ideas on God, soul and the world and to comprehend how that system reasons them out. It is an attempt to know which one of the three occupies the prime place, which one is the ultimate reality according to that system.

"Only the world is perceived and the other two entities are not. Therefore only the world is real and that is the only reality" — is one answer.

"It is sure that the soul exists; the world is only an appearance. It is an illusory world. It is like a dream; it is true while dreaming, and it is false when one wakes up. Therefore the world exists only in the projected idea of the dreamer, that is, the soul. Soul alone is there— only one Soul— an Absolute Soul— which is the only reality and nothing else is" —is another answer.

"Both the world and the soul exist; the world is dependent on the soul for its evolution. Both are real" —is yet another answer.

"It does not hold water to say that the world is dependent on the soul for its creation. God creates the world for the welfare of the innumerable souls and thrusts the souls into the womb of the created world to make them realize and reach Him. Therefore, all the three, God, soul and world are real" —is one more answer.

Apart from these views, there is a view that there are more than three realities and another view that there is nothing to be called real.

Of these various views, Tirumūlar confirms the fourth one, that is, all the three, God, soul and the world, are real.[1] From the standpoint of Tirumūlar the world is not an illusory entity but a perceived reality, the perceivers being the souls, and the One who helps the perceiving, being God. Tirumūlar names them as *pācam* (pāśa – the fetter), *pacu* (paśu – the soul in bondage) and Pati (God). Pāśa is that which binds. It binds the extensive knowledge of the souls. Paśu is that which is bound by pāśa. Pati is the Lord. Sivāgra-yogin explains: Pati is Paśupati, the Lord of the souls, the whole name is being apprehended through a part which the name signifies just as the full name Devendra is understood by the name Indra.[2] Tirumūlar's conception of the three will be analyzed in the following sections. The epistemological aspects in the *Tirumandiram* may be stated before we discuss Tirumūlar's views on Pati, paśu and pāśa.

2. The epistemological aspects in the Tirumandiram

Epistemology or theory of knowledge, a branch of philosophy, is concerned with the relation between subject and object in the process of cognitive activity, the relation of knowledge to reality, the possibility of man's cognition of the world, the criteria of the truth and the authenticity of knowledge.[3]

Before venturing into establishing their first principles, all the schools of Indian philosophy try to establish the validity of the sources that are engaged in establishing the first principles.

In the process of knowing, three things are involved: 1) the subject, 2) the object and 3) the knowledge that arises out of the relationship between the subject and the object. Without the involvement of these three, the process of knowing does not arise. These three are known in Sanskrit as jñātṛ, jñeya and jñāna respectively. The jñātṛ is also called jñāta. Tirumūlar says:

I have completely established
The *jñeya*, the jñāna, the *jñātṛ*

> The māyā, the *parai-āyam* that comes out of the *mā-māyā*,
> The Śiva and the *agōcara-vīya*.[4]

This verse which is placed in the section called *pāyiram* (Introduction) declares the aim of the *Tirumandiram*, that is, to explain completely and exhaustively the *jñātṛ*, i.e., the subject, the *jñeya*, i.e., the object, the jñāna, i.e., the knowledge that arises out of the subject-object contact, māyā, i.e., the primal substance that causes the objects, *parai-āyam*, i.e., the principles that operate the primal substance, (Sada) śiva, i.e., the principle that commands this *parai-āyam*, and the *agōcara-vīya*, i.e., the One, who is like the unperceived seed and who causes this world, the *sva-rūpa Śiva*.

Though Tirumūlar says that it is his aim to explain all the above, elsewhere, he also accepts that it is impossible to express the Lord in words. He ridicules those persons making such an effort, as "dumb fools are ye, trying to express the inexpressible."[5] The other mystics also share this view. Saint Māṇikka-vācagar says: "the One who is beyond word and thought."[6] Appar,[7] Sambandar,[8] Tirumaḻicai Āḻvār,[9] Siddha Avvai,[10] Abirāmi Baṭṭar[11]—all confirm this in a different phraseology.

The *Śiva-jñāṉa-siddhiyār* says that the lotus feet of the Lord is inexplicable even unto the Vedas, Brahma, and Viṣṇu.[12] In another place it says that God may be known by Scriptures and logic, that is, with the help of the Āgamic testimony and *pramāṇa* or *aḷavai* (in Tamil).[13] Does this not sound like a contradiction? V.A. Devasenapathy observes that the contradiction here is only apparent. He explains:

> What the Siddhāntin means is that while without God's grace neither the Scriptures nor Logic can help us to find God, illumined by His Grace we come to know Him from the Scriptures and also by Logic. The Siddhāntin feels the need

for Logic in addition to Revelation in the case of dull pupils who are likely to be confused by works of other faiths and who fail to grasp the fundamentals of the Siddhānta.[14]

2. 1. Aḷavai or pramāṇa

Pramāṇa is the means of acquiring valid knowledge. It is called *aḷavai* in Tamil. *Aḷavai* means measure. According to the *Naṉṉūl,* we measure the things of the world by four means, viz, *eṇṇal, eḍuttal, mugattal, nīṭṭal.*[15] That is, we measure things by computation *(eṇṇal),* or by weighing with the help of a balance *(eḍuttal),* or by the measure of capacity *(mugattal),* or by linear measure *(nīṭṭal).* Similarly we measure *Pati* (God), etc., with the help of the *pramāṇas* and hence they are called *aḷavai.*[16]

Tirumūlar uses the term *aḷavai* in the same sense.

I have measured the beginning and the end of this vast universe.
I have measured the Lord who is the beginning of this vast universe.
I have measured the male and female of this vast universe.
I have measured His grace and realized.[17]

Tirumūlar in this verse says that he has measured all the three entities, that is, the Pati (God), paśu (the souls which are divided into male and female in this universe) and pāśa (the fetters that cause the universe).

In the process of acquiring valid knowledge three things are involved in it. In Sanskrit they are: *pramāta* (the knower), *pramāṇa* (the means of knowing) and *prameya* (the object known). In Tamil they are known as *aḷappōṉ, aḷavai* and *aḷakka-p-paḍu poruḷ* respectively. Of these three, only the *pramāṇa* or *aḷavai* needs a deeper understanding, because only through *pramāṇa* one acquires valid knowledge. A Tamil work called *Aḷavai Viḷakkam* emphasizes the importance of *aḷavai* as follows: A verse without a musical tune cannot attract common people; it is of no use to them. A blind man cannot enthuse about an amazing beauty, since he could not see it. Likewise a person who is ignorant of the valid means of knowledge *(aḷavai)* cannot utter anything sensible.[18]

According to some, *aḷavai* is six in number. They are: perception (*pratyakṣa/kāṭci* in Tamil), inference *(anumāna/karudal)*, testimony *(śabda* or *āgama/urai)*, comparison *(upamāna/oppu)*, postulation *(arthāpatti/poruḷ)* and non-cognition *(abhāva* or *anupalabdhi/iṉmai)*. Some add four more *aḷavais* to this list and make it ten. They are: elimination *(pāriśeṣa/oḻibu)*, fact (relating to the properties of natural objects; it is the nature of wind to blow, of fire to burn, etc. – *saṃbhava/uṇmai*), evidence or authority from tradition *(aitihya/ulaga-vaḻakku)* and inherence (i.e., an inference by which a thing is determined from a predication of its nature – *sahaja* or *svabhāva-liṅga/iyalbu)*. There are people who speak of more than ten *aḷavais*.

The Śaiva Siddhāntins accept only the first three, viz., perception, inference and testimony (they call it by the name *āgama-pramāṇa*). In their opinion all the other *pramāṇas* may be reduced to these three *pramāṇas*.[19]

2. 1. 1. The aḷavais of the Tirumandiram

Though the *aḷavais* are not explained explicitly in the *Tirumandiram*, they are implicitly contained. Tirumūlar gives prime place to the *aḷavai* called testimony. Along with that perception and inference also find their due places. One verse of the *Tirumandiram* says that the objects of the world may be known through perception and God can be known by means of inference.[20]

2. 1. 1. 1. Perception

Cognition of reality through some kind of sense-object contact is called perception. This is called *indriya-pratyakṣa* or *vāyil-kāṭci* in Tamil. Tirumūlar calls this as *mugattilē kaṇ koṇḍu kāṇal.*[21] This is one type of perception. Another type of it is to know things with the help of the inner organs. This is called *mānasa-pratyakṣa* or *aga-k-kāṭci.* Tirumūlar calls this as *agattilē kaṇ koṇḍu kāṇal.*[22] One more type of perception is called *tan-vēdaṉai-k-kāṭci* or *sva-vedhana-pratyakṣa.* This is explained as perceiving pleasure, pain, etc. This also can be traced in the verses of the *Tirumandiram.*[23] Other than these the *Tirumandiram* speaks of a fourth type called *yoga-k-kāṭci* or *yoga-pratyakṣa;*[24] that is, perceiving without the aid of any external or internal organs.[25] Thus in the *Tirumandiram* we find four types of perception.

2. 1. 1. 2. Inference

Anumāna is the cognition of a mediate object through the ascertainment of concomitance. *Anumāna* is of two types: *svārthānumāna* (inference for oneself), and *parārthānumāna* (inference for another). Of these two, the *parārthānumāna* is stated as a five-membered syllogism so as to make others to understand the inference one has arrived at. The five members of the syllogism are: *pratijña (mēṟkōḷ), hetu (ētu), dṛṣṭānta (eḍuttu-k-kāṭṭu), upanaya* and *nigamana.* Of these five members even the first three would suffice to state an inference. For example, wherever there is smoke, there is fire, as in the kitchen. This hill has fire. Because it has smoke. In this inference, 'This hill has fire' is *pratijña* /

mēṟkōḷ; 'Because it has smoke' is *hetu / ētu*. 'As in the kitchen' is *dṛṣṭānta / eḍuttu-k-kāṭṭu*.[26] Traces of such type of inference is found in the *Tirumandiram*. The following may be considered as an example:

> ...The tender calf grows old into a bull and after some time dies;
> But this wonder-pageant of the world they do not comprehend.[27]

The logical form of this statement will be as follows: All the young ones will grow old as the calf. This one will grow old. Because this one is young. In this syllogism, 'This one will grow old' is *pratijña / mēṟkōḷ*; 'Because this one is young' is *hetu / ētu*; 'as the calf' is *dṛṣṭānta / eḍuttu-k-kāṭṭu*.

2. 1. 1. 3. Testimony

Testimony helps to know the objects, which cannot be cognized by perception and inference. God is beyond perception and inference.[28] Therefore Tirumūlar emphasizes testimony as the right *pramāṇa* to know the existence of God. Testimony (i.e., *Āgama-pramāṇa*) is given a special place because it is believed to be the utterance of God. Tirumūlar refers to the Āgamas that they are uttered out of the grace of the Lord.[29] The *Sivajñāṉa-siddhiyār* also endorses this.[30] The following verse from the Tirumandiram says how helpful the *pramāṇa* called testimony is in realizing the Lord:

> The way of dismantling and the way of assembling it,
> The way the soul goes out in a fraction,
> The Āgamas and the Vedas explain and thus
> They make realize Him.[31]

2. 1. 1. 4. Cit-śakti

Though it is said that the *pramāṇas* are three in number, they are only helping the cit-śakti (the principle of intelligence or literally the conscious power) to know things. *Pramāṇa* is defined as that which measures all but that which is not measured by anything else.[32] Hence cit-śakti is the only *pramāṇa*. It is the soul that measures the entities. The soul uses its cit-śakti as the instrument to measure these entities. This cit-śakti of the soul is called ātma-cit-śakti. Though it is said that the sense organs and the *antaḥkaraṇas* (the inner organs) measure things, the fact is that the cit-śakti of the soul is that which really measures. This is because the organs can perform only the functions allotted to them and they cannot perform the functions of the others. The eyes, for example, cannot hear. Since the organs do not have the capacity to apprehend anything other than their own respective objects, something capable of apprehending everything should be recognized. Such is cit-śakti and hence that alone is the *pramāna*. This view is also vouchsafed in the Pauṣkara-Āgama.[33] This is indicated in the following verse from the *Tirumandiram:*

> Devoid of knowledge
> Are Tattvas thirty and six;
> The Self that knows
> I know not;
> "You shall know"
> Thus blessed Nandi...[34]

The thirty-six principles or evolutes of māyā are unintelligent. The senses are included in the thirty-six principles. These unintelligent principles cannot measure and know. The knower is the soul with the potency of intelligence.

Even the ātma-cit-śakti cannot be said to be the *pramāna*, because the ātma-cit-śakti cannot measure Śiva. It can furnish only pāśa-jñāna (i.e., worldly knowledge – knowledge of the impermanent). It is only the Śiva-cit-śakti which can bestow paśu-jñāna and Śiva-jñāna. The following verse from the *Tirumandiram* presents this viewpoint:

> The soul neither knows by himself nor is he unintelligent;
> He knows that his knowledge is *sat-asat*.
> When he understands that both are bestowed by the Lord
> He knows the Lord and stands one with the Lord.[35]

That is, the soul cannot know unless it is revealed by the Lord. At the same time it is not an unintelligent inertia; because an unintelligent principle cannot be instructed upon. At one point of time it comes to know that it is capable of knowing both the intelligent entities *(sat)* as well as the unintelligent entity *(asat)*. The Lord does not and need not necessarily know the unintelligent, the *asat*. It is the soul, which is capacitated to know both the intelligent (the *sat*, viz., the Pati and paśu) and the unintelligent (the *asat*, viz., pāśa). Hence the soul is known also as *sat-asat*. When the soul realizes that its knowledge of the real and the unreal, the intelligent and the unintelligent is bestowed on it by the grace of the Lord, then whatever it knows is known by it because of the instruction of the Lord, it realizes the Lord and stands one with Him.

The following verse may also be considered for the purpose of clarification:

> For the people of subtle intelligence seeking the nuances
> The knowledge that operates from behind is that of the Lord...[36]

It is the Lord who drives from the behind. Unless the Lord reveals it, one can neither realize himself nor the Lord. It is the Pati, who is the knowledge behind the knowledge (of the soul). This knowledge of the Lord is known as Śiva-cit. So, ultimately it is the Śiva-cit, which is the real *pramāṇa*. "They know not the measure of grace" – exclaims Tirumūlar in verse 1798. This stands in conformity with the definition given to *pramāṇa* that a *pramāṇa* is that which measures all, but that which is not measured by anything else. The Śiva-cit-śakti can be measured only by itself and not by the ātma-cit-śakti. It is the *pramāṇa* (the means of knowing) and not the *prameya* (the object known) to some other *pramāṇa*. He is *prameya* only to His *pramāṇa*.

Pramāṇa can be viewed in two aspects: the *pramāṇa* that helps and the *pramāṇa* that is helped. The *pramāṇa* that is helped is the ātma-cit-śakti; the *pramāṇa* that helps is the Śiva-cit-śakti. This helps the soul in removing the concealment.

> The Light is unperceivable to the cataract eyes;
> Even those who are provided with eyes are unable to see that Light.
> Those are liberated who see the Light without effort
> With the Eye Divine.[37]

The Lord is beyond the reach of the ignorant; ignorance veils their eyes. The knowledge that one gains through the other *pramāṇas* (the pāśa-jñāna) is of no use; it does not help one to realize oneself and to realize the Lord. It is the Pati-jñāna or Śiva-jñāna, the Eye-Divine, that helps one to realize. Those who have realized are freed of their fetters. This way the Śiva-cit-śakti becomes the *pramāṇa* that helps. In the fettered state the organs help the soul to gain knowledge and in the state of liberation the Śiva-jñāna helps the souls to realize.

2. 1. 2. Prāmāṇya-vāda

The knower knows the objects only through the *pramāṇa*. If the *pramāṇa* is valid the knowledge gained through that also is valid. If the *pramāṇa* is invalid then the knowledge gained through that is invalid. The validity of the *pramāṇa* is called *prāmāṇya* and the invalidity of the *pramāṇa* is called *aprāmāṇya*. To the question which decides the validity and the invalidity of the *pramāṇa*, there are varying answers. According to some, the validity is intrinsic; only the invalidity is extrinsic; some others say that both validity and invalidity are extrinsic. The first answer is known as *svata-prāmāṇya-vāda* and the second one is known as *parata-prāmāṇya-vāda*. We find support to the *svata-prāmāṇya-vāda* in the *Tirumandiram*.

According to the viewpoint of the *parata-prāmāṇya-vādins*, the knowledge gained through one *pramāṇa* will be testified by the knowledge gained through another *pramāṇa*. If the first one corresponds with the second one, then it is valid; otherwise not.

This test confirms the knowledge gained in the first instance and does not produce a new knowledge. Further, if it is held that the validity of the knowledge gained in the first instance needs to be checked by a second one, then the validity of the knowledge gained in the second instance needs to be checked with a third one and it will go on endlessly.

According to the *svata-prāmāṇya-vādins*, true knowledge is by itself valid. Only invalidity is extrinsic and validity is not. To testify an invalid knowledge one needs the help of a valid knowledge and one valid knowledge is not needed to testify another valid knowledge. For example, one takes some food believing it to be good. If after taking it he finds it difficult to digest, then he realizes that the food he has taken is not a good one. He understands that his knowledge about the food is invalid. If nothing happens then it is all right; he does not go around checking the validity of his knowledge that the food is good. Hence invalidity is extrinsic and validity is intrinsic.

When valid knowledge is arrived at, one shall not go on doubting it and checking it. If one does so, the process of knowing will be hindered. Tirumūlar says: weigh well, and having weighed waver not.[38]

Therefore, the validity of the knowledge gained by the *pramāṇa* called cit-śakti, using the three *pramāṇas* (perception, inference and testimony) as instruments, is intrinsic.

3. The metaphysics of the Tirumandiram

In this section the views of Tirumūlar regarding Pati, paśu and pāśa are discussed.

3. 1. Pati – The Lord

God is beyond word and thought. It is impossible to explain His existence, His grace, His qualities. It is *a̱nubōga-k-kāmam* (the pleasure that is to be experienced) to use the language of Tirumūlar, and therefore it is inexplicable. All the mystics hold the same view. Saint Māṇikka-vācagar says: "Oh! The secret One who is beyond the reach of the wavering mind!"[39] Saint Appar says: "Without His grace, it is impossible to explain that God is of this nature, this color, these qualities and such and such is God."[40] Saint Sambandar orders: "Various and countless are the ways and the excellence of the Lord; do not ask for explanations."[41]

Tirumūlar says: He is the light which is beyond speech; He is interminable,[42] He is the bliss which is beyond speech; He is silence.[43] Though He is beyond thought and word He is verily accessible by love, says Tirumūlar and he expresses his weariness about the people who quarrel among themselves regarding the existence and the nature of God.

Well do they see
Life as a trice fleets away;
Yet they in contention stand;
What though these men get?
They stand not in ways righteous,
They adore not His Holy Feet
They know not the Primal One
In love endearing.[44]

Despite this, Tirumūlar renders some verses to establish the existence of God for the sake of those who want to reason it out:

Think of Him
As far as your thoughts go;
Speak His truth
As far as you can;
"Lord," they may say, "He is not,"
Very much He is, everywhere;
Seek the Holy Path
Of Hara that is ever good.[45]

One should use one's mental faculty as far as possible; as a result if one gets an answer that the Lord does not exist, that is because of one's lack of inquiry and not because that the Lord does not exist. Even if one says that God is not, God very much is. Every denial carries with it an affirmation. Though knowledge cannot help attain Him, the path shown by Lord Śiva can. In the *Tēvāram* Saint Sambandar says: "Do not test the Lord with your rhyme and reasons; as a blazing Light He exists,"[46] meaning, "when He is that much easy to comprehend why should one pain oneself?' Following the footsteps of Tirumūlar, Tiru-k-kaḍavūr Uyya-vanda-dēvaṉār, an author of a later date says: "I have inquired about Him as far as I can go and realized."[47]

To prove the existence of God for those who want to reason it out, Tirumūlar states his arguments and explains His nature.

3. 1. 1. Justifications for the existence of God

The three entities accepted by Tirumūlar cannot be established with the help of the *pramāṇa* called perception. Testimony can do, but it may not be acceptable to all. Therefore the *pramāṇa* called inference becomes the only resort to establish the existence of God. Measuring the unperceived through the perceived is inference. So it is possible to establish the existence of the unperceivable God through existence of the perceivable world. The justification is as follows:

That which is constituted of parts is subject to creation and destruction. World is constituted of parts. Therefore it is subject to creation and destruction. Many verses of the *Tirumandiram* highlight this aspect of the world that it is subject to creation and destruction.[48] Anything that is subject to creation and destruction is an effect and therefore there should be a cause for that effect. The world, which is an effect, must have a cause for its creation and destruction. That cause is God. Thus the *Tirumandiram* establishes the existence of God:

> When one is mindful of the creation and destruction
> And the grace of the Sacred One (which is the cause of those acts),
> One will realize the compassionate One,
> The One who pervades all the eight directions.[49]

It is the Destroyer who should be the Creator. Śiva is said to be the Destroyer *(caṅgāra-kāraṇaṉ/saṁhāra-kāraṇa)* and He should be the

Creator also. Because into which a thing gets absorbed, only from that it can emanate. One verse from the *Tirumandiram* says that the world, which is an assembly *(cavai* or *avai/sabha),* has Lord Śaṅkara— who is said to be the destroyer of the world— as its beginning.[50]

The following verse from the *Tirumandiram* explains that there can be no effect without a cause:

The potter mounts the clay on the wheel
The potter fashions as he conceives
Even as the potter our Lord Nandi is;
When He so decides, the inert world comes to shape.[51]

One may also consider the following verse from the *Tirumandiram*:

Where Tattvas are the Lord of Tattvas is;
Where Tattvas are not, the Lord of Tattvas is not;
When you know the truth of Tattva jnana
The Lord of Tattvas will there appear.[52]

The existence of the tattvas implies the existence of the Lord who created these tattvas. When one is enabled with this tattva-jñāna, he realizes the Lord of the tattvas.

Having given the cosmological justification for the existence of God, Tirumūlar also employs what may be called the moral justification.

The souls suffer the cycle of birth and death because of their karma. Karma (deed/action), one of the three fetters (pāśa), is unintelligent/inert. Therefore the fruits of the deeds cannot attach themselves to their doers/souls. There must be an administrator, an impartial judge, who will attach the fruits of the deeds to the respective doer at the time of fruition— in this birth or in the next birth(s). Thus the existence of God may be proved. This argument is subtly expressed in the following verse of the *Tirumandiram*:

> The Immaculate One creates all;
> And as He created me too,
> He animates within me
> A support to the body, a heir to karmic ills;
> Verily, the Lord is the verily Just.[53]

The Immaculate One, creates all, creates the bodies and milieus for jīvas too, according to their kārmic desert. This is His act of divine justice. Tirumūlar stresses this in one more verse:

> Being the Creator, the Destroyer,
> The One Who is inside the body and transmutes,
> The One who is all-pervading like a Light of grace,
> The One who is eternal, He is Just without prejudices/ contraction.[54]

The expression He is Just without prejudices, says it all about the moral administration of the Lord in this verse. This adds emphasis to the moral justification of the existence of God.

3. 1. 2. The cause of the world

Pati, paśu and pāśa, i.e., God, soul and the fetters are the three entities that are accepted by Tirumūlar as eternal. If the world is said to be a fetter, then it should also be eternal. If that is the case, in what way will the creation and destruction of the world be justified? An objection may arise that an eternal world does not need a Creator.

World is an effect. The cause of the world is an inert substance called māyā. This is articulated in the following verse of the *Tirumandiram*:

> The Sun, Moon, Agni and the celestials in-charge of eight directions,
> The space, air, water and earth
> The *tanmātras*, the *karmendriyas*, the *antaḥkaraṇas*
> All these came out of māyā along with *bindu*.[55]

Though the list of the evolutes given in this verse is not exhaustive, the verse clearly conveys the message that all these and the rest are caused by māyā.

Māyā is an inert but eternal substance. The world is evolved out of it and absorbed into it. The world in the evolution becomes gross and in the involution becomes subtle. On this ground it can be argued that the world, which is an effect of the māyā is real. This argument is called *satkārya-vāda*— the theory of causation that the effect exists prior to its manifestation in a latent state in the cause. This *satkārya-vāda* is expressed in the *Tirumandiram*:

> No seed-leaf without the seed; that seed-leaf
> In no way come out except that seed;
> The seed and the seed-leaf are together and not different... [56]

3. 1. 2. 1. The three causes

If the seed-leaf called the world is an effect of the seed called māyā, then what is the role of God? To manifest the latent, some power is needed. Even though the clay, the wheel and the stick all are available if there is no potter who activates these, the pot cannot be manifested. Here the unintelligent clay is the first cause. The intelligent potter is the efficient cause. The wheel and the stick are instrumental causes. So also the Lord, operates the inert māyā by His cit-śakti. Here māyā is the first cause. The Lord is the efficient cause and His cit-śakti (conscious power or intelligence) is the instrumental cause.

One may argue: why not the soul or paśu be the efficient cause? The soul is said to be intelligent; cannot it create the world? It cannot; because only when it gets entangled in the evolutes of māyā it realizes its intelligent potency.[57]

Māyā is in and of itself without power and intelligence and therefore it cannot create itself. It it can only be the first cause and not the efficient cause. Thus the reasoning zeroes in Pati as the efficient cause.

Himself fashions worlds all in detail minute
Himself fashions life, conferring birth
Himself fashions things big and small
  —The cauldron, the pitcher and the pot
Himself He fashions these and more
  —He the Architect Almighty.[58]

3. 1. 3. The five acts of the Lord

The five acts of the Lord are creation, sustenance, destruction, obscuration and grace (*paḍaippu, aḷippu, tuḍaippu, maṟaippu* and *aruḷ* in Tamil/*sṛṣṭi, sthiti, saṁhāra, tirobhāva* and *anugraha* in Sanskrit).

Jñāṉa-p-piragācar, one of the six commentators of the *Śiva-jñāṉa-siddhiyār* explains the five acts of Lord Śiva as follows:

1. Creation is the manifestation of the effect from its first cause, by the will of the Creator.
2. Sustenance is the stay of the effect in dependence on its first cause through the preponderance of the rajas element.
3. Destruction is the cessation of their duties by things and their disappearance into their first cause.

4. Obscuration is the power, which causes attachment in the soul for enjoying that which is condemned most, all the while believing it to be good.
5. Grace is the removal of pāśa and manifestation of Śivatva.[59]

Tirumūlar says:

Creation, Preservation, and Dissolution,
(That for Jivas grant rest from birth-and-death whirl)
Obfuscation and Grace
(That redeem Jiva after life below)
These, for Sakala souls He filled;
All these acts five,
Beginningless His are.[60]

Further he also symbolizes the Lord of five acts in the form of Naṭarāja. (This has been dealt with in detail in the chapter "Śaivism as conceived in the Tirumandiram"). None else other than Śiva is the reason for the five acts.

Himself creates; Himself preserves
Himself destroys; Himself obscures
Himself, all these He does
And grants Mukti after;
Himself the all-immanent Lord.[61]

3. 1. 3. 1. God is immutable

A potter who is the efficient cause of the pot is subject to mutation by his deed. But God, Who is the efficient cause of the world, Who performs the five acts, is not affected by His activities. When the sun shines, the lotus blossoms forth, the burning-glass emits fire and the water in the earth dries up. While the sun is responsible for these changes, it itself does not undergo any change. So it is with the Lord also. Śivāgra-yogin says that the creation of the universe is comparable to the blossoming of the lotus, the fructification of karma during the state of maintenance to the burning-glass emitting fire and the destruction of the universe to water drying up.[62] Tirumūlar says it is like a play without effort.[63]

Further, the efficient cause is of two types. The first type of efficient cause needs instruments to create. The second One does it at the mere resolve of it *(saṅkalpa-mātram)*.[64] The second type of efficient cause is the Lord alone. All the others can do nothing without instruments. Only those who do with instruments undergo change. The Lord who does at the mere thought does not undergo any change. The *Tirumandiram* clearly states that when the Lord so decides, the inert world comes to shape.[65] Here Tirumūlar uses the term Lord *(kōṉ)* meaning king to denote God intentionally. When the king resolves to do something he passes orders and it is done by his aides as desired by him. He needs somebody to carry out his orders. God needs none. The mere resolve itself will fructify *(vēṇḍil adu idu āmē)*. One more difference between the resolve of the king and God is the time factor. It takes some time to accomplish the order of the king. But there is no time-framework to accomplish the resolve of God. On the resolve it is done.[66]

Therefore it becomes clear that God is immutable.

3. 1. 3. 2. The purpose of the five acts

What is the Lord's purpose in performing His several activities? Some would say it is just a play quoting from sources including the *Tirumandiram*. Play does not mean amusement. It means to be at ease; that God performs all these acts with ease without undergoing any change. Therefore purpose of the activities of the Lord is not amusement. Then what? The reason for His activities is His love for the souls. It is His grace that actuates His activities. The reason is to help the souls to get rid of their malas or pāśa.

The following verse from the *Tirumandiram* clearly states this:

It was His grace that led me into Pāśa
It was His grace that freed me from that Pāśa
It was His grace that in divine love granted Mukti
It was His grace that granted me the love
For the state beyond Mukti.[67]

How can it be said that these are acts of grace when most of these other acts of the Lord plunge the souls into birth and death and thus make them suffer? The *Tirumandiram* answers:

In His Grace was I born,
In His Grace I grew up
In His Grace I rested in death;
In His Grace I was in obfuscation;
In His Grace I tasted of ambrosial bliss;
In His Grace, Nandi, my heart entered.[68]

That is, the act of creation is carried out by Him to enable the souls by giving them body etc., to work out their karma; sustenance is to make the souls experience the fruit of their action; destruction is to give rest to the souls; obscuration is to veil the nature of souls as cit and bring about indifference to fruits of actions, good and bad by first making them engage in action; grace is the grant of release. All these activities are thus indicative of His Grace.

3. 1. 4. The (accidental) nature of the Lord

Does the Lord have a form or not? Or is He a formless form? Does not the One Who performs the five acts need a form? He Who is eternally free and Who is of the form of intelligence has a form which can at once be said to be all the three, i.e., with form *(uruvam/rūpa)*, without form *(aruvam/arūpa)* and with and without form *(aru-v-uruvam/rūpārūpa)*.

If God is said to be any one of the above stated three forms, then it amounts to limiting the limitless. Everything in this limited world is either with-form or without-form or with-and-without-form. Of these various entities one cannot assume the nature of the other. For example, space – the *ākāśa*, is without-form and it cannot take a form. Earth is with-form and it cannot become formless. Candra, the moon, is with-and-without-form; it can neither be classified under the with-form category nor under the without-form category.[69] Therefore, these are limited entities unable to imbibe the nature of the other. If God is classified as One with-form or without-form or with-and-without-form He becomes limited; hence He is said to be the One of all the three— with-form, without-form and with-and-without-form. This is referred to in the *Tirumandiram*.[70]

Formlessness: If God is attributed with a form, will He not undergo changes as the other corporeal substances? The form of God is not a physical one. It is the body of grace.[71] Therefore He will undergo no changes. Only the souls need a physical body to carry out activities. God does not; because He is beyond the space-time limitations. He is birthless, deathless, and uninterrupted continuum.[72] He is formless in the sense that He is without a physique and therefore He will not undergo any changes.[73] He is supported by Himself, that is, He supports all the other things but He is supported by none.[74] He is *sui generis* (self-originating). He creates all the forms without a form for Himself. He has no birth yet He is the seed of all births.[75]

Form of the Lord: Sometimes it is said that the created world itself serves as the form of the Lord. Tirumūlar says: His form engages all the seven worlds.[76] Śiva-jñāṉa-yōgi says that the soul does not need another body to make its body to function.[77] So also the world being His body, the Lord does not need another body to activate the world. The following verse from *Śiva-jñāṉa-siddhiyār Cubakkam* clarifies this stand:

> The world being His form, the bodies being His limbs,
> The three potencies, volition, knowledge and action being the inner organs,
> The Lord enacts the drama of
> Illuminating the countless souls, playing five roles[78]

But unless God comes with a form to illuminate the souls, the souls will suffer. If He takes a physical body as a general rule it will undergo changes. To resolve this dichotomy Tirumūlar says that the body of the Lord is not a physical one subject to the fetters,[79] but it is a body of grace.[80] The Lord assumes form out of His limitless grace for the suffering souls. The *Tiru-k-kaḷiṟṟu-p-paḍiyār* asks:

> What can the sacred literature, the six religions,
> The practice of Yoga and the intelligence do to realize
> Unless the One takes the form with grace to inform
> Who can know the Greatest One? Tell me![81]

Tirumūlar in one place says that God is beyond word and thought; if God is said to be the One with a form, then He becomes subject to our thought. Besides that He becomes one among the many gods. Tirumūlar tackles this objection by saying that though He takes a form to inform the souls still He is beyond thought, because "Great is He, rising above the macrocosm vast *(viśvādhika);*"[82] He is the seed of the macrocosm *(viśva-kāraṇa);*[83] He stands in coherence and all pervading *(antaryāmin);*[84] He stands as the macrocosm *(viśva-rūpa).*[85] Only those who do not know this truth will speak of Him as one among the many like Viṣṇu and Brahma. They do not know the episode of Viṣṇu and Brahma vainly seeking to see the peak and the bottom of Lord Śiva who stood before them as a monument of fire.[86]

Of the forms assumed by the Lord for the sake of informing the souls, some are symbolic of *bhoga* (pleasure) and have been assumed so as to plunge the souls into *bhoga* (the form of Umā-maheśvara);[87] some are symbolic of anger and have been assumed so that the activities of the souls may be destroyed (the form of Kāmāri – destructing Kāma, the Indian cupid);[88] and some others symbolizing yogic meditation have been assumed so that the souls may gain release through Yoga (the form of Dakṣiṇāmūrti).[89] Only the ignorant will prattle that Śiva is one among the other gods.[90]

The following verse from the *Tirumandiram* speaks of the Lord's act of taking various forms:

Lord Nandi
That has form several,
And permeates life several,
Why does He in this Form
So open appear?
That He thus sports in joy
With Her of bangled hands
And Form bejeweled,
Is indeed a mystery, baffling![91]

V.A. Devasenapathy reasons out the Lord's act of taking various forms thus:

> 'If you must make me weep, you must weep yourself' is a maxim in art. Example here, as elsewhere, is better than precept. So also, the Lord appears to carry on certain vital functions in order that mortals may follow His lead. Besides, to trace the origin of these vital urges to Godhead is to sanctify them. If mortals are to enjoy the pleasures of life or engage in meditation in the right way, the Lord Himself must set them as example.[92]

The moment the form is accepted, the formlessness into which the form gets absorbed, follows naturally. When the formlessness emanates into a form, the formless-form stands as the intermediary.[93] The Lord's assuming these three— form, formlessness and formless-form— is out of grace.[94]

3. 1. 4. 1. Śiva and Śakti

It is clear that the forms of Lord Śiva are not the effects of māyā but of the Śakti called grace.

The holy feet of the One with matted locks
Is given as legacy (to the souls); the pure One Who holds Ganga
Has taken a body with the great Śakti and embraced by Her;
By this union all creation arises.[95]

Reaching the holy feet *(tāḷ)* is the ultimate goal of the souls. So it is said to be their legacy, by Tirumūlar. To ensure that they get their legacy, they need to be supported with bodily instruments and instructions. To support them with instruments and instructions the Lord takes forms. These forms are of grace. Grace is Śakti. In the union of Śiva and Śakti the universe is created.

Is Śakti different from Śiva? No. They are like the body and the soul;[96] they are like the part and the whole;[97] they are like the flower and its fragrance;[98] Śiva is not separate from Śakti.[99] Śakti is Śiva and Śiva is Śakti.[100] No Śiva without grace and no grace without Śiva.[101]

3. 1. 5. The (essential) nature of the Lord

Though God is attributed with-form, without-form and with-and-without-form, in His original nature *(svarūpa-lakṣaṇa)* is said to be beyond all these.

> He is not *tat-para;* He is not Sadāśiva;
> He is not *niṣkala*; He is not *sakala;*
> Extraordinary He is; like the sexual enjoyment
> He stood one with (the soul) stripped off imagination.[102]

God is not *para*, which is subject to change; He is not Sadaśiva (the name given to the with-and-without-form/*aru-v-uru*); He is not the without form *(aru/niṣkala)*; He is not the form *(uru/sakala)*; He is extraordinary and inexplicable like the sexual enjoyment, which cannot be explained but can be experienced. He is conceived to be with-form, without-form and with-and-without-form, because of the imagination enabled by His grace. When the true nature of the Lord is realized He will reveal Himself stripping off all the imaginative forms and names, and will stand one with the realized.

Tirumūlar characterizes God with eight attributes.[103] God is, unlike the souls, not subject to the three qualities (guṇas— *sattva, rajas* and *tamas*), which are the products of māyā. In this sense He is said to be the One without attributes. Though He is not subject to the three guṇas, which are impure, He is said to be the One with the pure eight guṇas. The Śaivāgamas list the eight guṇas of the Lord as follows:

1) being self-dependent *(taṉ-vayattaṉ ādal)*,
2) being immaculate in body *(tūya-uḍambiṉaṉ ādal)*,
3) having intuitive wisdom *(iyaṟkai-y-uṇaviṉaṉ ādal)*,
4) being omniscient *(muṟṟum uṇardal)*,
5) freedom, by nature, from all dross or other impurities which fetter souls *(iyalbāgavē pācaṅgaḷiṉ nīṅgudal)*,
6) being of boundless grace *(pēraruḷ uḍaimai)*,
7) being omnipotent *(muḍivil-āṟṟal uḍaimai)*, and
8) being in enjoyment of boundless bliss *(varambil-iṉbam uḍaimai)*.[104]

To be precise God is characterized as sat (satya), cit (jñāna) and ānanda, that is Satcitānanda.[105] Being Satcitānanda is the essential nature of the Lord.

The relation between the Lord and the other entities are one of identity-in-difference. That is, by His omnipresence He stands in identity with the world and the souls; by nature He stands different from them; by His helping grace He stands One with them yet different from them.[106]

3. 2. Pāśa – The bonds

Pāśa is the impediment that restrains the soul; that which binds the souls is pāśa. It is said to be of three varieties.[107] They are: āṇava, karma and māyā.[108] Of these three, āṇava is the ignorance called egoism;[109] māyā is the material cause of all that are created– the universe;[110] karma, which is divided into two– good and bad– is that which causes birth.[111] Of these three let us discuss māyā first.

3. 2. 1. Māyā

The word "māyā" is a combination of two syllables *mā* plus *yā*; of these two the first syllable *mā* stands for involution and the second *yā* stands for evolution. To spell out the first syllable *mā*, we close our lips, which signifies involution; while for the second *yā*, we widely open our mouth, which signifies evolution. The word "māyā" can also be derived in another way. That is the word is split into two words: *māy* plus *ā*. The first word *māy* means dying, coming to an end, to cease from existence, etc., and the second word *ā* means to become, to evolve, to come into existence, etc.

Māyā, the seed of the world, is so called because things come forth from it and go back into it. It is said to be of two kinds: śuddha-māyā (the pure māyā) and aśuddha-māyā (the impure māyā).[112] Taking also the prakṛti-māyā into consideration, which is a product of aśuddha-māyā, māyā is said to be of three kinds. Tirumūlar names these three māyās as *mā-māyā*, *māyā* and *ō-māyā*.[113]

Of these pure and impure māyās, the pure māyā is the mother; the impure māyā is the nurse; Paraśiva is the father. They thus help the souls to take birth, to undergo experiences, and finally to get liberated.[114]

What is the reason behind pushing the souls into the fold of māyā? Tirumūlar quips that it is to help the souls to get rid of their ignorance, the Lord, out of His unlimited grace, pushes the souls into the fold of māyā.[115]

What type of a grace is this to cause another impediment to the soul which is already impeded with āṇava? Tirumūlar comes out with an example to answer this objection: The washer men use the saline soil to remove the stains in cloths. Here, adding dirt to a cloth, which is already dirty is not to make the cloth dirtier but to clean it. Similarly, adding māyā, another fetter, to the already ailing soul is not to restrain it but to help with an instrument to gain knowledge. So it is nothing but a technique played by the Lord to help the souls improve themselves.[116] It is only because of the māyā the soul's natural potencies of knowledge, desire and action are activated.[117]

3. 2. 1. 1. The products of śuddha-māyā

From the śuddha-māyā sphere come out the first evolutes: 1. *nāda* (Śiva/formless), which is the principle of jñāna, directed by the jñāna-śakti of Parama-Śiva; 2. *bindu* (Śakti/formless), which is a principle of kriyā, directed by the kriyā-śakti of Parama-Śiva; 3. *sādākhya* (Sadāśiva/with-and-without-form), which is a principle of jñāna and kriyā, directed by the kriyā-śakti of Parama-Śiva; 4. *īśvara* (Maheśvara/with-form), which is a principle with a dominance of kriyā over jñāna, directed by the icchā-śakti of Parama-Śiva; 5. *śuddha-vidya* (Rudra/with form), which is a principle with a dominance of jñāna over kriyā, directed by the jñāna-śakti of Parama-Śiva. These are called the Śiva-tattvas or the śuddha-tattvas or the śuddha-māyā-tattvas.

Tirumūlar refers to the evolution of *nāda* and *bindu* from the śuddha-māyā.[118] From *bindu* the four *vāks* (forms of speech) called *vaikharī, madhyamā, paśyantī* and *sūkṣmā* come out.[119] *Vaikharī* is the gross form of speech. It can be heard by him who utters it and by him who hears it. It has the capacity to express what is thought and it helps to create determinate knowledge in the speaker and the hearer. *Madhyamā* is the form of speech, which is sub-vocal. It can be heard only internally, because it is a soft sound, residing in the throat and it helps to form determinate knowledge in the mind of him who utters it. *Paśyantī* possesses in a very subtle form, like the peahen's egg which does not show the five colors that are to be manifested later. It resides in the thought. It makes indeterminate knowledge possible. *Sūkṣmā* has two characteristics: (i) it exists as sound in the *kāraṇa-śarīra* and (ii) it makes knowledge possible. While *paśyantī, madhyamā* and *vaikharī* which evolve from *sūkṣmā* are destroyed, *sūkṣmā* persists as śuddha-māyā. He who is able to see it as it is, as a result of merit gained from his penance will derive the great enjoyment of the śuddha-māyā world (this is partial release) and comes to have unceasing wisdom, independence and eternality. He is freed from the weariness and changes caused by the cycle of births and deaths.[120]

3. 2. 1. 2. The products of aśuddha-māyā

Below the five Śiva-tattvas are the seven vidya-tattvas in the impure māyā (or *mā-māyā*) sphere, all directed by the five śuddha-tattvas: 1. aśuddha-māyā (impure māyā), which is directed by the *nāda-tattva*; 2. *kāla* (time); 3. *niyati* (necessity, destiny, law of causality or law of karma); 4. *kalā* (part or limited activity); these three are directed by the *bindu-tattva*; 5. *vidyā* (partial knowledge), which is directed by the *īśvara-tattva*; 6. *rāga* (attachment, desire), which is directed by the *śuddha-vidyā-tattva*; 7. *puruṣa* (the principle of consciousness or subjectivity), which is directed by the *sādākhya-tattva*.

The *Tirumandiram* identifies *kāla, niyati* and *kala* along with its products as the products of aśuddha-māyā and it also says that from these the other principles (tattvas) of evolution come out. The verses containing this information are scattered through out the eighth *tantra* of the *Tirumandiram.*[121] One verse says that all evolutes belong to the same clan called the products of māyā.[122] One verse explains the order of evolution of the *mahā-bhutās.*[123] One verse comes forth with the evolutes of the *mahā-bhūtās.*[124] Another verse attributes colors to the bhūtās.[125] Unlike in the

Sāṁkhya view (that *puruṣa* is the soul), *puruṣa* is only a product of māyā.[126]

One verse records that the Śaiva Siddhāntins accept thirty-six principles of evolution, the Vedāntins twenty-eight, the Vaiṣṇavites twenty-four and the Māyā-vādins twenty-five.[127]

Of the thirty-six principles twenty-four are aśuddha-tattvas (impure principles); seven are śuddhāśuddha-tattvas (pure-impure principles) and five are śuddha-tattvas (pure principles). The aśuddha-tattvas are the products of the prakṛti-māyā, also called the atma-tattvas. The seven śuddhāśuddha-tattvas are the products of āśuddha-māyā and are also called vidya-tattvas. The five śuddha-tattvas are the products of śuddha-māyā also called Śiva-tattvas.[128] All these three-fold tattvas, which are thirty-six in number, are made to associate with the souls.[129]

3. 2. 2. Karma

Viṉai is the Tamil equivalent of the Sanskrit term karma. Tirumūlar has used both the terms in his work.[130] Karma is action: action of mind, word and body. Tirumūlar warns: Don't think that only the deeds of the body are taken into account. Do not behave in such a way that your lips utter one thing, mind thinks another and the deed does a third.[131]

Karma is brought about by the activity of one's body. But how is the body itself brought into existence? What is the cause of the body? The body is the result of deeds done in a previous life.[132] Just as the seed and the sprout follow each other, these (bodies and acts) come in a series and as cause and effect of one another from time immemorial like a perpetually flowing stream *(pravāha-anādi)*. Hence there is no saying which is earlier and which is later of these two.[133] Though this point of view discourages further discussion on it, Muru. Pala. Rathinam Chettiyar makes an attempt to solve this imbroglio in his book:

> From time immemorial the souls are bound by the fetter called āṇava, their potencies of knowledge, desire and action being diminished by it. To help the souls out of āṇava, God creates subtle bodies for the souls first. Because He is creating out of unlimited grace, He creates the subtle bodies all alike. The subtle bodies of all the souls— from one-sensed beings to the six-sensed ones— are alike. The subtle body consists of the following eight constituents: the five subtle essences of the five elements *(tanmātras)*, i.e., taste, sight, touch, sound and smell (1-5), the mind (6), the ego-sense *(ahaṅkāra)* (7) and the intellect *(buddhi)* (8). After the Lord blesses the souls with subtle bodies, the souls' until untapped potencies of knowledge, desire and action are stimulated a little... The souls are essentially unlike each other. Because of this reason and the difference in the levels of concealment by the āṇanva-mala, each soul develops its own likes and dislikes. These likes and dislikes, although they are not clearly thought of, serve as the opening karmas. God creates the gross bodies taking into the account the foremost karmas (the rudimentary likes and dislikes) of the souls... With these gross bodies the souls continue to accumulate more karmas and as a result of these they are born again.[134]

Rathinam Chettiyar, in support of his argument, also quotes a verse from the Tamil work by name *Pōṟṟi-p-paḥṟoḍai* by Umāpati Śivācāriyār. In the verse quoted, Umāpati Śivācāriyār thanks the Lord for enabling the soul with the subtle body out of māyā to stimulate its potencies covered up by āṇava, and making the soul's deeds out of that stimulation the cause for creating the gross body to help the soul to gain jñāna. He compares this act of the Lord with that of helping a blind one with a stick.[135]

Tirumūlar has resolved the debate regarding whether karma precedes birth or birth precedes karma that birth (with the subtle body) precedes karma. Consider the following verses from the *Tirumandiram*:

> Of the two bodies that the Lord has created
> If sūkṣma (subtle) is to be explained,
> It is the puriyaṣṭa-kāya (body of eight constituents) made of
> Sound, touch, sight, taste, smell, intellect, mind and ego-sense.[136]

> Of these eight, five serve as sense organs
> And three serve as internal organs;
> This pāśa attached causes sentience in the souls
> Thus the Lord binds them and unbinds them.[137]

Because of its association with the subtle body which is a product of māyā, the soul becomes sentient and starts doing. This helps the Lord to bind and unbind the soul with the gross body. Therefore the gross body is the result of the subtle karmas (the likes and dislikes) of the soul in its subtle body.

3. 2. 2. 1. Classification of karma

Tirumūlar generally classifies the karmas into two: good and bad *(nal-vin̲ai* or *puṇya* and *tī-vin̲ai* or *pāpa)*[138] and calls them as *iru-vin̲ai* (the two deeds).[139] In accordance with the two deeds the souls will enjoy in heaven and suffer in hell.[140]

Karma is distinctively classified into three: *prārabdha, sañcita* and *āgāmya*. Of these, *prārabdha* is that karma from previous births which has started manifesting its consequences in the present birth. It is inescapable, however much one tries to escape it. Therefore, it has to be experienced and thus only eliminated. *Sañcita* is that past karma from previous births which will not manifest until a future birth and can be overcome by spiritual practices and destroyed entirely by jñāna. *Āgāmya* is karma which is created now by our present acts, which will mature in the normal course of events. It is open for us, so to act as to make our future or mar it.[141] In the *Tirumandiram*, it is said:

> The Tattva Jnanis realize the Self;
> The Gordian knot of Karma past
> They cut asunder;
> Future Karmas they seize and crush,
> By Grace of Siva,
> Whom they hold,
> High on their heads.[142]

Here Tirumūlar makes note of the *sañcita* and *āgāmya karmas* without referring to the *prārabdha-karma* leaving it to the understanding of the reader that there is no escape from the *prārabdha-karma.*

3. 2. 3. Āṇava

Āṇava is egoity, the primal bondage for the souls. It is eternal and beginningless. It is said that the āṇava-mala is to the souls as the verdigris is to copper. If āṇava-mala is removed, the souls will be restored to their essential nature as intelligence. Āṇava is one; but by virtue of its infinite capacities, it thwarts the three potencies of the soul.

Tirumūlar identifies the ego-sense as āṇava.[143] This ego-sense is due to ignorance. Only to help the soul out of this ignorance God associates it with māyā. In association with māyā, the soul also accumulates the third one, karma. Tirumūlar calls this āṇava as *iruḷ* (darkness).[144] The later Śaiva Siddhāntins would characterize āṇava-mala as worse than darkness; because in the case of darkness, it conceals only the objects which are in its fold, but reveals itself. In the case of āṇava, it not only conceals that which is in its fold but also itself.

3. 2. 4. Relation between the three malas

Tirumūlar explains the relation between the three malas in the following verse:

> Āṇava, māyā and karma are like
> The kernel, bran and husk to the soul, allowing not
> The soul to reach the Lord wrapping it;
> Rid of your pāśa and adore God.[145]

3. 2. 5 The other malas

Tirumūlar sometimes speaks of five malas.[146] The other two malas are *māyeya* and *tirodhāyī*.[147] Of these two, *māyeya* denotes the products of māyā, which are the locus for all the pleasures and pains. *Tirodhāyī* is Śiva's obscuring energy called tirodhāna-śakti, which impels each of the malas to its respective function and brings about the ripening of all the three. It is so-called because it prevents intuiting of the self and the Lord.[148]

3. 3. Paśu

That which is bound by pāśa is paśu.[149] It is also referred to by Tirumūlar by names such as *āṉmā*, *ādaṉ* and *uyir*. Let us first explore the nature of soul according to Tirumūlar. There are various views that soul is nothing but the gross body, senses, the subtle body, the prāṇa (vital air), Brahman, the *antaḥkaraṇas* (internal organs), etc. The verses of the *Tirumandiram* clearly state that soul is different from the aforesaid and it is the enjoyer of the results produced by these organs.[150]

According to the *Tirumandiram* souls are many in number.[151] These souls are not created entities according to Tirumūlar. If it is held that the souls are created then it leads to a contradiction; because that which is created is not eternal and it would also be difficult to explain why God who has no need, has created the souls. Hence Tirumūlar holds that the souls are eternal and that they are entangled in the chain of births and deaths because of their bondages— āṇava and karma.[152]

3. 3. 1. The nature of the soul

It is said that the soul is eternal. It is also intelligent. The following verse in the *Tirumandiram* explains this:

I know not that I am intelligent
The Lord made me know that I am intelligent
Now I know that I am intelligent out of His grace
And now I also know He is intelligent.[153]

Though the soul is intelligent it remains ignorant without even knowing its potency of intelligence because of its attachment with the fetter āṇava. Āṇava is so-called because it minimizes the triadic potencies of the soul to the size of an atom *(aṇu).*

The soul is attributed with two important characteristics. The first one is that the soul will never be on its own. It is always dependent. In the state of bondage it is dependent on pāśa, and in the state of liberation it is dependent on Pati.[154] The second characteristic of the soul is that it reflects the nature of that on which it depends. When it depends on the unintelligent existence— *asat,* i.e., on āṇava, it reflects the qualities of it. When it is in the company of the Intelligent Existence— *sat,* i.e., Pati, it reflects the qualities of Him. Hence the soul can associate with both, the *sat* and the *asat*, Tirumūlar calls it *satasat*.[155] He compares the soul with crystal, which reflects the thing kept nearby it.[156]

3. 3. 2. The states of soul

Depending on the association of the soul, there are three classifications for the states of the soul. These states of dependence are called *avasthas*. The three *avasthas* are: *kevalāvastha*, *sakalāvastha* and *śuddhāvastha*. Of these, *kevalāvastha* is the state of the soul in association with the āṇava alone. This is the primary state of the soul.[157] Along with āṇava, when the soul stands in association with the other two malas, māyā and karma, this state is called *sakalāvastha*. This is the intermediate state.[158] When the soul gets rid of these three malas and stands in association with Pati, the Lord, this state is called *śuddhāvastha*. This is the final state.[159] Tirumūlar puts these states in a nut shell: One who realized himself is a *śuddha*; the one who knows nothing is a *kevala*; and the one who knows with distortion is a *sakala*.[160] These three states are called *kāraṇa-avasthas* (the causal states).

There are also five states of consciousness, which are the resultants of the above said causal states. These states are known as *kāriya-avasthas* (the resultant states).[161] They are known as *jāgrat* or *naṉavu* (physical consciousness), *svapna* or *kaṉavu* (dream consciousness), *suṣupti* or *uṟakkam* (dreamless sleep),[162] *turiya* or *pēruṟakkam* (the fourth state), and *turiyātītam* or *uyirppaḍaṅgal* (beyond the fourth state).[163]

All the five *kāriya-avasthas* happen when the soul is in the *sakala* state. In each of these *kāriya-avasthas*, the soul acts in association with certain principles or instruments (tattvas) produced out of māyā. Accordingly the experiences of the soul differ. Tirumūlar explains the number of principles the soul is associated with and the place *(sthāna)* in which the soul positions itself to undergo the experience in each of the resultant states.

In the first state *jāgrat* or *naṉavu,* which is the waking state, the soul positions itself in the mid-brow (ājñā-cakra);[164] in this state the soul is active in association with thirty-five principles.[165] The thirty-five principles are: the ten organs— sensory and motor (five *jñānendriyas* and five *karmendriyas*), the five objects of the five senses (like sound, etc.), the resultant activities of the five motor organs (like speech, etc.), the ten airs (*vāyus* like prāṇa, etc.), the four *antaḥkaraṇas,* and the puruṣa.

In the second state *svapna* or *kaṉavu,* which is the dreaming state, the soul descends from the mid-brow to the throat (viśuddhi-cakra). Here it leaves association with the five sense organs and the five motor organs and remains with twenty-five principles.[166]

In the third state *suṣupti* or *uṟakkam,* which is sleeping state, the soul descends from throat to heart (anāhata-cakra), leaves association with the twenty-two principles and remains with three only (i.e., with the prāṇa, citta and puruṣa).[167]

In the fourth state *turiya,* the soul descends from heart to navel (maṇipūra-cakra), and remains with only two (i.e., prāṇa and puruṣa).[168]

In the fifth state *turiyātīta,* the soul goes to svādhiṣṭhāna-cakra, where it remains with puruṣa alone.[169]

The descendance of the soul from ājña to svādhiṣṭhāna is described as *kīḻāl-avastha* (the state of descendance) and the ascendance of the soul from svādhiṣṭhāna to ājña is described as *mēlāl-avastha* in the Śaiva Siddhānta parlance.

Apart from these *kāraṇa-avasthas* and *kāriya-avasthas,* the *Tirumandiram* also speaks of *para-avastha* and *nirmala-avastha.* These *avasthas* are the states of the soul where it is free of its bondage enjoying the bliss of being at the feet of the Lord. The *Tirumandiram* puts forth the achievement of *śuddha-avastha* as the final goal of the soul,[170] that is to become free from the fetters.

3. 3. 3. The categories of souls

Tirumūlar categorizes the souls into three *(mūvagai-c-cīva-varkkam)* and calls them as *vijñāna-kalas, praḷayā-kalas* and *sakalas.* Of these three types, the *vijñāna-kalas* are called as *kēvalattār,* i.e., those who have āṇava alone.[171] The *praḷayā-kalas* are called *iru-mala-pettar,* i.e., those who have two impurities (malas), āṇava and māyā.[172] (Though the *praḷayā-kalas* are generally identified with the two impurities of āṇava and karma, Tirumūlar identifies them with the two impurities of āṇava and māyā). The *sakalas* are called *mu-m-malattār,* i.e., those who have all the three impurities, āṇava, karma and māyā.[173] (See Appendix-B)

4. Liberation

Soul is intelligent; but not knowing its potency of intelligence it stays put in ignorance. To help the soul to come out of ignorance, the Lord, out of His grace, provides the soul with instruments by way of creating the world out of māyā. But these instruments, the tattva-tāttvikas, cannot enlighten the soul; they give only distorted knowledge. Hence the soul, forgetting the purpose of the instruments, engages itself fully in the worldly activities, completely lost in the gritty grip of the fetters. Tirumūlar depicts this graphically in the following verse:

> The ploughman ploughed; the heavens poured;
> By the ploughing, lily blossomed;
> Comparing it with his wife's eye,
> The ploughman ceased to plough it further.[174]

The ploughman ploughs his field to cultivate a particular crop and removes all weeds. Otherwise the weeds will have an effect on the growth of his intended crop. Though the lily is very beautiful and likeable, ultimately it is a weed. Instead of weeding it out the ploughman compares it with his wife's eye, and leaves it to grow. Thus he made the mistake of losing his purpose. Here the ploughman stands for the soul. Ploughing is the soul's efforts to get rid of the malas. The pouring of the heavens stands for the divine grace. Out of divine grace the world is evolved. The world is represented by the lily flower. The soul, instead of detaching from the world, lost itself completely in the worldly activities forgetting the original purpose. Tirumūlar calls such a soul as *kaḍum-paśu*, the severely fettered soul.[175]

The Śaiva Siddhānta works give another example to explain this:

> A prince, in ignorance of his parentage, joins some gypsies, loses his independence and dignity and allows himself to be brought up in gipsy ways, unbecoming of a prince. He does not realize that he is a prince and that his father is a king, until the king finds him, takes him away from the gypsies and restores him to his rightful place. Similarly, the soul forgets its essential nature, gets lost in the whirl of the senses, loses its intelligence and suffers, on account of not knowing itself and the Lord. When the soul as a result of certain austerities becomes fit, Śiva, who is the eternal, free, pure intelligence assumes the form of a preceptor, teaches it, destroys the efficiency of the mala (so that the soul may get rid of its subjection to the senses) and restores it to its essential nature.[176]

The following is the example given by Tirumūlar to explain this:

The cuckoo bird leaves its egg in the crow's nest;
The crow hatches it, nurses it. The young cuckoo,
Suspecting nothing neither dissociates nor asks why,
It allows the crow to nurse it out of ignorance.[177]

In this verse the crow is māyā; the cuckoo is the soul. It is out of the divine grace the soul realizes its mistakes and sets them right.[178] When the divine grace descends on the soul, it gets rid of the malas and attains liberation.

In the state of liberation— the souls do penance on their part;
And are in full receipt of divine grace; purified of the tattvas;
And rid of the karmas; stand in true devotion;
Immersed in the transcendental bliss.[179]

4. 1. Equanimity and the descent of grace

Is the divine grace accessible to all? Yes! It is there for all without any discrimination. But only the qualified knows the availa-bility of it and grabs it. To know that grace is readily available one has to do *tapas*, intensive practice of Yoga.[180] Even intensive practice is a result of previous *tapas*. Intensive practice comes handy only to those who have done it in their previous births.[181] To be blessed with such intensive practice one has to do action without attaching oneself with the fruit of that action. When this is done one remains unaffected even by his old karmas.[182]

...Sunder your desires and passions;
Having sundered,
The Lord's place, easy be.[183]

Sunder your desires, sunder your desires
Sunder your desires even like Lord;
The more the desires, the more your sorrows;
The more you give up, the more your bliss shall be.[184]

The souls, which have reached this state of non-attachment, are in a state of mental equanimity. They consider the merits and demerits all alike; that is, they do not enjoy at merit and are not disheartened at demerit. At this state, the divine grace will come in the form of a preceptor, to help the soul get liberated.

When Jīva attains the state of Neutrality
To deeds, good and evil,
Then does divine Grace in Guru form descend,
Removes attributes all,
Implants Jnana that is like a heavenly cool shade;
The Jīva thus rid of egoity,
And other Impurities Three,
Shall with Siva in union merge.[185]

The divine grace descends in accordance with one's efforts.[186] This descent is classified into four types according to the processing speed as *mandam* (slower), *manda-taram* (slow), *tīviram* (quick), and *tīvira-taram* (quicker).[187]

4. 2. The four ways of liberation

Tirumūlar teaches the four ways of attaining the feet of Śiva: *dāsa-mārga, satputra-mārga, saha-mārga,* and *sanmārga.*[188] These are also known as *caryā, kriyā, yoga* and *jñāna.*[189]

Dāsa-mārga or *caryā* is the path of servitude. In this, the relationship between the Lord and the soul is like that of the master and the slave. This path enjoins the following observances: cleaning and sanctifying the temple, weaving garlands, uttering the praise of the Lord, lighting the temple lamps, maintaining the temple gardens and offering one's services to any devotee of Śiva.

Satputra-mārga or *kriyā* is the path of the son. In this, the relationship between the Lord and the soul is like that of the father and the son. This path prescribes worship in the following way: collecting flowers, incense, light, water (for bathing the idol), food (for offering), etc.; the devotee has to perform the five kinds of purification (purification of the soul, the place, the things, the mantra, and the liṅga). Then a seat has to be made out of mūla-mantra for Śiva to occupy. He is to be contemplated as having occupied it, externalized, worshipped with true devotion and willingly praised.

Saha-mārga or *yoga* is the path of friendship. It requires the fulfillment of the following: The senses are to be turned away from their objects; inhaling and exhaling must be controlled, vital air must be directed along suṣumna when mental activities cease; the sequence of the mantras for the six ādhāras like the mūlādhāra must be learnt; the powers presiding over the ādhāras are to be worshipped internally. Uniting with the powers, one must go up from mūlādhāra to brahma-randhra. The lotus in brahma-randhra must be made to blossom. The nectar flowing downwards from the crown is to be circulated within the body; and contemplation of light that takes within itself every splendor is to crown all these.

Sanmārga is the path of jñāna. This path suggests the attainment of jñāna, without distinctions into knower, knowledge and the object of knowledge, i.e., the knowledge of unity with the one, eternal, pervasive, existent, intelligent and blissful Śiva.

These four paths lead to four progressive states of liberation respectively: *sāloka*, *sāmīpa*, *sārūpa*, and *sāyujya*.[190] *Sāloka* is living in the same world as Śiva. *Sāmīpa* is nearness to Śiva. *Sārūpa* is attaining similarity to the form of Śiva. *Sāyujya* is unity with Śiva, which is the supreme liberation.

Tirumūlar further explains the four states of release:

In Saloka Pasa Jnana (World knowledge) becomes
Pasu Jnana (Spiritual knowledge)
In Samipa it becomes Arul Jnana (Grace knowledge)
In Sarupa it is transformed into Pati Jnana (God knowledge)
In Sayujya it is for ever dissolved.[191]

4. 3. Nature of souls in the state of release

Tirumūlar explains the nature of souls in the liberated state: They have no impurities; they have no pride and prejudice; they have no families to look after and work for; they claim no excellence; they do not try to be in privileged circumstances; they have no self-interest.[192] They have no further births; they have now become one with God.[193] This state of being one with God is sweet like the combination of the juice of sugarcane, milk, jaggery, and the fountain water.[194] All their previous contradictions and sorrows of life are resolved.[195] They melt in their heart; they moan and rave; they feel like their bones are melting; they adore the Lord day and night; they feel like eating, biting and chewing Him out of love.[196] Their thoughts are filled with Śiva.[197]

5. Summing up

By taking into consideration the explicit and the implicit references to the philosophical concepts in the *Tirumandiram*, one comes to know that Tirumūlar was trying to evolve a systematic philosophy, with certain epistemological principles, a notion of God, soul and the world, which is the pre-cursor to the Śaiva Siddhānta school of philosophy.

The primary source for the Śaiva Siddhānta system is the *Śiva-jñāṉa-bōdam* of Mey-kaṇḍār. This work, which is dated to the thirteenth century A.D., has brought out the salient features of the

Śaiva Siddhānta system in just only twelve aphorisms each with three to four lines and not exceeding forty lines in total.

The *Tirumandiram* has brought out the essence of the system with just only four lines:

> Of the so-called three, the Pati, the paśu and the pāśa,
> Like the Pati, the paśu and pāśa are eternal;
> The paśu and the pāśa do not reach the Pati;
> If the Pati reaches the paśu, the pāśa will wane away.[198]

All the other verses of the *Tirumandiram* are only the superstructures on this foundation. No doubt that the primary purpose of Tirumūlar is to project the experiential aspect of religion, that is, the mystical element. But it could not be done without defining what is that which undergoes the experience, what is that which is experienced, and what is that which hinders the experience.

The Śaiva Siddhānta system of philosophy is an outcome of Tirumūlar's answers to these questions and it is Tirumūlar, who, for the first time calls it as Śaiva Siddhānta.[199]

In the history of Indian philosophy, Sanskrit is supposed to be the language of philosophy. The literatures of all the philosophical systems are written only in Sanskrit. Unless the source work is written in Sanskrit the system propounded will not be recognized. Even great philosophers like Śaṅkara and Rāmānuja, though they hailed from Tamil Nadu, and were well versed in Tamil, wrote only in Sanskrit.

Perhaps Tamil and Pali are the only exceptions, equally placed with Sanskrit, with a corpus of philosophical literature. All Buddhist treatises are in Pali and all primary sources of Śaiva Siddhānta are in Tamil. The *Tirumandiram* can be said to be the first systematic account of a particular philosophy in Tamil. Tirumūlar proves to be a path breaker and a leader by example, thus giving impetus to his future followers.

Notes on Chapter Two

1. *Tirumandiram*, 115.
2. Refer V.A. Devasenapathy, *Saiva Siddhanta*, p. 69
3. *Dictionary of Philosophy*, p. 114.
4. *Tirumandiram*, 90. Author's translation.
5. *Ibid.*, 2955; also refer 1593, 2648, 2844.
6. *Tiruvācagam*, "Pōṟṟi-t-tiru-v-agaval," 124.
7. *Tēvāram*, 4:260.
8. *Ibid.*, 1:122:5.
9. *Nālāyira-t-tivya-p-prabandam*, "Tiru-c-canda-viruttam," 11.
10. *Vināyakar Akaval.*
11. *Abirāmi Andādi*, 87.
12. *Siva-jñāṉa-siddhiyār Cubakkam*, 5.
13. *Ibid.*, 6.
14. V.A. Devasenapathy, *op.cit.*, p. 17.
15. *Naṉṉūl*, 290.
16. Mu. Tiruvilangam (Comm.), *Siva-jñāṉa-siddhiyār Cubakkam*, p. 14.
17. *Tirumandiram*, 1125. Author's translation.
18. Quoted in V.A. Devasenapathy, *op. cit.*, p. 17.
19. *Siva-jñāṉa-siddhiyār Cubakkam*, 7.
20. *Tirumandiram*, 1302.
21. *Ibid.*, 2944.
22. *Ibid.*, 2944.
23. *Ibid.*, 2946.
24. *Ibid.*, 689, 671, 675.
25. Refer *Siva-jñāṉa-siddhiyār Cubakkam*, 13, for explanations of *tan-vēdaṉai-k-kāṭci* and *yoga-k-kāṭci.*

26. Mu. Tiruvilangam (Comm.), *op. cit.*, 17.
27. *Tirumandiram*, 177. Translation of B. Natarajan with a slight modification.
28. *Ibid.*, 1793.
29. *Ibid.*, 58, 64.
30. *Siva-jñāṉa-siddhiyār Cubakkam*, 19.
31. *Tirumandiram*, 66. Author's translation.
32. Ci. Arunai Vadivel Mudaliyar, *Śiva-jñāna-bōda Māpāḍiya-p-poruḷ-nilai Viḷakkam*, p. 197.
33. P. Thirugnanasambandhan, "The Bearing of Saiva Siddhanta Epistemology on its Metaphysics," *Indian Philosophical Annual*, Vol. 14, p. 111.
34. *Tirumandiram*, 2323. Translation of B. Natarajan.
35. *Ibid.*, 2329. Author's translation.
36. *Ibid.*, 1228. Author's translation.
37. *Ibid.*, 2074. Translation of B. Natarajan with a slight modification.
38. *Ibid.*, 172.
39. *Tiru-vācagam*, "Śiva-purāṇam," 45.
40. *Tēvāram*, 6:97:10.
41. *Ibid.*, 3:54:4.
42. *Tirumandiram*, 3015.
43. *Ibid.*, 2844.
44. *Ibid.*, 2085. Translation of B. Natarajan.
45. *Ibid.*, 2103. Translation of B. Natarajan.
46. *Tēvāram*, 3:54:5.
47. *Tiru-k-kaḷiṟṟu-p-paḍiyār*, 56.
48. *Tirumandiram*, 393, 66, 323, 451.
49. *Ibid.*, 393. Author's translation.

50. *Ibid.*, 106. This can be compared with the first aphorism of the *Śiva-jñāṉa-bōdam.*
51. *Ibid.*, 443. Translation of B. Natarajan with a change in the last line.
52. *Ibid.*, 2817. Translation of B. Natarajan.
53. *Ibid.*, 394. Translation of B. Natarajan.
54. *Ibid.*, 15. Author's translation.
55. *Ibid.*, 410. Author's translation.
56. *Ibid.*, 1932. Author's translation.
57. *Ibid.*, 2229, 2334, 2344.
58. *Ibid.*, 417. Translation of B. Natarajan. Also refer 404.
59. Refer: V.A. Devasenapathy, *op. cit.*, p. 85, see footnote 20.
60. *Tirumandiram*, 2418. Translation of B. Natarajan.
61. *Ibid.*, 1809. Translation of B. Natarajan.
62. Quoted by V.A. Devasenapathy, *op. cit.*, p. 85.
63. *Tirumandiram*, 399, 492, 2369.
64. Ci. Arunai Vadivel Mudaliyar, *op. cit.*, p. 264.
65. *Tirumandiram*, 443.
66. This can be compared with the example verse 1.2.3 of *Śiva-jñāṉa-bōdam.*
67. *Tirumandiram*, 1802. Translation of B. Natarajan.
68. *Ibid.*, 1800. Translation of B. Natarajan.
69. V.A. Devasenapathy, *op. cit.*, 94.
70. *Tirumandiram*, 2790, 2762.
71. *Ibid.*, 2790.
72. *Ibid.*, 25.
73. *Ibid.*, 2941.
74. *Ibid.*, 889.
75. *Ibid.*, 2840.

76. *Ibid.*, 3004. Also refer: 3011, 373.
77. Refer: Ci. Arunai Vadivel Mudaliyar, *op. cit.*, p. 266.
78. *Śiva-jñāṉa-siddhiyār Cubakkam*, 237. Author's translation.
79. *Tirumandiram*, 2584.
80. *Ibid.*, 1806, 2424, 2722, 2790, 2732.
81. *Tiru-k-kaḷiṟṟu-p-paḍiyār*, 5. Author's translation.
82. *Tirumandiram*, 3006.
83. *Ibid.*, 4.
84. *Ibid.*, 28.
85. *Ibid.*, 10.
86. *Ibid.*, 372.
87. *Ibid.*, 1162, 2727, 2767, 2768, 2780.
88. *Ibid.*, 346, 421.
89. *Ibid.*, 2424, 1892.
90. *Ibid.*, 33.
91. *Ibid.*, 1248. Translation of B. Natarajan.
92. V.A. Devasenapathy, *op. cit.*, p. 97.
93. *Śiva-jñāṉa-siddhiyār Cubakkam*, 75.
94. *Tirumandiram*, 2790.
95. *Ibid.*, 1249.
96. *Ibid.*, 1066.
97. *Ibid.*, 1309.
98. *Ibid.*, 1137.
99. *Ibid.*, 1063.
100. *Ibid.*, 1772.
101. *Ibid.*, 475.
102. *Ibid.*, 2943. Author's translation.
103. *Ibid.*, 444, 1205.

104. Refer: *Tiru-k-kuṟaḷ*, Pari-mēl-aḻagar's commentary for verse 9.
105. *Tirumandiram*, 2833, 2834, 2860.
106. *Ibid.*, 2765, 2335.
107. *Ibid.*, 2406.
108. *Ibid.*, 2192.
109. *Ibid.*, 2421.
110. *Ibid.* 2421.
111. *Ibid.*, 2420.
112. *Ibid.*, 492, 2655.
113. *Ibid.*, 1045.
114. *Ibid.*, 2268.
115. *Ibid.*, 2421.
116. *Ibid.*, 2422.
117. *Ibid.*, 2334.
118. *Ibid.*, 382.
119. *Ibid.*, 1045.
120. V.A. Devesenapathy, *op. cit.*, pp. 139-140.
121. *Tirumandiram*, 2247, 2168, 2143, 2190, 2191.
122. *Ibid.*, 2025.
123. *Ibid.*, 385.
124. *Ibid.*, 2152.
125. *Ibid.*, 2145.
126. *Ibid.*, 2198.
127. *Ibid.*, 2179.
128. *Ibid.*, 2267.
129. *Ibid.*, 2419.
130. *Ibid.*, 2557, 2610, 2611, 2612, 2547, 2192, 1685.

131. *Ibid.*, 1683.
132. *Ibid.*, 2069, 2547, 2557, 143.
133. V.A. Devasenapathy, *op. cit.*, p. 170.
134. Muru. Pala. Rathinam Chettiyar, *Kaḍavuḷāl Muḍiyāda Ceyalgaḷ*, p. 85. (Translated from Tamil by the author).
135. *Pōṟṟi-p-paḥṟoḍai*, 10-13.
136. *Tirumandiram*, 2123. Author's translation.
137. *Ibid.*, 2124. Author's translation.
138. *Ibid.*, 1647, 1475, 1657.
139. *Ibid.*, 143, 2420, 2262, 1527.
140. *Ibid.*, 2420.
141. V.A. Devasenapathy, *op. cit.*, p. 183.
142. *Tirumandiram*, 2611. Translation of B. Natarajan.
143. *Ibid.*, 2421.
144. *Ibid.*, 1516, 1676, 1678, 2001.
145. *Ibid.*, 2192. Author's translation.
146. *Ibid.*, 118, 497, 2236, 2257, 2253, 2293, 2237, 2401, 2478.
147. *Ibid.*, 2229, 2259.
148. V.A. Devasenapathy, *op. cit.*, p. 193.
149. *Tirumandiram*, 2406, 2423.
150. *Ibid.*, 2279, 2264, 2586, 2132, 2133.
151. *Ibid.*, 2406, 1782, 1622, 2004.
152. *Ibid.*, 115.
153. *Ibid.*, 2357. Author's translation.
154. *Ibid.*, 2406.
155. *Ibid.*, 1420.
156. *Ibid.*, 114.
157. *Ibid.*, 2247.
158. *Ibid.*, 2261.

159. *Ibid.*, 2262.
160. *Ibid.*, 2227.
161. *Ibid.*, 2162, 2164, 2166, 2182.
162. *Ibid.*, 2142.
163. *Ibid.*, 2196, 2202.
164. *Ibid.*, 2147.
165. *Ibid.*, 2144.
166. *Ibid.*, 2200.
167. *Ibid.*, 2156, 2200.
168. *Ibid.*, 2156, 2200.
169. *Ibid.*, 2195.
170. *Ibid.*, 2209.
171. *Ibid.*, 494, 498, 2241, 2242.
172. *Ibid.*, 494, 498, 2241, 2243.
173. *Ibid.*, 495.
174. *Ibid.*, 1619. Author's translation.
175. *Ibid.*, 2505.
176. V.A. Devasenapathy, *op. cit.*, p. 236.
177. *Tirumandiram*, 488. Author's translation.
178. *Ibid.*, 2357.
179. *Ibid.*, 2633. Author's translation.
180. *Ibid.*, 1632.
181. *Tiru-k-kuṟaḷ*, 262.
182. *Tirumandiram*, 2547.
183. *Ibid.*, 2613. Translation of B. Natarajan.
184. *Ibid.*, 2615. Translation of B. Natarajan.
185. *Ibid.*, 1527. Translation of B. Natarajan.
186. *Ibid.*, 130.
187. *Ibid.*, 1514-1529.

188. *Ibid.*, 1502, 1495, 1492, 1477.

189. *Ibid.*, 1447.

190. *Ibid.*, 1507, 1512.

191. *Ibid.*, 1509. Translation of B. Natarajan.

192. *Ibid.*, 2957.

193. *Ibid.*, 2958.

194. *Ibid.*, 2959.

195. *Ibid.*, 2974.

196. *Ibid.*, 2980.

197. *Ibid.*, 2969.

198. *Ibid.*, 115. Author's translation.

199. *Ibid.*, 1421.

Chapter 3

Śaivism as Conceived in the Tirumandiram

KR. Arumugam

tērnda ara<u>n</u>ai aḍainda civa ne<u>r</u>i
pērndavar u<u>nn</u>i-p peyarnda peruva<u>l</u>i
ārndavar aṇḍattu-p pukka aruḷ ne<u>r</u>i
pōndu piṇaindu puṇar ne<u>r</u>i āmē.

It is this chosen Śaiva Path that helps reaching the Lord;
It is this Great Path to which even the deserters
returned realizing;
It is this Graceful Path that helps entering the cosmic world; and
No doubt it is this path that liberates and helps merging.

–*Tirumandiram, 1563*

3. Śaivism as Conceived in the Tirumandiram

KR. Arumugam

1. Introduction

Defining religion precisely is an impossible task. Each one will have one's own answer for the question what religion is. "Belief in God," "the art of living in perfection," "an internal experience" —may be the answers. Kant defines religion as "accepting our duties as divine commands;" according to Schleirmacher religion is "our dependence on something which is beyond our control but which controls us;" according to Hegal religion is "the bound soul realizing itself unbound."[1] Mathew Arnold defines religion as "morality touched with emotion."[2] Realising reality as it is, is religion according to the Indian point of view.[3]

The Sanskrit equivalent for the term "religion" is dharma. Dharma is classified into two. They are: *abhyudaya* and *nihśreyasa*. These two include the four *puruṣārthas*: *dharma* (morality), *artha* (wealth), *kāma* (pleasure) and *mokṣa* (liberation). Of these four, the first three are included in the *abhyudaya* and the last one is included in the *nihśreyasa*. It is defined that dharma (religion) is one which helps to attain *abhyudaya* and *nihśreyasa*.

Radhakrishnan compares philosophy and religion and expresses his views regarding them: Philosophy relies on logic; religion relies on faith. Philosophy tries to explain by ideas; religion, by symbols. A philosopher inquires and argues; a man of religion believes, follows, lives and loves.[4] This comparison of Radhakrishnan may be helpful in examining the position of Tirumūlar as a philosopher and as a man of religion.

Tirumūlar was a philosopher; but one cannot view him as a philosopher alone because his philosophy was built on his religious ideas. His philosophy was an outward expression of his inward attachment to Lord Śiva. This attachment was an offshoot of his boundless love and *bhakti* towards Śiva. In this regard one can say the religion of Tirumūlar is Śaivism.

Let us see some of the facts regarding the origin and development of Śaivism.

2. Śaivism: Origin and development

Śaivism is a religion, which holds Śiva as the supreme Lord. It is said to be the oldest and pre-historic religion.[5] Scholars wonder that the origin of Śaivism surpasses our imagination. Its traces were found in the Mohenjadaro-Harappa excavations. Sir John Marshall says: "Side by side with this Earth or Mother Goddess, there appears at Mohenjadaro a male god, who is recognizable at once as a prototype of the historic Śiva."[6] He further goes on to state that among the many revelations that Mohenjadaro and Harappa have had in store for us, none perhaps is more remarkable than this discovery that Śaivism has a history going back to Chalcolithic Age or perhaps even further still, and that it thus takes place as the most ancient living faith in the world.[7]

Śaivism is commendable not because it is the oldest religion, but because it is still a living religion practiced by multitudes.

2. 1. Is Śaivism pre-Vedic or Vedic?

There is a dispute among scholars whether Śaivism is Vedic or pre-Vedic. Scholars like Sir John Marshall, G.U. Pope, G. Slater, Maraimalai Adigal are of the opinion that Śaivism is pre-Aryan and pre-Vedic.[8] Scholars like K.A. Nilakanta Sastri have a counter-opinion and they advocate the Vedic origin of Śaivism.[9] Scholars like G.V. Tagare, though they believe that Śiva precedes Vedas and Āgamas, want to brush these kinds of arguments aside as they do not impress them.[10]

The subscribers of the Vedic origin point out the occurrence of the word Śiva in the Veda. The word Śiva means "the auspicious." But it is to be noted that the word Siva is used in the Vedas not as a noun but as an adjective to various gods, including Rudra.[11] Even those advocating a Vedic origin of Saivism admit that the Vedic Rudra came to be identified with Siva of the indigenous people. Regarding the question whether the two deities were originally identical or originally different, but later on identified, it seems to be a fairly accepted view today that the religion of Śaivism itself is anterior to the Vedic cult of the Rudra. The name "Śiva" itself, it has been shown with plausibility, is Dravidian in origin, though later on appropriated by Sanskrit.[12] Sir John Marshall says:

> It has been suggested that the name Siva is connected with Dravidic root meaning 'red.' Whether this surmise is correct or not, it is by no means unlikely that Sanskrit epithet of Siva (the auspicious), applied to this god by the Aryans, bore a phonetic resemblance to his original name.[13]

According to Maraimalai Adigal, the root meaning of the two terms, *Uruttiraṉ* (Rudra) and *Civaṉ* (Śiva) in Tamil, is "to be ruddy." Without mutilating or twisting the shape of these two terms, one can quite easily derive the one from the root *uru* and the other from *Civaṉ*, both meaning in Tamil "to be ruddy."[14]

2. 2. Exploring the word Śiva

In *Tolkāppiam*, the oldest available treatise on grammar in Tamil, God is referred to as *kaḍavuḷ*.[15] This word is said to be a combination of two words *kaḍa* plus *uḷ*. *Kaḍa* stands for transcendence and *uḷ* stands for immanence. This conveys the Tamil conception of God, which is both transcendental and immanent. According to some, *kaḍavuḷ* is a derivative of the root *kaḍavudal*, which means directing, to cause to go. To them *kaḍavuḷ* is taken to mean the One who directs. *Iṟaivaṉ* is another term to refer to God in Tamil. Tiruvaḷḷuvar uses this term twice in the opening section "Kaḍavuḷ-Vāḻttu" (In praise of the Lord) of his work *Tiru-k-kuṟaḷ*. *Iṟaivaṉ* in Tamil means the head.

It is to be noted that the Tamils' concept of God is expressed in the very words that denote God. When one uses the term *kaḍavuḷ* to refer to God, what is meant is that God has transcended and is beyond the entities and also immanent in the entities; that is, some other entities are also there. If we take the other meaning of the word, that is, God is the One who directs or the One who causes to go, here also it is implied that there are some other entities to be directed or to be activated by God. The same implication can be drawn from the other usage *Iṟaivaṉ* also. When God is called as *Iṟaivaṉ* (head) that means there is somebody else who is subservient. From this it becomes clear that the Tamils' concept of God is not the "God alone is" concept.

Tiruvaḷḷuvar uses the word *cemporuḷ* also to refer to the Absolute.[16] Pari-mēl-aḻagar, the gifted commentator of the *Tiru-k-kuṟaḷ*, clarifies the meaning of the term *cemporuḷ* thus: that which is eternal, that which permeates everything but not permeated by any other thing, that which is changeless, that which is as it is with nothing to support its existence, is called *cemporuḷ*.

The word *cemporuḷ* is made of two components, viz., *cemmai* plus *poruḷ*. The word *cemmai* has two meanings: 1. Redness;

ruddiness and 2. Perfection; equanimity; justness. The word *poruḷ* means an entity. The colour red stands for anger.[17] Red is considered to be sacred, most holy and efficacious in the Mother Goddess worship. Red is the colour of blood and the menstrual blood— which is known as *khā-puṣpa* in the Tāntric parlance— is considered to be a life giving power inherent in the female sex and thus red, the colour of blood, is sanctified. In the temple of Kāmākhya of Assam, India, a red liquid, prepared artificially, is sold to the devotees as the blood of the Goddess.[18] E. Mackay in his *Further Excavations at Mohenjodoro,* registers that most of the figures of the Mother Goddess from Mohenjodaro are painted over with a red slip or wash. The oldest extant figurines of the Mother Goddess, such as the Venus of Willendrof, are painted red. Some of the Egyptian, Maltese, Cypriot and Danubian figurines are also found ruddy.[19]

In the Tantras the menstrual blood of a virgin, which is known as *sayambhū-kusuma* or *rakta-candana,* has been regarded as so sacred that it is prescribed as an offering to the great God Śiva and his consort Devi. If it is not available, the menstrual blood of a Caṇḍāḷī (a woman belonging to the lowest caste of the caste hierarchy), which is known as *trisūla-puṣpa* or *vajra-puṣpa,* should be offered. If the blood of a Caṇḍāḷī is not available, red sandalwood paste may be used as a substitute.[20] The colour red thus gained importance in the primitive religions. In the later religious developments we come across a deeply ingrained dread of impurity and unholiness attributed to menstrual blood and the menstruating women. Almost all religious treatises have something in store for their followers about the uncleanliness of the menstrual blood and the menstruating women.

> If menstruation was the sign of blossoming, like blossoms, the blood was offered to the fields, rivers, canals, deities. How could that blood be dirty or unholy if blossoms were not?

asks B. Bhattacharya.[21] His view echoes the Siddhas' opinion on this subject.[22]

In Tamil the menstrual blood is called *tūmai*. It is a colloquial usage, which is taken to mean impurity, uncleanliness, etc., by the Tamil Lexicon.[23] According to the Lexicon the word *tūmai* is a probable distortion of *tūydaṉmai* (*tūydu* plus *aṉmai; tūydu* – that which is clean; *aṉmai* – a negative connotation). On the other hand it can also be interpreted that the word *tūmai* is a derivative of the word *tūymai*, which means cleanliness, purity, immaculateness, holiness. It is clear that the word *tūmai* is nearer to the word *tūymai* (which means immaculateness) and not to *tūydaṉmai* (which means uncleanliness).

It can be said that the menstrual blood is considered to be immaculate and holy in the Mother Goddess worship and the colour red stood as the symbolic representation of that holy menstrual blood. When the Mother Goddess worship was replaced by the Father God worship, red is attributed to the male God also. Ruddiness in Tamil is called *cemmai*, and the colour red, *civappu*. From the word *civappu, civaṉ* is derived. According to Tevaneya-p-pavanar, a great Tamil etymologist, the words *cemmai, civappu, ceyōṉ* and *civaṉ*, meaning red, are derived from one common root word *cuḷ*.[24] *Cuḷ* means red hot. Hotness is the quality of fire; fire is red in colour. The One who is red in colour is called *Civaṉ*. Red stands for anger. In this sense also it is apt to call the wrathful Lord, who is thedestroyer and creator of the universe, as *Civaṉ*.

The other meaning of the word *cemmai* is perfection, equanimity, justness. Like the red coloured fire, which burns anything that comes unto its fold without any reservation, the red coloured *Civaṉ* (Śiva) acts impartially. To use the definition of Tiruvaḷḷuvar God is beyond preference and beyond aversion *(vēṇḍudal vēṇḍāmai ilāṉ).*[25]

It becomes clear that the word *civaṉ* (Śiva) is of Tamil origin.

2. 3. The development of Śaivism

The controversy apart, Śaivism is a widespread and well-developed religion of India.[26] Keeping Śaivism as the religious back-up, different philosophies gained currency— Śaiva Siddhānta among the Tamils, Vīra-Śaivism among the Canarese (of Karnataka) and among some sections of the Tamils, Kashmir Śaivism among the Northerners, Pāśupatha school, Mahāvrata school, Kāpālika school, Vāma school, Bhairava school, Kālāmukha school and so many other religious sects.

While the Northerners concentrated on interpreting or reinterpreting Śaivism philosophically, the Southerners tried to keep the religious aspect of it alive and thriving. When the existence of Śaivism was threatened by Jainism and Buddhism, the Śaivites of Tamil Nadu launched a movement to revive Śaivism, for various reasons. This movement is popularly known as the Bhakti Movement. The Nāyaṉmārs led the movement from the forefront with productive results. A new corpus of literature was added to Tamil— the bhakti literature— which is an outcome of the Bhakti Movement. After consolidating the religious hegemony over the others, the need for a well-defined philosophy arose in Tamil Nadu. The tenets of the Tamil Śaiva philosophy were already there right from the days of Tolkāppiyar. It was Tirumūlar, who, for the first time made a mention of the word "Siddhānta" and dealt in detail with the philosophical aspects of Tamil Śaivism in his *Tiruman- diram.* "It is almost the only source to study the growth of Śaivism in Tamil Nadu during the fourth, fifth, and sixth centuries A.D.— which is known as the dark age of the Tamil country."[27] Taking his cue from Tirumūlar, Meykaṇḍār had expounded the systematised Śaiva Siddhānta philosophy in the thirteenth century.

3. Śaivism in the Tirumandiram

Śaivism is called *caivam* in Tamil. Tirumūlar defines the word *caivam* by way of characterising the four steps suggested in Śaivism to reach Śiva as follows:

> Śaivism is getting into contact with Śiva
> Śaivism is realizing oneself and depending on Śiva
> Śaivism is repealing the dependence on Śiva
> Śaivism is merging with and enjoying the bliss of Śiva.[28]

In the first step one enters into the fold of Śiva (*cālōgam – sāloka* – entering the world of Śiva). In the second step one comes close to Śiva and depends on Him for everything he does (*cāmībam – sāmīpya* – getting closer to Śiva). These two steps involve devotion and ritualistic worship. In the third step one learns to overcome his limitations and to continue on his own without rituals by way of practicing Yoga and he himself becomes the form of Śiva, i.e., he realizes Śiva personified by all the existing entities (*cārūbam – sārūpya* – getting the form of Śiva). In the fourth and last step one merges with Śiva and gets liberated (*cāyucciyam – sāyujya* – merging with Śiva). This is what Śaivism stands for. According to Tirumūlar,

It is this chosen Śaiva Path that helps reaching the Lord;
It is this Great Path to which even the deserters returned realizing;
It is this Graceful Path that helps entering the cosmic world;
and
No doubt it is this path that liberates and helps merging.[29]

Some verses in the fifth *tantra* of the *Tirumandiram* speak of the four gradations of Śaivism namely *cutta-caivam* (the pure Śaivism), *acutta-caivam* (the impure Śaivism), *markka-caivam* (the religious Śaivism) and *kaḍum-cutta-caivam* (the extremely pure Śaivism). Suba. Annamalai, in his critical edition of the *Tirumandiram*, rejects these verses on the ground that they speak against the intention of the author and concludes that these verses are interpolations. This conclusion is acceptable because Tirumūlar never encourages differentiations.

During the age of Tirumūlar there existed six different sects of Śaivism (Pāśupadam, Māviradam, Bairavam, Kābāligam, Vāmam, and Kāḷāmugam). Tirumūlar condemns heavily this sectarian attitude. All these sects– though all of them accept Śiva as the Lord unanimously– contending over superiority, lost their focus on the process of liberation.[30] These fools (the sectarian Śaivites), shouting their principles to no purpose like asses, do not know that Śiva is all pervasive. Out of ignorance, they will forget to hold on to the truth. They are forever entangled in the cycle of births and deaths.[31]

Six ways are there that lead to one great city. There is nothing superior or inferior about the ways. Those who contend are like the dog that foolishly barks at the hillock in vain.[32]

This shows that Tirumūlar was playing an important role of unifying Śaivism though not in a dogmatic way. To bridge the gap between the six sects he tries to define a new philosophy for Śaivism, viz., the Śaiva Siddhānta philosophy. This feature has been dealt with in the previous chapter of this book.

4. Mythological elements of Śaivism in theTirumandiram

The subject matter of religion is the worship of God with an ultimate aim to go to heaven or to attain liberation from the cycle of births. As God cannot be described in ordinary language, the religious expressions take refuge in myths and in rituals. A religion can never get rid of these two. The metaphysical truths are condensed in the myths, and the practical guidelines for experience are condensed in rituals. Tirumūlar is no exception to this. He represents Lord Śiva by symbolic images; worships and offers his verses as oblation; sings and rejoices; performs certain rituals; and guides others to follow suit. He tries to explain some metaphysical truths by reinterpreting the popular mythological stories.

The Lord Absolute Śiva is beyond word and thought;[33] there is none who knows him fully well;[34] there is none who had measured Him[35]— these utterances of Tirumūlar are expressions of his experience of Lord Śiva.

If one digs deep, it is understood that there are two aspects in the experience of Tirumūlar. One is the direct experience of Lord Śiva as the Absolute; another is Tirumūlar's experience of the myths and symbols regarding the Lord, passed-on to one generation by the previous ones.

There are many references to the mythological stories in the *Tirumandiram*. The second *tantra* of the *Tirumandiram* is a treasure trove of the mythical elements. The first eight sub-titles of this *tantra* are full of mythical references. The aim of this section of the *Tirumandiram* is to establish the primordial nature of Lord Śiva. Though all the Śaiva literary works speak of this, the tone of the *Tirumandiram* is somewhat different.

The mythical stories that narrate the primordial nature of Lord Śiva are many. They can be classified in some respects. One of these classifications is based on the valor of Śiva. The stories based on the valor of Śiva are eight in number. They are known as *aṭṭa-vīraṭṭam* and they are referred to in the *Tirumandiram* as *pati valiyil vīraṭṭam eṭṭu;* that is the eight episodes of destruction displayed by the valorous Pati, the Lord. These eight episodes are said to have taken place in eight holy places, all of which are within the boundaries of Tamil Nadu. They are: Tiru-k-kōvalūr, Tiru-p-paṟiyalūr, Tiru-k-kaṇḍiyūr, Tiru-viṟkuḍi, Tiru-v-adigai, Tiru-vaḻuvūr, Tiru-k-kaḍavūr and Tiru-k-koṟukkai.

All the mythical elements regarding Śiva can be contained in these eight episodes. They play an important role in the temple history of Tamil Nadu. There are also stories that explicate the aspect of grace of the Lord. In a way even the valorous destructive acts of Śiva can be said to be the acts of grace— the grace that chastises.

> ...while explaining the philosophical principles they are given a story-coating. This helps the ordinary people to have an easy access to the philosophical principles underlying. To drive the philosophical principles home, either they should be given a story-coating or they should be formatted in rituals...

> But as time moves on, these oft-beaten stories or rituals lose their significance. People may even forget that there is an inner significance in these stories or rituals.[36]

This is an observation of Chandrasekarendra Saraswati of the Kanchi Kamakoti Pitam. Tirumūlar had witnessed this loss of significance of the mythological stories pregnant with philosophical principles.

Though the myths on Śiva were popular amongst the masses at the time of Tirumūlar, they failed to create the right impact over the masses. Tirumūlar was concerned about this failure. Hence he reorganizes and reinterprets the myths. One may doubt that reorganizing and adding some touches to a myth will make it just a story. But the basic nature of myth is to change; because they are passed on from generation to generation and thus they are subject to change, like a stone in the flowing river gets polished, its rough edges get rounded-off and the stone becomes a pebble. To quote Kerenyi,

> A particular kind of material determines the art of mythology, an immemorial and traditional body of material contained in tales about gods and god-like beings, heroic battles and journeys to the Under world– "myhtologem" is the best Greek word for them– tales already well known but not unamenable to further reshaping. Mythology is the *movement* of this material: it is something solid and yet mobile, substantial and yet not static, capable of transformation.[37]

4. 1. The eight acts of valor of Lord Śiva

There is not much elaboration of the stories of the eight valorous acts in the *Tirumandiram*. It was not the aim of Tirumūlar to tell the stories since they were already popular. All that he was concerned about was to drive home the significance of these stories. But without missing a single episode Tirumūlar refers to all the eight. They are: 1. Destruction of Andagaṉ (Andhaka); 2. Destruction of Takkaṉ's (Dakṣa's) ego and his *yāga* (sacrifice); 3. Beheading Brahma; 4. Exterminating Calandaraṉ (Jalandhara); 5. Destruction of Tiri-puram (Tripura); 6. Killing and skinning Kayācuraṉ (Gajāśura – the elephant demon); 7. Kicking off Kālaṉ (Kāla, the God of death); and 8. Burning down Kāmaṉ to ashes (Kāma, the Cupid of Indian mythos).

Let us now consider the stories in brief and the way Tirumūlar interprets them.

4. 1. 1. Destruction of Andagaṉ

It is said that Andagaṉ was the son of Iraṇiyātcaṉ (Hiraṇyākṣa). Some say that he was the son of sage Kaciyabar (Kaśyapa). When Lord Śiva, in a playful mood, closed the eyes of Goddess Pārvati from behind, she was frightened and perspired. Out of this perspiration a demon took birth. Since the demon was blind he was named Andagaṉ (the blind). This demon called Andagaṉ was later given to Iraṇiyātcaṉ by Lord Śiva. Andagaṉ did penance concentrating on Brahma and got the eyes and invincible powers. This made him arrogant. He tried to lift Goddess Pārvati and the celestial tree called Pārijāta (night flowering jasmine– *Nyctanthes arbor-tristis*); he harmed the celestial beings. The celestials to escape from him went to Kailash to take the refuge of Lord Śiva and Andagaṉ followed them there too. The wrathful Lord pierced him with His trident and killed him. The subdued Andagaṉ appealed to the Lord to accept him as one of His gaṇas and it was granted by the Lord. This episode is said to have taken place in Tiru-k-kōvalūr.

Though this story is not that much popular in Tamil Nadu, Tirumūlar gives prime place to this story.

> Andagan̲, the blind-like demon, who dwells in the inner alcove,
> Fueled with boons harassed all living beings of the world:
> Thus appealed the celestials,
> And the Lord killed him with His sharp trident.[38]

The usage "inner alcove" *(karuttu)* suggests it all. That is the key word Tirumūlar uses to interpret the tale. Andagan̲ (the demon who acts like a blind) is not an external entity. He exists in the inner core of the souls. He plays the spoiling sport from within. He makes the souls blind and go astray. He is the personification of āṇava-mala. When the realized souls (*vān̲avar* – the celestials – the souls elevated to the possible extent by their knowledge, viz., paśu-jñāna, which is not strong enough to destroy the demon) appealed to the Lord, He out of grace, killed the demon Andagan̲, i.e., the āṇava-mala, the ignorance, with His trident called Śiva-jñāna or Pati-jñāna and thus helps the soul to get liberated. Here, one can interpret that the trident of Śiva stands for the three nāḍis — iḍa, piṅgala, and suṣumna.

4. 1. 2. Destruction of Takkan̲'s (Dakṣa's) ego and his yāga (sacrifice)

Tirumūlar seems to be very much attracted by the episode on Takkan̲. That is why he dedicates ten verses in the *Tirumandiram*, while allotting only one verse for the other episodes. Tirumūlar reads yogic messages in the sacrifice conducted by Takkan̲.

The destruction of Takkan̲'s *yāga* by Lord Śiva has many religious and historic implications. It not only brings out the differences between the Vaiṣṇvaites and Śaivaites but also tries to establish the superiority of Lord Śiva over the other gods.

This story of the destruction of Takkaṉ's ego and his sacrifice is found in various sources with some variations. Variations apart, the central theme of the story is this: Takkaṉ performed a historic sacrifice to which all the gods were invited except Lord Śiva and the offering, that Lord Śiva was entitled to, was not given to Him. This made Lord Śiva furious and the endnote of Takkaṉ was written.

> The prajāpati fatally erred; deadly was his sin.
> The Lord smote his head and consigned it to flames
> Thinking such like are needed for this world
> Fixed a head and let him be.[39]

Prajāpati was Takkaṉ. It was a honorary title conferred on him and on some others. He was known as Takka-p-piracāpati (Dakṣa Prajāpati). He was the father of Lord Śiva's consort Tāṭcāyaṇi (Dākṣāyaṇī), i.e., the father-in-law of Śiva. When Takkaṉ started the sacrifice without an invitation to Śiva, which made Him furious, Tāṭcāyaṇi wanted to attend it since it was performed by Her father. Even though Lord Śiva denied permission to Her to attend the sacrifice, She proceeded. Takkaṉ insulted Her too. She had thrown Herself in the sacrificial fire and she died. The enraged Śiva wiped out the sacrifice of Takkaṉ, beheaded him and burnt his head into ashes. Śiva wanted to have him as an example to those egotistic miscreants and hence he fixed Takkaṉ with the head of a goat and resurrected him. This episode is said to have taken place in Tiru-p-paṟiyalūr.

The sacrifice performed by Takkaṉ was an act of denial of the primordial nature of Śiva. It is an act out of disagreement that Śiva is the Premier of all sacrifices.

> ... Fire, His eye is; transcending all the seven worlds
> He is the Lord of the cool flame of the sacrificial fire.[40]

But is it just to exemplify His primordial nature that Lord Śiva destroyed the sacrifice of Takkaṉ? The *Tirumandiram* throws new light on this. Tirumūlar gives a new meaning to sacrifice. Instead of growing fire and through it offering oblations to the celestials to gain wealth for oneself and others, one should raise the fire that resides in him, the kuṇḍalinī-śakti, make it reach all the cakras and thus achieve the final goal.[41] This is sacrifice according to Tirumūlar.

While commenting on the third fraction *(adhi-karaṇa)* of the ninth sūtra of the *Śiva-jñāna-bōdam*, the description of a *homa* (sacrifice) given by the commentator Śiva-jñāna-muṉivar is worth noting here:

> The abdomen is the place of the sacrifice [the kuṇḍalinī]. The ghee that is to be poured in the sacrificial fire is the nectar secreted from in between the eye-brows. The ladle [which is used to pour the ghee] and the spatula [which is used to kindle the fire] are the suṣumna and iḍa nāḍis respectively. The fire grown out of these is jñāna.[42]

To do this inner sacrifice, directing the seminal energy upwards is the technique; to direct the seminal fluid upwards prāṇāyāma is the modus operandi. The movement of *bindu* is closely connected with the circulation of the life energy in the form of breath.

Mircea Eliade quotes the following passage from the *Vaikhānasa-smārta-sūtra*, II:18, which refers to the *prāṇāgnihotra* — that is, the daily sacrifice in respiration.

> The self-luminous *ātman* is the sacrificer; the intellect is the bride; the lotus of the heart is the *vedi* ; the body hair is the

herb *dharba;* the *prāṇā* ... the *apāna* ... the *vyāna* ... the *udāna* ... the *samāna* ... are the five fires [of the sacrifice]. The sense organs, the tongue, etc., are the sacrificial vessels; the objects of the senses, taste, etc., are the sacrificial substances.[43]

In the *Tirumandiram* there are many references to interpret *yāga* (sacrifice) as an inner activity of Yoga.[44]

In this "*kuṇḍalinī-yāga,*" when the prāṇa is controlled, the passage of suṣumna-nāḍi gets opened, and kuṇḍalinī goes up through that, piercing the six ādhāras and finally merges with Para-Śiva. The roots of liberation are in the upward. As Pāmbāṭṭi-c-cittar portrays there is no birth for those who have uprooted the roots planted upwards.[45] An anonymous poem of a Baul of Bengal runs as follows:

The roots of the tree
are planted in the sky
and the branches
lie on the earth.[46]

This is how the whole Kuṇḍalinī-Yoga is structured. The inwardness and upward movement are the primary characteristics of it. To perform this, prāṇāyāma is the key. Prāṇāyāma helps the yogin to divert his down flowing seminal fluid and direct it upward. This act of diverting and directing the seminal fluid upward is called *vindu-maṟittal*[47] (diverting the seminal fluid) and *vindu-cayam*[48] (conquering ejaculation) by Tirumūlar. This act of directing the semen energy upward is called as ulṭā-sādhana in Yoga. The one who has held the *vindu*— the semen— intact is the yogin, the jñāni and the perfect Siddha. He is called as *aṇṇal* by Tirumūlar.[49] *Aṇṇal* is an epithet which means "the superior master;" it is used to denote God sometimes. It is the statement of

Tirumūlar that the steadfast yogins do not emit the semen even when they unite with a woman passionately.[50] Tirumūlar warns sternly that the loss of semen will bring devastation.[51]

Let us consider the Takkaṉ episode in this background. The following verse from the *Tirumandiram* highlights the intention of Tirumūlar:

> The Father was outraged about the sacrifice of Takkaṉ;
> Walked through the fires of that sacrifice; Due to wrath of the Lord,
> The celestials spilled out hither and thither,
> Without any direction, without the worship accomplished.[52]

Here Takkaṉ is the soul; worship is worshipping the Lord while the prāṇa is set in motion in the suṣumna. Tirumūlar says in another verse that worshipping the Lord while the prāṇa does not move around in the *indu* (iḍa) and *bānu* (piṅgala)– that is, worshipping the Lord while the prāṇa moves in suṣumna– is the greatest of all worships offered to the Lord.[53] When the prāṇa is activated in the suṣumna, and the fire of kuṇḍalinī is kindled, control over the semen energy is achieved.[54] Worship offered to the Lord while the prāṇa moves in the iḍa and piṅgala nāḍis is not auspicious; that lends a hand to the bad elements gain strength and helps spill the semen and bring destruction[55] and that is what happened to the sacrifice of Takkaṉ. Worship offered while the prāṇa is moving in the iḍa and piṅgala means that there is a personal desire, a prayer for some results, some benefits, say, a desire for a child, to cure a disease of the body or mind, or for success in some endeavor. One's prayer has a worldly underlying energy attached to it. When worship is offered while prāṇa is moving in the suṣumna, worship of the Lord is pure, for the prayer or offering arises from the fire of inner devotion, pure love and never desire. There is pure self-giving. And so grace descends.

Tirumūlar makes one to read between the lines and take home the message. Tirumūlar wants to underline in the verses that speak of the destruction of the sacrifice of Takkaṉ that without the helping grace of the Lord the soul can never perform the *kuṇḍalinī-yāga*. When the root-fire, the kuṇḍalinī-agni is placed in the crest, it burns the malas (the fetters) and thus yields liberation due to the grace of the Lord; and those who know well the nature of the Lord need not worry; those who melt in love for Lord will surely reach Him.[56]

4. 1. 3. Beheading Brahma

Brahma, the creator, had five heads. When Brahma mistreated the Lord, He assumed the form of Bairavar (Bhairava) and beheaded the crest head of Brahma. Blood poured out heavily from the cut. Bairavar held that blood in the skull of Brahma's head that was beheaded, using it as a bowl. Thus Brahma was left with only four heads and accepted the superiority of Lord Śiva over him. There is a second part of this story found in the *Dakṣa-kāṇḍa*. When Bairavar went with the skull of Brahma using it as the begging bowl to Viṣṇu, the sustainer, begging a bowlful of his blood, Viṣṇu tore his forehead and poured it in the skull-bowl so as to fill it. But the skull-bowl could not be filled up even after a time-span of thousand years and Viṣṇu was drained out. These two mythological stories emphasize the superiority of Lord Śiva over the other two, Brahma and Viṣṇu. This episode is said to have happened in Tiru-k-kaṇḍiyūr.

All pervasive are the Lord's feet
All worlds they support

All life they sustain;
That this the Heavenly Beings may know
In mounting anger He nipped Aya's head
And in the skull drained Achutha's blood.[57]

To have sexual pleasure one need to have an erection. Erection needs more blood flowing to the genital. To avoid erection one should avoid blood flow to the genital. Instead, the blood flow should be redirected to the upper regions. By concentrating on the crest one can curtail the flow of blood to the lower regions and thus avoid erection and emission. Cutting the top head of Ayaṉ (Brahma) and make him bleed in the crest and begging the blood of Achutaṉ (Viṣṇu) from his forehead and draining him, suggest this. There is a Siddha usage *uccuiyilē piccai eḍuttal*— begging at the top.[58] This usage is highly suggestive of the act of Lord Śiva.

Another verse of the *Tirumandiram* also hints the same:

The Lord begged in Brahma's skull
The Lord begged to commit the virtue of inseparability
The Lord begged by showing Brahma's skull
The Lord begged to make Brahma to become the absolute.[59]

Brahma here can be interpreted as the individual soul. The virtue of inseparability suggests keeping the semen energy intact with oneself without emitting it. The Lord begs by showing the skull of Brahma to remind the individual soul of checking and diverting the blood flow to the crest by which act, the individual soul becomes one with the Lord.

4. 1. 4. Exterminating Calandaraṉ (Jalandhara)

When Lord Śiva burnt the Tiri-puram (Tripura – the three forts of the three demons) to ashes the fire that was produced from the eye of the Lord in the forehead fell in the Sindhu River.

That fire cooled down in the river and produced a son called Calandaraṉ. By virtue of his penance he got a boon that no one else could kill him. He became all powerful and started harassing the celestials. They complained to Lord Śiva. Calandaraṉ also wanted to have the company of Śiva's consort Pārvati. He challenged Śiva for a duel. Since Calandaraṉ was blessed with the boon that nobody could kill him, Śiva played a trick to kill him. He drew a circle with His toe and challenged Calandaraṉ to lift it. He did it. The disc turned into a powerful discus and killed Calandaraṉ. This heroic deed is said to have taken place in Tiruviṟkuḍi.

The Premier who pervades all including my heart,
The One whom the holy books extol,
Was challenged by the boiling Calandaraṉ;
The Lord marked a circle with His finger coolly.[60]

Here Calandaraṉ refers to the *apāna-vāyu. Apāna* is a wind that is associated with the anus, the genital and the abdominal regions. This wind helps one with the required pressure for excretion, urination, ejaculation of semen, and child delivery.[61] This wind always tend to flow down. By flowing down it causes loss of semen energy. By doing *uddhiyāna-bandha* (the "upward-going" lock— performed by drawing back the abdomen) this down flowing wind can be pulled up. To sustain the wind pulled up to the throat *jalandhara-bandha* (Jalandhara's lock— done by contracting the throat) is to be performed.

In this way the old myth can be redefined in new terms. It is to be noted that here too, the accomplishment of diverting the seminal energy is emphasized.

4. 1. 5. Destruction of Tiri-puram (Tripura)

It is an age old story that Lord Śiva burnt the three flying fortresses to ashes. One Cōḻā King by name Toḍi-t-tōḷ Cembiyan̲ was honoured as "tūṅgeyil eṟinda" Toḍi-t-tōḷ Cembiyan̲, which means the one who has burnt the flying fortress. This shows the proximity of the Tamils to this myth. The Caṅgam classic *Puṟa-nān̲ūṟu* describes the myth of Śiva burning the three air-fortresses, while paying tributes to a Pāṇḍiya king by comparing him to Lord Śiva.[62] The dances performed by Lord Śiva while burning the air-fortresses and after that, namely *koḍukoṭṭi* and *pāṇḍaraṅgam*, are referred to in the *Cilappadigāram.*[63] Though this episode is said to have taken place in Tiru-v-adigai, it also relates the nearby villages Acciṟu-pākkam (the place where the axis of the cart broke down) and Pēraṇi (the place where the procession of the Lord took place).

The central theme of this mythological account is this: The demon called Tāragācuran̲ who was killed by Lord Muruga had three sons by name Tāragāṭcan̲ (Tārakākṣa), Kamalāṭcan̲ (Kamalākṣa) and Vittiyun̲māli (Vidyunmāli). They did severe penance and were blessed by Brahma to be unconquerable and with three flying fortresses made of gold, silver and iron to each one of them. By virtue of the boon they can be destroyed with one single arrow and in one single attempt. Śiva has made Mount Meru as the bow, the king of snakes Vāsuki as the string to be tied in the bow and Lord Viṣṇu as the arrow and destroyed the three flying fortresses in which the demons took refuge.

Now let us consider how Tirumūlar views the tale:

Fools are they who behold that the primal One,
Who is having water in His matted hair has destroyed the three fortresses;

The three fortresses are the three malas
Who understands that the Lord destroyed thus.[64]

Those who repeat the same old story that the Lord has destroyed the three flying fortresses are fools. The three fortresses stand for the three malas, the fetters— the āṇava-mala, the karma-mala and the māyā-mala. When the Lord is sought after He will destroy these three fetters. This is how the myth of burning the three fortresses is to be understood.

4. 1. 6. Killing and skinning Kayācuraṉ (Gajāśura)

The demon called Kayācuraṉ (the elephant demon) was creating a hell of troubles for the celestials. They complained to Lord Śiva who killed the demon, skinned him and wore the skin as his upper garment, a tiger's skin being His lower. It is something special and symbolic that the Lord attired Him with the skin of the elephant, because it was believed in ancient times that one who even comes into contact with the freshly skinned skin from the body of an elephant would promptly die.[65] So this act of the Lord demonstrates a symbolic conquest over death.

Some sources present a slightly different and detailed version of the story: There were some sages in a forest called Tārugā-vaṉam. It was their conviction that it is enough if one lives out the karma meant for him; that alone can yield the desired results; there is nothing that a God can do and hence there is no need of a God. The wives of these sages were of the opinion that maintaining chastity was more important than a God. Lord Śiva and Viṣṇu decided to prove them wrong. Viṣṇu took the form of a beautiful damsel, walked in front of the sages who were doing the sacrifices and the other related rituals— the karma meant for them— and lured them away. They left all their duties undone and went after her.

Śiva took the form of Piṭcāḍaṉar (Bhikṣāṭana – a beautiful form of the Lord, naked) and went in front of the wives of the sages. They, forgetting all their loud advocacy of chastity, fell in love with Him and lost their chastity mentally. When the sages came back, they were shocked to see their wives standing incapacitated in front of a nude Male. They were irate. They started a sacrifice to kill the nude Male. From the sacrificial fire came many forms; but their attempts to kill the nude Male were in vain. An army of *bhūtas* (goblins – described as dwarfish with huge pot-belly and very small legs) arose from the fire; but the *bhūtas* were unable to subjugate the nude Male and instead became His personal army. A venomous snake came out of the fire; it was tamed and was worn as a necklace by the nude Male. A demon called Muyalagaṉ came out of the fire; he was crushed under the foot of the nude Male. A small drum tapering in the middle called *uḍukkai* came out of the fire; it was made His personal musical instrument and kept in one of His many hands as a symbol of creation. A weapon called *maḻu* and then a trident came out the fire; they were taken as His weapons. A deer came out of the fire; it was taken and kept in one of His many hands. A skull came out of the fire; it was taken for His begging bowl. Fire came; it was taken and kept in one of His many hands as a symbol of destruction. Then came a tiger from the fire, which was killed and skinned by the nude Male and the skin was used to cover the lower part of His body. Then came the elephant (Kayācuraṉ), which was also killed and skinned by Him— the Male who was then half-attired in the skin of the tiger— and the skin of the elephant was used to cover the upper part of His body. Seeing all their attempts failing, the sages of Tārugā-vaṉam cursed Him. He withstood that also. Tired of the failures, they asked Him who He was. He simply said that He resides in Kailash and disappeared. The sages soon became subject to diseases. They approached Indra for cure. On his instruction they meditated on Śiva and were cured by His grace. This episode is said to have taken place in Tiru-vaḻuvūr.

The *Tirumandiram* follows the second version of the story:

> They do not know the significance of the Lord's skinning the elephant,
> Which came out of the sacrifice with the roaring three fires.
> Those who came out of that fire
> Desiring empowerment were killed.[66]

The three sacrificial fires are: *gārhapatya*, *āhavanīya* and the *dakṣiṇāgni* (these three will be replaced in the inner sacrifice respectively by prāṇa, *apāna* and *vyāna*, the first three of the five primary winds, the other two being *udāna* and *samāna*).

The fools think that by conducting sacrifices they can achieve something and empower themselves; they do not know the significance of the Lord's skinning of the elephant and the killing of the other entities that came out of the sacrifice. Sacrifice is not an outward one; instead it is inward. When one does sacrifice in the inner alcove (that is the *kuṇḍalinī-yāga*) with the three fires (using the three winds) the elephant called ignorance will completely come out of its hide out to be killed by the grace of the Lord. The other products of ignorance will also be extinguished.

The message that Tirumūlar puts forth by rereading this episode should be this: ignorance binds one with the undependable; like a frenzied elephant it makes one indulged in the senses and in the pleasures that come through them and to roam aimlessly. This sensual indulgence will implant one in deep trouble. To get out of this trouble one should come out of the hold of the elephant called ignorance and kill it.[67] To do this one should stop searching outside and turn in; do the inner sacrifice and by the grace of the Lord kill the elephant called ignorance.

4. 1. 7. Kicking off Kālaṉ (Kāla)

Conquering death is the oldest dream of mankind. The Śaivites have hid the key to live this dream in the myth of Mārkkaṇḍēyaṉ (Mārkaṇḍēya). The achievement of deathless life by Mārkkaṇḍēyaṉ brings death to death. The story of Mārkkaṇḍēyaṉ was very popular. In the Tamil Saṅgam literature we come across an irony that the name of a poet who sings about the momentariness of life was Mārkkaṇḍēyaṉār.[68] Tiru-vaḷḷuvar in his *Tiru-k-kuṟaḷ* also hints at the story of Mārkkaṇḍēyaṉ:

> Behold the men that have acquired power by austerities: they can succeed even in conquering death.[69]

The story is: The sage Mirugaṇḍu (Mṛkaṇḍu) was without a son and did penance aspiring one, meditating on Lord Śiva. Lord Śiva appeared and Mirugaṇḍu asked for progeny. Śiva gave him a choice of a foolish son who will live long and an intelligent son who will live only for sixteen years. Mirugaṇḍu chose the second option and thus he was blessed. His offspring was named Mārkkaṇḍēyaṉ. When Mārkkaṇḍēyaṉ reached the age of sixteen the parents started grieving, counting his days. Not knowing the reason, he asked for it and he was informed. He sat in meditation in front of the Śiva-liṅga. Kālaṉ, the God of death, came to take over the life of Mārkkaṇḍēyaṉ and threw the noose of death on him. Mārkkaṇḍēyaṉ embraced the Śiva-liṅga. The noose fell on the Śiva-liṅga too. The Lord came out of the Śiva-liṅga, kicked

Kālaṉ furiously and blessed Mārkkaṇḍēyaṉ to live forever as a sixteen year youth. This episode is said to have taken place in Tiru-k-kaḍavūr.

The interpretation of Tirumūlar is:

The one who is kindled in the hollow of the root
Should be coursed to the hollow in the top
By doing this Yoga of Fire with wind, he scorched the God of Death
And remained undisturbed in this world.[70]

The term *kāl* means foot as well as wind. This term is used by Tirumūlar in the verse under reference to denote both the meanings. By controlling the wind prāṇa, one can raise the kuṇḍalinī fire which is in the mūlādhāra, the root, to the sahasrāra, the top. On achieving this one can kick the God of death, Kālaṉ, and be in this world undisturbed. Those who have realized this fact can leap in joy when the God of death approaches them to take their life and thus humiliate Him.[71]

4. 1. 8. Burning down Kāmaṉ (Kāma) to ashes

Tāṭcāyaṇi (Dākṣāyaṇī), the daughter of Takkaṉ, after committing self-immolation in the sacrificial fire, took birth as Pārvati, the daughter of Imavāṉ (Himavān, the king of the Himālayas) to get married to Lord Śiva. At the same time three demons, who were brothers— Cūra-padumaṉ, Ciṅga-mugaṉ and Tāragaṉ— were troubling the celestials. The son of the Lord only can destroy them. But the Lord was without a better half after the death of Tāṭcāyaṇi and entered into deep meditation after that episode. Nobody dared to wake him up. At the breaking point, unable to tolerate the atrocities of the three demon brothers, the celestials decided to wake the Lord up from His meditation. For this they approached Kāmaṉ (Kāma, the Indian Cupid) to throw his arrows of love on the Lord and thus stimulate Him. Kāmaṉ did what he was told but only succeeded partially. He woke up the Lord from His deep meditation but that did not have the desired result. The Lord out of infuriation burned Kāmaṉ with the fire of His third eye. This episode is said to have happened in Tiru-k-koṟukkai.

> Fastening the mind comfortable and steadfast
> Nullifying the exit through the sexual organ and
> Thus making the acts of Kāmaṉ void, fixing the gaze at the ājña
> Did exceptional penance the place being Koṟukkai.[72]

Here the point that Tirumūlar wants to make clear is that one should not fritter away one's energy through sex. That will cost him dear. Keeping the mind steadfast and nullifying the emission of the semen energy is exceptional penance.

Through all these eight acts of valor of Lord Śiva, Tirumūlar attempts to convey only one message: Ignorance misleads. Hence ignorance should be annihilated. This can be done only with the grace of the Lord. The grace of the Lord can be achieved only through the inner sacrifice. Inner sacrifice is Kuṇḍalinī-Yoga, through prāṇāyāma and other related practices. By doing this properly one can divert seminal energy upwards, which helps to kick out the God of death. If this seminal energy is allowed to flow down or is released, one's spiritual progress is hindered. Those who understand this will remain unperturbed.

4. 2. Śiva drinking the poison

To get the nectar which consecrates immortality, and which is hidden in the milky ocean, the celestials and the demons decided to churn the milky ocean. To churn the ocean they used Mount Mandhara as the churning staff and Vāsuki, the king of snakes, as the rope. The celestials took the tail side of the snake and the demons took the head side of the snake and started churning. On churning, first came the deadliest venom called *ālālam (āla-hāla)*, scorching the celestials and the demons. Unable to bear it they surrendered unto Lord Śiva. To save them, Śiva drank the poison. Goddess Pārvati, who was sitting nearby Him, stopped the poison by pressing the throat of the Lord. The poison, unable to enter into the system, stayed put there in the throat of the Lord making His throat black in color. After this episode the Lord acquired one more name Nīla-kaṇḍaṉ (Nīla-kaṇṭha – the black-throated One).

When speaking of this myth Tirumūlar says:

> People do not know the significance of the throat of the down-facing face
> Of the Lord with spreading tresses and the garland of skulls,
> Who supports the universe in all the eight directions, becoming black;
> The senseless will say that it is because of the intake of poison.[73]

Tirumūlar did not shy away from condemning people of misinterpretation. According to him the reason for the blackness in the throat of the Lord was not the intake of poison. Then what? Tirumūlar read poison as semen. Because the vital *vindu* (semen) when wasted, brings death; it was interpreted as poison by Tirumūlar.[74] He had also noted the dire consequences of wasting the *vindu* and the benefits of retaining it.[75] Since the down-flowing *vindu* brings disaster it is considered as poison. The *vindu* preserved and directed upward becomes nectar. This conversion is made possible by igniting the kuṇḍalinī fire.[76] Saint Māṇikka-vācagar praises the Lord: "Obeisance to You, for You drank the poison as nectar delightfully."[77]

It becomes clear that Tirumūlar's reading of the episode takes a turn in interpreting poison. The seminal energy, when uncultivated, becomes poison and when cultivated becomes nectar. Lord had cultivated the seminal energy by directing it up and fastening it in the throat region. His throat's being black symbolizes this.

Why the throat region should be chosen to symbolize this? Why not some other region in the body? Because,

The feet are earth; the navel is water;
Below the breast is fire;
Above the breast and below the shoulder is air;
The neck and above is space.[78]

The region of earth is mūlādhāra; the region of water is svādhiṣṭhāna; the region of fire is maṇipūraka; the region of air is viśuddhi; and the region of space is ājña. The region of space, that is, the ājña-cakra and the sahasrāra (which represents the transcendental space – *para-veḷi*) alone is conducive for Yoga. To mark the boundary line, the throat of the Lord was blackened.

Churning the milky ocean is churning one's inner resources. The celestials and the demons are the good and bad elements in one's self.

4. 3. The dance of Śiva

The world being His form, the bodies being His limbs,
The three potencies, volition, knowledge and action being the inner organs,
The Lord enacts the drama of
Illuminating the countless souls, playing five roles.[79]

This verse from *Śiva-jñāṉa-siddhiyār Cubakkam* brings out the import of the dance of Śiva. The five roles played by the Lord are: creation, sustenance, destruction, obscuration and grace. Another work *Uṇmai-viḷakkam* clearly spells out the implied results of the dance of Śiva in different words:

> Shaking off the māyā, burning the karma and
> Pressing hard the subdued āṇava, out of love and grace
> Immersing the soul in the ocean of bliss
> Is the dance of our Father.[80]

Of the many names given to the Lord, the name Naṭarāja (the King of dances) is a special one. Tirumūlar calls this dancing Lord, Kūttaṉ[81] (*kūttu* – dance; Kūttaṉ – the dancer). The entire universe is His stage for play.

4. 3. 1. Classification of the dance of Śiva

Tirumūlar mentions a variety of dances played by the Lord. They are: *civāṉanda-k-kūttu, cundara-k-kūttu, poṉ-padi-k-kūttu, poṉ-tillai-k-kūttu* and *aṟpuda-k-kūttu.*[82] Along with these five, Tirumūlar also notes some other dances *koḍukoṭṭi, pāṇḍaraṅgam, kōḍu, caṅgāram* and also the eight dances, the five dances and the six dances.[83]

Of these dances the *koḍukoṭṭi* is the dance preformed by the Lord after the destruction of all. *Pāṇḍaraṅgam* is the dance performed after burning the three flying fortresses to ashes, smearing those ashes over his body. *Kōḍu* is the dance performed after beheading Brahma. *Caṅgāram* is the dance after the complete destruction of the universe. According to Viswanatha Pillai, the eight dances are the respective dances for the acts of creation, sustenance, destruction, obscuration, grace and along with them the dances called *muṉi-tāṇḍavam, aṉavarada-tāṇḍavam* and *āṉanda-*

tāṇḍavam. The five dances are the respective dances of the five acts, which are known as *aintoḻil-naḍaṉam.* The six dances are the five dances along with the *āṉanda-tāṇḍavam.*[84]

4. 3. 2. The purpose of the dance of Śiva

Redeeming the souls from ignorance is the purpose of the dance of the Lord. The suṣumna-nāḍi is called *Śiva-bhūmi*[85] and it is the place where the Lord dances.[86] When Lord Śiva dances and abides there, the mind will never go out wandering.[87]

> He danced out of love for the souls; then the novel dance;
> He danced in the forest; He danced in the thought;
> He danced in the suṣumna and He danced in the infinite jñāna;
> Thus My Lord completed.[88]

Although the Lord has no business on His own, He steps into business for the sake of the souls out of love. To redeem the souls from ignorance, He creates the world so as to provide the instruments of knowledge to the souls. This is a novel act, which leads to the other acts of the Lord. Now the world has been created and thus the souls are provided with the necessary tools to cut asunder their ignorance. But the tempted souls fall prey to delusion and their ignorance proliferated. This intensified ignorance is compared to a dense forest in which finding the exit root is impossible without a proper guide. The Lord acts as the guide. Now the souls start realizing slowly. They start thinking in the right way. The Lord strengthens this right thinking. For those who seek, He is readily available in the inner recesses by staying in the suṣumna. As a result, jñāna dawns and the Lord abides by the souls forever, completing his businesses as far as the redeemed souls are concerned.

The Lord is said to be dancing in the *ciṟṟambalam* (the *cit-ākāśa*). This *ciṟṟambalam* is situated twelve finger-measures above the crown (this is also called *tuvātacānta-p-peruveḷi*, i.e., *dvādaśānta*).[89] By concentrating in between the eye-brows one can identify the *ciṟṟambalam*, the stage where the Lord dances.[90] Those who identify and adore the dancing feet of the Lord will— out of love— sob, fear, fall, rise, get exhausted, be unaware of themselves; their ego will be lost.[91] They will stop seeking material wealth; for them no more bewilderment; no more harassment due to the body; no more distractions of the senses; no more desires; only seeking after the bliss gets intensified.[92] Making one realize the three aspects of the Lord, the sat, the cit and the ānanda within one's self, that is, helping one to attain jñāna, is the purpose for which the Lord dances.

> The fulfillment of the blissful dance of Śiva,
> Which is beyond the word, is in the enlightenment of
> The aspect Light, the aspect Existence and the aspect
> Blissful mergence with the graceful Śivakāmi.[93]

The aspect light is cit; the aspect existence is sat and the aspect mergence with Śivakāmi denotes the boundless bliss.

4. 3. 3. The symbolism of the dance of Śiva

Of the four hands of the Lord of Dance— Naṭarāja, one of the left hands holds fire and one of the right hands holds the hand-drum called *uḍukkai*. Another left hand is uplifted in air across the chest with the wrist and fingers tilted downward, palm facing down, the index finger indicating the left foot uplifted in the air. Another right hand is raised in blessing (*abhaya-hastha* – the fear-not gesture), the palm outward and the fingers pointing upward. Of the feet of the Lord of Dance, the left foot is uplifted in the air and the right foot is fixed firmly on Muyalgaṉ, a demon representing the āṇava-mala (see Appendix-C).

Tirumūlar deciphers the symbolism of the form of the Lord of Dance.

> The Lord's drum represents creation and the protective hand, sustenance;
> The Lord's fire represents destruction so to say;
> The Lord's fixed foot represents obscuration; and
> The Lord's raised foot is liberation.[94]

The same idea is echoed in the later work on Śaiva Siddhānta, *Uṇmai-viḷakkam* also.[95] To Tirumūlar the dance of Śiva also represents the five-letters, the Pañcākṣara, ci-va-ya-na-ma:

> *Ci* is the hand that shakes off;
> *Vā* is the flower-like hand held close to the chest as if embracing the ascetics.
> *Ya* is the golden hand with the fear-not gesture;
> *Na* is the hand with fire and *Ma* is the foot fixed.[96]

The letter *ci* is represented by the right hand that holds a drum. The dancing Lord shakes off His right hand to play the drum held in it. The Lord dances to the rhythmic sound created of the drum. This playing of the drum symbolises the act of ceaseless creation by the Lord. In this connection it is worth noting here that the first evolute in the process of creation is *nādam* (sound). In the Tamil context, when one shakes off something, either physically or mentally, he produces a sound *ci* out of disgust. Since creation is the output of the māyā-mala, the Lord shakes off His hand in disgust as if He wants to clear off the dirt from His hand. This is to make the souls understand that they should also follow suit by shaking off the worldly attachments, concentrating on the Lord.

The left hand of the Lord is stretched across and held close to the chest, the palm of which looks like a down-facing lotus represents the letter *vā*. *Vā* is an expression used in Tamil to welcome a person, which literally means 'come.' The hand under reference is posing as if it welcomes all the ascetics who do rare penance and hugs them. The index finger of this hand points to the uplifted foot to show the destination of the souls.

The right hand that poses the fear-not gesture represents the letter *ya*. It is the golden hand that protects.

The letter *na* is represented by the left hand that holds fire. Fire represents destruction. Fire is just. It destroys everything that comes unto its fold, both the good and the bad. Destruction is a blessing in disguise. For it helps the realized souls to relinquish their body, which is the only remaining link that connects them to this world. It helps the unrealized souls also by way of providing them with a break, so that they can rest them and come back to the world afresh. Even destruction is an act of grace.

The letter *ma* is represented by the foot fixed firm on the demon called Muyalagaṉ, who represents the āṇava-mala. By pressing the demon under His foot, allowing him no space to raise his head, the Lord helps the souls. This foot is said to represent the act of obscuration.

Thus the Body of the Lord represents the five-letters and hence Tirumūlar asks us to treat the five-letters as the Body of the Lord.[97] Seconding the proposal of the *Tirumandiram*, the *Uṇmai-viḷakkam* says: Aum is the *tiruvāci* (the fiery ring that surrounds the image of the Lord); and the Lord dancing inside it is the five-letters.[98]

5. Temple worship

As already observed the metaphysical truths were condensed in myths and symbols. These myths and symbols were represented by images of drawing and sculpture. When the general public acclaimed these creative images, they became objects of worship. For accessibility to all, they were kept in public places. To keep them safe, temples were built. When the concept of the temple made deep inroads into the minds of the people, it became part and parcel of their life. The Āgamas helped the temples with a definite architectural format conforming to the symbolism. The involvement of the society in building and maintaining the temple made the temple a social institution.

5. 1. The term kōyil (temple)

Kōyil is the Tamil word that denotes temple, which is made of two words *kō* and *il*. *Kō* means the Lord and *il*, His abode. In the ancient times there were no built-temples. Instead the Lord was worshipped in the natural locations. The *Tiru-murugāṟṟu-p-paḍai* notifies the natural locations where Lord Muruga was worshipped.[99] The *Paṭṭiṉa-p-pālai* makes a mention of *kanduḍai-p-podiyil.*[100] *Podiyil* is a temple in which a *kandu* is installed. *Kandu* is a post representing a deity. Similarly, the *Malaipaḍu-kaḍām* refers to a hill called Naviram as the abode of Lord Śiva.[101]

Though there were numerous references to the gods and their abodes in the Saṅgam literature and the later works such as *Cilappadigāram*, *Maṇimēgalai* and others, the term *kōyil* was not found in any of these literary works in reference to the temple. The term *nagar* was used to refer to the temple in the Saṅgam literature;[102] sometimes the term *podiyil* was also used. We find the term *kōṭṭam* in the place of temple in *Cilappadigāram* and

Maṇimēgalai.[103] The term *kōyil* was used to refer to the palace of the king in those times.[104] One finds no reference to the word *kōyil* denoting the temple in the *Tiru-k-kuṟaḷ* and the other didactic works.

Of the saints of Bhakti Movement, Kāraikkāl Ammaiyār and Tirmūlar representing Śaivism, Pēy-āḻvār, Pūdattāḻvār and Poygai-āḻvār representing Vaiṣṇavism were the predecessors. Of these saints one finds no reference to the term *kōyil* signifying temple in the verses of Kāraikkāl Ammaiyār, Pēy-āḻvār and Pūdattāḻvār. It was probably Tirmūlar and Poygai-āḻvār, who for the first time used the term *kōyil* to refer to the temple.[105]

5. 2. The structure of the temple

During the time of Tirumūlar worshipping the Lord at the temple had been in vogue. Thanks to the Āgamas and the Tantras. In one time temples were built with bricks, wood and plaster. The Pallava king Mahēndra-varmaṉ revolutionized temple building. In his period the temples became rock-cut temples, known as cave-temples *(kugai-k-kōyilgaḷ)*. This way of structuring temples gave them elongation. But this type of temples can be built only where huge rocks were available. The successors of Magēndra-varmaṉ turned back to the traditional way of building temples. But this time they used stone blocks instead of bricks to some extent.

The sanctum sanctorum of the presiding deity and the tower built on it was the first structure of the temples. The other structures such as the central hall, the compound walls, the walk-way inside the compound walls going round the shrine and the precincts of the other deities like Caṇḍēcar, Gaṇēcar (Gaṇeśa) and Cuppiramaṇiyar (Subramaṇya) were all later additions. Small towers over the compound gateways of the temples were built. These small towers were later made into huge ones. Tanks were created either inside or outside, adjacent to the temples. The Goddess was kept in a separate shrine. The inner walkways were decorated with paintings and sculptures depicting the mythological stories.

5. 3. The role of temple in society

The temples played not only a religious role but social, artistic, educational and political roles too. They became places of refuge to the sculptor, drawing artiste, dancer, musician, philosopher, religionist, mythologist, administrator, poet and the like. They lodged the armies of the kings during the war times. They were used as the court halls for hearing the cases by the local authorities. In those days the public documents, the donations and the other charitable activities were recorded by way of inscribing them on the temple walls and thus the temples also acted as the local archives. The temples with various activities were taken under the control of the government. The governments provided the temples with tax-free lands for the welfare and to administer. This way the temples grew rich and they started lending money. The interest on the money that was lent was credited to the temple. Regarding the economic activities of the temples of the Pallava age, C. Minakshi says:

> The functions discharged by the temple were of varied nature. As one of the biggest landowners in the locality it looked after the interests of the agriculture in the area. It cultivated lands, extended cultivation to uncultivated areas (A.R. 258 of 1919) and for the rehabilitation of dilapidated villages. As a consumer it purchased different articles for various services connected with the worship in the temple... The temple

encouraged rural industries like weaving by granting to the families of weavers lands round the temple precincts... . The temples during the later Pallava days were functioning as a substantial economic institution to which the villages could turn for help at times of famine, floods or economic depression.[106]

5. 4. Temple worship in the Tirumandiram

Though Tirumūlar was for inner worship, he did not undermine the place of the temples in a society. He had insisted that the temples should be properly preserved. He had also warned people of the calamities if the temples were not maintained properly.

If the worship in the temples is not done properly there will be no rain fall in that region; this will result in diseases; due to this the king will be weakened; theft will be on the increase.[107] Even if a single stone is dislocated in a temple the king and the priest will be ruined, because of their carelessness.[108] If the already installed liṅga is transplanted in some other place, before the completion of the transplantation, the king will be dethroned and will die.[109] The following verse shows the importance given to temple worship.

Wander you through town and villa
Seek Him through shrine and temple
Sing of Him as "Siva, Siva, my Lord"
And thus do you offer, worship meek,
And the Lord will make your heart His temple.[110]

6. Worship: The essence of religion

The aim of philosophy is to discover the underlying reality; the aim of religion is to help the souls to get liberated by releasing them permanently. For a mystic like Tirumūlar both— knowing the reality and realizing it— are important. They are like the two sides of the same coin.

Worship is an important part of realizing the reality. Cēkkiḻār defines worship as an outward expression of love.[111] The mother-cow comes hurriedly when the calf seeks and cries for the mother. Like that, when the seeker cries earnestly yearning for the Lord, He will come definitely.[112]

Worship is an element of *bhakti.* Tirumūlar says that *bhakti* and jñāna are the two steps that lead to *para-siddhi,* that is, the ultimate goal called liberation.[113] In one place Tirumūlar goes to the extent of saying that the sincere *bhaktas* have envisioned that Light which is difficult even for the Siddhas.[114] Tirumūlar not only appreciates the *bhaktas* but also condemns them when they become cheaters. He calls them *mattagar* (intoxicated persons), those who sell *bhakti* and make a business out of it.[115]

Before attempting to understand worship in the *Tirumandiram,* let us look into the features of worship. Generally speaking worship contains some acts which may be internal or external or both. These acts are called rituals. John Woodroffe says:

> Ritual is an art, the art of religion. Art is the outward material expression of ideas intellectually held and emotionally felt. Ritual art is concerned with the expression of these ideas and feeling, which are specially called religious. ...
>
> The ultimate object of the ritual— that is, the realization of God— is effected by the transformation of the worshipper into likeness with the worshipped.[116]

6. 1. The four stages of worship

The Āgamas have classified a four-fold path to achieve the spiritual goal. They are: carya, kriya, yoga and jñāna. By the time of Tirumūlar this four-fold worship was in trend and Tirumūlar notes them in a number of verses. He defines the four in the following way:

> Knowing the Lord one with oneself is worship by jñāna;
> Seeing the Lord as the Light of one's life is worship by Yoga;
> Invoking the Lord in an idol is worship by outward means kriya;
> Collecting materials of worship with tender-heart is Śiva-pūja— carya.[117]

6. 1. 2. Carya

The practice of caryā is basic to salvation and it is the breath of the Śaivites.[118] Carya-ites, that is, those who stick to the path called caryā, are those who seek the Lord in cities and villages, in temples, singing His glory, offering their meek souls unto Him.[119] They are called the bhaktas.[120]

6. 1. 3. Kriya

The kriya-ites, that is, those who tread in the path called kriyā, are those who do not fail even for a single day to praise and worship the Lord.[121] They are external worshippers.[122] They wear the holy marks. These external worshippers are called devotees *(toṇḍar)*.[123]

6. 1. 4. Yoga

The yogins are those who course the kuṇḍalinī fire through the six ādhāras single-mindedly and make themselves like a wooden post unaware of the external pressures operating on them. Those who can do this will realize the Lord within. In them the fragrance of the Lord will bloom.[124] When this happens the cycle of births and deaths is terminated.[125] Those who stick on to this path of Aṣṭāṅga-Yoga— the eight-limbed Yoga starting with *yama*— are called the pure yogins *(tū-yōgar)*.[126] Tirumūlar also classifies Yoga into three types: Caryā-Yoga, Kriyā-Yoga, Yoga-Yoga. Of these, Caryā-Yoga helps one to get rid of his desires and to reach the abode of God *(sāloka)*. The Kriyā-Yoga helps one to get closer to God *(sāmīpya)*. The Yoga-Yoga helps one to stick on to God steadfastly with everlasting love and realizing God in one's own self *(sārūpya)*.[127]

6. 1. 5. Jñāna

The jñānis are those who become He.[128] The self is disturbed because of the ripples of thinking *(vṛttis)*; thinking is due to *citta* (the mental faculty); *citta* is fueled by the sense of egoity, but also by the intelligence and the mind; the mind is a creation of the primal sound *nāda*. To cease the disturbances one has to stop the *citta-vṛttis*. One has to stop fueling the *citta* with egoity, intelligence and mind. One has to finally transcend them by realizing the source of the primal sound— the *nādānta*. Realizing the *nādānta* is jñāna. This path is also called *sanmārga*.[129] Tirumūlar refers to these people as Siddhas.[130]

Of these four paths Tirumūlar gives a special place to the path of jñāna.

Than Jnana,
There is no better ethical path, here below;
No better religious faith;
Nothing else than Jnana can confer liberation true;
They that are exalted in Jnana
Are truly exalted among men.[131]

Though he emphasizes jñāna as the highest path to stick on to, he also insists that there is a process of reaching that. To him, all the four paths are the steps in the ladder to unite with the Lord.

The Bhakta to begin with practices Chariya and Kriya,
Then blessed with grace takes to Yoga pure;
And that way reaches the path of Jnana
And in the end by guru 's grace becomes one with Siva.[132]

7. A bird 's eye view of religion as conceived in the Tirumandiram

It is true that Tirumūlar did not speak in praise of any religion and that he was secular. It is also true that in one place he had said that even the founders of the six faiths have not found the Lord.[133] But his shaking off the religions does not mean that he denied religions altogether. It means that he condemns the show-biz attitude of the religions, which are full of sound and fury signifying nothing.[134] It means that he condemns those who contend that this religion is good and that religion is bad.[135]

In the same way Tirumūlar gives importance only to internal worship; but that does not mean that he has denied a place to external worship. For those who believe that the Lord resides within and outside He is so; for those who deny His existence He is neither inside nor outside.[136]

Idol worship does not mean *worshipping an idol*; instead it means *worshipping the Lord in an idol*. For those who worship the Lord in an idol sincerely, the idol is not simply an image made of stone or wood or metal; it *is* the omnipresent Lord Itself.

The idol worshipper should have the sharpness of an archer. There is an incident in the epic Mahābhārata. Once Droṇācārya, the guru of the Pāṇḍavas and the Kauravas, asked Arjuna, one of the five Pāṇḍava princes, to hit at a mango in a mango tree, to prove the prowess of Arjuna in archery to others. Arjuna took his bow and an arrow, aimed at it.

Droṇācārya asked Arjuna: "What is that you are aiming at now? The tree?"

Arjuna said: "No!"

"The leaves?"

"No!"

"The mango?"

"No! The stalk that supports the mango!"

That should be the concentration exercised by the idol worshipper. He should not concentrate on the external decorations of the idol and be lost in it; instead he should be able to see God in it. Tirumūlar makes an appeal to the seeker to be a good archer, hitting straight the mark.[137] This is the beginning stage of worship. Starting from the external worship the seeker slowly grows in maturity to worship the Lord without an image. As already pointed out the final stage of becoming one with the Lord through jñāna is processed through the other steps caryā, kriyā and yoga.

For those who have achieved the state of jñāna, the external worship and other rituals may be meaningless. Even though these measures are to be stuck on to for the sake of the ordinary folk who are yet to cross the bridge. To avoid distortions in the myths, the spiritual message-bearers should reinterpret them, bringing out their significance; otherwise they will become dead stories and just fun.

That is what is attempted by Tirumūlar in the *Tirumandiram.* To avoid the religions going blunt, he reinterprets the mythological stories, brings out the symbolism of the form of Lord Naṭarāja, and reasons out the preservation of the temples. This care of Tirumūlar is an expression of his social concern.

Camayam is the Tamil word for religion, which comes from the root *camai,* and which means "that which is mature," "that which creates," "that which prepares."[138] Making *camayam,* religion, true to its meaning was the sole aim of Tirumūlar and not denying it. The religion of Tirumūlar was the one that prepares the jīvas to become Śiva, that is, Śaivism.

Notes on Chapter Three

1. Refer: Albun G. Widgery, *The Comparative Study of Religions*, p. 2.
2. Quoted in E.E. Kellett, *A Short History of Religions*, p. 9.
3. Radhakrishnan, *The Hindu Way of Life*, p. 13.
4. S. Radhakrishnan, *The Reign of Religion in Contemporary Philosophy*, p. 5.
5. G.U.Pope (Tr.), *Tiruvachagam*, p. LXXIV.
6. Sir John Marshall in his *Mohenjadaro and Indus Civilization*, quoted by T.B. Siddalingaiah, "Śaiva Siddhānta: Its Origin and Development up to Umāpati," R. Balasubramanian (ed.), *History of Science, Philosophy and Culture in Indian Civiliza tion*, Vol. II, Part 3 - *Theistic Vedanta*, p. 642.
7. *Ibid.*, p. 642.
8. T.B. Siddalingam, *Caiva-camaya-t-tōṟṟamum Vaḷarcciyum*, pp. 11-13.
9. T.B. Siddalingaiah, "Śaiva Siddhānta: Its Origin and Development upto Umāpati," *History of Science, Philosophy and Culture in Indian Civilization*, p. 642.
10. G.V. Tagare, *Caiva-tattuvam*, Ka. Sri. Sri. (tr.), p. xxiv.
11. T.B. Siddalingam, *op.cit.*, p. 9.
12. T.B. Siddhalingaiah, *op.cit.*, p. 623.
13. Quoted by T.B. Siddhalingaiah, *Ibid.*, p. 642.
14. *Ibid.*, p. 642.
15. *Tolkāppiyam*, "Poruḷadigāram," 85.
16. *Tiru-k-kuraḷ*, 358.
17. *karuppum civappum veguḷi-p-poruḷ. Tolkāppiyam*, "Colladigāram," 372.
18. N.N. Bhattacharyya, *History of the Tantric Religion*, p. 133.
19. *Ibid.*, p. 134.

20. *Ibid.*, p. 136.
21. B. Bhattacharya, *Saivism and the Phallic World*, Vol. 1, pp. 11-12.
22. Refer the verses of Śiva-vākkiyar, 48, 129-134.
23. Tamil Lexicon, Vol. IV, part I, p. 2019.
24. Tevaneyan, *Tamiḻar Madam*, pp. 37-39.
25. *Tiru-k-kuṟaḷ*, 4.
26. For a detailed analysis of the development of Śaivism from the point of view of the Vedic tradition, refer R. Balasubramanian's "The Tradition of Śaivism," in *History of Science, Philosophy and Culture in Indian Civilization*, pp. 1-39. To know the development of Śaivism from the point of view of the Tamil tradition, refer T.B. Siddalingaiah, "Śaiva Siddhānta: Its Origin and Development up to Umāpati," *Ibid.*, pp. 623-641.
27. Quoted by T.B. Siddalingaiah, *Ibid.*, p. 625.
28. *Tirumandiram*, 1512. Author's translation.
29. *Ibid.*, 1563. Author's translation.
30. *Ibid.*, 1535.
31. *Ibid.*, 1538.
32. *Ibid.*, 1558.
33. *Ibid.*, 2854.
34. *Ibid.*, 2126.
35. *Ibid.*, 95.
36. Ra. Ganapathy, *Deivattiṉ Kural*, Vol. I, pp. 170-171.
37. Quoted by P.S. Somasundaram, *Tirujñāṉasambandhar: Philosophy and Religion*, p. 144.
38. *Tirumandiram*, 339. Author's translation.
39. *Ibid.*, 340. Translation of B. Natarajan with a slight change.
40. *Ibid.*, 221. Author's translation.

41. *Ibid.*, 223.
42. C. Arunai Vadivel Mudaliyar, *Śiva-jñāṉa-bōda-māpāḍiya-p-poruḷ-nilai viḷakkam*, p. 705.
43. Mircea Eliade, *Yoga: Immortality and Freedom*, Willard R. Trask, (tr.), p. 111.
44. *Tirumandiram*, 337, 338.
45. Pāmbāṭṭi-c-cittar, 113.
46. Quoted by T.N. Ganapathy, *The Philosophy of the Tamil Siddhas*, p. 93.
47. *Tirumandiram*, 1965.
48. *Ibid.*, 1962.
49. *Ibid.*, 1950.
50. *Ibid.*, 1961.
51. *Ibid.*, 1936.
52. *Ibid.*, 353. Author's translation.
53. *Ibid.*, 1852.
54. *Ibid.*, 1962.
55. *Ibid.*, 1852.
56. *Ibid.*, 357, 360, 361.
57. *Ibid.*, 341. Translation of B. Natarajan.
58. T.N. Ganapathy, *op.cit.*, p. 87.
59. *Tirumandiram*, 1887. Author's translation.
60. *Ibid.*, 342. Author's translation.
61. Ka. Cu. Uttamarayan, *To<u>r</u><u>r</u>a-k-kirama Ārācciyum Citta Maruttuva Varalā<u>r</u>um*, p. 24.
62. *Pu<u>r</u>a-nā<u>n</u>ū<u>r</u>u*, 55.
63. *Cilappadigāram*, 6:40-45.
64. *Tirumandiram*, 343. Author's translation.
65. Nacci<u>n</u>ārki<u>n</u>iyar (Comm.), *Cīvaga-cindāmaṇi*, p. 1367.

66. *Tirumandiram*, 344. Author's translation. This episode is hinted in verse 21 also.
67. *Ibid.*, 2034.
68. *Puṟa-nāṉūṟu*, 365.
69. *Tiru-k-kuṟaḷ*, 269. Translation of V.V.S. Aiyar.
70. *Tirumandiram*, 345. Author's translation.
71. *Ibid.*, 172.
72. *Ibid.*, 346. Author's translation.
73. *Ibid.*, 521. Author's translation.
74. *Ibid.*, 1951.
75. *Ibid.*, 1957.
76. *Ibid.*, 1949–51, 1958–59, 1962, 1971.
77. *Tiru-vācagam*, "Pōṟṟi-t-tiru-agaval," 173.
78. *Tirumandiram*, 1974. Author's translation.
79. M. Tiruvilangam (Comm.), *Śiva-jñāṉa-siddhiyār Cubakkam*, 237. Author's translation.
80. *Uṇmai-viḷakkam*, 36. Author's translation.
81. *Tirumandiram*, 2723, 2741–43.
82. *Ibid.*, 2723.
83. *Ibid.*, 2733.
84. M. V. Viswanatha Pillai (Ed.), *Tirumandiram*, p. 580.
85. *Tirumandiram*, 2747.
86. *Ibid.*, 2748.
87. *Ibid.*, 2735.
88. *Ibid.*, 2736. Author's translation.
89. *Ibid.*, 2764.
90. *Ibid.*, 2770.
91. *Ibid.*, 2744.
92. *Ibid.*, 2745.

93. *Ibid.*, 2726. Author's translation.
94. *Ibid.*, 2799. Author's translation.
95. *Uṇmai-viḷakkam*, 35.
96. *Tirumandiram*, 2797. Author's translation.
97. *Ibid.*, 2798.
98. *Uṇmai-viḷakkam*, 34.
99. *Tiru-murugāṟṟu-p-paḍai*, 223-226.
100. *Paṭṭiṉa-p-pālai*, 249.
101. *Malaipaḍu-kaḍām*, 82-83.
102. *Puṟa-nāṉūṟu*, 6; *Tiru-murugāṟṟu-p-paḍai*, 244.
103. *Cilappadigāram*, "Padigam," 1; *Maṇimēgalai*, 6:53.
104. *Maṇimēgalai*, 20:96.
105. *Tirumandiram*, 517, 1445; *Nālāyira-t-tivviya-p-pirabandam*, "Periya Tiru-moḻi," 5.
106. Quoted by P.S. Somasundaram, *op.cit.*, p. 167.
107. *Tirumandiram*, 517, 518.
108. *Ibid.*, 516.
109. *Ibid.* 515.
110. *Ibid.*, 1446. Translation of B. Natarajan.
111. *Periya-purāṇam*, "Tiru-k-kūṭṭa-c-ciṟappu," 8.
112. *Tirumandiram*, 2627.
113. *Ibid.*, 1585. Also refer: 2623, 2624, 2626, 2628,1454, 1455.
114. *Ibid.*, 284.
115. *Ibid.*, 2069.
116. Quoted by P.S. Somasundaram, *op.cit.*, pp. 171-172.
117. *Tirumandiram*, 1444. Author's Translation.
118. *Ibid.*, 1443.
119. *Ibid.*, 1445.
120. *Ibid.*, 1446.

121. *Ibid.*, 1447.
122. *Ibid.*, 1444, 1448.
123. *Ibid.*, 1446.
124. *Ibid.*, 1457, 1459.
125. *Ibid.*, 1460.
126. *Ibid.*, 1446.
127. *Ibid.*, 1465.
128. *Ibid.*, 1447.
129. *Ibid.*, 1468.
130. *Ibid.*, 1446.
131. *Ibid.*, 1467. Translation of B. Natarajan.
132. *Ibid.*, 1455. Translation of B. Natarajan.
133. *Ibid.*, 1533.
134. *Ibid.*, 1556.
135. *Ibid.*, 1558.
136. *Ibid.*, 1532.
137. *Ibid.*, 269.
138. Tevaneyan, *Tami̲lar Madam*, pp. 3-4.

CHAPTER 4
THE YOGA OF THE TIRUMANDIRAM

T.N. Ganapathy

yōga-c camādiyiṉ uḷḷe agal iḍam
yōga-c camādiyiṉ uḷḷe uḷaroḷi
yōga-c camādiyiṉ uḷḷe uḷa catti
yōga-c camādi ugandavar cittarē.

In Yoga Samādhi is Space Infinite;
In Yoga Samādhi is Light Abiding;
In Yoga Samādhi is Śakti Omnipotent;
They that delight in Yoga Samādhi
Are verily Siddhas great.

–Tirumandiram, 1490.

4. The Yoga of the Tirumandiram

T.N. Ganapathy

1. Definition of Yoga

Any attempt to define Yoga in terms of *per genus et differentia* will be an unsuccessful attempt for "only by Yoga is Yoga known." Really Yoga means many things for it is many things. To start with one can indicate the denotative aspect of the term and gradually, though not successfully, attempt to comprehend its connotative aspect. Through denotation, we can say that Yoga is the *lingua franca* that has crossed doctrinal, regional, linguistic and geographical frontiers. As Mircea Eliade says Yoga is a "living fossil," a modality of spirituality which has existed for a long time and still "un-fossilizable."[1] Patañjali calls Yoga as *anuśāsana*, which means "direction coming down from traditions."[2]

Though etymologically the term "Yoga" means "to bind together," it has acquired many other connotations such as "method," "activity," "force," "meditation," "renunciation," "concentration," "evenness," "practice of inner isolation," etc. Theos Bernard gives seventeen meanings of the term "Yoga."[3] It is the method of actualizing what is always potential in one's nature. It helps one to understand the untapped silent areas of one's consciousness. The nucleus of Yoga is practice. He who tastes knows it, not by philosophic argument. As *dhyāna-sukham*— joy of contemplation— Yoga provides man with the joy of self-discovery. The Tamil Yoga Siddhas have indicated the connotation of the term Yoga. According to Śiva-vākkiyar, a Tamil Siddha, the aim of Yoga is to attain "seedless consciousness,"[4] or pure or integral consciousness, which is an emergence from time and abolition of history. It is a "perception beyond perception."[5] The Tamil Yoga Siddhas call Yoga figuratively as an esoteric path of taking honey without flowers as base. Yoga, in short, may be interpreted as a method by means of which the basic aspects of the individual, namely, the vital current, mind, consciousness and energy are mobilized and harmonized. It is an esoteric technique, a method of inner development of a human being. In short, Yoga is ecstasy that is samādhi. It provides practical method for self-realisation.

1. 1. Yoga is different from religion

Yoga may be associated with religion *per se*, but it is distinctly distinguishable from religion and religious practices. While religion speaks of God-realization, Yoga speaks of self-realization. To achieve self-realization jñāna is the method adopted by Yoga. Tamil Siddhas insisted on the supreme importance of jñāna and they do not emphasize bhakti as the method of realization. In bhakti the heart weeps for what is lost whereas in jñāna the spirit delights in what it has found. Hence the Tamil Yoga Siddhas are critical about idol-worship and religious practices. They are against the fundamentalist attitude of religion. In their literature there is almost a total absence of any local cult or the deity. No genuine Siddha in Tamil Literature has sung in praise of any local God. One of the chief characteristic features, the *differentia,* to determine a genuine Siddha is to find out whether he/she has sung in praise of any local God or Deity. According to Śiva-vākkiyar, a Siddha never worships a deity in the temple.[6] This is a feature that distinguishes Siddhas from other saints, especially Āḻvārs and Nāyaṉmārs. Yet the Siddhas believed in the Supreme Abstraction and called it as "That" or "It" or "Suchness" or "*Parāparam*" in Tamil. The Siddhas are against any institutionalized religion, which produces habits, customs and ritualistic practices which prevent one from being spiritually alert and fully conscious. Formalities threaten to become more important than knowing one's own inner nature or self and hence rituals and scriptures become only fetters. One who is bent on enlightenment should be careful about the road-blocks such as rituals, scriptures, temples, churches, mosques, etc., which hinder the spiritual pathway and progress. According to the Siddhas the cause of the prevalence of delusion in our lives is institutional rather than personal.

2. Yoga as understood by Tirumūlar

In discussing Yoga as understood by Tirumūlar one has to take into consideration his definitions of a Siddha; that is, his views regarding Yoga *inter alia* are connected with his understanding of who a Siddha is. His views on Yoga and his definitions of a Siddha are the two sides of the same coin.

2. 1. Yoga is Śiva-Yoga

First of all Tirumūlar calls the Yoga discussed in the *Tirumandiram* as *nava-yoga* (new type of Yoga) or *tava-yoga* (Yoga of penance) or Śiva-Yoga (Yoga that bestows *Śiva-ānanda*).

The verse runs as follows:

Śiva-Yoga is to distinguish the *cit* from the *acit*;
Yoga of penance is to attain self-illumination;
Other types of Yoga are not Yoga proper; to attain Śiva-ānanda
Nandi has bestowed this new type of Yoga.[7]

Tirumūlar says that Nandi (Śiva) has bestowed this new type of Yoga *(nava-yoga)* discarding the previous types of Yoga as Yoga not proper. The term that Tirumūlar uses for the other types of Yoga is *ava-yoga. Ava-yoga* refers to the useless types of Yoga that were in vogue previously, which do not bestow anything good for the yogin. G. Varadarajan interprets the term *ava-yoga* as Haṭha-Yoga, which deals mainly with bodily discipline.[8] But this interpretation is far-fetched, for *ava-yoga* simply means Yoga which is useless.

Śiva-Yoga, also called Śiva-rāja-Yoga distinguishes by means of *viveka* (discrimination), the *cit* (intelligence, consciousness, knowledge) from the *acit* (non-conscious, that which lacks knowledge). Suba. Annamalai distinguishes between *cit* and *acit* in the following manner: Though the atman or individual soul or consciousness by nature is *cit*, it does not know due to ignorance that it is *cit* and it is treated as *acit*; but when once wisdom dawns, the ignorance that it is *acit* is removed.[9] This interpretation powerfully reminds us of the story which Swami Vivekananda is fond of narrating. It is as follows:

> There is a story about a lioness, who was big with young, going about in search of prey; and seeing a flock of sheep, she jumped upon them. She died in the effort; and a little baby lion was born, motherless. It was taken care of by the sheep, and the sheep brought it up, and it grew up with them, ate grass and bleated like the sheep. And although in time it became a big, full-grown lion, it thought it was a sheep. One day another lion came in search of prey and was astonished to find that in the midst of this flock of sheep was a lion, fleeing like the sheep at the approach of danger. He tried to get near the sheep-lion, to tell it that it was not a sheep but a lion; but the poor animal fled at his approach. However he watched his opportunity and one day found the sheep-lion sleeping. He approached it and said, "You are a lion." "I am a sheep," cried the other lion and could not believe the contrary, but bleated. The lion dragged him towards a lake and said, "Look here, here is my reflection and yours." Then came the comparison. It looked at the lion and then at its own reflection,

and in a moment came the idea that it was a lion. The lion roared, the bleating was gone.[10]

Śiva-Yoga is the Yoga method by which the atman identifies itself with Śiva. It is a process of attaining Śivahood at the top of the head *(sahasrāra)*. It is called in Siddha literature as "Yoga which touches the top"[11] Here the yogin is said to "drink" the "ambrosial juice" oozing from the sahasrāra. Hence this Yoga is called by some Siddhas as a process of "begging at the top" or "quenching the thirst at the top."

Śiva-Yoga is attained by *tava-yoga* (Yoga of penance). It is a new type of Yoga *(nava-yoga)*, which has been bestowed to humanity by Nandi (Śiva) Himself. By calling as *nava-yoga*, Tirumūlar indicates that this new type of Yoga was not in vogue before him in the Tamil country. It is for the first time that this Yoga is explicitly explained and discussed in the *Tirumandiram*. (Though Tirumūlar does not use the expression Kuṇḍalini-Yoga, what is discussed by him is only that. In the sections that follow, the term Kuṇḍalini-Yoga is used as the alternate term for Śiva-Yoga). That is, the *Tirumandiram* is not only an Āgama treatise but a treatise on Yoga as well. Though the *Tirumandiram* is listed as the tenth *Tirumuṟai* (bhakti works of Tamil Śaivism), it is distinctly different from the other *Tirumuṟais* in that it discusses a new type of Yoga *(nava-yoga)* dealing with cakras, prāṇāyāma, Pariyaṅga-Yoga, twilight language, etc., The *Tirumandiram* develops Aṣṭāṅga-Yoga as Śiva-Yoga. Hence its message is wider than Patañjali's *Yoga-Sūtras*.[12] It is the first treatise in Tamil on Śiva-Yoga known as Kuṇḍalini-Yoga. As Tamilannal says Tirumūlar, in his *Tirumandiram*, struck a new tradition in Tamil.[13]

According to Tirumūlar, yogins who practice Śiva-Yoga are called Śiva-yogins or Siddhas:

Śiva yogins are they that the seed destroy;
Who, in waking state, the pure awareness induce;
Who in harmony unbroken, achieve the tranced breath
When life, senses, body-alike simulate death.[14]

Siddhas are those who are alive, but "dead" so far as the external world is concerned. They are jīvan-muktas who live in their bodies, but yet liberated; they are yogic adepts of immortality. As they call in Tibet they are *amṛta-siddhi-yogins*. That is, jīvan-mukti is living liberation. A jīvan-mukta has a body made of enlightened awareness and equal to that of Śiva, but a physical body nevertheless. To be liberated in life is to be Śiva— the Supreme Abstraction unbounded by form or times. (Śiva is the symbol used to connote a divinized human state of liberation, and every yogin should strive to be Śiva, the Lord of yogins). Tirumūlar, therefore, calls a Siddha as *Śiva-muṉi-Siddha*[15] or *nirāmayattōr* (one who does not suffer birth).[16] Tirumūlar calls himself such a Siddha.[17]

There are several verses in the *Tirumandiram* to show that Yoga is Śiva-jñāna. Tirumūlar defines a Siddha as one who has attained Śiva-jñāna.[18] He calls a Siddha as Śiva-mukta.[19] According to Tirumūlar Śiva-jñānis are dead to the world, though living in body and senses.[20] Śiva-jñānis are jīvan-muktas.

Jīvan-mukti or living liberation is a state of embodied wisdom in which the yogic attainments transform all aspects of human existence. Tirumūlar calls a jīvan-mukta as *cōmbar.*[21] *Sōmbar* in Tamil stands for the state of tranquility. He also calls a jīvan-mukta as *tūṅgi-k-kaṇḍāṉ*. It means one who has attained realization by "sleeping." A jīvan-mukta is one who "sleeps" (is quiet) and sees Śiva's world and experiences Śiva-Yoga.[22]

In a work called *Amṛta-siddhi* or *The Attainment of Immortality*[23] the author Avadhuta Candra describes a jīvan-mukta as follows:

When the attainments of
Body, speech, and mind are manifest,
The great attainment, the bestowal of the fruit of living liberation
Is to be known. (30.3)

The yogin is blissful,
Omniscient, he has vision,
He makes an offering of all elements,
Pledged to the three worlds. (30.5)

He is not burned by fire,
Nor does he sink in water,
The master of Yoga is invincible,
He has cast off the things of the world. (30.8)

Such a yogin is made of everything,
Composed of all elements,
Always dwelling in omniscience,
He has the respect of the entire world. (30.9)
Endowed with all the qualities of Siva,
With limitless all-pervading wisdom,
The yogin, following the great adepts,
Is the locus of all accomplishments. (30.7)

So do these beings live,
Beheld replete with spiritual attainments,
Those adepts who posses the body of Siva,
Are known as the Living Liberated. (30.14)

Thus the blissful yogin (achieves),
A wisdom body, magnificent,
Indestructible, unchanging, and pervasive,
All-encompassing, omnipresent, (he is) Siva. (35.1)[24]

A genuine yogin is equal to Śiva. It is appropriate that Tirumūlar defines Yoga as Śiva-Yoga.

2. 2. Śiva-Yoga is Kuṇḍalinī-Yoga

Tirumūlar speaks of Yoga as Śiva-Yoga and says that it shows the way.

Neither mantra, nor song, nor arts four and sixty
Ever sunder birth and its accursed bonds
Then did I take to Yoga's way,
And lo! I met the Sun, Moon and Fire on the way to Cranium,
And they showed the Supreme Way.[25]

The Śiva-Yoga way is the Kuṇḍalinī-Yoga way for he speaks of the Sun (piṅgalā), Moon (iḍā) and fire (suṣumnā) by means of which he reaches the cranium (the sahasrāra). Therefore one can safely substitute the term Kuṇḍalinī-Yoga for Śiva-Yoga. Tirumūlar has not used the term "Kuṇḍalinī-Yoga" anywhere in his work. He uses the term *kuṇḍali* in verse 2419. Here the term *kuṇḍali* is used in a different sense to mean the term tirodhāna-śakti, which provides worldly experiences for the souls, hiding spiritual truths from view. However Tirumūlar refers to *aruḷ-śakti* (a benevolent energy) as a śakti, which resides in the human body. When the yogin attains the sahasrāra by diverting the *aruḷ-śakti* residing in him, he attains the eternal bliss. The energy that guides him to pass through the six adharas and reach the sahasrāra is the *aruḷ-śakti* residing in him. This *aruḷ-śakti* (as residing in the human body) is what is commonly referred to as kuṇḍalinī-śakti.

Tirumūlar uses the term *kuṇḍali* in verse 580 in the specific sense of the kuṇḍalinī energy. Tirumūlar calls *aruḷ-śakti* as *yajña,* which cuts asunder rebirth.

(Arul-sakti)
Cuts the bonds of birth asunder;
Grants the prowess of mighty *tapas;*
Scorches the soul's forgetfulness;
And leads you to liberation path.[26]

Tirumūlar calls Kuṇḍalinī-Yoga as *tapas*[27] and calls it as the Great Way.[28] He also refers to Yoga as sublimation of sex.[29]

2. 3. Aspects of Yoga as discussed in the Tirumandiram

In the *Tirumandiram* apart from Śiva-Yoga, Tirumūlar speaks of the following aspects of Yoga.

1. Aṣṭāṅga-Yoga;
2. Kechari-Yoga;
3. Candra-Yoga; and
4. Pariyaṅga-Yoga.

Before we discuss them, let us pass in review, the three types of yogins and the benefits of Yoga and Kuṇḍalinī-Yoga as explained in the *Tirumandiram.*

2. 4. Three types of yogins

Tirumūlar speaks about the three types of yogins. One type is the *kāmattōr,* who indulge in sex for its pleasure; they are the *vāmācārins* or *vāmattōr.* The other type is *ōmatttōr* of the *dakṣiṇācāra* school of Yoga, who find the light in their inner flame through the method of Śiva-Yoga. The third type of yogins is called *nāmattōr,* people who indulge in the *bhakti* method of singing the praise of God.[30]

2. 5 Benefits of Yoga

Throughout the *Tirumandiram* the value of Yoga (Śiva-Yoga) is stressed. In one place he says that the hairs of the yogin will emit light.[31] The following verses may be quoted for understanding the benefits of Yoga.

They who knock about
Reach not the Refuge of Blossom Feet;
Containing not the Kundalini fire within;
Their body a prey to fire becomes;
They who know the Way
And seek His Victorious Feet
See the heavenly Dancer
Through their spinal hollow.[32]

They who sought the Dancer as their goal
Gained many things good;
And so stood in the path of the holy scriptures;
Seeking Him within and experiencing His presence
In eagerness they sit
And one with Siva become.[33]

Well may they thus live for aeons and aeons,
And they tire not in their devotion;
And thus see the mind's end,
And within see Him as Entity non-separate;
And as one with Siva they live filled in divinity
And so see countless ages of Life Exalted.[34]
They who seek
Know death none; evil none;

They who seek
Will become lords of earth;
They who seek

But know this true;
And well may it be told
To those that aspire.[35]

Yogi attains siddhis eight
He experiences the divine Nada State;
He is of Karma rid
He is of calm mind
He pursues the Four Ends of Human Goal,
He courses the Sakti Kundalini
Through centers six within the body;
That way he reaches the one
And union in Him attains.[36]

2. 6. Appropriate days for commencing Yoga

Even though any day is good for starting to learn Yoga, it is significant that Tirumūlar indicates the appropriate days for commencing Yoga.

The birthday, The first, second, third and the eighth day following it,
Any one of these is day appropriate for commencing Yoga;
Find the day suitable most,
And easy shall be your entry
Into the Mystic House within.[37]

3. Kuṇḍalinī-Yoga

Any study on the translation and commentary of the poems of the *Tirumandiram* requires a background note on Kuṇḍalinī-Yoga. The Tamil Siddha movement is a part of the pan-Indian Tāntric Yoga tradition. It insists on the value of the Tantra-Yoga as a means for the attainment of freedom and immortality. Yoga is essentially the cultivation of awareness. It emphasizes practice rather than philosophy. Tantra-Yoga is basically Kuṇḍalinī-Yoga. The principle of polarity and the principle of identity are among the most important aspects of Tantra. The aim of Tantra is to transcend all forms of duality by the total merging of the dual principles into one within the yogin's body. The duality is symbolically put as two poles: male and female, as Śiva and Śakti. One of the main tenets of Tāntric Yoga is that whatever is in the macrocosm, *aṇḍa*, is in the microcosm, *piṇḍa*. The entire Kuṇḍalinī-Yoga is an expression of the micro-macro unity. The individual being and the Universal Being are one. Jīva is Śiva; the microcosm is the macrocosm.

Yoga has many forms and of these the main four are: Mantra-Yoga, Haṭha-Yoga, Laya-Yoga, and Rāja-Yoga. The simplest form of Yoga is Mantra-Yoga in which the aspirant is selective about the object of his contemplation, such as gods in images, emblems, pictures, markings, *maṇḍalas, yantras, mudrās*, etc. The practices, which comprise Haṭha-Yoga, are concerned primarily with the control of the physical body for conditioning the subtle body. A basic knowledge of Haṭha-Yoga is necessary for anyone who wants to understand the Siddhas. Laya-Yoga is the highest form of Haṭha-Yoga and is connected with the functioning of the kuṇḍalinī. The Tāntrics and the Siddhas lay great emphasis on this form of Yoga. The method of arousing the kuṇḍalinī and uniting her with the Supreme Spirit is the essential part of Laya-Yoga. Rāja-Yoga stands for the concentration of the mind through the control of the vital airs.

Laya-Yoga is a yogic method practiced by all the Siddhas. It is deep absorptive concentration, which takes one to the final goal of oneness with the infinite or what Siddhas call *Śiva-aikya*. Since arousing the kuṇḍalinī is the fundamental aspect of Laya-Yoga, this Yoga has been called Kuṇḍalinī-Yoga. Kuṇḍalinī-Yoga is called by Tirumūlar as Śiva-Yoga leading to *Śiva-aikya*. *Śiva-aikya* is a reality, because the basis of it is love. Śivam is love. The basis of Yoga is love and its method is jñāna.

3. 1. References in the Tirumandiram of Kuṇḍalinī-Yoga (Śiva-Yoga)

Though in *tantra* Seven of the *Tirumandiram* one finds a reference to the six ādhāras (section 1), the *mudrās* (section 17), the importance of controlling the five senses (section 32) and how to control the senses by way of sublimation (section 33), the concept and the function of the Kuṇḍalinī-Yoga (Śiva-Yoga) is diffused throughout the work. In this connection it may be noted that the entire section one on *Agattiyam* and section two on the *Eight Heroic Deeds of Śiva* of the *tantra* Two may be interpreted symbolically in terms of Śiva-Yoga. A case in point is that in verse 337, the term *naḍuvuḷa aṅgi Agattiya* means "admidst the blazing sacrificial fire" which refers to the Kuṇḍalinī energy, i.e., *aruḷ-śakti*, arising at the mūlādhāra. In verse 339 the term *cūlam*, i.e., the trident refers to the iḍā, piṅgala and suṣumnā nāḍis. Verse 345 speaks of the mūlādhāra from where kuṇḍalinī-śakti is awakened and courses to the hollow on the top, i.e., the sahasrāra. The section four on *Dakṣa's Sacrifice* may also be construed as a subtle symbolic reference to Kuṇḍalinī-Yoga. Verse 360 speaks of the *nava-kuṇḍam*, which refers to the six ādhāras, the two eyes and the sahasrāra as if they form the *agni* (fire) of the *homa-yajña*. It also refers to praṇava by using the term *vil* (in Tamil), i.e., bow. The phrase "Dakṣa's sacrifice" itself refers symbolically to the wasting of *aruḷ* or kuṇḍalinī-śakti without properly directing it to attain the Śiva at the sahasrāra.

In section 12 of *tantra* One, called *Andaṇar O̱lukkam*, i.e., the dharma of the brahmins, Tirumūlar uses the term *andaṇar ākuti*, i.e., the *yajña* performed by the brahmins, to refer symbolically to the arousing of the kuṇḍalinī.[38] Similarly he compares Kuṇḍalinī-Yoga with *yāga* or *yajña*.[39] Further he specifically refers to Kuṇḍalinī-Yoga when he speaks of those who fail to scale the height (i.e., the sahasrāra) through the thread of the kuṇḍalinī.[40] In one verse he refers to the passage of kuṇḍalinī as the ladder of threads (in Tamil *nūl-ēṇi*).[41] In a similar fashion he refers to the kuṇḍalinī-yogins, as those who stand in the middle path.[42] Verse 523 of *tantra* Two and verses 424 and 470 of the same *tantra* specifically refer to the process of kuṇḍalinī energy. The following verse speaks of the process of Kuṇḍalinī-Yoga.

> Open and drink deep the nectar that gushes from the spring;
> Unfold the petals of the Holy Master's Lotus feet;
> Lead the yoga-breath through the spring channel up
> Reach the Divine Good in holy meet.[43]

In one verse in *tantra* Three, Tirumūlar speaks of Yoga as *ādhāra-yoga* and *nirādhāra-yoga*.[44] Experiencing the appropriate powers at the six ādhāras and ascending them one after another is *ādhāra-yoga*. *Nirādhāra* means beyond the ādhāras of the body. Beyond the sahasrāra, there is the *dvādaśānta* space (the twelfth end). *Nirādhāra-yoga* is ascension from sahasrāra to *dvādaśānta* space, which is beyond thought and speech. Tirumūlar describes kuṇḍalinī as one which cuts the bonds of birth, grants the powers of *tapas* and leads one to the path of liberation.[45] In a section called the *Grace of Guru's feet,* Tirumūlar says that the passage of kuṇḍalinī to the head is due to the real grace of the guru. In this connection one may refer to section 17 of *tantra* Eight which speaks of *Head and Foot Knowledge.* To quote Tirumūlar:

They know not
The Head and Foot (of Lord) is within body,
The Head is in Sahasrara (cranium)
The Foot in Muladhara;
Those who visioned thus in the Yogic way,
Remained in Prayer
Their heads bowed at Lord's feet.[46]

3. 2. Kuṇḍalinī-Yoga as described in the Tirumandiram

Kuṇḍalinī-Yoga is called Ṣaṭ-cakra-Yoga because in it we come across the six subtle centers called cakras. The Siddha Yoga practice is primarily based on the cakra organization and the nāḍi system.

3. 2. 1. The cakra System

In *tantra* seven, section 1, Tirumūlar discusses the six ādhāras, their petals, their letters, etc.[47] The cakra system is one of the subtle power operations. The cakras are inner power phenomena and centers of psychic energy. The power that is hidden and waiting to be aroused is the kuṇḍalinī. There are seven cakras in the human system. In addition to the general power called kuṇḍalinī or *aruḷ-śakti*, each of these cakras contains specific power phenomena, that is, śaktis. The cakras are figuratively referred to as lotuses even though the term cakra literally means a wheel or a circle. The term cakra refers to the internal centers symbolized as lotus flowers through which the yoga-kuṇḍalinī-śakti flows producing various spiritual phenomena in life, body, and consciousness. In principle, each cakra has a certain number of petals, numbering four, six, ten, twelve, sixteen and two. The number of petals indicates the rate of psychic vibrations of that particular cakra.

Each petal of the cakra represents a syllable, a sound vibration. The sum of these sounds is the mantra of the cakra. In the center of each cakra a letter represents the root, the *bīja*, of the mantra. Similarly, each cakra has a color. Apart from the sounds and colors, each cakra has a shape, represents an element called *deva* and its principle, has a God and Goddess representing spiritual forces manifest and latent in the cakra, and represents a *loka*, world, and an animal. The gods and goddesses represented by the cakras are not of the religious pantheon, but just names given for the particular forms of consciousness manifested and exhibited in each cakra.

Awakening of the cakras, in general, corresponds to the predominant psychological states and the levels of spiritual consciousness attained by the sādhaka, or aspirant. That is, each cakra is identified with certain level of meditative achievement. (The lower three are egoistic, and concerned with sex, security and power to realize desires. The upper three are concerned with love, creativity and intuition). The seven cakras are, then, the thresholds or spiritual gates in the human body leading one to the attainment of the Absolute Reality. The seven cakras are:

1) Mūlādhāra–The root center. Tirumūlar calls it as *mūla-dhvāra.*[48]
2) Svādhiṣṭhāna–The support of the life-breath center. Tirumūlar calls it as *kamalam.*[49]
3) Maṇipūra–The center embedded with gems. Tirumūlar calls it as blacksea.[50]
4) Anāhata–The unstruck sound center. Tirumūlar calls it as the *nāda* sphere.[51]
5) Viśuddha–The great purity center. Tirumūlar calls it as *nādānta* sphere.[52]

6) Ājña–The command center. Tirumūlar calls it as the *mēdhā* sphere.[53]
7) Sahasrāra–The thousand-petaled lotus center. Tirumūlar calls it as the *bōdhānta* sphere.[54]

The first six are called the six ādhāras (props or supports). We have, in all, six ādhāras and seven cakras. The seven cakras are called the seven worlds by Tirumūlar.[55] At the top of all the six ādhāras, there is the sahasrāra, known as *brahma-randhra* or *nirvāṇa-cakra*. When prāṇa is coursed up through these cakras, the yogin is oblivious of his personal self. With the support of prāṇa the yogin should evoke AUM and proceed beyond the ādhāras to ascend further the six steps called *adhvas*, viz., *kala*, *bhuvana*, *varṇa*, *mantra*, *pada* and *tattva*. When this is practiced the yogin experiences himself as the *parāparam*, infintite bliss.[56] Tirumūlar says that over the fifty letters of the petals of the six ādhāras there is the basic letter AUM.[57]

Sahasrāra is called by different names by Tirumūlar. He visions it as an eight-petaled lotus.[58] It is so called because its petals are facing the eight directions. The eight directions are: eastern, south-eastern, southern, south-western, western, north-western, northern and north-eastern. Tirumūlar speaks of the petals of the ādhāras in verse 746 of *tantra* Three and in verse 1704 of *tantra* Seven. Tirumūlar also speaks of the root syllables of the ādhāras.[59] Suba. Annamalai has explained this in the form a chart.[60] It is as follows:

Five elements	Five letters	Symbols	Energy symbolized	Place in the body
Space	ya	o	ō	middle of the eye-brows
Air	va	e	ē	neck
Fire	ci	u	ū	heart
Water	ma	i	ī	navel
Earth	na	a	ā	base of the spinal column

Sahasrāra is called the celestial lake *(cēṇ-paḍu-poigai,).*[61] the stony arena, i.e., the Mount Meru within *(podu)*;[62] the cave *(koy)*;[63] the mango fruit;[64] the purest gold *(cempoṉ)*[65] the moon-sphere *(nilā-maṇḍalam)*,[66] hundred by hundred *(nūṟu-nūṟu)*;[67] the golden temple *(poṉ-ambalam)*;[68] cirrambalam (microcosm), *cidambaram, tiruvambalam* (the temple of god);[69] *tarātalam;*[70] *podu ambalam* (common temple);[71] *kuṇḍigai* (top vessel);[72] *candra-maṇḍala,*[73] *aṣta-taḷam.*[74] It is conceived of as a lotus of a thousand petals. This cakra is the quintessential consciousness where the integration of all polarities is experienced. Even Vedas are hesistant to speak of this experience.[75] Yet Tirumūlar attempts to give a picture of the experience of the eight petaled lotus.[76] It is called Mount Meru. The verse is as follows:

> He is in this world
> Yet if He is beyond reach,
> Seek Him in Heaven,
> Where the elephants roam
> And the Celestials wander,

Where fire, rain and wind abide;
In that Space seek Him.[77]

When one attains this state there is no death for him. It is the state that embraces all. To quote Tirumūlar:

Who seeks the luminous nada atop
And of its sweetness savour
Know of death— no more;
The Lord is the seed of all
Of Sun, Moon and Fire
Of the Universe Vast
The Architect that builds all as well.[78]

Through self-effort based on wisdom, inquiry into Self, one can reach the Supreme Abode and burn up all desires. In this state of samādhi, there is eternal satisfaction and clear perception of the reality of the universe. Once this abode is reached one rules his own world with an enlightened mind, radiant with bliss, peace and sweet purity.

Tirumūlar suggests the sun as piṅgala-nāḍi, moon as iḍā-nāḍi and fire as the kuṇḍalinī awakened in the suṣumnā. When moon and *agni* (fire) join, the rays of the sun become active or dominant. Tirumūlar explains further that when the moon and sun and fire join, one's soul, or spark of the soul *(tāraka)* one's True Self, which is found deep in the heart center, anāhata or within the ājña reveals itself and becomes everything, all existence.[79]

Once a yogin reaches the sahasrāra and experiences the Supreme Self there is a transformation of the mind, body and life to the extent to which all the bindus or kalās are intergrated. This is a state of void or no mind. In this state of no mind, consciousness is free of all limitations, free of all taints and impurities of concepts or percepts and is in its essential nature is Supreme Intelligence.

3. 2. 2. The Kuṇḍalinī

The location of the kuṇḍalinī is given by Tirumūlar. Here he specifically uses the term *kuṇḍali.* The verse is as follows:

> Two finger length above the Muladhara
> Two finger length below the sex organ
> Four finger length below the navel visible
> There within is Kundalini
> A flaming fire lambent. [80]

The term *āṟu-mugaṉ* in verse 520 of the *Tirumandiram* may be symbolically interpreted as the kuṇḍalinī power that passes through the six ādhāras. In this connection it would be interesting to note what Tirumūlar says about two mothers.[81] According to him life in the body is fastened by two powers, the kuṇḍalinī power and the cit-śakti (energy of Supreme Consciousness/the cosmic power). He also calls kuṇḍalinī as *tēci* and life śakti as *tēcaṉ.*[82] The life in the body should attain jñāna through kuṇḍalinī-śakti. Tirumūlar in section eight of *tantra* Four, describes kuṇḍalinī-śakti and her nature in one hundred verses.[83]

Kuṇḍalinī is the individual bodily representation of the great cosmic power. It is symbolized by the sleeping serpent with three and a half coils. This latent sleeping energy is to be awakened and sent upward to the sahasrāra where it becomes fully awakened consciousness, called samādhi. Kuṇḍalinī-Yoga is the technique for transforming normal consciousness into supreme consciousness. Tirumūlar uses a significant expression to refer to kuṇḍalinī as the spark that kindles all the lamps around (The Tamil term is *tūṇḍu viḷakku*).[84]

The three coils of the kuṇḍalinī represent the three states of mind *(avasthās)*, namely, waking *(jāgrat,* in Tamil *naṉavu)*, dreaming *(svapna,* in Tamil *kaṉavu)*, and deep sleep *(suṣupti,* in Tamil *uṟakkam)*. There is a fourth state *(turiya,* in Tamil *niṭṭai* or *pēruṟakkam)*, combining and transcending the other states; this is represented by the half coil. The homology between kuṇḍalinī and the serpent is significant. In India a serpent is viewed as a symbol of immortality. The serpent inserting its own tail in its mouth is a symbol of eternity, because a circle has no beginning and no end. Indian folklore credits the serpent with vitality, with the possession of the knowledge of life-giving plants. This is the reason why the Siddhas who practiced Kuṇḍalinī-Yoga are recognized as genuine medicine men. We have to view the kundalinī as a sort of dormant force in the body, but when it is roused and reaches its destination, this force is transformed into *amṛta*, the immortal nectar of liberation.

The awakening of the kuṇḍalinī is the sole aim of Yoga. When kuṇḍalinī reaches a cakra, the head or face of the cakra (or lotus) turns upward and the cakra "blooms." The dynamization of kuṇḍalinī when it passes from one cakra to another is an unfoldment of spiritual consciousness stage by stage and also the acquirement of certain yogic powers called siddhis. Yoga-sādhana consists in raising the kuṇḍalinī-śakti, the coiled force from one pole, the mūlādhāra, to the other, the sahasrāra, the abode of Śiva. When kuṇḍalinī reaches and merges into the sahasrāra, the yogin becomes conscious of what is conscious. Here he is said to "drink" the "ambrosial juice" *(rasa* or *amṛta)* oozing from the "moon" of the sahasrāra. This *amṛta* is called by many names in the Siddha literature.

3. 2. 3 The nāḍi system

In Yoga, the nāḍi system is not the nervous system. The term nāḍi is used in a technical sense. It is the most important component of the subtle body. It is the channel of activated energy; it is an etheric channel. The energy that is carried by this channel is called the prāṇa energy. According to the *Haṭha-Yoga-Pradīpikā* there are about 72,000 nāḍis, which spread and move the cosmic energy in the body. The chief nāḍis are ten in number. (Tamil Siddha terminology is given in brackets) They are: iḍā *(iḍakalai)*, piṅgalā *(piṅgalai)*, suṣumnā *(suḻumuṉai)*, *gāndhārī (kantari)*, *hastijihvā (atti)*, *puṣa (puruḍaṉ)*, *yaśasvinī (ciṅkuvai)*, *alambuṣa (alamputai)*, *kuhu (kuku)*, and *saṅkhinī (caṅkini)*. All these *nāḍis* start from the *kanda* above the anus. The spinal cord tapers down into a bunch of soft threads called *filium terminale,* which is the portion of the *kanda.* The iḍā, piṅgalā, and suṣumnā are the most important nāḍis from the Yoga point of view.

The iḍā and the piṅgalā stand to the left and the right of the suṣumnā respectively. Tirumūlar calls iḍā as *kaṇṇaṉ*, i.e., the moon and piṅgalā as the sun.[85] He also calls them as two rhythms.[86] G.Varadarajan identifies the three threads worn by the Hindus as representing the iḍā, piṅgalā and *suṣumnā.*[87] Taking its origin from the navel, the iḍā has its terminus at the left nostril. Taking its origin from the same area, the piṅgalā terminates at the right nostril. These two subtle psychic arteries run parallel and close to the suṣumnā until they cross and the right-left position is reversed. In Tāntric lore, these two nāḍis signify opposite poles. The confluence or commingling of the three together, iḍā and piṅgalā with suṣumnā at the level of the ājñā-cakra, is known as the sacred triple-stream or *triveṇi* or *prayāga*. From the ājñā-cakra, the iḍā and the piṅgalā, proceed to the right and the left nostrils respectively, and the suṣumnā enters the sahasrāra. Tirumūlar calls iḍā as the left hand and piṅgalā as the right hand and the suṣumnā as the trunk *(tudikkai)*. If one knows the technique of breathing through these nāḍis Tirumūlar says one achieves immortality. The verse is as follows:

> Alternating breath's course from left to right and vice versa,
> They who can force breath through spinal Sushumna
> Shall know tiring none;
> They can abolish sleep forever
> And attain god-awareness;
> They die not;
> Immortal they shall be.[88]

It is significant that Tirumūlar uses an expression in verse 1069 in *tantra* Four. The Tamil word is *nīdi*, which may be interpreted as the middle path of not swerving to any one side. This term, according to Suba. Annamalai, is to be interpreted as the act of an yogin who passes the prāṇa through the suṣumnā. Hence a yogin is also called the *naḍuvu ni̲n̲r̲ār*, a person who courses prāṇa through suṣumnā.[89]

3. 2. 4. Aṣṭāṅga-Yoga

Laya-Yoga follows the various stages of control that are referred to as Aṣṭāṅga-Yoga or the eight-limbs of Yoga. They are *yama* (abstention), *niyama* (observance), *āsana* or *sthūla-kriyā* (posture or muscular control process), *prāṇāyāma* or *sūkṣma-kriyā* (breath-control process), *pratyāhāra* (sensory control), *dhāraṇa* (holding concentration), *dhyāna* (deep concentration), and *samādhi* (cognitive absorption). In *tantra* Three, sections 1 to 9, verses 549 to 631 Tirumūlar discusses in detail the eight-limbs of Yoga. He lists the eight limbs of Yoga in the following verse:

Yama, Niyama and Asana numberless
Pranayama wholesome and Pratyahara alike,
Dharana, Dhyana and Samadhi to triumph
-These eight are the steely limbs of Yoga.[90]

Yama consists of a number of do's and don'ts. It is an ethical preparation for Yoga. Tirumūlar speaks of one who follows the ten ways of *yama* as follows:

He does not kill, he does not lie, he does not steal;
Of marked virtues is he; good, meek and just;
He shares his joys, he knows no blemish
Neither drinks nor lusts
This the man who in Iyama's ways stands.[91]

A man who stands in *niyama* should have firm faith in the first cause, i.e., the Supreme Being and that He is the kuṇḍalinī-fire. Tirumūlar speaks of the way of *niyama* as follows:

The Being First,
The Meaning-Central of Vedas all,
The Light Divine,
The Fire within that Light
He who shares Himself
Half-and-Half with His Śakti
And the Divine justice thereof
-Them, he in Niyama's path knows.[92]

He also speaks of the ten virtues of *niyama* and an additional ten virtues of the same in two verses. They are:

Purity, compassion, frugal food and patience
Forthrightness, truth and steadfastness
-These he ardently cherishes;
Killing, stealing and lusting, he abhors,

-Thus stands with virtues ten
The one who Niyama's ways observes.[93]

Tapas, meditation, serenity and holiness
Charity, vows in Saiva way and Siddhanta learning
Sacrifice, Siva puja and thoughts pure
-With these ten, the one in Niyama perfects his way.[94]

According to Tirumūlar there are many āsanas (eighty and hundred) of which *padmāsana* (lotus posture), *bhadrāsana* (the happy posture), *kukkuḍāsana* (the cock posture), *simhāsana* (the lion posture) are important. He speaks of the eight important āsanas:

Bhadra, Gomukha, Padma and Simha,
Sothira, Veera, and Sukha,
These seven along with eminent svastika
Constitute the eight, Eighty and hundred, however,
Are asanas in all reckoned.[95]

Since there is a separate section on praṇāyāma we shall leave the discussion of it here.

Pratyāhāra is the restraint of the senses and the withdrawal of the mind from external things. It is not a mere control of the senses but a sublimation of the senses.[96] It includes maintaining an inner focus and avoidance of dispersion and distraction. The yogins, says Tirumūlar, like the turtle, withdraw their senses within and know this world and That.[97] The *vairāgya* or firmness of the yogins in withdrawing their sense is compared to that of the Varamus lizard, which tenaciously holds to the object it seizes and does not swerve, however hard you pull the reptile.[98] Tirumūlar, in his work, in *tantra* Seven, devotes two sections on the importance of subduing the five senses,[99] and how to subdue the senses by way of sublimation.[100] One cannot resist the temptation of quoting the following verses, which speak of the sublimation of the senses.

"Control, control the senses Five,"
Thus say those who know not;
None, not even the Immortals;
The senses Five control;
When you the senses Five control;
Verily are you an inert mass;
(There is a way alternate open)
Sublimate them toward the Lord;
That Wisdom's Way, I learned.[101]

If the senses Five you sublimate
Then all worlds are yours;
That is tapas rare;
That is the Lord's Feet too;
That indeed is the way to Grace receive.[102]

Daily think of the Living Nandi
Gently control your thoughts distracting,
Course your thoughts through Muladhara
Then your thoughts a temple become,
From north to south extending.[103]

According to Tirumūlar sublimation is the best way. According to him,

Tie the prancing senses five
To the post of Jnana that illumineth;
Thus you attain grace that is Bliss;
This the Way of Yore, high and true.[104]

Dhāraṇa means to retain the mind and keep it steadfast inside, which has been obtained by *pratyāhāra*. Tirumūlar says that one should sit calm in singleness of thought like a stork at streams-head waiting for a catch.[105] Tirumūlar explains *dhāraṇa* in the following verse:

> To contain body's harassing senses five
> In elements five,
> To contain elements five
> In organs cognitive internal,
> To contain cognitive organs internal
> In their Tanmatras
> To contain the Tanmatras
> In the being Uncreated
> That, verily, is Dharana
> In stages practiced.[106]

Dhyāna is consistent, uninterrupted meditation. According to Tirumūlar it is of two kinds. the verse is as follows:

> The Ten-
> The five elements and the five senses
> Being contained, one by the other,
> The internal organ Buddhi
> In turn contains the senses,
> Thus is Dhyana born;
> The para Dhyana first;
> That is on Sakti centered,
> And Siva Dhyana next
> That is by Guru blessed.
> These two are the Ways of Dhyana Yoga.[107]

If one practices *dhyāna* one gains liberation. The verses are as follows:

If your eyes twain are
On nasal point fixed,
No sorrows befall you;
Perishes not your body;
Agitation none shall you have;
Feelings none:
Seekings none;
None that is "I;"
You and Siva one become.[108]

Fixing the gaze on nasal point
Retaining the roaming breath within
They who can thus still the nadis,
Will sure reach the Goal
No fear of birth to be for them.[109]

A yogin who practices *dhyāna* enjoys varied sound experiences:

Bell, sea, elephant, flute, cloud
Bee, dragon-fly, conch, drum, and lute
The subtle sounds of these ten are heard
For them alone
Who have stilled their mind in God.[110]

The roar of sea, the thundering of cloud,
The trumpeting of elephant, the euphony of lute,
The music of the orbs
That glow in firmament vast,
The melody of the flute; the resonance of conch,
All these
The yogi true alone hears.[111]

Dhyāna leads to the grace of being one with Śivam.

Transcending Tattvas six and thirty unreal,

Destroying Maya's layers thick,
Transformed into Jnana Pure by Grace
Themselves that Grace inseparable Becoming
They who achieved thus
Were the good souls
That the Way of Dhyana knew.[112]

Samādhi is the final goal of Aṣṭāṅga-Yoga. It is the attainment of tranquility.

Samadhi attained, Siva is attained;
Sakti too will be caught in its fold;
Distracting passions will be dispelled;
In equanimity perfect,
Like unto a balance
Will be the mind
All this, for those who in Samadhi sleep.[113]

In almost all the editions of the *Tirumandiram* there is a separate section called the *Fruits of the Eight-limbed-Yoga.*

They who seek Lord
Of the matted locks bedecked with flowers
Will sure reach the Abode of Gods;
"What this devotee of mine seeks,
That I grant,"
Thus blesses the Lord
That mounts the Bull
And dances to His Consort's delight.[114]

Transcending Jiva's caused limitations
And accepting the Causal Tattvas
Extinguishing the Causal sources themselves
Thus do tapasvins unite in the Being Uncaused
That, in truth is Samadhi supreme.[115]

According to Suba. Annamalai this section containing eight verses (verses 632-639) is an interpolation since it does not fit in with the title, differs from the original style of Tirumūlar's writing and contains words/terms, which are being used at a later period than at the time of Tirumūlar.

3. 2. 5. Prāṇāyāma

Prāṇāyāma is the practice of ordered breathing; it is not a mere physical technique but a vital step in yogic discipline. Prāṇāyāma makes the restless mind fit for concentration. The process of prāṇāyāma consists of three acts: inspiration *(pūraka, apāna, āhāra)*, expiration *(recaka, prāṇa,)* and suspension of breath *(kumbhaka, vyāna, rucira, dhāraṇa)*. The terms *pūraka, recaka,* and *kumbhaka* are used by the Tāntrics and the Siddhas and not by Patañjali. The real object of prāṇāyāma is to help one attain *ekāgrata* or one-pointedness of the mind. The cakras are unfolded by prāṇāyāma, so that the aroused kuṇḍalinī can pierce through them. The prāṇa energy causes the kuṇḍalinī to uncoil itself. Prāṇāyāma opens the passage of the suṣumnā and prāṇa joins the kuṇḍalinī when it enters the suṣumnā. When the whole current of prāṇa is infused into the suṣumnā, it generates heat that causes kuṇḍalinī to be roused. The kuṇḍalinī then "hisses," uncoils, and straightens itself and pierces the six ādhāras. To achieve this, the sādhaka sits in the prescribed āsana and steadies his mind by the *kechari-mudrā*. When the kuṇḍalinī in the sādhaka enters the sahasrāra and becomes one with Śiva, he becomes one with the witness of the universe, a Siddha, and emergence from time and history is accomplished. When prāṇa ascends through the suṣumnā the yogin experiences

... Seven sounds he hears
Five colours he sees
Three odours he smells,
Two tasks he knows...[116]

These sounds, colors, smells can be symbolic or representative of the inner secrets of our nature. As we become clearer in our inner sensing we are able to trace thoughts and feelings and sounds and colors and odors back to their source and feel their origin and receive their messages immediately.

According to Tirumūlar the prāṇāyāma practice consists of the following:

You who enter the land of yoga practice!
Know that it consists in this
The measure of breath inhaled is twelve inches
Having measured accordingly
Exhale eight matra consciously
The four matras retained
Are in the six adharas to suffuse
And thus breathing examine to Tattvas twenty and five.[117]

As explained by B. Natarajan, this verse means: Yoga consists in the following: inhalation of twelve *mātras* (unit of time); exhalation of eight *mātras*; retention of four *mātras*. Breathing in this measure continuously, Yoga suffuses the six ādhāras with prāṇa, which ascends beyond the twenty-five tattvas.

There are said to be three points for *recaka* (exhalation), *kumbhaka* (retention) and *pūraka* (inhalation): 1. outside the nose, 2. from below the place known as *dvādaśānta* (above or in front of the forehead at a distance of twelve fingers); 3. the source at the heart.

Contact with the source of this prāṇic force, which is located downward to the length of twelve fingers in the heart lotus is known as pūraka or inhalation. When the apāna has ceased to move and when the prāṇa does not arise and move out of the heart (and until these begin to happen) it is known as kumbhaka. The natural and effortless movement of the life force at all times is the movement of the vital air up to the extent of twelve fingers from oneself and this constitutes recaka.

If one practices suspension of breath after exhaling the prāṇa to a distance farther where the apāna rises (twelve finger breath distance), he is no longer subject to pain and suffering. If he is able to see the space within himself, where the inhaled breath turns into the impulse for exhalation (infront of, or at the root of the nose), it is said he is not born again. By seeing where the prāṇa and apāna terminate their motions, and by holding oneself in that space one's mind does not arise. This is an effortless suspension of the breath and is a Supreme state.

In two sections of *tantra* Three, Tirumūlar speaks of the *measurement of life span* (by the process of breathing) (section 15) and the *breath rhythm in days of the week* (section 16). We shall summarise below the above two sections in the words of Yogacharya Shantikumar as quoted by B.Natarajan.[118]

According to B.Natarajan Indian astrology has developed a branch of techniques in measuring the life span based on observation of the breathing rhythm. This is known as *cara-v-ōṭṭam* in Tamil. In Sanskrit it is known as *pavana-sarvodaya-śāstra*.

> Learned Indian yogis of yore had critically studied the movement of air through the whole respiratory passage during inhalation and exhalation. They had discovered that just as the current of a river sometimes flows on the one side, and at

another time on the other side, the air also changes sides in the nasal passages during inhalation and exhalation. They had discovered a close connection between the mental states and such sideway movement of air.

It has been observed that we sometimes breathe through the left nostril and sometimes through the right one. The nostrils thus work alternately. The left channel for the passage of the air is known as '*ida*' while the right channel is the *pingala*. The left one is known as the lunar channel *(chandra nadi)*, while the right one is the solar channel *(surya nadi)*. When a person has obtained mastery over pranayama, and when he is physically and mentally healthy and ready for higher spiritual practices, his breathing is from the middle channel known as '*susumna nadi.*'

In the bright half of the month and on the first, second, the seventh, eighth, ninth and fourteenth days, and on the full moon day one breathes (editor's note: initially) through the left nostril in the mornings, but every hour this alternates with the right nostril. In the remaining days of the bright half of the month, one breathes (editor's note: initially) through the right nostril in the mornings, the direction changing every hour, the right and left nostrils alternating.

In the dark half of the month and on the first day one breathes through the right nostril, but alternating every hour with the left nostril. Then there is reverse movement every third day.

When one breathes through the left nostril – lunar channel – the breath comes under the invisible influence of the moon and such lunar qualities as coolness, steadiness, sobriety, discretion, etc., are thus born or nourished.

When one breathes through the right nostril – solar channel – the breath comes under the invisible influence of the sun and solar qualities such as heat, light, bravery, dynamism, enthusiasm, strength, etc., are thereby born or nourished.

Breathing can be changed from the right nostril to the left one and vice versa. The technique is very simple. If you are breathing through the left nostril, and you want to breathe through the right one, lie down on the right side for sometime. If you are breathing through the right nostril and wish to breathe through the left, lie down on the left side for a short time.

When one breathes through the right nostril, one should undertake such work, which requires greater exertion, eg., walking, running, arguing, physical exercise, eating or cleaning the bowels. Ancient Indian medical science advises people to rest on the left side after meals so that one breathes through the right nostril and the food is thus well digested.

When one breathes through the left nostril, one should undertake such work, which requires less exertion, such as light mental work, discretionary work or work of a permanent nature. Sleeping on the right side relieves mental stress, strain, and tension and gives mental rest. In this state of breathing, holy activities may be undertaken. This is an ideal state for studies as well.

When one breathes through the middle channel, one should practice concentration, meditation and spiritual activities. A true yogi or for that matter even a perfectly healthy person constantly breathes thus and maintains mental peace and equanimity even under the most trying circumstances.

Ancient Indian astrology had developed a particular branch,

which was based on this. If one breathes through the left nostril and if a person sitting on his left asks if a certain work undertaken or to be undertaken would be successful, the answer should always be in the affirmative; but if one breathes through the right nostril and if a person sitting on his left asks if a certain work undertaken or to be undertaken would be successful, the answer should always be in the negative.

When one constantly breathes through the middle channel, one develops intuition, knows future events, can practice telepathy and transform the personality of others easily. Such breathing is compared with a mother-in-law who is difficult to be pleased but if once pleased becomes an additional blessing. (Quoted from *The Science of Yogic Breathing* by Yogacharya Shantikumar, pp. 30-32).

According to Tirumūlar if one knows the rhythm of breath, one is aware of the *nāda*. That is *nāda* and God are one in consciousness.[119] If breath is coursed upwards, it will give steadiness of mind.[120] If one practices breathing from the left to the right nostril and from the right to the left in rhythmic alteration, it purifies the prāṇa-nāḍis. If one practices this carefully, it helps one to have mastery over the senses and one can live for hundred years.[121] Tirumūlar speaks of the retention of breath *(kumbhaka)* and speaks of the practice of retention for certain number of days when one experiences certain visions.[122] In one verse Tirumūlar identifies Kuṇḍalinī-Yoga with prāṇāyāma. The verse is as follows:

None knows kundalini that spans high
None knows the science of breath control
They who know it not perish away
I knew the truth that none know.[123]

In section 16, *tantra* Three, Tirumūlar speaks of the differences of the breath rhythms between the left and right nāḍis on different days of the week.[124]

3. 2. 6. Bandhas and mudrās

Along with āsanas, we have *bandhas* and *mudrās,* which play an important part in Haṭha-Yoga. *Bandhas* are locks or concentrations pertaining to isolated muscles or groups of muscles. They are the special bodily manipulations or devises that are designed to confine the life-force within the trunk and thereby stimulate it. The Siddhas speak of *mūla-bandha, uddiyāna-bandha,* and *jalan- dhara-bandha. Mūla-bandha* (i.e., the root-lock) is executed by contracting the perineum and vaginal muscles. *Uddiyāna-bandha* is performed by drawing back the abdominal muscles.[125] It is a preliminary exercise to the performance of *kechari-mudrā.* It is an exercise in the lower regions parallel to the *kechari-mudrā* at the higher regions. It is damming the course of downward *apāna* at the mūlādhāra. To quote the *Tirumandiram*:

> The exhaling breath will inside retained be;
> The retained breath will from escape prevented be;
> In due time,
> From the Moon's region starts ambrosial flow;
> If it is not checked it will merge in the Kundalini.[126]

Jalandhara-bandha is done by pressing the chin and the chest together tightly. These *bandhas* are performed to withdraw the prāṇa from the iḍā and the piṅgalā. The prāṇa withdrawn from the iḍā and the piṅgalā enters the suṣumnā and goes upwards towards the sahasrāra. When the whole current of prāṇa is infused into suṣumnā it generates heat, causes kuṇḍalinī to be roused and uncoils it. The uncoiled animated kuṇḍalinī by piercing each of the lotuses absorbs into itself the regnant tattvas (the five elements) contained in each of them. When the ascent is made, each of the tattvas enters the state of dissolution called the *laya* state. This is the part played by *bandhas* in Laya-Yoga.

Mudrās are psycho energetic gestures involving the hands, fingers, eyes or tongue while performing meditation or breathing practices. It is also a non-verbal mode of communication and self-expression; it is a stylized form of gestural communication. Of these, the *yoni-mudrā*, the *sāmbhavi-mudrā* and the *kechari-mudrā* are very important for rousing the kuṇḍalinī.

Tirumūlar says that *mudrās* are used to transcend the *avastas* eleven. *Mudrā* directs the eleven organs— five *jñānendriyas*, five *karmendriyas* and *manas* on the silent letter AUM.[127]

3. 2. 6. 1. Yoni-mudrā

Tirumūlar refers to *yoni-mudrā* as *mauna-mudrā*.[128] *Yoni-mudrā* (womb-seal) is performed by sitting in the upright posture and closing the eyes, ears, nostrils and the mouth with fingers so as to shut out all external impressions followed by breath suspension and simultaneous contemplation of the six centres (cakras) with concentration at the same time on a light behind the eyes. The *mudrā* that is *mauna* is the *mudrā* for those who seek *mukti*.

3. 2. 6. 2. Sāmbhavi-mudrā

It consists in gazing at the spots between the eye-brows while inwardly contemplating on the transcendental self. According to Tirumūlar *sāmbhavi-mudrā* brings grace and terminates the cycle of birth.[129] He calls it as the lion among mudrās that leads to the eight siddhis.[130]

3. 2. 6. 3. Kechari-mudrā

It is the *jñāna-mudrā,* whereas *sāmbhavi-mudrā* is the *mudrā* of grace of Śiva. In *kechari-mudrā* the tongue is lengthened; for the lengthening of the tongue certain processes are advised. They are: (1) *Chedana*– the cutting gradually at intervals of the band that holds the tongue to the base of the mouth, i.e., the *lingual frenum;* (2) *Chalan*– this tie being removed, the tongue is then moved from side to side by holding it between the fingers; and (3) *Dohana*– the tongue is stretched in the manner of milking the cow's udder. In *kechari-mudrā* when the tongue has been lengthened one has to practice turning it upward and backward so as to touch the palate until at length it reaches the holes of the nostrils opening into the mouth. Close the holes with the tongue and fix the gaze at the space between the eyebrows. This position of the tongue in the mouth is said to permit or facilitate the flow of current along the iḍā, the piṅgalā, and the suṣumnā nāḍis to the sahasrāra. This *mudrā* is said to be the king among *mudrās,* and hence some Siddhas call Kuṇḍalinī-Yoga, the "Yoga of the inner tongue." *Kechari-mudrā* is called Kechari-Yoga by Tirumūlar. It is also called *nirādhāra-yoga.* The term *kechari* is not to be confused with the term *kesari. Kesari* means lion whereas *kechari* means to traverse in space. Kesari may stand for the lion-posture. But *kechari* has nothing to do with postures. When *kechari-mudrā* is performed, the mystic nectar will begin to ooze from the sahasrāra. One who drinks the nectar obtains bodily immortality. It is interesting to note that Kechari-Yoga is interpreted as the Yoga, which bestows rains from the head or sahasrāra.[131] Through mastery of the *kechari-mudrā* the yogin can engage in sexual activity without the risk of seminal discharge. Regarding the practice of *kechari-mudrā* Tirumūlar writes:

Control the spiration
And see that breath is wasted not;
Bind it tight,
Dam the source of Kundalini at Muladhara,
Lock the chimney up in the mouth;
Bolt the cavity above with thy tongue's tip
And sit erect in yoga Samadhi
No more shall there be death for you.[132]

Kechari-mudrā leads to youthfullness. To quote Tirumūlar:

If you can send the breath twain
Into the mouth's upper cavity
You shall then know death none;
And the gates of nectar will open be;
Greying and wrinkling will disappear
For all to see;
Young will the Yogi be;
True this, I say, in the name of Nandi Holy.[133]

Kechari-Yoga is a pre-requisite to Pariyaṅga-Yoga.

3. 2. 7. Mantra and Maṇḍala

Any discussion of Tantra-Yoga would be incomplete without an account of mantra and *maṇḍala,* for they have an important place in the Tāntric system. Mantra is a vehicle of power and consciousness. It is a process by which the mind is controlled and concentration is established. It is learned from the master's mouth. It is symbolized reality. In discussing the cakras we have noted that each syllable on the petals of the cakras indicates sound vibrations and the varying degrees of energies working in the various centers, and the sum of these sounds is the mantra of the cakra. In the center of every cakra there is a seed sound, *bīja-*

mantra. The *bīja-mantra* is the prāṇic force concentrated to a point where its sound-emitting power is exhibited. *Bīja-mantras* are seed syllables whose concentrated power is revealed through repetition. By repeating a *bīja-mantra* the sādhaka awakens the state of consciousness associated with each cakra realizing its potential power and consciousness, that is, kuṇḍalinī.

The *Tirumandiram* speaks of *Bhairavi-mantra* (section 6 of tantra Four), which is *AUM-AIM.* Along with these AUM and AIM there are twelve *bīja-mantras.* To quote Tirumūlar:

> ... With letters Twelve and Two
> From OM to AIM they fourteen are
> That Her Mantras... [134]

Let us quote B.Natarajan to understand what the twelve *bīja-mantras* are:

1. Haum— 'Ha' means Siva, 'au' means Sadasiva, 'm' means Sivaya who dispels sorrow.
2. Dum— 'Da' means Durga, 'u' means save, 'm' means mother of the universe.
3. Krim— 'Ka' is Kali, 'ra' is Brahma, 'i' is Mahamaya, 'm' means mother of the universe.
4. Hrim— 'H' is Śiva, 'ra' is prakriti, 'i' is Mahamaya, 'm' means mother of the universe.
5. Srim— 'S' is Mahalakshmi, 'ra' is wealth, 'i' is satisfaction, 'm' is nada.
6. Aim— 'Ai' is Sarasvati, 'm' is nada.
7. Klim— 'Ka' is Kamadeva. 'l' is Indra, 'i' is contentment, 'm' is nada.
8. Hum— 'H' is Siva, 'u' is Bhairava, 'm' is nada.

9. Gam— 'G' is Ganesha, 'm' is nada.
10. Glaum— 'G' is Ganesha, 'l' is what pervades, 'au' is tejas, 'm' is nada.
11. Kṣraum— 'Kasa' is Nrshimha, 'ra' is Brahma, 'au' is teeth pointing upwards.
12. Strim— 'S' is deliverance, 't' is saviour, 'ra' is liberation, 'i' is Mahamaya, 'm' is bindu.[135]

Tirumūlar also speaks of sthūla-pañcākṣara-mantra, sūkṣma-pañcākṣara-mantra and ati-sūkṣma-pañcākṣara-mantra.[136]

According to tradition the sacred five letters are *na-ma-si-va-ya* called pañcākṣara-mantra. The five letters are called by different names in Śaiva tradition.

- The mantra, *na-ma-ci-va-ya* is called sthūla-pañcākṣara (sthūla means gross).
- The mantra, *ci-va-ya-na-ma* is called sūkṣma-pañcākṣara (sūkṣma means the subtle form of a grosser object).
- The mantra, *ci-va-ya-va-ci* is called ati-sūkṣma-pañcākṣara (ati-sūkṣma means intensely subtle).
- The mantra, *ci-va* is called kāraṇa-pañcākṣara (kāraṇa means the source or origin).
- The mantra, *ci* is called mahā-kāraṇa-pañcākṣara (mahā-karaṇa means the exalted or immense source or origin).

Those who desire enjoyment in the world should mentally repeat the sthūla-pañcākṣara and those who desire the enjoyment of liberation along with the enjoyment in the world should mentally repeat the sūksma-pañcākṣara. Those who desire only liberation *(mokṣa)* should mentally repeat the ati-sūkṣma, the kāraṇa and the mahā-kāraṇa-pañcākṣaras.

- If one repeats these mantras to be heard by oneself and others, it is called *vācagam* (audible muttering of the mantra).
- If one utters the mantras to be heard only by himself (arising from the heart), it is called *upañcu* (*upañcu* means recitation of a mantra so as to be heard by the reciter alone).
- If one recites a mantra mentally, it is called *paśyanti.*

One can recite the sthūla and sūksma-pañcākṣaras by *vācagam* and *upañcu.* But one should recite the ati-sūkṣma, the kāraṇa and the mahā-kāraṇa-pañcākṣaras only by *paśyanti.*

There is a difference of opinion as to whether *ci-va-ya-va-ci* or *ci-va-ya-ci-va* is the sūkṣma-pañcākṣara. According to Śiva-vākkiyar *ci-va-ya-va-ci* is the sūkṣma-pañcākṣara.

The five letters are represented by the five faces of Śiva. The five faces of Śiva are: *Vāmadeva* (face turned northward), *Tatpuruṣa* (face turned eastward), *Sadyojāta* (face turned westward), *Aghora* (face turned southward), *Iśāna* (face turned upward). (There is also a sixth face called *Adho-mugam*, face looking downward).

Agastya in his *Tirumandira Viḷakkam*-22 (an exposition of *Tirumandiram* that is pañcākṣara) says that for each face of Śiva there are twenty-five variations of the five-lettered pañcākṣara, thus making a total of one hundred and twenty-five variations.

Tirumūlar shows how AUM and the five letters are distributed in the six ādhāras.

In the six Adharas (centres) within
Are distributed the Five Letters and Aum;
That comprise Aum Nama Sivaya

In the Muladhara is Na
In the Svadhisthana is Ma,
In the Navel Centre is Si,
In the Heart Centre is Va,
In the Throat Centre is Ya,
In the Eye-brow Centre is AUM.[137]

Maṇḍala and *yantra* are the two tools of Tāntric worship. *Maṇḍalas* are employed in the worship of deities (energies) in general. *Yantras* are employed for a particular deity (energy) and for a specific purpose. *Maṇḍala* has been variously translated by experts as "cosmogram," "cosmogenic model," "map of the soul," "cosmic plan," "lay-out of the psyche," "mystic circular diagram," etc. It means literally "circle;" it may also mean "center" or "that which surrounds." It is a pictorial representation of the process of the descent or devolution of the One Supreme Consciousness, layer by layer, into the creation of multitudinous forms. Equally it provides the scheme for the return of the individual into the plenitude of the fundamental consciousness. *Maṇḍalas* are an early and common device employed by the Tantras as a support for meditation.

3. 2. 8. Yantra

The simplest *yantra* is a series of triangles surrounded by several concentric circles that are framed in a square with four "doors." A *yantra* is a powerful diagram, an energy pattern, an ideo-gram. We may say that the cakra system is the *yantra* or the real dynamic graph of the prāṇic operation. Probably the cakra system and the *maṇḍala* system represent two different attempts made by Tāntric yogins to attain liberation. They also probably represent a major separation of monastic communities and also a sectarian split among them. The Siddhas of Tamil Nadu adopted the cakra system. The Tamil Siddhas concentrated more on the cakra system than on the *maṇḍala,* since the *maṇḍala* is employed in the worship of deities. This is the reason why Tirūmular treated *yantras* as cakras. *Yantras* are called as cakras by him.

The symbols used in Kuṇḍalinī-Yoga have a message and meaning for the initiated. The circle occurs very frequently in *yantras.* It symbolizes wholeness or stability. The square pattern, with relevant gates used in *yantras,* symbolizes elemental earth. The four gates represent the earthly plane, which one must transcend. The triangles used in *yantras* have similar significance. A triangle *(trikoṇa)* represents the three guṇas (qualities): *sattva, rajas,* and *tamas.* The triangle with its apex downward represents the female organ. The triangle pointing upward represents the male principle, Śiva. The two interlocking triangles in the form of a hexagon represent the union of Śiva-Śakti, and the creation of the objective universe.

Tirumūlar speaks of the following cakras *(cakkaram/yantras)* in his work. They are: *Tiru-v-ambala-ccakkaram; Tirupurai-c-cakkaram; Ēroḷi-c-cakkaram, Bhairavi-ccakkaram, Sāmbhavi-maṇ- ḍala-c-cakkaram, Bhuvaṉāpati-ccakkaram, Navākkari-ccakkaram,* etc.

Tiru-v-ambala-ccakkaram (section 2 of *tantra* Four) is the diagrammatic representation of the pañcākṣara-mantra. To quote B. Natarajan,

> *Tiruvambala chakra*: ref. Mantra 904, ante. This and the mantras following give a detailed exposition on the configuration of this chakra (ideo-gram). While commentrators widely differ in their interpretation of these mantras, an ideogram into which much research has gone is one attempted by Sri. G.Varadarajan in his book, "Tirumantira Neri," (Tamil) pp.111-115.

This rather extensive section on certain yantras has been condensed by the translator into a synoptic commentary, consequently, it is not amenable to enumeration.

Tirumular previously expounded the truth of the ajapā mantra, 'Soham,' that becomes Aum, which, in turn, becomes A and U; and again, in turn, Si and Va. 'Si' and 'Va' expanded into the Five-Lettered mantra, Sivayanama and further on into the 51 letters of the Sanskrit alphabet. He now proceeds to reveal the yantra or the diagramtic representation of the Panchakshara (Five-Lettered) mantra. He calls this the Tiruambala Chakra, or the yantra for the Divine Dance Arena. (The yantras are referred to as chakras here).

The Tiruambala Chakra seems to be a cluster of several Chakras. Its several variations are represented in different diagrams. Tirumular also lays down the rules for chanting the bija mantras, and expounds on their esoteric significance.

There is a diagram with 121 chambers filled by the mantra, Sivayanama. This is called the Sivaya nama Chakra.

There is another Chakra dedicated to the mantra, Hara Hara. The significance of the letters, Si, and the letter, Aum, are explained. This is the Hara Hara Chakra.

The Five-Letter mantra has both sthula (manifest) and sukshma (subtle) aspects. The manifest Panchakshara is 'Namasivaya.' The subtle Panchakshara is 'Sivayanama'. Thus the same mantra is both manifest and subtle. This is represented in a Chakra— the Panchakshara Chakra.

There is also a yantra for the Siva mantra, 'Siva.' This is called the Siva Chakra.

There is yet another Chakras of 48 squares in which the six letters, Aum Namasivaya, are distributed. This seems to be a variation of the Siva Chakra. The six letters are the quintessence of the six faiths. This is the Six-Letter Chakra.

Umapathi Chakra is formed by drawing eight vertical lines and eight horizontal lines, and filling the chambers with the Five-Letter mantra.

Tirumular winds up his exposition of the *Tiruvambala Chakra* by describing six other *Chakras*, whose worship by incantation of appropriate mantras, confers certain earthly powers. These are:

1. Sthambana Chakra— renders enemies powerless.
2. Mohana Chakra— gives the power of fascination.
3. Ucchatana Chakra— confers the powers to exorcize.
4. Marana Chakra— renders the destruction and death of enemies.
5. Vasiya Chakra— confers the powers of seduction.
6. Akarshana Chakra— confers the power of placing men and things under the will and desire of the sadhakas.

These six Chakras, although designed for wordly ends, are yet based on the mantra, Aum, with its incantation and ritual variations.[138]

Tirupurai-ccakkaram (section 5 of *tantra* Four) is the popular *Śrī-yantra*, or the six-pointed cakra: It consists of two triangles one inverted over the other representing the male and the female principles in couple with *bindu* or the drop of semen in the centre.

Ēroḷi-c-cakkaram (section 9 of *tantra* Four), (cakra of Supreme Light): From the central kuṇḍalinī (i.e., the fire kuṇḍalinī) arises the mighty four letters *va, ca, ṣa, sa*. These four letters of the kuṇḍalinī are expanded into 144 letters of the cakra. From these letters *nāda-cakra* i.e., praṇava is formed. The praṇava expands into the six-letter mantra *Aum-na-ma-ci-va-ya.*

Bhairavi-ccakkaram (section 10 of *tantra* Four): One should meditate on this cakra (Bhairava is an aspect of Lord Śiva) to remove obstacles.

Sāmbhavi-maṇḍala-cakkaram (section 11 of *tantra* Four) Sāmbhavi is Śiva-Śakti. As the mother of this cakra, Sāmbhavi confers one with wealth, great estate, pilgrimage to holy waters, delicious food, pleasant emotions, sound sleep and gold. One should chant the five letters in the form of fifty-one letters.

Bhuvaṉāpati-ccakkaram is also known as *Śri-vidyā-cakra,* which is formed of 15 letters. They are: *Ka, Aa, E, la, hrim,* called *vākbhava* group; *ha, sa, ka, ha, la, hrim* called *kāmarāja* group; *sa, ka, la, hrim* called *śakti* group; with the colors golden-hued, red-hued and white-hued respectively. The *bhuvaṉāpati-mantra* is the form of Śiva.[139] This cakra should be in the form of six-pointed star.

Navākkari-ccakkaram is a mantra of nine letters. To quote Tirumūlar:

> With Klim, as mantra-foot
> Srim, Hrim, Aim, Gaum
> Krim, Haum, Aum, and Saum
> Thus in order is the mantra Navakkari
> At the end chant Sivayanama,
> At every rotation,
> Then you attain the fruitfulness of Navakkari.[140]

This cakra is explained in one hundred verses by Tirumūlar (verses 1319 to 1418).

4. Candra-Yoga

Candra-Yoga is not a separate kind of Yoga as is Pariyaṅga-Yoga. Kuṇḍalinī acquires different Tāntric names in its passage from mūlādhāra to sahasrāra. Kuṇḍalinī extending from mūlādhāra to anāhata is called *agni* or fire kuṇḍalinī. This is technically called in Tamil as *agni-maṇḍalam*. Kuṇḍalinī extending from anāhata to ājñā is called *sūrya* or sun-kuṇḍalini. This is called *sūrya-maṇḍalam* in Tamil. Kuṇḍalinī extending from ājñā to the end of suṣumnā, i.e., top of the head, is called *candra* or moon-kuṇḍalinī. This is called *candra-maṇḍalam* in Tamil. Kuṇḍalinī, which is beyond suṣumnā and residing at sahasrāra, has been termed as *turiya-kuṇḍalinī.*

There are sixteen *kalās* or aspects of the moon (the sixteen phases are the 14 phases of the moon along with the New Moon and the Full Moon). The sixteen *kalās* are: 1) *kṛpa* (mercy), 2) *mṛdutva* (gentleness), 3) *dhairyam* (patience, composure), 4) *vairāgya* (dispassion), 5) *dhṛti* (constancy), 6) *sampat* (prosperity, i.e., spiritual), 7) *trasya* (cheerfulness), 8) *romance* (rapture), 9) *vinaya* (sense of prosperity, humility), 10) *dhyāna* (meditation), 11) *susthirata* (quietitude, restfulness), 12) *gāmbhirya* (gravity of demenanor), 13) *udyama* (enterprise, effort), 14) *akshoba* (emotionless), 15) *audārya* (magnanimity), 16) *ekāgrata* (concentration); also "time."[141]

The twelve *kalās* of the sun are the twelve months. Fire as such has no *kalās*; but the ten energies contained in the fire are treated as the ten *agni-kalās*.

In the words of B. Natarajan, Candra-Yoga may be described as follows:

> In that journey in kundalini-yoga, the ten kalas of fire are first absorbed by the 12 kalas of the sun. Together the kalas of the sun and fire are absorbed in the 16 kalas of the moon. Thus the kalas of three different origins merge into one. Into them finally merge the four kalas of kundalini in the cranium top. There in the sahasrara, the yogi pays homage at the Feet of the Lord. Those who have learned to merge the kalas of fire and sun in the kalas of the moon, verily become masters of themselves.[142]

To quote Tirumūlar,

> Rouse Kalas of Fire
> Merge them in Sun
> Merge all in Moon,
> Of senses and sense organs rid,
> That verily is Chandra yoga.[143]
>
> This, in short, is Chandra yoga. Through kundalini yoga rouse the kalas of fire. Merge them in the kalas of the sun. Merge them in the moon's kalas. Finally merge them all in jiva, of senses and sense organs rid. This verse describes the Kalas and how they should be handled.[144]

By Candra-Yoga death is conquered:

> The yogis who thus practice incessantly
> Conquer Death;
> They will live in this world aeons beyond;
> They are worthy of our obeisance,
> They who, this Moon's yoga in success practice.[145]

5. Pariyaṅga-Yoga

Maithuna-Yoga is one special version of Yoga called "contrary practice" or *ulṭā-sādhana.* Immortality is made possible by adopting this method which consists of the following: Instead of emitting the semen in its usual downward motion it should be sublimated upwards, which is possible by a Yoga process called Maithuna-Yoga. The upward flow of the nerve-energy, partly used for reproduction, is called *ūrdhva-retas* in Sanskrit. In the *Taittirīya Āraṇyaka* (10, 12) one meets with the term *ūrdhva-retas,* literally meaning 'with erect semen.' The *Mahābhārata* also refers to sages *(yatis)* who are *ūrdhva-retas.* This should not be interpreted to mean that these sages have an erection. The underlying idea is that an ascetic gains power by directing his semen upward. In Taoist practice also there is mention of making the seminal essence *(ching)* return. It is said that in Hebrew language, "to know" originally had a sexual meaning.

The *Tirumandiram* calls this arresting and upward flow of semen as *vindu-maṟittal* (in Tamil) and speaks of a characteristic feature of a yogin as one who does not emit the semen even though he has intercourse with a woman. This reversal of all vital forces, called *ulṭā-sādhana* in Yoga, leads to the control and finally to the paralyzing of the mind, *citta.* At the sahasrāra the yogin finally conquers his mind. The upward movement suggests a progression away from worldliness and ignorance and tends towards purity, enlightenment and immortality. The concept that the semen should be sublimated upwards to attain immortality is an ancient discovery of Yoga. The yogic technique of non-spilling of semen is called *skanda.* As long as complete control of semen is not attained in the practice of Yoga, *skanda* is not born. *Skanda* is born only when the ejaculation is arrested by specific techniques including prāṇāyāma and the semen is sublimated and reaches the sahasrāra. In Yoga, the man who discharges the semen is called a *paśu,* an animal, and the man who retains it during *maithuna,* i.e., sexual union, is called *divya,* divine or *vīra,* hero. The *Agastiyar Jñāṉam* and the *Tirumandiram* speak of this process and assure us that there is no death for a person who adopts this method perfectly. Tirumūlar calls such a yogin as *veṇyogattaṉ* (a white yogin) and Maithuna-Yoga as Pariyaṅga-Yogam,[146] which unfortunately has been translated as "bedstead Yoga" by Kamil Zvelebil.[147]

As examples of the treatment of Maithuna-Yoga, Bōgar's (a Tamil Siddha) poem *Aṣṭāṅga-Yogam* and Saint Ramalingam's poem *Aṉubava-Mālai,* may be taken for consideration.

The title *Aṣṭāṅga-Yogam* itself is couched in "twilight language" for nowhere in the poem Bōgar discusses the eight limbs of the Yoga. Bōgar's *Aṣṭāṅga-Yogam,* the "eight limbed" Yoga, may be interpreted as a coupling and union of four arms and four legs in an act of sexual union. Interpreted in this way, *bhoga* alone has become Yoga. A genuine interpretation of this Aṣṭāṅga-Yoga would be that in the identity of opposites, called man and woman, the *antaḥkaraṇa* (the internal organs) of both parties involved in the Yoga become one and the same. The four *antaḥkaraṇas* of the man, called *buddhi, manas, ahamkāra* and *citta* and the four *antaḥkaraṇas* of woman, become one and the same, conceptually and physically inseparable. This is the real Aṣṭāṅga-Yoga or Maithuna-Yoga.

In *Aṉubava-Mālai,* Saint Ramalingam gives a narrative of the experiences of a supreme love between the lover and the beloved. The lover is the human soul represented as a lady devoted in love to the beloved, the Supreme Lord. They embrace each other which is a pure state of supreme love without any mixture of any lower desire, much less of sex. His embrace imparts deathlessness to the body of the lover, the human soul, which becomes of the nature of the golden body of the beloved Lord. Explaining this state of *maithuna,* Saint Ramalingam says that it is a state which has become blissfully One, Two, and a state which is neither One nor Two, a state in between One and Two as the state of one-in-one and two-in-one.[148] He also asks "How can I express the subtlety by of the inner union?" and says that in that *maithuna* state, "I became He."[149]

Similarly Jayadeva's *Gīta-Govindam* has strong erotic overtones In it one finds a beautiful description of sexual pleasure i.e., bridal mysticism. To quote Georg Feuerstein:

> Secretly at night I went to his home in a concealed thicket where he remained in hiding. Anxiously I glanced in all directions, while he was laughing with an abundant longing for the delight *(rati)* (of sexual union); O friend! Make the crusher of (the demon) Keshin love me passionately. I am enamored, entertaining desires of love! (2.11).
>
> I was shy at our first union. He was kind toward me, (showing) hundreds of ingenious flatteries. I spoke through sweet and gentle smiles, and he unfastened the garment around my hips. (2.12).
>
> He laid me down on a bed of shoots. For a long time he rested on my breast, while I caressed and kissed him. Embracing me, he drank from my lower lip. (2.13).
>
> I closed my eyes from drowsiness. The hair on his cheeks bristled from my caresses. My whole body was perspiring, and he was quite restless because of his great intoxication with passion. (2.14).

> Radha pines for her lover, as the awakened heart yearns for God. Reflecting the radical spirit of Tantra, the *Gita-Govinda* extensively employs sexual metaphors to convey the bodily passion that the devotee feels when he or she contemplates God.[150]

This conjugal union, known as *maithuna,* is a mystical equation, standing for the spiritual Brahman-Ātman equation. It does not refer to the numerical or the logical identity of man and woman, Śiva and Śakti, Brahman and Ātman. It is the assertion of a meta-logical identity. The equation between the "He-She," belongs to experience or direct apprehension and not to the interpretation. The oneness that is experienced in *maithuna* is an experienced certainity. It is an experience of the dissolution of the separate personality, a fading of the "I" into the Boundless Experience. *Maithuna* is a conceptual framework of the oneness between Śiva-Śakti. The "oneness" is of an extraordinary character. For want of a better expression this oneness is sometimes termed in Tamil Siddha literature as *maithuna,* as *yāmula,* as *veṇ-yōgam.* This super union is termed as Yoga. Yoga, in essence, is oneness. As a method Kuṇḍalinī-Yoga, as well as Maithuna-Yoga make us realize this oneness. In one sense this oneness is "selfless" because in the broadest sense it is not selfish, that it does not have an element of ego, or "I"ness in it. In another sense the "oneness" is the Self, the self with a capital "S," a supreme Self because it is no other than one's own self in a new dimension, the "newly discovered self." This oneness is an undivided oneness. The *aikya* or oneness of male and female, of Śiva and Śakti is called Maithuna-Yoga and is called the best of all unions. The *pañca-tattva* (See Appendix-D) of the Maithuna-Yoga, or the old *vāmācara* tradition, has unfortunately degenerated into mere sexo-yogic practice.

The original significance and import of the Tāntric practices have been misused by unscrupulous sādhakas and misunderstood by ordinary people who are not trained in Tāntric sādhana. These have contributed to the development of a general abhorrence and antipathy towards the Tantras and the Tantric practices among the orthodox circles. Further, the degenerated *vāmācāra* tradition has reduced itself to sexual forms of ritualistic religion and worship. Bōgar says that in ignorance those who do not understand may condemn the sages who practice these *(maithuna)* techniques.

The employment of sex imagery is frequent in the Tāntric lore. It works both ways— making it adorable and making it abominable, although sex is employed in Tantra not for direct gratification but for reversal and restraint. Unfortunately we live in an erotic age of "sex affirming culture" where for better or worse the lid is off the *id* (the part of the mind relating to a person's unconscious instincts and impulses).

5. 1. References to Pariyaṅga-Yoga

Even though there is a separate section on Pariyaṅga-Yoga (section 19 of *tantra* Three) there are references to this Yoga in other places in the *Tirumandiram.*

In verse 140 of *tantra* One, there is the first suggestion of the sublimation of senses, which is a prelude to Pariyaṅga-Yoga. Tirumūlar uses a significant expression in this verse and says that the senses will turn inward *(pulaṉ maḍai māṟum).*

In verse 216 of the same *tantra* Tirumūlar specifically indicates the idea of Pariyaṅga-Yoga.

When the sacrificer in the company of his consort,
Offers oblations to the outer fire and the inner fire

Maintaining the discipline of yama, etc.,
They proceed along the correct yogic path.[151]

The summary of the verse may be indicated as follows: When the yogin's inner fire (i.e., kuṇḍalinī-śakti) reaches the ājñā-cakra, the ultimate Reality, (which is in the form of the inner fire), is the guiding spirit. The purpose of creating the male and the female and making them mutually inter-dependent is to experience this inner fire or light in their union, i.e., *maithuna.* When the male and the female embrace each other in the act of *maithuna,* this type of Yoga helps them to experience the inner guiding light. In this act of *maithuna, bhoga* in its spiritual dimension becomes Yoga. Tirumūlar uses the expression "pure path" *(tūya-neṟi)* for this type of Yoga.

In verse 283 of *tantra* One there is a fine reference to Pariyaṅga-Yoga.

Like the sweet love in sex experienced,
So, in the Great Love, let yourself in Him succumb;
Thus in Love sublimed, all your senses stilled,
Bounding in Bliss Supreme, That this becomes.[152]

Here Tirumūlar says that the union between the male and the female in micro-sex, is the same as the union between *ātman* and Śiva, that is macro-sex. This verse suggests that there is a one to one correspondence between sensual / carnal pleasure and the pleasure of identity between jīva and Śiva. *Tiru-v-undiyār,* a Śaiva Siddhānta work, also says that the sexual pleasure that one experiences is the same as the pleasure that one gets in the union between jīva and Śiva. In this connection we may also refer to the following:

In the *Bṛhadāraṇyaka Upaniṣad* the realization of the self has been compared to the transcendental realization of bliss arising through the deep embrace of a woman.

As, when deeply embraced by the dear woman, one knows neither anything external nor anything internal— so also a man deeply embraced by the *ātman* through perfect knowledge knows neither anything external nor anything internal.[153]

Sri Ramakrishna Paramahamsa says:

Nitya-śuddha bodha-rūpam – the Eternal and ever-pure consciousness. How can I make it clear to you? A young girl once asked her friend: 'Well, friend, your husband is here. What sort of pleasure do you enjoy with him?' The friend answered, 'My dear, you will know it for yourself when you get a husband. How can I explain it to you?'[154]

Tirumūlar likens the mystical bliss to sexual enjoyment and calls it *a<u>n</u>ubōga-k-kāmam* (felicity of union in sex). The three verses dealing with *a<u>n</u>ubōga-k-kāmam* are as follows:

Tat-Para He is not,
Sadasiva He is not,
Formless is He,
Formed is He not,
Wondrous indeed like felicity of sex-union enjoyed
Imagination baffling,
He in me in union stood.[155]

Thou fools who see with fleshy eyes
Know! To see with inner eye is bliss true;
How can mother tell the daughter
Of the felicity in the union with her husband?
In what terms will she that describe?[156]

As salt in water, in Lord I mixed,
Transcending Param and Paraparam states,
Beyond word and speech I in union merged;
"How was It?"–you ask
"It was It"–I say.[157]

Tirumūlar warns people who indulge in the mere sex act without sublimating it. In *tantra* Two he warns that if one enters into mere sexual pleasure one is doomed. The verse is as follows:

The Lord is within them,
Yet they know Him not,
They of faith false;
Limitless the flow of their evil deeds
Down down the deep drain it goes,
Never its destination to know.[158]

"Limitless the flow" (in Tamil *veḷḷattai nāḍudal*) in this verse suggests one who wants to enjoy physical sex. Just as the floodwater is drained and wasted, those who enjoy sex for the sake of sexual pleasure only, are wasting the energy. They have not conquered/ sublimated sex as a physical act *(vindu-jayam)*.

People who waste their sexual energy without sublimating it is like those who dropped gold in sea and looked hard for it in a pond.[159] This indicates that one should sublimate the sexual energy generated at the glands at the mūlādhāra and divert it by merging it with the kuṇḍalinī-śakti, pass it through suṣumnā to ājñā-cakra and from there realize the blissful light.

Tirumūlar describes what happens to the sexual energy *(vindu)* when associated with the three gunas. When the *bindu* mixes with *tamas* it becomes black. When the *bindu* mixes with *rajas* it becomes red like the red fire (i.e., kuṇḍalinī energy) at the ājñā-cakra. When it mixes with *sattva* it becomes a white bright light at the same cakra.[160]

Śiva-vākkiyar refers to this experience as *svarga-lōga-veḷi*,[161] i.e., infinite space where the body is seen as white and red. This is a significant experience of the yogins where white stands for the *prakāśa* aspect (the light of consciousness or the principle of self-revelation) of the God-head and red stands for the *vimarśa* aspect (experience which brings about the world process). This is called *raktoha śukla prabhā misram* in Sanskrit. Kambaḷi-c-caṭṭaimuṉi calls this experience as *Śiva-bōga-jñāṉam* (knowledge of the experience of the enjoyment of Śiva).[162]

In this context it is significant to refer to verse 521 of the *Tirumandiram*. The verse runs as follows:

> (Siva) He sports the garland of white skulls,
> His spreading locks are matted;
> He supports Universe vast,
> He fills Space in directions eight,
> On the throat of His Downward-directed Face
> Darkness suffuses;
> They say, "He swallowed poison;"
> They are ignorant, they know not the truth.[163]

People, who are ignorant, do not know the significance of "the throat of His downward-directed Face darkness suffuses." This phrase means that the body-space below the throat stands for darkness or ignorance. When the sex-energy *(śukla)* is directed below in this body-space it is dark. When the *śukla*-energy is sublimated above the throat, it stands for *amṛta* and it illuminates the body-space above the throat. "Śiva has swallowed the poison" means that he has prevented the sex-energy as physical dark energy going downward and sublimated it as *amṛta* above the ājñā-cakra (i.e., the middle of his eye-brows where He has the third eye). Since He has sublimated the sex-energy as physical energy at the throat, His throat has become black. The significance of Śiva's black throat (*Nīla-kaṇḍa<u>n</u>, nīla* means black, *kaṇḍa<u>n</u>* means throat) stands for the sublimation of the sex-energy. The term *adho-mugam,* i.e., "downward-directed face" refers to the redirection of the downward sex energy and sublimating it above that face (or throat). That is *adho-mugam* blossoms and transforms itself into limitless energy redirecting the semen energy and sublimating it. "The eyes must not see nor the ears hear, this is the way to eternal life."[164] That is, just as the eyes and ears must be redirected from the enjoyment of the sense organs to the enjoyment of supreme bliss by sublimating them, the sex-energy must be sublimated.

The process of sublimation is indicated in two verses in the *Tirumandiram*, the process of sublimation is suggested as follows:

> ...If breath that is controlled spurts there upwards
> Then will this dark body
> As a temple lamp lustrous bejeweled be.[165]

Tirumūlar uses the term *cuṇaṅgiḍa* in verse 821 to suggest sublimation. There is a clear explanation of sublimation in the following verse.

> They that have sported in the waters of virgin...
> No more shall wallow in the filthy waters of virgin's lust;
> If they but seek to sport in the Holy Virgin's Waters...
> No more births shall they in future take.[166]

The meaning of the verse is: Those men who have wallowed in the indulgence of sex with women do not know the method of sublimation. Once they know how to direct the sex-energy and sublimate it then they need not wallow in the series of births. That is, if sex is sublimated, the chain of birth and death is snapped.

In *tantra* Seven Tirumūlar speaks of ātma-linga. This ātma-liṅga is the result of the intercourse between Śiva and Śakti. Śakti is the *bindu,* which is in the form of a circle. Śiva is in the form of a rod, which is tubular. The cohabitation between them is called the linga copulation or *liṅga-p-puṇarcci* in Tamil. Śakti is in the form of *bindu* from the mūlādhāra to the throat region and Śiva is in the form of the macrocosmic *ākāśa* (space) above it. This combination of Śiva-Śakti is the form of the liṅga. Here liṅga is not a mere sexual cohabitation but it stands for the sublimation of the sexual energy leading to liberation or *mahā-ākāśa* or "beyond the beyond." Therefore liṅga stands for the sublimation of the sex-energy. In liṅga, *bindu* is the base and *nāda* is the rod inserted in it. Tirumūlar gives an explanation of the liṅga-tattva.

> The grand pedestal of Sakti holds the Atma Tattvas,
> The central part of Sakti holds the Vidya Tattvas,
> The Linga of Sakti, the Siva Tattvas,
> Sadasiva is Sakti's Soul Divine.[167]

It is unfortunate that liṅga worship is considered to be a worship of *Śisna-devata* (phallic God) in a degrading tone in the non-Siddha tradition.[168]

There are two sections in *tantra* Seven (sections 20 and 21), which speak about the rise of *bindu* (and the conquest of *bindu,* i.e., regulation of *bindu*) flow respectively. In both the sections there are fifty-two verses (verses 1923-1974). Though all these verses are important in a discussion on Pariyaṅga-Yoga, let us note only the very significant verses. The verses from 1923 to

1936 deal with cosmogony viewed from the special angle of evolutes as *bindu* and *nāda* of the primal cause. Tirumūlar laments in verse 1936 that people know not the destruction that wasting of *bindu* results in; they are ignorant who emit the sex-energy. They do not know to prevent it by determined will power. They are ignorant of knowing how to sublimate this energy for their true liberation from *samsāra*, that is, the act of recreation and procreation.

Tirumūlar speaks of the sublimation of the sex act as follows:

Embrace the damsel,
Your five sense organs with her five conjoining
But, detached your passion for the women be;
Like the senses that are God-Ward sublimated,
Be calm; excited be not;
Control your breath, senses and mind,
Concentrated be your thought,
Thus emit your bindu.[169]

According to Tirumūlar those who stand in Yoga-way, even though unite with woman in passion they do not emit their bindu.[170] According to Śiva-vākkiyar, even when a Siddha is enjoying the breasts of a woman, because of his disinterested attitude, (that is due to the sublimation of sex) he cuts asunder the knots of karma and becomes one who does not suffer rebirth.[171] That is, by conserving and sublimating the sex-energy the yogins kindle the kuṇḍalinī-śakti and coursing upward through the suṣumnā, they reach the state of illumination. The following verses/expressions from the *Tirumandiram* are significant:

In ignorance the folks waste it daily,
And destroyed by senses, in pain weep;

If in wisdom, they conscious perform Yoga supreme,
The Bindu disappears, divinely assimilated.[172]

Tirumūlar says that he who has conquered bindu has conquered time.[173]

When the Bindu of the body
Thus perishes (by Yoga)
It is into Divine Bindu transformed,
Of the ambrosial Lunar Sphere within;
When the Bindu of the body,
Perishes in the fire of Kundalini,
The ambrosial waters flow and fill the body;
Then indeed is Siva Bhoga that is ambrosial sweet;
And thus bathed in divine waters of ambrosia
The yogi attains Siddhis rare.[174]

By sublimating the sex-energy the yogin's body glitters as gold and it becomes immortal.[175] In another verse Tirumūlar says that when the bindu subsides (that is when it is sublimated) then it is Śivoham.[176]

In this connection it is interesting to note the directions given by Tirumūlar for sublimating the sex-energy. First he advises to clean the body of the woman before embracing her.

If you desire woman's love intense to excite,
The day before you in sexual union indulge,
Cleanse the woman of her bowel, phlegm and bile,
Then in union embrace her.[177]

Tirumūlar also gives the regulation days for sexual union to achieve sublimation.

Those who wish to sleep with women,
Let them observe the periodicity thus;
Of the two phases of the moon,
The first eight days of the waxing moon
For union appropriate are not,
In the six days that remain,
And in the first six days of the waning moon
Can they in union be.[178]

He gives the regulation days for the practicing yogins too.

Let those that Yoga practise
Avoid the fifth, the sixth and the eleventh days
After the woman menstruates;
The rest, who the pleasure seek,
Take the six days in the middle,
Of the three weeks that follow.[179]

Tirumūlar speaks about the duration of sexual union and the rules for the release of the *bindu*.

When on union they decide on,
Let it be for muhurtas four,
Following the injunctions of the Kama Sastras,
Let them the sexual act perform,
When the Moon's Kalas (left nadi) shine bright,
And breath in Sun's nadi low runs
Emit Bindu, the breath holding,
Breathing through nostril right, quelling left.[180]

The last line means breathing only through the right nostril, the left remaining closed. Here one *muhurta* is one and a half hours. The significant expression for sublimating the sex energy, the term used by Tirumūlar, is *vindu-maṟittal*[181] (that is arresting *bindu* from emission). He also calls it as "frying the *bindu*."[182] If one sublimates the *bindu*, one will live for hundred crores of years.[183]

Tirumūlar also gives a secret way to conquer/sublimate *bindu*.

Intone sound "Si" (the first sound of Panchakshara)
In your Prana (life breath)'s silent thought
Merge in "AUM"–the sound cluster of "A, U, M"
Thus Para Sakti reach,
That indeed is the way of Bindu Conquest
This the Mystic Secret (upadesa)–you hold.[184]

In pañcākṣara the letter "ci" stands for Śivam. When the yogin meditates on the pañcākṣara this letter stands for life's breath. The life's breath is the kuṇḍalinī-śakti. When it reaches the ājñā-cakra through the suṣumnā, there will be illumination, which is the gift of Parāśakti. This illumination is represented by the letters *va, ya, na, ma*. At this stage the *bindu* will be conquered. This conquering of the sex-energy is the result of the mantra *ci, va, ya, na, ma*.

5. 2. Translation of Pariyaṅga-Yoga

For the sake of a clear understanding of Pariyaṅga-Yoga, the entire section of 19 of *tantra* Three, as given by B. Natarajan in his translation of the *Tirumandiram* is reproduced in Appendix-E, with due acknowledgement to him.

5. 3. Tāntric Celibacy – A Vāmācāra Concept

Since Pariyaṅga-Yoga, which deals with sexual act in terms of Yoga is a *vāmācāra* concept, one should understand what *vāmācāra* stands for.

If an individual is initiated into *dakṣinācāra*, he must follow the path of jñāna or knowledge. If he is initiated into *vāmācāra*, the individual must follow the path of *pañca-tattva* called the five "m"s or *pañca-makāras* in Tāntric literature. The five "m"s are: *madya, matsya, māmsa, mudrā,* and *maithuna.* In *vāma-śrota* these terms refer to their literal meanings, that is, wine, fish, meat, parched cereal and sexual union respectively. But in *dakṣiṇa-śrota* they are hypostatized into mental configurations, and these terms are intended to denote a progressive course of *sādhana* leading to the realization of the Absolute Self. *Madya* becomes the symbol for intoxicating knowledge, *matsya* is symbolic of prāṇāyāma, *māmsa* stands for the control of speech and withdrawl from world phenomena, *mudrā* refers to the yogic state of concentration and *maithuna* is the merging of the sāḍhaka with the Reality.

Some Tantras call *vāmācāra* as *kulācāra* and *dakṣiṇācāra* as *samayācara,* which is a contemplative technique involving Kuṇḍalinī-Yoga. *Vāmācāra* is more or less a synonym for *kaulācāra. Kaulas* combine enjoyment *(bhoga)* with renunciation *(tyāga).* There are two classes in *kaulācāra*— *pūrva-kaula* and *uttara-kaula. Pūrva-kaulas* uphold the indulgence in the five "m"s. The *uttara-kaulas* do not use any external aid for worship. They are known as *vīras* as they perform yogic practices on cremation ground. The sādhaka creates within himself the cremation ground for burning out the dead corpse of desires or *vāsanas.* The conception of *dakṣiṇācāra* as opposed to *vāmācāra* seems to be a later development and it is possible that the first word in the term *vāmācāra* is not *vāma* or left, but *vāma,* woman. Originally, there was no rightism or leftism in the Tantras. In some Tantras it is stated that the efficacy of *dakṣiṇācāra* is limited and painful. It is like crossing a river with the help of a jar. *Vāmācāra* system is like crossing a river on a nice comfortable boat.[185] From early times both the paths, *vāmācāra* as the way of delight and *dakṣiṇācāra* as the way of knowledge, have been treated with equal respect, though later on *vāma-mārga* fell into disrepute.

Tirumūlar seems to have a leaning towards *vāmācāra* when he speaks that Yoga and *bhoga* are both conjoined by the yogins. The verse is as follows:

> Both Yoga and bhoga, yogis may have;
> Through Yoga is attained Siva's form divine,
> Through bhoga all earthy blessings;
> Thus he may enjoy both— he, yogi immortal.[186]

When Yoga becomes *bhoga, nirvāṇa* equals *samsāra.* Tāntric Buddhism defines the condition of bodhi-mind in Nirvāṇa as in the embrace of a woman. To quote Georg Feuerstein:

> The great dictum of *Tāntrism* is that the transcendental reality and the conditional world are coessential – nirvāṇa equals *samsāra.* In other words, transcendental ecstasy and sensory pleasure are not finally incompatible.[187]

In other words, there seems to be a correspondence between inner and outer reality, and one also encounters what C.J. Jung calls the notion of synchronicity, which is an attempt to explain the fact that there is a coincidence between external events *(bhoga)* and internal experience (Yoga).

In this context it would be worthwhile to note certain views on the *vāmācāra* concepts expressed by Abhinavagupta as elaborated in chapter 29 of the *Tantrā-loka.*[188] According to Abhinavagupta bliss is the supreme Brahman and it resides in the body in three ways.[189] Amongst the three, two are wine and meat. The other is intercourse.[190] Those who abstain from the three are called "bonded animals."[191] He who observes the last of the three, i.e., *maithuna* is called a *brahmacāri*, that is, Tāntric sublimity is a form of celibacy. It is Tāntric *brahmacarya*. It is an existential sexuality. It is an erotic liberation. It is enlightened sexuality.[192] A *brahmacāri* according to Abhinavagupta, is one

> ... who is at ease...and who, even while involved in sexual union, is perfectly mindful, his body utterly tranquil, who is fully acquainted with the rules of unlawful behaviour mentioned in the Atimarga (tradition), who is fully enlightened as well, who indeed is composed of consciousness, is autonomous at all times, who comes in contact with the particular object in order to acquire the supernatural power of experiencing his own consciousness and not because of an attitude of greed, who is free of the attitude of the 'bonded animal;" he is certainly committed to the great path.
>
> He, whose conduct shows attentiveness to his own self both in the midst of worldly affairs and during the performance of the ritual of the left, always retains his seed during the observance (of the ritual intercourse). (The word *skhalana* has been used for the word seed. This word can also refer to the emission of semen. The yogi who holds his seed could be described as "unfaltering"). He whose mind, at the moment of emitting semen, i.e., within the split-second of time has spontaneously settled in respect of all the fluctuations of thought, all at once there arises in his mind the consciousness of bliss. The resulting form is perfectly described as 'pertaining to Brahman.'[193]

Describing emission, Abhinavagupta says that emission *(visarga)* is three-fold: union, risen and rested.[194] Quoting from the *Gama-śāstra* Abhinavagupta states:

Śakti is the fire pit; Śiva is the liṅga, their blending is the supreme plane. Emanation, re-absorption and 'that' *(tad)* derive from these two. The emission is three-fold according to the Gama.

The fire pit, i.e., the female-śakti, is the 'risen' form. Śiva is the 'rested' form (Then) blending is the union. With regard to (those three): the emergence of emanation, in the sense of being 'risen, is because of the śakti; (the emergence) of reabsorption, in the sense of being 'rested' is because of Śiva; and the emergence of the ineffable *(anakhya)*, in the sense of absence of all division is because of the union, i.e., because of what is called 'the supreme plane.' Such is the three-fold emission according to the Gama-śāstra.[195]

In a work called the *Yoni-Tantra* there is a description of *yoni-pūja*, the premilinary rites to be performed before the sexual act.[196]

The preliminary rites:

1. The Adept procures a woman who is wanton.
2. He places her in the *maṇḍala* and
3. He offers her a narcotic drink.
4. He places her on his left thigh and
5. He honours her *yoni*, which is to be unshaven.
6. He anoints the *yoni* with sandal paste to look like flower or menses, *puṣpam.*
7. He gives her wine to drink.
8. He paints a 'half-moon,' *ardhacandra*, on her forehead with vermilion.
9. He places his hands on her breasts and mutters the *bhagabīja*, which is identified with the *māyābīja* (HRIM).
10. He kisses her on the cheeks and moulds her breasts.

11. He recites the mantra or a *stotra*.
12. The śakti anoints the *liṅga* with sandal paste and saffron.

One finds a beautiful description of the sexual partner in *Tantrā-loka*:

> Let him, then bring a sexual partner to the place (of ritual), her eyes reeling with desire; her lips are red as *bimba* fruit, her teeth are lovely, her face is furrowed at the brow, she is beautiful; her eyes are like those of a trembling fawn; pleasantly she smiles; her a bundant hair is like a glittering swarm of large black bees; her eyes are tremulous because of the furrowing of her brows which are shaped like cupid's bow; her complexion is the colour of liquid gold; she is tranquil; she is made very beautiful in a hundred ways by the varied beauty of her ear-ornaments; she is adorned with a lovely necklace on her lovely conch-like throat; she is bent down by the weight of her breasts which are as haughty as the frontal lobes of an elephant in rut; she is adorned with *kandali* flowers on her well-rounded arms; the fingers of her hand flare like cobra's hood; she is adorned with a finger-ring streaming with the variegated flames of a glittering jewel; her face, with the lovely charm of the full moon, ravishes the heart; her slim lovely waist resembles a noble lion or a rainbow; the languid movement of her loins reveals the triple row of folds (over her navel); her lovely thighs are like a plantain tree and her lovely calves are like the trunk of an elephant; she is most beautiful, with feet and ankles like cupid's chariot wheel; she is adorned with a string of beautiful (pearls) which tinkle like ghee falling (into the sacrificial fire); she makes a clinking sound with her trembling anklet

and jingling girdle; she makes a murmuring hum with her bracelet and jingling armlet; her gait is like that of a huge elephant in rut, her navel is deep; her speech is beautiful like the man stammering cries of the goose; she is adorned with a garland of fragrant flowers on the thread of her armlet; she is perfectly eager for the gift of harmless betel-nut from 'the huge cobra;' she dances, she sings and makes cries of pleasure *sit*, she plays and pretends to repulse a lover's caress; she is untroubled and she retains her composure, her mind is devoted to the goddess alone; greed and folly having disappeared from her mind, she is consciousness itself; her one attitude is that of savouring the unique wonder of Bhairava: she is the sexual partner, the enchantress, the *mudrā* in this world of the movable-and-immovable."[197]

5. 4. Pariyaṅga-Yoga – An evaluation

In explaining *rāsa-krīḍa* to people who listen to him the *paurāṇika*, (the person who expounds the Purāṇas to public at large gatherings) used to say that in explaining the principle behind it, he feels like walking on the razor's edge. *Rāsa-krīḍa* deals with Śrī Kṛṣṇa's "dealings" with the young *gopis* (girls). If one interprets it carefully, it will mean how the Lord in the form of Śrī Kṛṣṇa tries to liberate the young *gopis* by his pranks. If it is interpreted loosely the same thing would become only a mean sexual act. In the same way one has to be careful in evaluating Pariyaṅga-Yoga; otherwise it will degenerate into a mere physical sexual act.

Pariyaṅga-Yoga is a type of Yoga in which the heroic yogin *(vīra)* and his consort *(duti)* participate in the great banquet *(mahotsava)*, a secret sex ritual which culminates in their act of intercourse under Tāntric laboratory conditions. It is an expression to show that the yogin's sensory tumult is stilled, permitting to achieve an ever-increasing identity with cosmic consciousness. Pariyaṅga-Yoga may be translated as ritual sex, whose purpose is two-fold:

> (1) It is the means to the attainment of spiritual greatness through the identity (union) of Śiva and Energy. The aspirants become identified with the Absolute or the Tremendous God—the highest state realized by a yogi—and remain there even in the most adverse conditions. (2) It is a test to see if the votary can have such control over bodily senses as to remain impassible to emotion and pleasure (especially during the climax of the sexual union) and to concentrate on the pure self.[198]

Pariyaṅga-Yoga, as we have already seen, is an erotic celibacy; the principle behind it is sublimation and not suppression. It is an alchemy of emotional transmutation. It is *ūrdhva-retas.* This means the upward-flow that refines the juice-current of life. The yogins by this process discovered the erotic continuum from desire to *vīrya.*

Special care must be taken in deciphering sexual metaphors and symbols used by the Siddhas and the Tāntrics who divinized sex in order to take away sex-mindedness. It is very true that in this imperfect world the way to hell is paved with very good intentions. As a washer man makes a dirty cloth clean with some matter which itself is dirty, or as some water accidentally goes into one's ears is taken out by the help of some additional water itself, the Siddhas and the Tāntrics feel that one can get rid of the *kāma* by *kāma* itself. *Kāma* becomes a bondage only when it is resorted to by the foolish and not by the wise in whose case it serves as the cause of emancipation. It is said that the joy of sexual union is a foretaste of heaven. It is also observed that when an animal's sexual instinct is over-whelmingly strong, its instinct for self-preservation or self-identity is reduced practically to zero. During sexual union one loses one's sense of personality and merges oneself into a greater whole. Sexual union is the 'obscure silence where all lovers lose themselves.'

Due to our notion of morality, sex-act has become the cloaking taboo, the busting secret, the covering shame. But actually according to Tantra it contains "a sharing mystery." It is said that due to their high sense of morality the victorians covered the legs of their furniture! In Tantra there is a loss of the sense of the holy and the moral. In this connection one should understand the import and significance of the Khajuraho Temples. To quote Rajneesh:

> These temples of Khajuraho were no ordinary temples. They were a kind of therapy; they exist as a therapy. Whenever somebody was suffering from some sexual perversion he was sent to Khajuraho. He had to watch and meditate on all those abnormal, bizarre things. He had something perverted in his mind; that perversion was inside the unconscious. What does psychoanalysis do? It tries to bring things from the unconscious to the conscious, that's all. And psychoanalysis, says that once something comes from the unconscious, to the conscious, it is released you are free of it. Now this was a great psychoanalysis this Khajuraho. These temples were tantra temples; one of the greatest experiments ever done. They are not obscene, they are not pornographic, they are spiritual— a great experiment in spirituality, a great experiment in

> transforming human energy towards higher levels. Change your focus from having to being.
>
> Without understanding the significance of these temples the tourist assumes that the Hindus are as lecherous as he is.[199]

It is unfortunate that sex has been treated as an unnatural thing to be hidden from the purview of people. The institutionalized customs are responsible for these attitudes. Normality and abnormality are culturally defined concepts suppressing sex, instead of sublimating, is like dividing the bud and the blossom into two separate categories. In *Śatapata Brāhmanas* sexual union is identified with *yajña* (1.9.2.7; 1.9.2.77, VI, 4.3.7 etc.,) It is said in *Rudra-yāmala* and *Brahma-yāmala* that ṛṣi Vasiṣṭa went to China to obtain *vāmācāra* practices. In Tantra the designations of the male and the female or of the seed and the ovum are used to explain the two aspects of the absolute reality, static and dynamic, negative and positive; and their union refers to the unity in the ultimate truth. This is represented as *ardha-nārīśvara* (a God whose one half is male and another half is female one of the forms of Śiva). This integration of duality of male and female, static and dynamic, etc., is called *yuga-naddha.* In Vajrāyana Buddhism the principle of *yuga-naddha* is represented by the deity embracing his consort closely in the act of sexual union. According to the Tantras this polarity between male and female is blended in every human being and *maithuna* is the nearest approximation to this blending, in which, act the embracer and the embraced are lost, (forgetting that they are two) in the act of embracing. In *maithuna* state "we" becomes "one," multiplicity becomes singleness. It is a state of "I am Thou." Micro-sex (small blending) is the biological foundation of macro-sex (great/or absolute blending). In its existential content the ritual of union is functionally detachable from the conceptual.

Here the male and the female are both playing the roles at the absolute level in the form of Śiva and Śakti. In short, the intense bliss derived from sexo-yogic practice has got homogeneity in the mystical states and processes. In this connection we may mention the role of alchemy, which leads to a "chemical marriage" as a model where the opposites are melted into a unity. In the same way male and female are melted into unity in the act of *maithuna*. In this *maithuna*– *kāma* (carnal love) is transformed into *prema* (understanding love). The sublimation of sex may be called "transubstantiation" a metamorphosis comparable to the transubstantiation of bread and *idli* into the body. In this connection one may note the significance of the following: According to one ancient text "where cows have sported with bulls, or where beautiful woman have dallied with their lovers, that place is an appropriate site for a temple."

Tāntric sex reveals to us that we are not mere human beings having a spiritual experience but really spiritual beings committed to human experience. Through Tāntric-sex a man / woman is liberated from the tyranny of the senses and the sensuous. Trying to explain the significance and import of Pariyaṅga-Yoga to worldly people, as Kabir says, is like a barren woman rocking an empty cradle.

6. The Siddhis as discussed by Tirumūlar

The siddhis are mystic accomplishments or miraculous powers attained in the process of Yoga. Patañjali in his *Yoga-Sūtras* enumerates different possible causes for the emergence of the siddhis, such as *janmaja* (siddhis obtained by some from the time of birth); *auṣadhija* (siddhis obtained through the use of herbs); *mantraja,* (siddhis acquired by the practice of sound powers called mantras); *tapoja,* (siddhis attained through meditation); and *samādhija* (siddhis attained through samādhi i.e., entasis).[200] According to Patañjali siddhis are obstacles to cognitive absorption (samādhi) but are accomplishments in the waking state.[201] It is unfortunate that in the Indian literature and folklore, siddhis have become the subject of fables, fairy tales, legends and mythologies and also objects of worship. It is stated that in some areas of Punjab the siddhis are worshipped under different names and under the forms of stones.[202] In Tamil Nadu Siddhas are identified with the raw alchemists, reducing them to miracle men or magicians who turn base metals, brass (*pittaḷai* in Tamil) into gold (*āḍagam* in Tamil). *Liṅga-purāṇa* refers to siddhi as impediments and calls them *upasarga,* an ailment in the soul of the yogin. It is true that though the siddhis may "tempt the monk with a vain magical mastery of the world and, in addition, are likely to cause confusion in the minds of the unbelievers... they, as it were, constitute the new experiential categories... of the monk"[203] This is the reason why Pattiṉattār, a Tamil Siddha, calls siddhi as "bitter sugarcane"*kacakkum karumbu* to indicate its dual nature. In truth, the siddhis are not merely negative by-products, but rightful phenomena of a successful Yoga practice. To the genuine Siddha, the siddhis are of immense value, for they indicate that he is in the process of deconditioning himself from the laws of nature and from karmic determinism forever.

6. 1. Aṣṭa-mā-siddhis

The eight siddhis have been enumerated as follows by Tirumūlar in section 11 of *tantra* Three (verses 640 to 693).

Himself the atom, himself the cosmos
Himself light, himself heavy
Himself invisible air,

Himself migrating into mortal bodies other,
Himself possessing prowess of the Truthful One
Himself immanent in all
–These eight are the Siddhis Great.[204]

Tirumūlar says that *sāmbhavi* and *kechari mudrās* are necessary to attain the siddhis.[205] He also opines that twelve years of continuous practice of these mudrās is necessary to attain the eight siddhis.[206] When the yogin attains *aṇimā-siddhi* he becomes lighter than the flimsiest cotton wool.[207] After attaining this siddhi the yogin should persevere for five years to attain the *lagimā-siddhi* which is the power to penerate anywhere at will.[208] When the yogin attains this siddhi he will glow with divine light.[209] A year after *lagimā,* the yogin attains *mahimā-siddhi,* that is, the power of becoming great.[210] He attains *prāpti,* one year after he visions the celestial *bhutas* in *mahimā.*[211] *Prāpti* is the power to attain all desired objects. A year after attaining *prāpti, prakāmya,* that is, the power to transmigrate into another body is achieved.[212] A year after attaining *prakāmya, īśatva-siddhi,* that is the power to control and to create, to preserve and to destroy is attained.[213] After one year of *īśatva* the yogin attains *vasitva,* the power to become immanent like god.[214] A year after attaining *vasitva,* the yogin attains *kāmavasayitva-siddhi,* the power to pervade. Tirumūlar calls this siddhi as *kāmaru-tattva.*[215] One who has mastered all these eight siddhis will be the Lord of the entire globe.[216]

NOTES ON CHAPTER FOUR

1. Mircea Eliade, *Yoga: Immortality and Freedom*, p. 361.
2. Yoga Sutras, 1.1.
3. Theos Bernard, *Heaven Lies within Us*, pp. 52-53.
4. Śiva-vākkiyar, 43.
5. *Ibid.*, 288.
6. *Ibid.*, 21.
7. *Tirumandiram*, 122. Author's translation.
8. G. Varadharajan (Comm.), *Tirumandiram*, Vol. I, p. 61.
9. Suba. Annamalai (Ed.), *Tirumandiram*, Vol.1, p. 67.
10. *The Collected Works of Swami Vivekananda*, Vol. II, p. 86.
11. Śiva-vākkiyar, 363
12. For a comparison between the *Tirumandiram* and the *Yoga--Sutras* refer Marshall Govindan's book *Kriya* Yoga *Sutras of Patanjali and the Siddhas*, Introduction.
13. Refer his Foreword to Suba. Annamalai (Ed.), *Tirumandiram*, Vol 3, p. IX.
14. *Tirumandiram*, 121. Translation of B.Natarajan.
15. *Ibid.*, 83.
16. *Ibid.*, 102.
17. *Ibid.*, 641.
18. *Ibid.*, 1446; refer also 1447.
19. *Ibid.*, 1475.
20. *Ibid.*, 1671, 1678.
21. *Ibid.*, 128.
22. *Ibid.*, 129.
23. A Buddhist Tibetan work whose microfilms of the MSS are said to be preserved in the Nepal National Archives.

24. These verses are quoted by Kurtis R. Schaeffer in his article on "The Attainment of Immortality: From Nathas in India To Buddhists in Tibet" in the *Journal of Indian Philosophy*, Vol. 30, 2002, pp. 515-533.
25. *Tirumandiram*, 1461. Translation of B. Natarajan.
26. *Ibid.*, 1524. Translation of B. Natarajan.
27. *Ibid.*, 1641.
28. *Ibid.*, 132.
29. *Ibid.*, 1950.
30. *Ibid.*, 327.
31. *Ibid.*, 93.
32. *Ibid.*, 754. Translation of B. Natarajan.
33. *Ibid.*, 755. Translation of B. Natarajan.
34. *Ibid.*, 759. Translation of B. Natarajan.
35. *Ibid.*, 764. Translation of B. Natarajan.
36. *Ibid.*, 1898. Translation of B. Natarajan.
37. *Ibid.*, 743. Translation of B. Natarajan.
38. *Ibid.*, 224.
39. *Ibid.*, 223.
40. *Ibid.*, 295.
41. *Ibid.*, 296.
42. *Ibid.*, 320
43. *Ibid.*, 336. Translation of B. Natarajan.
44. *Ibid.*, 702.
45. *Ibid.*, 1524.
46. *Ibid.*, 2427. Translation of B. Natarajan.
47. *Ibid.*, 1704 to 1711.
48. *Ibid.*, 345.

49. *Ibid.*, 377.
50. *Ibid.*, 60.
51. *Ibid.*, 1705.
52. *Ibid.*, 1705.
53. *Ibid.*, 1705.
54. *Ibid.*, 1705.
55. *Ibid.*, 659.
56. *Ibid.*, 1708.
57. *Ibid.*, 1709.
58. *Ibid.*, 2528.
59. *Ibid.*, 892.
60. Suba. Annamalai (Ed.), *Tirumandiram*, Vol. I, p. 489.
61. *Ibid.*, 434.
62. *Ibid.*, 789.
63. *Ibid.*, 593.
64. *Ibid.*, 624.
65. *Ibid.*, 626.
66. *Ibid.*, 802.
67. *Ibid.*, 813.
68. *Ibid.*, 887.
69. *Ibid.*, all in 886.
70. *Ibid.*, 890.
71. *Ibid.*, 894.
72. *Ibid.*, 1207.
73. *Ibid.*, 1329.
74. *Ibid.*, 2527-2536.
75. *Ibid.*, 2546.
76. *Ibid.*, 2527-2536.

77. *Ibid.*, 2525. Translation of B.Natarajan.
78. *Ibid.*, 442.
79. *Ibid.*, 864.
80. *Ibid.*, 580. Translation of B.Natarajan.
81. *Ibid.*, 475.
82. *Ibid.*, 723.
83. *Ibid.*, 1155-1254.
84. *Ibid.*, 178.
85. *Ibid.*, 184.
86. *Ibid.*, 189.
87. *Ibid.*, 230. G.Varadarajan (Comm.), *Tirumandiram*, Vol. I, p. 110.
88. *Ibid.*, 801. Translation of B.Natarajan.
89. *Ibid.*, 320, 321 and 322.
90. *Ibid.*, 552. Translation of B.Natarajan.
91. *Ibid.*, 554. Translation of B.Natarajan.
92. *Ibid.*, 555. Translation of B.Natarajan.
93. *Ibid.*, 556. Translation of B.Natarajan.
94. *Ibid.*, 557. Translation of B.Natarajan.
95. *Ibid.*, 563. Translation of B.Natarajan.
96. *Ibid.*, 2023-2043.
97. *Ibid.*, 133.
98. *Ibid.*, 539.
99. *Ibid.*, 2023-2030.
100. *Ibid.*, 2031-2043.
101. *Ibid.*, 2033. Translation of B. Natarajan.
102. *Ibid.*, 2035. Translation of B. Natarajan.
103. *Ibid.*, 2039. Translation of B. Natarajan.

104. *Ibid.*, 2038. Translation of B. Natarajan.
105. *Ibid.*, 591.
106. *Ibid.*, 597. Translation of B. Natarajan.
107. *Ibid.*, 598. Translation of B. Natarajan.
108. *Ibid.*, 604. Translation of B. Natarajan.
109. *Ibid.*, 605. Translation of B. Natarajan.
110. *Ibid.*, 606. Translation of B. Natarajan.
111. *Ibid.*, 607. Translation of B. Natarajan.
112. *Ibid.*, 617. Translation of B. Natarajan.
113. *Ibid.*, 629. Translation of B. Natarajan.
114. *Ibid.*, 632. Translation of B. Natarajan.
115. *Ibid.*, 639. Translation of B. Natarajan.
116. *Ibid.*, 723. Translation of B. Natarajan.
117. *Ibid.*, 744. Translation of B. Natarajan.
118. B.Natarajan (Tr.), *Tirumandiram*, p. 120.
119. *Tirumandiram*, 771.
120. *Ibid.*, 772.
121. *Ibid.*, 773.
122. *Ibid.*, 778 and 785.
123. *Ibid.*, 786. Translation of B. Natarajan.
124. *Ibid.*, , 790-796.
125. *Ibid.*, 818.
126. *Ibid.*, 819. Translation of B. Natarajan.
127. *Ibid.*, 1892.
128. *Ibid.*, 1900.
129. *Ibid.*, 1894.
130. *Ibid.*, 1897.
131. *Ibid.*, 2409. Refer Suba.Annamalai (Ed.), *Tirumandiram*, Vol. I, p.228.

132. *Ibid.*, 799. Translation of B. Natarajan.
133. *Ibid.*, 805. Translation of B. Natarajan.
134. *Ibid.*, 1075. Translation of B. Natarajan
135. B.Natarajan (Tr.), *Tirumandiram*, p.169.
136. *Tirumandiram*, sections 5, 6 and 7 of *tantra* Nine.
137. *Ibid.*, 2701. Translation of B. Natarajan
138. B.Natarajan (Tr.), *Tirumandiram*, pp.146-147. (pp. 4-9 to 4-10 of Babaji's Kriya Yoga and Publications, Inc. edition).
139. *Tirumandiram*, 1308.
140. *Ibid.*, 1320. Translation of B. Natarajan
141. M. Govindan (Ed.), *Thirumandiram*, Glossary, pp. VIII-IX.
142. B.Natarajan (Tr.), *Tirumandiram*, p.136.
143. *Tirumandiram*, 862, Translation of B. Natarajan
144. B.Natarajan (Tr.), *Tirumandiram*, p.137.
145. *Tirumandiram*, 874.
146. *Ibid.*, III *tantra*, section 19.
147. *The Poets of the Powers*, p. 78.
148. Saint Ramalingam, *Tiru-v-aruṭpā*, "Aṉubava-Mālai," 65.
149. *Ibid.*, 94.
150. Georg Feuerstein, *The Yoga Tradition*, pp. 382-383.
151. *Tirumandiram*, 216. Translation of B. Natarajan.
152. *Ibid.*, 283. Translation of B. Natarajan
153. *Bṛhadāraṇyaka Upaniṣad*, 4-3.21.
154. *The Gospel of Sri Ramakrishna*, Tr. Swami Nikhilananda (abridged edition), p. 440.
155. *Tirumandiram*, 2943. Translation of B. Natarajan.
156. *Ibid.*, 2944. Translation of B. Natarajan.
157. *Ibid.*, 2945. Translation of B. Natarajan.
158. *Ibid.*, 511. Translation of B. Natarajan.

159. *Ibid.*, 513.
160. *Ibid.*, 514.
161. Śiva-vākkiyar, 86.
162. *Kambaḷi-c-caṭṭai-muṉi-Muṉjñāṉam-100*, 15.
163. *Tirumandiram*, 521. Translation of B. Natarajan.
164. *Ibid.*, 588.
165. *Ibid.*, 820. Translation of B. Natarajan.
166. *Ibid.*, 1519. Translation of B. Natarajan.
167. *Ibid.*, 1758. Translation of B. Natarajan.
168. In this connection it would be instructive to study the book Phallic-Worship written and signed by the author George Ryley Scott, which deals with a history of sex and sex rites in relation to the religions of all races from antiquity to the present day. Seven hundred and seventy five copies of the book have been privately printed for subscribers only by T.Werner Laurie Ltd., House 24 and 26, Black Friars Lane, E.C. 4, 1941, and the author of this section on Pariyanga-Yoga has got a numbered copy (number 242) of this book which is a very rare work.
169. *Tirumandiram*, 1942. Translation of B. Natarajan.
170. *Ibid.*, 1961.
171. Śiva-vākkiyar, 182; refer also Bhadragiriyār, 53.
172. *Tirumandiram*, 1952. Translation of B. Natarajan.
173. *Ibid.*, 1954.
174. *Ibid.*, 1959. Translation of B. Natarajan.
175. *Ibid.*, 1966.
176. *Ibid.*, 1969.
177. *Ibid.*, 1955. Translation of B. Natarajan.
178. *Ibid.*, 1939. Translation of B. Natarajan.

179. *Ibid.*, 1940. Translation of B. Natarajan.
180. *Ibid.*, 1941. Translation of B. Natarajan.
181. *Ibid.*, 1965.
182. *Ibid.*, 1970.
183. *Ibid.*, 1953.
184. *Ibid.*, 1967. Translation of B. Natarajan.
185. *Gandharva Tantra*, ed., R.C.Kak and H.B.Sastri, Vol. XXXVI, pp. 33-34.
186. *Tirumandiram*, 1491. Translation of B. Natarajan. *Bōgam* or enjoyment is of eight kinds. They are: woman *(peṇ)*, dress *(āḍai)*, ornaments *(aṇikalaṉ)*, food *(bōjaṉam)*, betel leaves with areca nuts *(tāmbūlam)*, perfumes *(parimaḷam)*, music, i.e., fine arts *(pāṭṭu)* and bed of flowers *(pūvamaḷi)*.
187. *The Yoga tradition*, p. XXXI.
188. John R. Dupuche, *Abhinavagupta: The Kula Ritual.*
189. *Ibid.*, p. 241.
190. *Ibid.*, p. 242.
191. *Ibid.*, p. 242.
192. *Ibid.*, p. 242.
193. *Ibid.*, pp. 244-245.
194. *Ibid.*, p. 277.
195. *Ibid.*, p. 278.
196. Quoted by Abhinavagupta, *Ibid.*, p. 125.
197. *Ibid.*, pp. 245-246.
198. Paul E. Murphy, *Triadic Mysticism*, pp. 56-57.
199. Rajneesh, *The Tantra Vision*, Vol. II, pp. 176-177.
200. *Yoga-Sutras*, IV.1.
201. *Ibid.*, III. 37.

202. Briggs, *Goraknāth and the Kāṇphaṭṭa Yogis*, p. 137.

203. Mircea Eliade, *Yoga: Immortality and Freedom*, p.177.

204. *Tirumandiram*, 649. Translation of B.Natarajan.

205. *Ibid.*, 642.

206. *Ibid.*, 645, 646.

207. *Ibid.*, 673.

208. *Ibid.*, 674.

209. *Ibid.*, 675.

210. *Ibid.*, 676.

211. *Ibid.*, 679.

212. *Ibid.*, 682.

213. *Ibid.*, 684.

214. *Ibid.*, 688.

215. *Ibid.*, 691.

216. *Ibid.*, 693.

Chapter 5

The Mysticism of the Tirumandiram

T.N. Ganapathy

mugattil kaṇ koṇḍu kāṇginṟa mūḍarkāḷ
agattil kaṇ koṇḍu kāṇbadē āṉandam
magaṭku-t tāy taṉ maṇāḷaṉōḍu āḍiya
cugattai-c colleṉṟāl collumāṟu eṅṅaṉē.

Thou fools who see with fleshy eyes
Know! To see with inner eye is bliss true;
How can mother tell the daughter
Of the felicity in the union with her husband?
In what terms will she that describe?

–*Tirumandiram, 2944.*

5. The Mysticism of the Tirumandiram

T.N. Ganapathy

1. What is mysticism?

1. 1. Western conception of mysticism

Mysticism may mean many things to many people. Etymologically the term is derived from the Greek word "muein" which means, "to close the lips and eyes." It is said that when the lips and eyes are silent, the heart has a hundred tongues. Bertrand Russell has said that mystical emotion "is the inspirer of whatever is best in man."[1] According to him mystical philosophy is characterized by certain beliefs. They are:

(i) the belief in insight as against discursive analytic knowledge; an insight into a hidden wisdom, an insight which is "contrasted with sense, reason and analysis, which are regarded as blind guides leading to the morass of illusion."

(ii) the belief in unity which refuses to admit opposition or division anywhere. This sense of unity is associated with a feeling of infinite peace.

(iii) the belief in the unreality of time.

(iv) the belief that all evil is mere appearance.[2]

William James in his *Varieties of Religious Experiences* says that the mystical state is characterized by ineffability, transciency, passivity, consciousness of oneness of everything, sense of timelessness and immediacy. W.T. Stace has made a search to find out "the universal core of mysticism" and he has laid down the following seven propositions:

1. There is a unifying vision, in which the One is perceived by the senses in and through many objects, so the "All is One."

2. The One is apprehended as an inner life, or presence in all things, so that "nothing is really dead."
3. This brings a sense of reality, which is objective and true.
4. There is a feeling of satisfaction, joy and bliss.
5. There is a feeling of the holy and the sacred, which is the specifically religious element of the experience.
6. There is a feeling that it is paradoxical.
7. There is a feeling that it is inexpressible in words.[3]

According to Albert Einstein, even science is mystical in nature. He wrote that the finest thing we can experience is mystery. It is the fundamental emotion that is at the roots of true science. Those who do not know it, those who cannot admire, those who are no longer capable of experiencing a sense of wonder might as well be dead.[4]

Aldous Huxley's series of experiments with drug mescaline is an attempt to describe mystic experiences in terms of drugs.[5]

Generally mysticism is termed as consummation, but what that consummation would be no one can say in words. It is an instantaneous, intuitive insight loaded with the feeling that it is not accessible to common sense, rational training or learning.

With these Western definitions in the background, we may better appreciate mysticism as exemplified in the *Tirumandiram* and grasp its scope as we proceed further.

1. 2. Mysticism and poetry

The first point that is to be noted is that the mysticism of the *Tirumandiram* is couched in the poetic form. This suggests that there are intimate connections between the mystical and the poetic forms. Arnold Toynbee has said that the truth apprehended by mystic experience finds its natural expression in poetry.[6] The Siddhas feel that only in the poetic form can intense, spiritual, mystical experiences be indicated. Language other than poetry is inadequate even to hint at the experience of the mystics. Poetry can express insights and intuitions. It conveys a great deal more while saying less; and it suggests a world of meaning different from all other verbalized forms of expression. Kenneth Bryant has made an important distinction between *saguṇa* (with attributes) and *nirguṇa* (attributeless) poetry. Whereas *saguṇa* poetry is based on a story, the only basis for *nirguṇa* poetry is the poet's personal intuitive experience. While the *saguṇa* poet presents a narrative or a drama, all that the *nirguṇa* poet can present is moments of realisation.[7] Since the *Tirumandiram* expresses an openness to a wonderful transcendence, with its conciseness and intensity, we may call it *nirguṇa* poetry. As poetry, the *Tirumandiram* exhibits a profound connection between the mystical and the aesthetic.

1. 3. Bōgar's understanding of mysticism

Before continuing with the mysticism of the *Tirumandiram*, let us pass in review Bōgar's views.

In *Śiva-Yōga Jñāṉam-12*,[8] Bōgar uses a technical phrase *vēdānta-t-turiyam*. It is the super-conscious state of experience, which is the state of silence itself. In verse 12 of the same poem Bōgar uses the term samādhi to refer to the mystical super-conscious state of experience. Samādhi is a state of the self knowing itself; it means self-knowledge where the experiencer (self) and the experienced (Self or Brahman) are lost in experiencing (ecstasy). Samādhi is a mystical state of experience which is a realization of one's original identity or oneness with the Reality, which state of experience is completely indescribable. It is a state where the experiencer becomes the experience and the one melting and merging with existence. In verse 7 of *Samādhi-Dīkṣai-10*,[9] Bōgar uses "stopping of time" as the state of samādhi. Samādhi means an experience of eternal presence; an eternal nowness. That is, mystical experience is an experience of the death of time. In verse 11 of *Aṣṭāṅga-Yōgam-24*,[10] Bōgar defines mystical experience as "an experience beyond Vedānta knowledge" *(vēdāntam kaḍanda iḍam)*. In verse 76 of *Upadēśa-Jñāṉam-156*,[11] Bōgar uses a significant paradoxical expression, *tēṅgāmal tēṅgum yōgam* which indicates the nature of mystical experience. *Tēṅgāmal tēṅgum yōgam* means "non-stagnating, stagnating Yoga," like the paradoxical expression "sleepless sleep." It means "non-stagnating, fullness (stagnating) of Yoga" Anything that is full does not develop further, hence it stagnates. But in the case of mystic experience there is the fullness of experience without stagnation. This fullness of mystical experience is not static, nor does it stagnate; it is always dynamic full of energy and activity, yet transcendental. This "non-stagnating stagnation of mystical experience" is one more paradoxical expression indicating the nature of mysticism.

1. 4. Tirumūlar's insight into mysticism

Tirumūlar uses *yoga-samādhi* as a term to indicate mystic experience. *Yoga-samādhi* is infinite space, abiding light and omnipotent energy, which are other expressions for mystic experience.[12] He calls mystic experience "a state of deeper inner nature" or *corugi-k-kiḍakkum tuṟai* in Tamil.[13] This term *corugi-k-kiḍakkum tuṟai* (literal translation is "penetrating field") means a hidden, deep, unexpressed and inexpressible state of consciousness, which can be experienced by "the penetration of the self into itself," i.e., by *yoga-samādhi*. This term is the exact

Tamil equivalent for mystical experience as used by Tirumūlar. Tirumūlar uses another expression, "the place (of tranquility) where Vedas terminated" *(curudi muḍinda iḍam)*.[14] *Tiru-viḷaiyāḍal-purāṇam* uses a similar expression to indicate mystic experience as "the inexpressible (hidden) purity to describe which even Vedas hesitate"*(vēdam kiḍandu taḍumāṟum vañca veḷi)*.[15] The other expressions used by Tirumūlar to indicate mystic experiences are:

(i) *Niradicayāṉandam,*[16] meaning eternal bliss;

(ii) *oppilā-āṉandam,*[17] meaning peerless bliss;

(iii) *cōmbu,*[18] meaning divine tranquility;

(iv) *cutta-caṅgāram,*[19] (pure mergence or pure dissolution or pure absorption) meaning "being completely actionless," "the merging of the mental cognates in the infinite," "soul remaining completely free" and "the soul merging in primal quiescence;"

(v) *Śivānaṉda,*[20] meaning the blissful state of Śiva, attained by the soul after it has renounced all its connections with birth and death;[21]

(vi) *amuda-nilai,*[22] meaning the state of ambrosial bliss;

(vii) *Siddha-atīta state,*[23] meaning pure state of beyond;

(viii) *cugōdayam,*[24] meaning blissful experience/knowledge;

(ix) *tiru-neṟi,*[25] meaning the divine state of consciousness where one attains Śiva's nature;

(x) *taṉṉai aṟiyum aṟivu,*[26] means the experience which knows the self as Self.

According to Tirumūlar mystical experience is a state of transcendental awareness or a state of oneness. The state of oneness or mystical state is described by him as follows:

Meditating in oneness, I visioned paraparam,
Meditating in oneness, I realized Siva-State,
Meditating in oneness, I experienced Awareness Transcendental
Meditating in oneness, I witnessed aeons and aeons.[27]

He further says that this mystical state is one, which cannot be comprehended even by an artist who always has a deeper insight into things. [28]

1. 5. Mystics and their characteristics

What mystic experience is may be indicated by taking into consideration the terms used by Tirumūlar to refer to the mystics and also the characterization he makes of them. He uses such terms as "discoverers in sleep" *(tūṅgi-k-kaṇḍār),*[29] "those who realize by non-verbal experience" *(urai-aṟṟu-uṇarvōr),*[30] "one who realizes oneself as Self" *(tām-aṟivār)*[31] "Lord of tattvas" *(Śiva-tattuvar)*[32] "Śaivas of pure intensity" *(kaḍum-cutta-caivar)*[33] "and unwavering yogins" *(naḍukkaṟṟa-yōgigaḷ).*[34]

The following verses of the *Tirumandiram* give an idea of mysticism by delineating the characteristic features of the mystics, *(kaḍum-cutta-caivar)* which require no further explanation. One can understand what mysticism stands for by going through the following (sample) verses.

The Jnani masters all sacred lore on earth,
And the attainments sixty and four
And espies the Land of Mauna
And all other land besides;
He sees the goal of all Vedas
And sees Lord and himself united in one.[35]

He stills the incessant flow of thought
That even Yoga's severity stills not,
With Jnana he effaces the Self
And in Bhava identifies with Siva;
That in brief is worthy Jnani's story. [36]

You and He are not two separate
You and He are but one united;
Thus do you stand,
Freed of all sectarian shackles;
Adore the Feet of Paraparai
And with Siva become One;
That the way Siddhanta fulfills.[37]

They are not for outward form and attire,
They are not for pomp and ceremony,
Uprooting all bond and desire,
Abiding in the Immaculate Lord,
They bring to die destruction,
The Soul's egoity and its bondage beginningless
Thus they onward leap,
With Siva's light suffused
They, of Suddha Saiva Way.[38]

When you scorch Impurities five
And listen to the Voice of Silence
You become a pure Mukta;
And I and you in one merge;
You shall joy of the Bliss Divine;
Verily, then by Sanmarga Path
You become He indeed.[39]

The heart of the holy trembles not in fear,
All passions stilled, it enjoys calm unruffled;
Neither is there death
Nor pain, nor night nor day,
Nor fruits of Karma to experience;
That truly is the state of the desire-renounced.[40]

The annihilating of the Self
The Self-becoming He
The identity in Siva
The Mudra setting the state ultra
All these and the rest they had,
They who received deliverance at the Feet of Nandi.[41]

They the Awareness have, see world all,
They the Awareness have, know sorrows none,
When they that Awareness have truly realized,
They indeed have the truth... seen.[42]

1. 6. The method of appreciation

All the efforts to present a "picture" of mystical experience clearly show that ineffability is the common characteristic of mysticism. As Tennyson says it is an experience "which does often lie too deep for tears." Since mystic experience is wholly unconceptualizable, the method to be adopted for an "understanding" of mysticism is the method of appreciation and not the method of description. Mystic experience is a meaningful one though not in verbal terms. To use Russell's familiar phrase it can be understood only by "knowledge by acquaintance." To indicate this experience Tirumūlar uses a significant expression, "an experience without a name" *(nāmam a͟ra ni͟r͟ral)*.[43] Bōgar in his *Jñā͟na-cūttiram-1* uses a beautiful expression, "which is not understandable in verse, but grasped in one stroke by sharing."[44] Bōgar says that even poetry, where intense spiritual experiences can be verbalized, cannot express them adequately. Felt experiences cannot be translated fully in expressible language. Our language is but a broken light to convey the significance of felt experiences. Only by "sharing" one can indicate the meaning of such experiences. "Sharing" is the one and the only way of "understanding" the great felt truths, which in essence is intimate appreciation. Intimate appreciation is felt explanation and it only can take us to the "spirit" of mystical experience, which is the quality of the heart. When the mystic tries to communicate what is incommunicable by its very nature, one lands in paradoxical language and sometimes in twilight language, which form the integral part of Siddha mysticism.

2. The Phenomenology of Consciousness

The phenomenon of consciousness remains a mystery not only to modern science but to every thinker. It expresses itself in different forms and under different names, but its own nature is ineffable and mystical.

Consciousness is not a substance nor an illusory phenomenon or epiphenomonon. Nor can it be understood or controlled as a machine or an animal body. Consciousness is the deepest *telos* immanent in the evolutionary process of nature and society. To realize the full nature of consciousness would be to realize divinity on earth.[45]

It is said that within the "atoms" of consciousness lie particles of all experience even as in taste of honey lie all riches of flowers, fruit and leaf.

Consciousness is a large complex of awareness, which includes our ordinary mind, the subconscious ones below the mind, and the super-conscious ones above the mind and the subliminal consciousness, which includes non-ordinary levels of consciousness. In Yoga a lotus flower indicates the different levels of consciousness. In India the subliminal consciousness is spoken of as a field having the five inner sheaths or the *kośas,* called the *annamaya-kośa,* the sheath of matter consisting of the physical body, the *prāṇamaya-kośa,* the sheath of life, the *manomaya-kośa,* the sheath of conscious activity, the *vijñānamaya-kośa,* the sheath of intelligence and the *ānandamaya-kośa,* the sheath of bliss. The individual consciousness or self is enveloped within these bodies. Each sheath is within the previous one and thus it becomes subtler and subtler, one within the next.

The individual soul, the jīva, undergoes five states of experience or consciousness—*jāgrat,* waking experience, *svapna,* dream experience, *suṣupti,* deep sleep experience, *turiya,* the fourth state of consciousness, which is beyond the changing modes of existence, and *turiyātīta,* the state of consciousness which is in a totally blissful condition. *Turiyātīta,* i.e., the fifth state of consciousness is not there in the Vedānta. These five states of consciousness and the five bodies *(kośas)* are discussed in the *Tirumandiram,* under the section "the five divisions of the body."[46]

The individual states of experience are called *avasthās* in Indian philosophy. These are states of consciousness. According to Tirumūlar *avasthās* or states of consciousness are broadly classified into five. They are *kīḻāl-avasthā* (lower *avasthā*), *madhya-avasthā* (the middle *avasthā* also known as *sakala-avasthā*), *śuddha-avasthā* (also known as *kevala-avasthā*), *parā-avasthā* (the dynamic state of pure consciousness), *mēlāl-avasthā* (also called *Śiva-avasthā* or *nirmala-avasthā*). Each of these five *avasthās* (states of consciousness) has the following five sub-divisions—*jāgrat, svapna, suṣupti, turiya* and *turiyātīta*. For a detailed description of these broad states and inner states of consciousness one has to make a special study of *tantra* Eight of the *Tirumandiram*, which is not within the scope of this chapter.

Consciousness is the common denominator of both the jīva-consciousness and Śiva-consciousness. The jīva-consciousness is entangled in the senses and other extraneous factors and once it forces itself from all the shackles of jīva-experience that surround consciousness, it is the same as Śiva-consciousness. Jīva-consciousness *does not become* Śiva-consciousness, but it *is* Śiva-consciousness itself. When the jīva-consciousness is engulfed in delusion, it is *acit*-consciousness; but when the delusion is removed, it is *cit*-consciousness, an integral aspect of Sat-cit-ānanda. The jīva-consciousness "becoming" one with the Śiva-consciousness is called *viśva-grāsam* or total absorption by Tirumūlar.[47] Let us quote three verses from this section on total-absorption from the *Tirumandiram*, to understand the absolute merging of the jīva-Śiva consciousness.

> Even as shadow disappears with body,
> Even as bubble returns into water,
> Even as flame of camphor leaves traces none,
> So is it when Jiva into Param unites.[48]

> When body and Jiva
> As unbroken unite (in Yoga)
> Then shall Grace of Siva Sakti be;
> Then does Jiva, Param become;
> Jiva that leaves this body,
> Pervasive then becomes;
> With beginning and end none
> In Siva forever it merges.[49]

Jiva becomes Para;
That Para pervasive stands;
Immanent too in all creation it is;
A mighty Power it is,
That can dissolve and create universe vast,
This was the boon granted to me;
And thus is my state exalted.[50]

In this connection it is worthwhile to note how Bōgar tries to explain the process of absorption and merging, i.e., *laya*, by providing certain similes. The process of merging should be like the wick and the ghee being absorbed in the light-lamp, like the rain water being absorbed by the sun, like the colors being absorbed by the crystal, like the bubble being absorbed by the deep water, like the produced sound being absorbed and lost in the ether.[51] Similarly jīva-consciousness should be merged in the Śiva-consciousness. Though the *laya* state cannot be explained by similes, yet Bōgar uses them as indicators of it without being that one itself.

2. 1. Yoga as the science of consciousness

Regarding Yoga as the science of consciousness G.C. Pande writes as follows:

> Yoga is the practical aspect of the science of consciousness. It aims at the direct intuitive knowledge of consciousness in action. The principal means of *yoga* is the cultivation of a cognitive state of the mind called *samādhi* or putting together, concentration or integration. It is different from the states of sleep and dreaming because it is a state of high alertness and lucidity. It is also different from the waking state because it is free from the distraction of speech and thoughts, sensations

> and images, feelings and desires. It is a lucid and tranquil flow of the mind in which the ripples of objectivity and mediated subjectivity subside. The non-selfhood of the momentary mental states is easily understood and along with it is glimpsed the timeless and noumenal transcendental nature of consciousness. But *yoga* is a long process of withdrawl and ascent to ever higher levels of consciousness which is in reality the infinite matrix of all possible universes as also the hidden *telos* of Evolution or the very process of Time. Since the detached and objective exploration of one's own consciousness requires that one should not be ruffled by physical and social distractions and since yoga is a long time search like emptying the ocean with a blade of grass, it requires a long ascetic training. Yoga is a science but it is not amoral or value-free. Knowing the true self requires a firm detachment from one's habitual lower self. As to the phenomenology of consciousness in action, several models have been presented in yogic systems.[52]

The *Tirumandiram,* as a Yoga treatise, provides one such model with the knowledge of various states and levels of consciousness. Not only that, it also gives us the practical methods of verifying them by fresh achievements in one's own being. If one studies deeper the verses of the *Tirumandiram,* one can have a vast and opulent treasure of the knowledge of consciousness in Yoga. One can adopt what Kireet Joshi has said about Yoga to the *Tirumandiram* as well.

> Yoga affirms that there are extraordinary states of consciousness, accessible to us by a methodized effort. These include not only states and powers of the subliminal consciousness and of dreams and visions but also the following:

a. Presence of the invisible;
b. Consciousness of Purification;
c. Psychology of Concentration: Meditation and Contemplation;
d. Waking consciousness, dream consciousness, sleep consciousness, transcendental consciousness *(jagrat, swapna, sushupti, turiya)* in the light of the psychology of *Samādhi*;
e. Awakening of *kundalini* and consequent realizations;
f. Soul-consciousness; *Chaitya Purusha* and *Jivatman;*
g. Cosmic Consciousness;
h. Liberation from the Ego; *Jivan Mukti, Videha mukti, Nirvana, Kaivalya.*
i. Liberation and perfection of Nature: *Sadharmyamukti*;
j. *Ashtasiddhi*;
k. Status and action of Equality *(Samattvam)*;
l. Consciousness of infinity and Eternity: Space-time and spaceless–timeless;
m. Super conscious planes: Higher Mind, Illumined Mind, Intuitive Mind, Overmind and Super mind;
n. Consciousness of Sachchidananda (Existence-Consciousness-Bliss).

In the new awaking in the world which leads us to concentrate on the theme of Consciousness, it would be highly relevant to make a detailed study of these and other experiences and realizations which give us a direct access to what may significantly be called the Infinite Ocean of Consciousness.[53]

One may say that another name for mystical experience is Cosmic Consciousness.

2. 2. Are there mystic experiences?

Before concluding this section a question may be raised and answered. Can any one doubt or deny mystic experience? No. An "interpretation" of mystic experience can be doubted, but the experience itself is indubitable; for the mystic is absolutely certain of the truth of his/her experience beyond the possibility of arguing him/her out of it. As the world-renowned Advaitin, Professor R. Balasubramanian used to write:

> What is affirmed by consciousness through its intentional performance can never be denied and what is denied by consciousness through its intentional performance can never be accepted.[54]

Mystic experiences cannot be considered as "true" or "false" in the ordinary sense in which empirical facts are true or false, for they go beyond the "either-or" pattern of the logic of understanding. As Suzuki says mystical experience is a state of absolute Suchness, of absolute emptiness, which is absolute fullness[55] which cannot be understood by the categories of understanding, but which can be "caught" in one's own individual moments of experience. It is a deep participation through the heart not through discursive intellect. Mystic experience is "poetic truth;" the language of "poetic truth" is depth or expressive language; and the language of empirical truth is the steno-language, the language of science.[56] In short, mystical experience is free from all theories of explanation and proof. A mystic has no proof. He is the only proof. To quote W.T.Stace:

> The mystics of all countries and ages have always with one accord affirmed their experiences were "above reason or outside reason"... they meant what they said, and that what they said is true. That their experience is beyond reason

means simply that it is beyond logic. And we cannot reject this testimony unless we reject the whole of mysticism as a fraud. It is evident that all those who have mystical experience feel that there is some sense in which that experience is utterly unique, utterly unlike any commonsense kind of experience, completely incommensurable with the sense experience of the space-time world. He who reaches up to the mystical consciousness has reached a plane utterly outside and beyond the plane of everyday consciousness, not to be understood or judged by the standards or criteria of that plane. It is very clear that mystics feel this. But all attempts to show that the mystical paradoxes can be got rid of by some logical or linguistic device are just so many attempts to reduce mysticism to common sense, to take away its unique character, and reduce it to the level of our everyday experience. There is nothing wrong with common sense or with everyday experience. But we cannot have it both ways. We cannot both believe that the mystical consciousness is unique, different in mind from our ordinary consciousness, and yet at the same time that there is nothing in it which cannot be "reduced" to our ordinary consciousness.[57]

3. The corugi-k-kiḍakkum tuṟai

Liberation or *mokṣa* or *vīḍu* (in Tamil) is a mystical state which is referred to as *yoga-samādhi* by Tirumūlar.[58] Liberation is a process of giving up. To quote Tirumūlar:

To give up thoughts of women
To think no more of kith and kin
To be meek in learning
To abound in jnana

To be sparing of speech
To listen to deeds of Siddhi
To sit unruffled
These the ways of the aspirant of yoga samadhi.[59]

Liberation is renunciation; it is true *sanyāsa*. True *sanyāsa,* it is said, is to renounce your son, i.e., pride, your brother, i.e., wealth; your wife, i.e., desire and your house, i.e., delusion. Yājñavalkya characterized renunciation as the transcendence of attachment to everything, including the desire for renunciation itself. Tirumūlar goes to the extent of suggesting the abandonment of everything, including the abandonment of the desire to attain Godhead.[60] He has defined Vedānta as a process of achieving desirelessness. Vedānta is the way of renouncing desires.[61] Liberation or mystical experience is in itself an existential fact. *Mukti, mokṣa, vīḍu,* nirvikalpa-samādhi, *sahaja* and nirvāṇa are some of the names for the mystical state of being. Liberation is a disentanglement of oneself from every narrow, limited identification. Tirumūlar says that the mystical state is one where the self is free from any religious identification.[62] In short, mystic experience simply means the moment when there is nothing to be experienced. All experiences are dissolved. One sits alone in one's purity. One cannot call it an experience even.

3. 1. Divine vision

Tirumūlar's mysticism is *vivekaja-jñāna,* an experience which is pulsating with undecipherable mystery. *Vivekaja-jñāna* is referred to as *aruṭkaṇ,* divine vision, by Tirumūlar.[63] As Bhadragiriyār says it is "knowledge which knows knowledge through knowing knowledge."[64] The term jñāna has been used by Tirumūlar to mean an insight into the nature of the self. He often used the simile of light when talking about self or consciousness. He calls jñāna or wisdom or knowledge as *teḷivu* in Tamil. He also uses the term *saṇmārga* for the path of jñāna.[65] *Teḷivu* means "illuminative wisdom" or "proper understanding." According to Tirumūlar without *teḷivu,* one cannot attain the blessed state of *mukti* or selfhood.

> Without wisdom one shall never know Śiva;
> Without wisdom one shall never be jīva
> Without wisdom one shall never become Śiva;
> Without wisdom one shall never terminate the bondage of birth.[66]

He confirms the significance of this verse in another verse by saying that only the truly wise attain heavenly bliss *(kaṟṟavar pēriṉbam uṟṟu niṉṟarē).*[67] Only jñāna can unite the limited self with the unlimited Self just as understanding unites perceptions with concepts.

3. 2. Self-realization

Tirumūlar calls self-realization as "the knowledge, which knows the Self."[68] It is a state of being a leader of one's own self.[69] He regrets that earlier he was ignorant of that which knows itself.[70] and feels happy that once he knows his self, he does not know, nay, need not know, anything other than that.[71] He calls self-knowledge as genuine knowledge and the rest is but knowledge demented.[72]

Self-knowledge, according to the Siddhas, is a realization of one's original identity or "oneness" with Sivam or God. Tirumūlar defines samādhi or self-knowledge as a state where the "I" becomes the "He."[73] Self-realization reveals that what we call God is inside one's own self.[74] This should be interpreted as an insight of not "my" awareness, but the Being's awareness of Itself in "me." Tirumūlar is emphatic that self-realization is a process where the jīva (as self) identifies itself with Śiva (as Self) and he calls this "as the great seal of jñāna.[75] When the mystic attains Śivahood he is thrown into an abyss of love, possessing simultaneously the mystic light, vision, peace and joy. Mystical realization finds its achievement in absorption in Śiva—the ultimate realization of one's true nature. Self-realization is the bliss of the Siddha, the bliss being the knowledge that the ultimate is in oneself. According to Tirumūlar's view the self in man is the ultimate substance behind the world of phenomena. Tirumūlar exhibits his love of Tamil language by comparing *mukti* and jñāna with the "sound of music of the three kinds of literature of Tamil— *iyal* (literature), *icai* (music), *nāḍagam* (drama).[76]

3. 3. How does self-realization take place?

Now a question may arise: How does self-realization take place? How is it possible that the self in "me" is the Self in Him and vice versa? Self-realization can be achieved only when one can realize the immensity within one's soul as detached from one's ego. In the words of Śiva-vākkiyar the moment the "I" dies, it is achieved.[77] All mental and physical actions of the human being are the expressions of the "I-ness." From the Siddha point of view this "I-ness" is the indication of a narrow expression of consciousness in which the real self has been "isolated" and remains unknown. The highest spiritual attainment is to make the "restricted I" completely absorbed in the "Supreme I." It is not a state of the annihilation of the self, because Self is immortal. It is a self emptied of profane desires and worldly attachments. Immortality can be experienced only when the self is free from the bondage of "I-ness." The individual self does not exist independently of the Highest Self. It is not a separate entity as it is in essence the Highest Self itself. Indeed there is no "thou" nor "I" nor "other." In the supreme state the "I" in the human being and the "He" have become one and the same. It is a "Thou-I" state, not a state of "I and Thou," which represents pluralism. All is self. Tirumūlar is emphatic that there is no "I' and "mine."

I sought Him in terms of I and You
But He that knows not I from You
Taught me the truth, "I" indeed is "You"
And now I talk not of I and You.[78]

According to Tirumūlar in the ultimate state of the self one is not even aware of the effacing of the ego.[79] This ultimate state is a unitive experience where there is no distinction between "I" and "Thou."[80] Self-realization is a state where the sense of otherness disappears, but the sense of integrity persists. It is a state where "I" experience the "other" in myself and the "other than myself" experiences me.[81] Self-realization is a state of spiritual impersonality not because it denies ego but because it transcends it. Impersonal is used as opposed to the thing dependent on name, body and form, what is called personality. "Impersonal" here means the infinite dimension underlying the finite ego. In this sense to attain liberation is to become impersonal.

3. 4. Sanmārga

Tirumūlar calls the method or process of "I becoming "He" as the *sanmārga* (which literally means the path of virtue),[82] and calls mystic vision itself as the vision of the *sanmārgi*. The term *sanmārgi* as used by Tirumūlar is the equivalent to the word mystic. *Sanmārga* is the path of illumination *(oḷi-neṟi)*, which makes the yogins to realize that he is none other than Śiva. It is *Śiva-neṟi*, "the way of Śiva."[83] A *sanmārgi* is called by Tirumūlar as Śiva-Yoga-Siddha,[84] and *sanmārga* is called Siddha-Yoga.[85] *Sanmārga* leads to supreme bliss.

When you scorch Impurities five
And listen to the Voice of Silence
You become a pure Mukta;
And I and you in one merge;
And by the unsullied grace Jnana grants
You shall joy of the Bliss Divine;
Verily then by *Sanmarga* path
You become He indeed.[86]

The five impurities are: āṇava (egoity), karma (action), māyā (delusion), *māyeya* (results of delusion), and *tirodhāyi* (concealment). He also says that *sanmārga* merges "I in You" by transcending the limits of the *turiya* state.[87] According to Tirumūlar *sanmārga* "gives the jīva the "rest" that knows no commotion ever."[88]

3. 5. Oneness of jīva and Śiva

According to Tirumūlar once self-realization is attained jīva and Śiva become one and the same,[89] making the jīva discard the four forms[90] of āṇava, karma, māyā and attachment to self. As Eddington pointed out the mystic self-realization is like the idem potent symbol of modern mathematical physics the square of which is equal to itself, ($J^2 = J$).[91] Tirumūlar makes a mystic equation between the "I" and the "He," between the self and the Absolute.[92] This mystical equation does not refer to a numerical or logical identity of the self and the Absolute. It is the assertion of a meta-logical identity. The identity between the jīva and Śiva belongs to experience or direct apprehension and not to the interpretation. The "oneness" is an experienced certainty. It is an experience of the dissolution of the separate personality, the jīva melting, dissolving in the thought of Śiva,[93] a fading of the "I" into the Boundless Being. Tirumūlar likens the emergence and absorption of jīva into Śiva as follows:

> The fierce rays of the sun beating upon the water,
> The dissolved salt does in crystal shapes emerge;
> That salt in water dissolved becomes liquid again,
> So does Jiva in Siva get redissolved.[94]

Tirumūlar compares this mergence as follows:

> The tiny atom, swimming in the universe vast,
> Merges in the Vast– no separate existence knows.[95]

That is "I" have known not myself as Śivam, but have known myself as not different from Śiva. "That is, Śivam made me know as Self *(tvam)* transformed me into That *(tat)* and made me known as Śiva *(asi)*." That is, *Tat Tvam Asi* "That Thou Art."[96] The "oneness" between the "I" and the Absolute is of an extra-ordinary character. It is said that this "oneness" is a technical one (it is a *paribhāṣa*). For want of a better expression the "oneness" is termed as "super union" and this is what is termed Yoga. Yoga in essence, is oneness; it is ecstatic transcendence. This mystical oneness between the self and the Self is an undivided oneness. As Tirumūlar says that when one light merges in another light there will be only light.[97] Due to ignorance this oneness between Brahman or Śiva and ātman or jīva is not known. The eye sees several things, yet it does not see itself.[98] We are Brahman/Śiva, but we do not know that we are. Pattiṉattār's lament is significant. "We are inside the river, but yet we are in search of the bathing ghat to go to the river."[99] It is like hearing of a fish in water as athirst. When jīva-Śiva identity is attained, all other things pale into insignificance. Tirumūlar writes:

Within them,
(Who have attained Siva-State)
There is fire, water and air;
The sun and the moon are there seated;
Hari, Brahma and Rudra
Are also in their heart.[100]

3. 6. Vettaveli

In Siddha literature, liberation is referred to as *veḷi,* or *para-kāyam,* eternal space. Tirumūlar uses the term *kaḍuveḷi* for liberation.[101] He also calls the state of liberation as unsullied, untinged, immaculate *veḷi.*[102] *Veṭṭaveḷi* is a common term used by many Siddhas. *Veṭṭaveḷi* is *ākāśa*— as *ākāśa* it is pervasive in character. Tirumūlar refers to this pervasive nature of *ākāśa* when he speaks of *ākāśa* as external and as internal— *jagat-ākāśa* and *ākāśa* in Śivam.[103] The term *veṭṭaveḷi* refers to an infinite transcendental awareness; it is not my or your or our awareness, but the awareness of Being itself. *Veṭṭaveḷi* also stands for freedom from time. It is a "place" where there is neither night nor day.[104] Hence the perfected yogin is referred to as *kāla-atīta* or "one who has transcended time." The yogin is liberated from the future as well as the past and lives in *akāla* or "non-historical time" or "primordial time." *Akāla* has neither a before nor an after; it is an eternal now. In that realm of *veṭṭaveḷi,* which is nowness, which is always an instant eternity or eternity in-itself, which is "time" rediscovered by the yogin, where the small personal pronouns become meaningless. The sense of timelessness or emergence from time constitutes one of the meanings of *veṭṭaveḷi.*

3. 7. Śūnya/Nirvāṇa

The term *kaḍuveḷi* is used by Tirumūlar to refer to *veṭṭaveḷi.*[105] *Kaḍuveḷi* is indeterminate void and it is called śūnya by the Siddhas.

Śūnya is not emptiness; it refers to "unsubstantiality;" it is an open dimension which is not bound by concepts and percepts and is beyond the space-time matrix. It is free of duality and discursive thought. It is not nothingness but fullness itself. It is content-less consciousness, which has no content except itself, it being the oneness of the totality of things. It is not the negation of "is-ness" but the negation of all determinations. It is a state of undifferentiation. It is empty space without a centre. Śūnya is not a "theory" advocated by the Siddhas; in fact, it is the end of "all theories" about Reality. It is the absence of subjectivity and objectivity; where all distinctions are emptied. It is a state of bliss and tranquility, which is referred to by Tirumūlar as *yoga-nirvāṇa* or *jñāna-nirvāṇa*.[106] The term nirvāṇa used by Tirumūlar[107] is significant, because to call that state as existence or non-existence or even a state of bliss would impose a limitation. Nirvāṇa is loss of all sense of personality in a boundless cosmic consciousness, which is *perum-cuga-veḷi*, the great blissful state.[108]

In one sense nirvāṇa may mean absence of things. As such it may mean negation. Speaking about the mystical negation Eckhart observes:

> The divine One is a negation of negations... what does One mean? Something to which nothing is to be added.... The One is a negation of negations. Every creature contains a negation: one denies that it is the other. An angel denies that it is any other creature, but God contains the denial of denials. He is that One who denies of every other that it is anything except himself.[109]

In this sense nirvāṇa is not a positive word. In Upaniṣadic thinking all positive words have boundaries. Negative words do not have any boundaries. As such nirvāṇa may mean the unbounded, the limitless, infinite peace. Although nirvāṇa may mean complete negation, a mere absence, yet it is also a positive experience, in the sense that it is consciousness, which is not a consciousness of any particular existence. It is an experience without any images. It is imageless emptiness, an imageless vision. As Eckhart says:

> If you are to experience this... you must depart from all crowds... The crowds are the agents of the soul and their activities: memory, understanding and will in all their diversifications. You must leave them all: sense perceptions, imagination.[110]

The concept of śūnya or nirvāṇa is a paradoxical one and W.T. Stace calls it as the Vaccum-plenum paradox.[111] *Veṭṭaveḷi* or śūnya also stands for *oḷi* or blazing light. Tirumūlar uses the expression light vision of space, i.e., *kaḍu-oḷi.*[112] It is said that a yogin's body is a countless tissue of lights. In one of the verses, Tirumūlar says that he lived for seven crore *yugas* (aeons).[113] This phrase "lived for seven crore years" has been interpreted by G.Varadarajan in his commentary on the *Tirumandiram* that Tirumūlar lived "as blaze of light."[114] In the *Tirumandiram* we have a whole section dealing with this blazing light, which is an expression of divinity where images and metaphors relating to luminosity such as light, flame, fire, lamp, etc., are used.[115]

Another term that is used for *veṭṭaveḷi* or *kaḍuveḷi* is *pāḻ* or *muppāḻ,* which means vast expanse or emptiness.

3. 8. Muppāḻ

The concept *muppāḻ* is a significant one in Siddha literature. Almost all the Siddhas use this concept in their poems. People who have studied Siddha literature use the term *muppāḻ* as referring to eternal space without comprehending what constitutes *muppāḻ*. The Siddhas use this term *muppāḻ* to conceal certain things from the ordinary reader. Commonly *muppāḻ* is referred to as *veṭṭaveḷi* or eternal empty space or the pervasive nature of *ākāśa*. The Buddhist text *Guhya-samāja Tantra* speaks of "stainless sky," which is the same as *veṭṭaveḷi* or *pāḻ* or *muppāḻ*.

Among all the Siddhas only in Bōgar and Tirumūlar one finds a hint of the meaning and significance of the term *muppāḻ*. Bōgar speaks of *muppāḻ* in many places in his works, but in verse 1 of *Jñāṉa-cārāmcam-100* and in verse 124 of *Upadēśa-jñāṉam-156* one finds a clear elucidation of the term *muppāḻ*.[116]

The translation of verse 1 of *Jñāṉa-cārāmcam* runs as follows:

Inside that open space there (is) bright empty space;
The protective empty space (is) open space of empty space;
The fact being the Absolute inside the Absolute;
Itself becoming Śiva inside Śiva;
Becoming the source as Śakti inside Śakti;
The self inside the source is the sound;
Inside the sound experiences the renowned Sadāśivam.
(Author's own translation).

The summary of this verse is: Real wisdom consists in comprehending the attributeless, the featureless empty space, which is known as "three empty spaces" (in Tamil *muppāḻ*). The three empty spaces are spaces "within" the empty space. It is like the Absolute within the Absolute, Śiva itself becoming Śiva, Śakti itself becoming the source of Śakti. The self inside this source is the sound; inside the sound one should experience Sadāśivam.

Here we find that there is a kind of tension when Bōgar tries to speak about the Absolute reality as empty space, etc. Bōgar feels that the experience is inexpressible and translinguistic and at the same tries to describe it in such language as "inside open space there is bright empty, empty space; the protective bright space is open space." This is the paradox of mystical experience, expressing in language the one, which is really inexpressible.

Translation of verse 124 of *Upadēsa-jñāṉam-156* is:

> View with interest the body and the (five) elements in the first eternal space;
> If realized with care one will become a scholar;
> If the shining second eternal space is reached
> (One) will become a Siddha of sixty-four;
> Leaving that if one enters the third eternal space
> It is the place of the origin of the strong vital air (prana);
> If perceived with concern the place where the despising four geneses go
> One will seek a remote place (where) the Lord of Death will tremble.
>
> (Author's own translation).

The summary of this verse is: The first eternal space *(mudal-pāḻ)* is the space of the existence of the five elements (the *mahā-bhūtas*) and the body constituting them. If one understands this eternal space, he is a scholar. The second eternal space is where one becomes a Siddha by attaining the sixty-four *siddhis*. The third eternal space is the place of the vital air, *prāṇa*. If one understands with concern where the four modes of genesis of life go, one (the yogin) will seek a remote place where the Lord of Death cannot visit. In this verse Bōgar refers to "open space," "bright space" and "empty space." This is referred to as three "empty spaces," *muppāḻ* in Siddha literature.

Muppāḻ means three levels of eternal space. The first eternal space constitutes the five elements earth, water, fire, air and ether and the body constituted by them. A scholar studies these dimensions of reality with interest and care. In so saying Bōgar emphasizes the value of such study, as much as scientists would say today.

The second eternal space constitutes the attainment of the sixty-four siddhis, or the attainment of *Siddha-deha*, through yogic exercises and techniques of control, called "bodily siddhi."

A sādhaka who has acquired a *Siddha-deha* becomes the master of his "body." It is a "body" bereft of all limitations and bondage of the spatio-temporal world and is not governed by the physical laws; it is a supra-normal body. To a person who has attained the *Siddha-deha* the world of sense impressions does not operate. There is also the disappearance of the ego, the "I consciousness." Since the "I" is lost, one can be everywhere at any time in any form.

The third eternal space is the place of prāṇa. According to the Bhagavad-Gītā prāṇa is a conscious spiritual entity, co-existent with *ākāśa*. Prāṇa is not just respiratory breath; it is a conscious force, a subtle cosmic element. It is the dynamic counterpart of the coiled kuṇḍalinī, which is potential energy. It is the spirit which animates the universe and by which man breathes. The third eternal space is the *praṇava-deha* or *mantira-mēṉi*. It is the body of *nāda* or sound.

Bōgar uses the expression *oḷi-p-pāḻ* "bright empty space," meaning *ākāśa* and the root word of *ākāśa* is *kās,* which means to radiate, to shine. In mystical literature, light is an expression of divinity. In the Upaniṣads light is declared identical with Being and immortality. Tirumūlar also speaks of the inner light of the soul.[117]

A further elucidation of *muppāḻ* is to be found in the *Tirumandiram.*[118] A suggestive indication of what the *muppāḻ*, the three empty spaces are, is indicated by Tirumular in two verses:[119]

Experiencing the seven Caused states
The Maya space is left behind;
Experiencing the seven Causal States
The Bodha space is left behind;
Experiencing and sundering the Cause-Caused states (above)
The Upasanta Space is left behind;
Then alone is End finale.[120]

The three empty spaces *(muppāḻ)* are called the *māyā* space, the *bodha* space (or the *jīva* space), and the *upa-cānta* space (or *vyoma* space).

Māya-p-pāḻ, māyā space (or space of deception) consists in differentiating the atman from the seven caused states, that is, 1. *vidyā-tattvas,* i.e., from the five *bhūtas,* 2. from the five *tanmātras,* 3. from the five *jñānendriyas,* 4. from the five *karmendriyas,* 5. from the four *antahkaraṇas,* 6. from the prāṇa and 7. from the *prakṛti.*

Bōdha-p-pāḻ (or *jīva-p-pāḻ*), consists in differentiating the atman from the seven causal states that is, *kāla, vidyā, rāga, kāla, niyati* (the five *kañcukas*), *puruṣa* and their source aśuddha-māyā.

Upa-cānta-p-pāḻ (or *vyoma-p-pāḻ*) consists in differentiating and sundering the impressions of the above fourteen, (i.e. the seven caused states and the seven causal states). Liberation (of jīva) consists in discarding and leaving these three empty spaces. (See Appendix-F).

In verse 2496, Tirumūlar speaks of the three empty spaces of *māyā-p-pāḻ, jīva-p-pāḻ* and *vyoma-p-pāḻ* and says that due to Śiva-Śakti, these three spaces are stilled in the jīva and that the jīva realizes its pervasive character as that of the omnipresence and pervasion of Śiva. That the jīva is comprised in Śivam is the significance of the mahā-vākya— *tat-tvam-asi.*

The continuation of the idea that the jīva has become Śiva is expressed in the following verse:

Jiva having become Siva
And the triple Malas extinguished;
Ascending into the Triple voids
In Desire and Not-desire ceased
Pass into the holy state of
Satya-Jnana-Ananda Bliss;
There in that farthest Turiya of Jiva,
The Self-illuminating Manifestness (Svarupa) is.[121]

The triple voids *(muppāḻ)* referred to above may mean either the three malas (impurities), āṇava, karma and māyā or the three voids called *maya-p-pāḻ, bōdha-p-pāḻ* and *upa-cānta-p-pāḻ,* or the three aspects of māyā called prakṛti-māyā, aśuddha-māyā and śuddha-māyā. When jīva leaves these three voids either due to grace or due to its jñāna, it reaches the state of *turiya* where it passes on to the state of *satya-jñāna-ānanda,* i.e., it attains the state of *Sat-cit-ānanda* and becomes one with Śiva.

The concept of *muppāḻ* is elucidated further in the following verse:

As the brilliance, color and luster of the ruby
Being reflected in the nearby crystal

The three-termed word is in the *muppāḻ;*
With the inexpressible praṇava as the
Mudrā of jñāna one attains realization.[122]

Explanation: By contemplating on the praṇava-mantra, the Aum, which is the *mudrā* of jñāna (i.e., *cin-mudrā*), one can attain liberation. The mantra Aum is referred to as ati-sūksma-pañcākṣara in that it contains the sacred five letters *na-ma-ci-vā-ya*. This form of the mantra is a mahā-vākya, i.e., *tat-tvam-asi*, Thou Art That. *Tat* stands for Śiva, *tvam* stands for "thou" (jīva) and *asi* stands for "becomes" or "is." Thou Art That means jīva is Śiva. A whole section, section 36, is devoted by Tirumūlar in *tantra* Eight, to explain the mahā-vākya, *tat-tvam-asi.*

How can jīva become Śiva? It is explained that just as the crystal reflects the ruby in all its aspects, when it is near to it the jīva reflects Śiva in all its aspects. That is, if the jīva transcends the *muppāḻ* by contemplating on the meaning of praṇava which is the same as the mahā-vākya, *tat-tvam-asi,* then jīva has become or reflects Śiva in all its facets like a clear crystal. In this sense the three terms of the mahā-vākya and the three empty spaces (i.e. *muppāḻ*) convey one and the same thing.[123]

Having deliberated all this, Tirumūlar says that this one empty space (called śūnya), which transcends all the three empty spaces, cannot be described except that it is Śiva-knowledge-bliss, that is, *tat-para-jñāna-ānanda.* It is a state of beyond the beyond, a state of *turiya.*

Some Siddhas speak of *muppāḻ* as three spaces. The three spaces referred to by them are: 1. the outer space *(mahākāśa)*, that is the space where the universe, stars and planets are posited; 2. mental space *(cittākāśa)*, that is the space where dream world and the objects of imagination exist; 3. knowledge space *(citākāśa)*, that is the space where genuine mystical/spiritual experiences take place. In fine one may say that the term *muppāḻ* suggests that mystical experience has no "structure," it being "formless." *Kathā-Upaniṣad* says that mystical experiences are "soundless, formless, intangible." It is a formless experience and as such indescribable. Mystics usually say that their experiences are ineffable, incommunicable and indescribable.

3. 9. Indescribability

The term *veṭṭaveḷi* or *kaḍuveḷi* stands for the indescribability of the mystic experience. Tirumūlar likens mystical experience to what he calls *aṉubōga-k-kāmam*, i.e., the experiencing of the pleasure of love.[124] He also says that just as a mother cannot explain or express to her daughter her enjoyment with his father, similarly mystical experience cannot be expressed or explained in words.[125] The nature of blissful experience can be understood only by self-experience and Tirumūlar has gone to the extent of saying that the experience cannot be understood even by artists who always have a deeper insight into things.[126] He also says that even Brahma and Viṣṇu cannot understand the mystical experience of Śiva.[127] In other words, it is difficult to pin down, catch and grasp with accurate concepts and words what mystic experience stands for. One can "enjoy" mystic experience by being and living through it. Tirumūlar likens mystic experience to the enjoyment-experience of the truly learned *(kaṟṟavar pēriṉbam)*.[128] The term samādhi also expresses an experience that is completely indescribable. When something is indescribable one has to remain silent. Inviolable silence accompanies the mystic state until all is absorbed in the void or *kaḍuveḷi*. The term *veṭṭaveḷi* or *kaḍuveḷi* as an expression for mystic experience gradually led to convey the meaning of silence.

3. 10. Cummā

The concept *cummā* in Siddha literature refers to the mystical silence, even though no spoken word can name that silence without breaking it. Tirumūlar uses a strong language by calling those people fools, who try to speak or write about that which is indescribable.[129] According to Tirumūlar there is liberation in the state of silence.[130] He calls silence as the seal of the *mukta* or liberated soul.[131] *Cummā* (silence) is the silent language of the heart. It is a mystical metaphor often used for distinctionlessness. It is a state where the Absolute is not an ultimate but an intimate. Silence is a state of consent, in which all is quiet and one remains as a witness. Silence implies the witnessing consciousness. Tirumūlar makes a distinction between *mauna* (silence) and the state of dumbness.

To attain stillness of Speech and Thought at once is *mauna*

Mauna sans Speech alone
Is but state of dumbness;
Only when Speech and Thought are alike in mauna
Are you in State Suddha (Perfection)
Who but knows
That Suddha state to bring about?[132]

Silence is stillness of both thought and speech. *Mauna* without speech alone is but the state of dumbness. Perfection is stillness of both thought and speech. The "silence" stands for the unspeakable level of reality—the non-verbal, the non-symbolic and the wholly indefinable one. In the words of Tirumūlar *cummā*, then stands for "imageless liberation" or "unsepeakable bliss"[133] or a motionless state of liberation or a state where words have died.[134] It is a state where one is not able to express one's blissful experience, not even aware of the feeling that one is enjoying the bliss, a state without any "luggage" of attachments, which can be compared to a sea where no wave lashes, a state transcending the four forms of sound—*sūkṣma, paśyanthi, madhyama* and *vaikhari,* a state going beyond birth and death (another interpretation for "words have died").[135] All these words such as *veṭṭaveḷi,* śūnya, nirvāṇa, *mauna* etc., stand to describe the undifferentiated unity of mystical consciousness.

Further Tirumūlar says that the moment one has attained this state of jñāna, one becomes actionless.[136] He says that a jñāni is "sitting unmoved like a painted picture."[137] He calls such people "men without action"[138] or in Tamil *cōmbar.*[139] Hence Siddhas who have attained the state of eternal bliss are called *cōmbargaḷ.* According to Tirumūlar, only to those who are actionless, is there the divine message.[140] It is not a state of idleness, or laziness but a state of Siddhahood, which is "the occupation of all occupations." It is perfect stillness which involves no running about, no going to temples, no pilgrimages, no heated discourses, no sharp-brained discussions, etc. Tirumūlar calls *cōmbar,* "men without action," as holy ones in Śiva's robes.

> Sans illusions, sans ignorance, sans intelligence,
> Sans the embraces of fish-eyed damsels and their attachment,
> Themselves as themselves; in solitude remain one in Siva-Sakti
> Thus are they, the Holy ones in Siva's robe.[141]

Even today in Tamil Nadu it is a common thing to ask a mischievous child to keep quiet by saying "be like Śiva." The term *cōmbar* in Tamil stands for the saint[142] and not for lazy people as the present day connotation of the word goes.

3. 11. Sleepless sleep

The Siddhas say that the mystical state is the state of "sleepless sleep" which means the stilling of the mind. One should make one's sleep conscious, not to eliminate sleep altogether, but to transform it. "Sleepless sleep" is a state of restful alertness or operative rest or what the Siddhas call *aṟi-tuyil* or *yoga-nittirai* (yogic sleep or vigilant sleep). It is a state of choiceless awareness. It is a passionless state, a state where the cloud of obscurity is lifted from the soul. Tirumūlar calls it the Siddha-state and refers to it as *tūngi-k-kaṇḍār,* a state of "knowing while sleeping."[143] It is the state of unqualified emptiness. The "sleep" in "sleepless sleep" refers to the state where the senses are asleep and where the consciousness is alert. It is a mystical sleep and quietitude in which the yogin forgets all that is external. Bōgar uses the expression "awareness in sleep."[144] This may also mean "the awakened consciousness" from the sleep of daily life. It is an "egoless awareness," without any "otherness" in it.

3. 12. Beyond the beyond

Tirumūlar uses an expression "beyond, beyond the beyond," to express the mystic state of experience.[145] He calls "beyond the beyond" as *kevala-in-kevala.* This expression stands for the fact that the Absolute is beyond the three thresholds of man—the threshold of the world, the threshold of time and the threshold of his limiting consciousness. Tirumūlar uses a significant expression in Tamil, *aṇḍam-ūḍu-aṟuttāṉ,* which means "to transcend beyond the universe."[146] In all mystic literature one finds that there is a kind of tension when the saints try to speak about the reality as inexpressible and translinguistic and at the same time try to describe it in such language as "beyond the beyond." This is the paradox of mystical experience, which has been referred to by

Tirumūlar as expressing in language the one, which is really inexpressible.[147] The term "beyond the beyond" also suggests the nature of Reality as understood by Tirumūlar. It means exceeding or wider than relations. Reality includes all relations but it is "beyond" all these relations. Whereas "you" and "I" as persons have "sets" of relations, reality does not have such a "set." In this sense reality is the Absolute, i.e., Irrelative; to use Tirumūlar's expression it is *cemporuḷ*, Reality which is significant, momentous. If the Absolute is beyond relations, it must be a state of "not-two-ness," i.e., it must be one. But it is not a "one" of the many. Tirumūlar uses a significant expression, *kaḷimbu-aṟuttāṉ* to refer to the irrelative nature of the Absolute.[148] *Kaḷimbu-aṟuttāṉ* not only means dispelling primordial impurities but it also suggests doing away with relations or forms. It stands for going beyond birth and death, a state which has no coming, no going, no perishing.[149] Tirumūlar names it as *upa-cāntam*, a state where there is no *pōkku-varattu* (no going and returning).[150] If the Absolute is one and beyond all relations, it cannot be the God of religion, for the God of religion implies the relation between the worshipper and the worshipped. This relationship creates a rupture in the oneness of God. This is why Tirumūlar says: there is no "particular God;"[151] only ignorant people speak of "this or that God"[152] and those who speak of this one God as Śiva, Viṣṇu and Brahma are nothing but prattling.[153] "God" (in the sense of the Absolute) is the one institution that can never be grasped in a particular religious concept. Though it is always being defined differently by many religions, it is never being fully or finally defined or grasped by those religions.

3. 13. The Great Aloneness

The One is always alone. To use the expression of Tirumūlar, the Absolute (or Pati) is "Great Aloneness."[154] It is Being, not *a* being; it is not an object of awareness; it is awareness itself. This is the meaning of the term *kaivalya* or *kēvalam* that we find in the *Tirumandiram. Kēvalam* is Aloneness; it is a Great Isolation which is empty or free from all relations. It is a state of "unoccupation." In this sense Yoga is the power to practice inner isolation, to retire within oneself. It is the flight of the alone to the Alone. Tirumūlar had leanings towards viewing the Absolute as non-dual. The undifferentiated unity which is the ultimate ideal of the Siddhas is very often explained in terms of perfect sexual union like the oneness of Śiva and Śakti. That is, in the *maithuna* state the "we" becomes "one," multiplicity becomes singleness. In a deeper sense it means the realization of the oneness amidst all diversities. It is said that when Śiva and Śakti are united then results *samarasa*. In the state of *samarasa*, Absolute Bliss, where the ātman is identical with the Brahman, it is not that something different is seen, but that one sees differently. As Tirumūlar says it is a state of "I am Thou."[155] In this sentence the copula "am" is not a logical one, but a mystical copula of "oneness."

3. 14. Aum Namaśivāya

Almost all the Siddhas refer to the mystical mantra, Aum Namaśivāya; Tirumūlar says that this Aum is the *Śiva-svarūpa*[156] and calls it "the one word."[157] He also says that the "great light" "the peerless light," has turned into the sound praṇava.[158] It means that at the height of the yogic mystic experience, light and sound are the same. Tirumūlar vouchsafes that the "five letters" will help one to cut the account of rebirth.[159] According to him the whole world consists of these five letters.[160] The utterance of the five letters will make one (eternally) young.[161] It will also convert "copper into Gold," i.e., it will make the body immortal.[162] Tirumūlar speaks of the fifty-one letters that is the mantra sounds that one experiences while undergoing the process of Kuṇḍalinī-Yoga as constitutive of the Vedas and the Āgamas and says that the fifty-one letters are ultimately reduced to the five letters.[163] Śivāyanama is the mystic key to open the threshold of *mukti*. It is a key of the mystic "opening." According to Tirumūlar, it is a mahā-vākya. *Śiva* stands for *tat, nama* stands for *tvam* and *aya* stands for *asi*. Hence Śivāyanama means *tat-tvam-asi*, That Thou Art. He calls *tat tvam asi* and thereby the mantra Namaśivāya as the end of all Vedas.[164] As he says, a thrilling unstuck mantra when practiced will lead to realization.[165] Māṇikka-vācagar reflects the same idea in his *Tiru-vācagam* where he says:

> He (God) is not to be known by them who resort to the sound of uttered words or books.[166]

God can be realized only through mantras, which are the light of gnosis. Tirumūlar says the Lord is in the form of unstruck sound.[167] Describing the mystical state Tirumūlar writes:

> Milk, honey, juice of fruit
> In ambrosial sweetness mixed;
> Like it is when the triple States of Turiya—is crossed,
> And Jiva enters in Satya-Jnana-Ananda;
> It is a sweetness that permeates
> Every root of body's hair.[168]

In another place Tirumūlar says that beyond difference and non-difference is that state of bliss; in every hair root its ambrosial sweetness floods.[169] Such is this blissful state after enjoying which sugarcane tastes bitter and honey tastes sour.

In this body of pleasures
Like sugarcane and honey mixed
Sprouted the Fragrance of Siva Bliss
In eagerness my heart sought it
And I visioned the Void;
Then did the cane taste bitter
And honey sour.[170]

Once this state is attained Tirumūlar says that no one can dare to threaten him thereafter and that he will be no more with any one else.

None can intimidate me hereafter,
The Lord came and entered my thoughts,
There will I sport and wander in joy;
No more will I with anyone else be.[171]

Not able to express further Tirumūlar speaks of the mystical state as a state of enjoying "the fruit called Namaśivāya.[172] By following the foot steps of the *Tirumandiram* let us enjoy the Namaśivāya fruit, by "eating" which one sees everything dressed in divinity.

Notes on Chapter Five

1. Bertrand Russell, *Mysticism and Logic*, p.18.
2. *Ibid.*, pp.15-17.
3. W.T. Stace, *Mysticism and Philosophy*, pp. 79; 110-111.
4. Quoted in Girgio Zunini, *Man and His Religion: Aspects of Religious Psychology*, p. 324.
5. Aldous Huxley, *The Doors of Perception.*
6. Arnold Toynbee, *An Historian's Approach to Religion*, p.122.
7. Kenneth E.Bryant, "Sant and Vaiṣṇava Poetry: Some Observations on Method" in Mark Juergensmeyer and N. Gerald Barrier, eds. *Sikh Studies; Comparative Perspectives of a Changing Tradition*, pp. 65-74.
8. T.N.Ganapathy, *The Yoga of Siddha Bōganāthar*, Vol. I, pp. 85-87.
9. *Ibid.*, pp.123-124.
10. *Ibid.*, pp. 203-204.
11. T.N.Ganapathy, *The Yoga of Siddha Bōganāthar*, Vol. II, pp. 180-182.
12. *Tirumandiram*, 1490.
13. *Ibid.*, 1987.
14. *Ibid.*, 128, refer also 1602, where the end of the Vedas is referred to as the nectar of truth, which is awareness of the Self.
15. *Tiru-viḷayāḍal-purāṇam*, "Nāṉmāḍa-k-kūḍal-āṉa-paḍalam," 1.
16. *Tirumandiram*, 78.
17. *Ibid.*, 113.
18. *Ibid.*, 127.
19. *Ibid.*, 425 to 428. In verses 425 to 428 Tirumūlar speaks of four kinds of mergence or dissolution or absorption. They

are: 1. *nitta-caṅgāram*, daily mergence, i.e., sleep; 2. *vaitta-caṅgāram*, fixed or determined mergence, i.e., waking state; 3. *cutta-caṅgāram*, the pure mergence, i.e., the mystical state and 4. *uytta-caṅgāram*, the experienced mergence, i.e., final state of merging into the Absolute. In 422 Tirumūlar speaks of three *layas* or *praḷayas* i.e., ends, (i) daily praḷaya – sleep; (ii) *middle praḷaya* – death and (iii) *maha-praḷaya*, the great deluge.

20. *Ibid.*, 1605.
21. *Ibid.*, 1614.
22. *Ibid.*, 1605.
23. *Ibid.*, 2311.
24. *Ibid.*, 2843.
25. *Ibid.*, 54.
26. *Ibid.*, 2355.
27. *Ibid.*, 2953. Translation of B. Natarajan.
28. *Ibid.*, 956.
29. *Ibid.*, 129.
30. *Ibid.*, 134.
31. *Ibid.*, 251.
32. *Ibid.*, 251.
33. *Ibid.*, 1425.
34. *Ibid.*, 1435.
35. *Ibid.*, 1426. Translation of B.Natarajan.
36. *Ibid.*, 1434. Translation of B.Natarajan.
37. *Ibid.*, 1437. Translation of B.Natarajan.
38. *Ibid.*, 1438. Translation of B.Natarajan.
39. *Ibid.*, 1481. Translation of B.Natarajan.
40. *Ibid.*, 1624. Translation of B.Natarajan.

41. *Ibid.*, 1675. Translation of B.Natarajan.
42. *Ibid.*, 1786; Translation of B.Natarajan. see 2938 also.
43. *Ibid.*, 2082.
44. T.N. Ganapathy, *The Yoga of Siddha Bōganāthar*, Vol. I , pp. 81-82.
45. G.C.Pande, *Consciousness, Neuro Science and Philosophy*, ICPR Consciousness Series: 3, p.10.
46. *Tirumandiram*, 2122-2138.
47. *Ibid.*, *tantra* Eight, section 37.
48. *Ibid.*, 2587. Translation of B.Natarajan.
49. *Ibid.*, 2588. Translation of B.Natarajan.
50. *Ibid.*, 2590. Translation of B.Natarajan.
51. T.N. Ganapathy, *The Yoga Siddha Bōganāthar*, Vol. II, pp. 332-334.
52. G.C. Pande, *op. cit.*, p. 5.
53. Kireet Joshi, *Yoga and Consciousness*, ICPR Consciousness Series: 2, pp. 8-9.
54. R. Balasubramanian, his unpublished paper entitled "Indian Systems of Knowledge;" paper presented during the International Conference organized by the ICPR in 2003.
55. D.T. Suzuki, *Zen Buddhism*, p. 69.
56. Philip Wheel Wright, *The Burning Fountain*, pp. 3 and 4.
57. W.T. Stace, *op. cit.*, pp. 264-265.
58. *Tirumandiram*, 1490. Å
59. *Ibid.*, 705. Translation of B.Natarajan.
60. *Ibid.*, 2615.
61. *Ibid.*, 1702.
62. *Ibid.*, 2838.
63. *Ibid.*, 1808.

64. Bhadragiriyār, 192 and 23; refer also *Tirumandiram*, 1360.
65. *Tirumandiram, tantra* Five, section 9.
66. *Ibid.*, 1480. Author's translation.
67. *Ibid.*, 298.
68. *Ibid.*, 2355.
69. *Ibid.*, 896.
70. *Ibid.*, 2181.
71. *Ibid.*, 2366.
72. *Ibid.*, 2318.
73. *Ibid.*, 2320, 2381, 1783.
74. *Ibid.*, 1740, 1748, 1762 and 2994.
75. *Ibid.*, 2331. Refer also 136, 604, 766, 767, and 1825, where the self-realized jīva is identified with Śivam. Tirumūlar refers to the realized self as "inner jiva" *(uṭcīvaṉ)* and says that it indicates Śivam.
76. *Ibid.*, 2115.
77. Śiva-vākkiyar, 482; refer also *Tirumandiram*, 2820.
78. *Tirumandiram*, 1441. Translation of B.Natarajan; refer also 1527 and 1607.
79. *Ibid.*, 2951.
80. *Ibid.*, 1788 and 2348.
81. Paul Deussen has brought out beautifully the implications of *Tat tvam asi* in a lecture he delivered at Bombay in the year 1893. He says: "...The highest and purest morality is the immediate consequence of the Vedanta. The Gospels fix quite correctly as the highest law of morality: "love your neighbour as yourselves." But why should I do so, since by the order of nature I feel pain and pleasure only in myself, not in my neighbour? The answer is not in the Bible... but it is in the

Veda, is in the great formula "*tat tvam asi,*" which gives in three words metaphysics and morals altogether. You shall love your neighbour as your selves— because you are your neighbour, and mere illusion makes you believe, that your neighbour is something different from yourselves. Or in the words of the *Bhagavad gita*:- he, who knows himself in everything and everything in himself, will not injure himself by himself, *nahinasti atmana atmanam.* This is the sum and tenor of all morality, and this is the standpoint of a man knowing himself as Brahman. He feels himself as everything,— so he will not desire anything, for he has whatever can be had;— he feels himself as everything,— so he will not injure anything, for nobody injures himself... and so the Vedanta, in its unfalsified form, is the strongest support of pure morality, is the greatest consolation in the sufferings of life and death,— Indians, keep to it!" Paul Deussan, *The Philosophy of the Vedanta in its Relations to the Occidental Metaphysics*, an address delivered before the Bombay branch of the Royal Asiatic Society, Saturday, the 25th February, 1893. Published by Tookaram Tatya for the Bombay Theosophical Publica tions Fund, 1894, pp. 30-32.

82. *Tirumandiram*, 1481 and 1483.
83. *Ibid.*, 1478.
84. *Ibid.*, 1477.
85. *Ibid.*, 1487.
86. *Ibid.*, 1481. Translation of B.Natarajan.
87. *Ibid.*, 1483.
88. *Ibid.*, 1487.
89. *Ibid.*, 1823 and 2958.
90. *Ibid.*, 1592.

91. Arthur Eddington, *The Philosophy of the Physical Sciences*, pp.162, 202.
92. *Tirumandiram*, 1011, 1772, 1789, 1825, 2017, 2277, 2280, 2381, 2660, 2846 and 2958.
93. *Ibid.*, 2539 and 295,
94. *Ibid.*, 136. Translation of B.Natarajan.
95. *Ibid.*, 137. Translation of B.Natarajan.
96. *Ibid.*, 1609.
97. *Ibid.*, 135.
98. *Ibid.*, 440.
99. Paṭṭiṉattār, "Podu," 40.
100. *Tirumandiram*, 2315. Translation of B.Natarajan.
101. *Ibid.*, 1357 and 2303.
102. *tōyāda tu-veḷi*, *Ibid.*, 1768.
103. *Ibid.*, 2812.
104. *Ibid.*, 80 and 1856.
105. *Ibid.*, 1357.
106. *Ibid.*, 1466 and 1476.
107. *Ibid.*, 2864.
108. *Ibid.*, 123.
109. Quoted by W.T. Stace, *op. cit.*, p. 225.
110. *Ibid.*, pp. 99.
111. *Ibid.*, pp. 162-163.
112. *Tirumandiram*, 2303.
113. *Ibid.*, 74.
114. G. Varadarajan (Comm.), *Tirumandiram*, Vol.1, p. 35.
115. *Tirumandiram*, 2681-2697.
116. Refer T.N. Ganapathy, *The Yoga of Siddha Bōganāthar*, Vol. II.
117. *Tirumandiram*, 1818 and 1819.

118. *Ibid.*, 2483, 2825, and 2834.

119. *Ibid.*, 2495 and 2496.

120. *Ibid.*, 2495. Translation of B.Natarajan.

121. *Ibid.*, 2834. Translation of B.Natarajan.

122. *Ibid.*, 2483. Author's translation.

123. *Ibid.*, 2488 to 2494.

124. *Ibid.*, 2943; In the *Bṛhadāraṇyaka Upaniṣad* the realization of the self has been compared to the transcendental realization of bliss arising through the deep embrace of a woman. "As, when deeply embraced by the dear woman, one knows neither anything external nor anything internal— so also a man deeply embraced by the *ātman* through perfect knowledge knows neither anything external nor anything internal." (4-3.21).

125. *Ibid.*, 2944.

126. *Ibid.*, 956.

127. *Ibid.*, 97.

128. *Ibid.*, 298.

129. *Ibid.*, 2955.

130. *Ibid.*, 1611.

131. *Ibid.*, 1895 and 1900.

132. *Ibid.*, 1896. Translation of B. Natarajan

133. *Ibid.*, 1595 and 2635.

134. *Ibid.*, 1593.

135. *Ibid.*, 1593.

136. *Ibid.*, 2075.

137. *Ibid.*, 1459.

138. *Ibid.*, 2319.

139. *Ibid.*, 128.

140. *Ibid.*, 2319.

141. *Ibid.*, 1678. Translation of B. Natarajan.

142. Refer Toṇḍar aḍi-p-poḍi Āḻvār, "Tirumalai," 38.

143. *Tirumandiram*, 129.

144. Verse 13 of Bōgar's *Jñāṉa-cārāmcam-100*. See T.N.Ganapathy's *The Yoga Siddha Bōganāthar*, Vol. II, pp. 362-365.

145. *Tirumandiram*, 1768. (Refer Śiva-vākkiyar, 9 and 12, refer also 211. Paṭṭiṉattār, "Neñjoḍu Pulambal," 3. Bhadragiriyār, 149. In this connection it would be worthwhile to note that the *Guhya-samāja Tantra* is described in the colophon as the "beyond the beyond in the Tantra" *(tantrānām uttarottaram).* Saint Appar also describes the Absolute as one who is "Beyond Beyond the Beyond." Kabir also states "the knowledge beyond the knowledge is my knowledge." *The Bijak of Kabir*, p. 112. Refer also "the great Being beyond boundaries and beyond beyond," "the Beyond-Beyond God" of Meher Baba's philosophy.

146. *Tirumandiram*, 181.

147. *Ibid.*, 2648 and 2955.

148. *Ibid.*, 113 and 114.

149. *Ibid.*, 2854 and 1614.

150. *Ibid.*, 2506.

151. *Ibid.*, 109.

152. *Ibid.*, 105 and 1154.

153. *Ibid.*, 110 and 1087.

154. *Ibid.*, 2450, The Tamil expression is *taṉi-uṟṟa-kevalam.*

155. *Ibid.*, 2660.

156. *Ibid.*, 2676 and 2677.

157. *Ibid.*, 884 and 885.

158. *Ibid.*, 693.

159. *Ibid.*, 2705, 2716 and 2717.

160. *Ibid.*, 2775.

161. *Ibid.*, 169.

162. *Ibid.*, 903 and 907.

163. *Ibid.*, 696 and 965.

164. *Ibid.*, 1602.

165. *Ibid.*, 85.

166. *Tiru-vācagam*, "Aṟputa-p-pattu," 8.

167. *Tirumandiram*, 1542.

168. *Ibid.*, 2831. Translation of B. Natarajan.

169. *Ibid.*, 2856.

170. *Ibid.*, 2976. Translation of B. Natarajan.

171. *Ibid.*, 2960. Translation of B. Natarajan.

172. *Ibid.*, 2962.

Chapter 6

The Twilight Language of the Tirumandiram

T.N. Ganapathy

tuṟu paḍarndu kiḍandadu tū neṟi
māṟi-k kiḍakkum vagai aṟivār illai
māṟi-k kiḍakkum vagai aṟivāḷarkku
ūṟi-k kiḍandadu eṉ uḷḷaṉbu tāṉē.

The Holy way is by thorny bushes covered
They know not how to remove it;
They who know how to remove it
Are they for whom my heart yearns.

–*Tirumandiram, 2867.*

6. The Twilight Language of the Tirumandiram

T.N. Ganapathy

In the ninth *tantra*, section 17, Tirumūlar uses the expression *śūnya-sambhāṣaṇai*, which may be translated as twilight language. Its literal meaning is "the conversation about the void." In this section there are seventy verses (verses 2866 to 2935). Before deciphering these verses, it would be better to have a background of what is meant by twilight language.

1. The background

To express their mystical experience, the Siddhas have used a paradoxical language which is characterized by a deceptive simplicity (in Tamil it is called *ēmāṟṟum eḷimai*). Using the common language of the people, the poems are written for both the uninitiated, common people and also for the initiated. The meaning of the poems operates at two levels—one, the exoteric and the linguistic, the other, the esoteric and the symbolical. The poems are noted for using pedestrian symbolism, that is, symbols and words used by ordinary common people. They really conceal the spiritual doctrines and the mystical aspects of Kuṇḍalinī-Yoga from the uninitiated. The esoteric meaning can be understood only by the initiated. The twilight language is a clothed language in which the highest truths are hidden in the form of the lowest, the most sacred in the form of the most ordinary, the transcendent in the form of the most earthly and the deepest knowledge in the form of the most grotesque paradoxes. For example in one of the verses, Tirumūlar uses the following paradoxical Tamil expression whose literal translation is: those who possess a lizard eat the snake knowingly.[1] Its significant meaning is: "those who have firmness of mind (those who possess a lizard, i.e., varamamus), flourish high in Kuṇḍalinī-Yoga (eat the snake knowingly). It is a language, which is not literal but suggestive, epigrammatic, and enigmatic, discernible only to those who have been initiated to the secret lore. The essential characteristic feature of the twilight language is "its polysemantic nature, its multivalence, its capacity to express at the same time a number of meanings both at the level of ordinary experience and at the level of transcendence."

The Siddhas are very particular that there is no use in giving the secret treasures to people who do not have a control over their senses, that is, those who do not deserve them. They are very particular that great truths should not be given to the agnostics, the cynics and the indisciplined. Kabīr, the mystic poet of India, used to say: Do not display one's diamonds in the vegetable stall. There is a Sanskrit expression, *ācārya-muṣṭi*, which means the "closed fist." This is an expression, which has been applied to gurus who withhold their teachings from others so that they are not misunderstood and misapplied. The maintenance of secrecy is not due to the opprobrium of orthodoxy. It is only a protection both against the vulgarizing or institutionalizing of a habit of thought only proper to those who understand it and against accusations of heresy. In this connection it is worthwhile to mention a palm-leaf manuscript available in the Kerala University MSS library, Tiruvananthapuram (India), called *Jñāṉa-bōdhagam* in which it is said that some who have made an attempt to study Siddha poetry have left it as a "nuisance," because they could not decipher the meaning. It speaks of the dual meaning of the language of the Siddhas as a "merciless language" since in it they conceive one thing and express another. It warns people not to take the language of the Siddhas at its face value and if one were to do it, it will be like a farmer who wants to plough one's fields on the support of the mist-formation. In short, *sandhyā-bhāṣā* entails a sort of systematic ambiguity.

1. 1. Sandhyā-bhāṣā – Two views

The Sanskrit term for *śūnya-sambhāṣaṇai* (as used by Tirumūlar) is *sandhyā-bhāṣā*. There are two views about the correct form of the term *sandhyā-bhāṣā*. One set of scholars use the term *sandhyā-bhāṣā* meaning twilight language and another set of scholars use the term *sandhā-bhāṣā*, meaning intentional language. Hariprasad Shastri uses the term *sandhyā-bhāṣā* to mean the "language of light and darkness, partly light and partly darkness; some part can be understood while the other cannot."[2] Vidhu-shekhara Bhattacharya (Sastri), says that *sandhyā* is a wrong spelling and it must be *sandhā-bhāṣā* and interprets it as *abhiprāyika-vacana* or *neyārtha-vacana* meaning "intentional speech."[3] He says that it is wrong to call it "twilight language." Intentional language is a purposely-created mode of communication having a concealed meaning. Following Vidhushekhara Sastri, P.C. Bagchi, Burnouf, Kern, Max Muller, Mircea Eliade and Agehananda Bharati, use the term *sandhā-bhāṣā*. Eliade informs us that Burnouf translated it as "enigmatic language," Kern as "mystery," and Max Muller as "hidden sayings" and that he himself prefers as "intentional language." But Lama Angarika Govinda in his *Foundations of Tibetan Mysticism*, Snellgrove in his translation of *The Hevajra Tantra* (Vol.1), and Alex Wayman in his *The Buddhist Tantras: Light on Indo-Tibetan Esotericism*, use the term *sandhyā-bhāṣā* and its literal meaning is "twilight language," which is said to bear a double meaning, the ordinary and the mystic. It is the great riddle of the yogins, which the disciples and others cannot unravel. Hence Snellgrove translates the term *sandhyā-bhāṣā* as "secret language." The term "twilight language" is an approximate one to refer to the Siddha writings.

According to Buddhadasa, the Thai-monk, scholar-meditator, certain aspects of Gotama's teachings as we find them in the *Tri-piṭaka* are couched in a kind of symbolic language. This he terms "dhamma language" as opposed to everyday language.[4] He assumes that certain aspects of Buddhist teaching are unintelligible unless they are assumed to be symbolic. He cites as an example the attempt by Māra and his daughters to distract Buddha in his meditations. Māra is a personification of unwholesome thoughts. His daughters' three names Tantra, Ārati and Rati are the Pāli terms standing for craving, discontent and desire. The story of Māra and his three daughters represents symbolically the events that occur in the mind of the meditator. As Buddhadasa says this account of Māra symbolizes the arising of distracting thoughts or any mental state opposed to spiritual progress. Similarly he identifies the various hells and heavens of the Buddhist cosmology with states of consciousness. In short, the necessary information for the meditator is there in the unintelligible teaching of the *Tri-piṭaka*, but concealed in symbolic language. The Zen Buddhists use a term *koan* to refer to a paradoxical expression or question or action of the master.[5]

1. 2. The purpose of twilight language

Twilight language is a purposely-created mode of communication. Its purpose is to seek, to search for, to enquire after the meaning behind the hidden language. In fact, it is a sort of technical language, whose technique is to express in words that which is beyond expression. The purpose of rendering great truths in symbolic, yet simple language is:

1. to prevent the uninitiated from comprehending the hidden meaning by making them satisfied with the super ficial meaning;

2. to preserve the real message intact by making the people sing them in popular folk song forms so that the message may survive beyond any breaks in the line of oral transmission and to facilitate rediscovery at a later time; that is, to ensure against the loss of the precious teaching;
3. to make the message reach anyone who is interested in it without discrimination of sex, or caste;
4. to camouflage such instructions as may be resented by the orthodox public;[6]
5. to express the highest experiences of the mind since common parlance is not adequate;[7]
6. to entice people from orthodox observance and to lure them into the Tāntric web;[8]
7. to use it as a mnemonic device;[9]
8. to annoy the orthodox, that is teasing the orthodox religious bourgeois; perhaps a sort of linguistic catharsis.[10]
9. to project the yogin into the paradoxical situation indispensable to his training.[11]
10. to provide the yogin with a means of describing supernormal experiences for which ordinary language is inadequate.
11. to provide a working basis for the interpretative analysis of the *maṇḍalas* and the cakras used in secret meditative transmission to be revealed to the initiated disciples only.
12. to ensure that knowledge about advanced practices would remain concealed from all those known to be incapable of applying those practices effectively;[12]

13. to supplement and illustrate the instructions given by gurus, each symbol suggesting in vivid graphic form some essential characteristic of the technique to be practised;[13]

To understand the twilight language requires a total hermeneutic of reading, an awareness, in fact, of the total religious and philosophical structures, which infuse into it.

How the twilight language of the Siddhas originated is a problem that scholars have yet to confront. Let us note some of the suggestions regarding its origination without entering into a discussion.

1. The twilight language may be due to the love of paradox common to all spiritual traditions.
2. It may be viewed as a special extension of mantric language.
3. The twilight language may perhaps have been merely another of the many diagressions from the path of medita tion.[14]
4. It originated because the common parlance is inadequate to express the highest experiences of the mind.

1. 3. The number "eighteen"

In Tamil Nadu, tradition speaks of the eighteen Siddhas *(padiṉeṇ-cittargaḷ)*. The number "eighteen" has got a twilight element in it, in that it admits of a multivalence of meanings in Tamil Siddha literature.[15] The number "eighteen" does not refer to the number of Siddhas, for Siddhas are innumerable. The Siddhas are those who have attained the "eighteen" siddhis. That there are eighteen siddhis is vouched by Śrī Kṛṣṇa in the *Bhāgavata*[16] and by

Śrī Rāmakṛṣṇa in his *Gospel.*[17] Experienced Tāntrics explain that kuṇḍalinī after reaching the sahasrāra region, has to cross further through eighteen *mahā-vidyās,* i.e., eighteen energized subtle centres encircling the sahasrāra region, finally to unite with Śiva in an act known as Maithuna-Yoga. Kāka-pucuṇḍar, a Tamil Siddha, refers to these eighteen energized centres in one of his verses.[18] The English translation of the verse is rendered here:

> One should reach the top Lotus
> And reach the eighteen ridge (summit of the hill).

Bōgar in his *Jñāṉa-cārāmcam-100* says that after reaching the top house, i.e., sahasrāra, if one concentrates on the eighteen energized centres, one will attain wisdom.[19]

1. 4. An interpretation of the five 'm's

In Tāntric literature and in Siddha poetry we come cross the *pañca-makāra* which refers to the five rites which all begin with the letter 'm,' *madya, māmsa, matsya, mudrā* and *maithuna.* (See Appendix-D for a detailed account of *pañca-makāra*).

Apart from the five 'm's certain twilight terms have been used in Tāntric literature. Some of them are:

1. Blind woman – ignorance;
2. Potter – kārmic formations;
3. Monkey – mind;
4. Two men in a boat – mind and body;
5. House with six windows – six senses;
6. Guru's head – sahasrāra;
7. Tiger – master of initiation;
8. Diamond – absolute reality;
9. Wine – moon/piṅgalā;

10. Father and mother – egoism and craving.

1. 5. Twilight Language in Tamil Siddha literature

Before we deal with Tirumūlar's *śūnya-sambhāṣaṇai* in detail, it will be worthwhile to note certain expressions used by the Tamil Siddhas in general. The use of numerals to denote facts or ideas or allusions is a favorite device of the Tamil Siddhas. This can be shown in the following verse of Śiva-vākkiyar:

añce̲luttile(1) *pi̲randu añce̲luttile*(2) *vaḷarndu*
añce̲luttai(3) *ōdukin̲r̲a pañca*(4) *būta pāvikāḷ!*
añce̲luttil(5) *ōre̲luttar̲indu kūr̲a vallirēl*
añcal añcal en̲r̲u nātan̲ ambalattil āḍumē.[20]

Here the word 'five' *(añcu/pañca)* occurs five times in the poem, each having a different meaning. The first 'five' means the five senses or the five *kośas*, the second 'five' stands for the five prāṇas; the third 'five' and the fifth 'five' stand for the five sacred letters; the fourth 'five' stands for the five elements.

Alphabet symbolism is a common technique that we find in the Tantras and especially in Siddha poetry. We find several mystical syllables, a large number of short unetymological vocables, such as *krīm, hrīm, hum*, etc., in Siddha poetry. They are said to be the abbreviations of the deities, i.e., the psychic energies and their functions, located in each cakra. In uttering these syllables the cakras are said to react and function. To a sādhaka they certainly have a value of a secret, initiatory language. These sounds are said to reveal their message only during meditation. For the uninitiated these letters remain unintelligible because their meanings do not belong to rational language, the language that serves to communicate ordinary experiences. To take an example, according to one interpretation given by a Siddha friend, the letters *k, r, i, m* in the mantra *krim*, suggest *dharma, artha, kāma* and *mokṣa* respectively. In yet another interpretation, *k* stands for the creative aspect, *r* – the destructive aspect, *i* – the restraining aspect and *m* – the equilibrium aspect of the ultimate reality.

The mantra Aum is a 'dumb word' wherein *A* stands for creation of the universe, *u* for protection and *m* for destruction. In this connection it would be worthwhile to find the equivalents of the letters, A, U, M as found in Alain Danielou's *Hindu Polytheism.*[21] From the foregoing analysis, we can safely say that the monosyllables that we find in Siddha poetry are no longer gibberish. They have a meaning and a message. Their combination as mantras is not merely a string of isolated items but they form an organic whole of meaning and sense 'to those who know."

In Tamil Siddha poetry we find a lot of references to Kuṇḍalinī-Yoga couched in twilight language. The process of the self merging with the reality in the *amṛta*, secreted at the sahasrāra is referred to in a twilight language as *asti-karaittal. Asti-karaittal* literally means dissolving the ashes. Bhadragiriyār couches the process of the prāṇāyāma in twilight language. He speaks of prāṇa as a 'twelve-legged horse' (just to indicate its quickness of mobility) and refers to iḍā and piṅgalā as the two chains. Śiva-vākkiyar refers to suṣumnā as *tārai* (long trumpet) and iḍā and piṅgalā as two conchs.

We also come across the following symbolic terms in Tamil Siddha literature (only a few representative samples are given. The list is neither complete nor exhaustive). For human body the following terms are used: *kuppai, āḍu-tuṟai, tiru-mēṉi, tañjāvūr, vīḍu, uppu-k-kūḍu, kōyil, atti-p-paḻam, muṭṭai, vēṅkaṭam, paṉai, śrī-raṅgam, kurambai, aindagam, pandal. Pūraka* stands for *caryā-*

mārga, *kumbhaka* stands for *kriyā-mārga*, *rechaka* stands for *yoga-mārga*, *vāsi* stands for *jñāna-mārga*. The terms used for piṅgalā are: *ravi*, *andi*, *teṟku*. The terms used for iḍā are: *madi*, *sandi*, *vaḍakku*. For suṣumnā the following terms are used: *ucci*, *cuḍar*, *andaram*, *tarppai*, *guru-muḻi*, *pūṇḍu*; the *vilvam* is used for the bottom end of suṣumnā and *tēr-ōḍi-t-teru* is used for the route of the suṣumnā. The term *neruppaṟai* and the letter *n*, are used for sahasrāra. While *kaḍuveḷi* and *māṅgāy* stand for Brahman, *kandagam* is jīva that is bound; the six ādhāras are referred to as 'street' or *vīdi*. The terms *vēṅgai*, *uragam*, *cummā*, refer to the kuṇḍalinī. The middle of the eyebrow is variously designated as *kaṉaka-pīṭam*, *tillai*, *nelli-k-kāy* and *kumba-kōṇam*. The terms 'deer' and 'tree' stand for mind. The branches of the tree stand for the senses while the leaves and fruits for hopes and passions. "Monkey" stands for consciousness and *nāṉmugaṉ* refers to eye, nose, ear and tongue. *Nandi-vāhaṉa* is the *sthūla-deha*; and 'forest' stands for external objects. *Ahamkāra* is called *ūmattaṉ* root; viśuddhi is called *kaḍu-k-kāi*. The term *chīṉa* stands for concentration.

The term *parama-hamsa* is also symbolic. Figuratively it is said that the swan *(hamsa)* is playing in the waters of the Ganga and the Yamuna. The Ganga and the Yamuna stand for the in-going and out-going of the vital air, i.e., iḍā and piṅgalā. *Parama-hamsa* is a man who has stopped playing in these rivers and has chosen the course of the middle stream, that is suṣumnā, thus leading to sahasrāra, a place of infinite and immeasurable joy. Similarly lotus is a flower that has caught the Indian imagination not only by its beauty and delicacy but by its layer of multiplicity of petals, vitality and purity. The element of sumptuous fecundity is not excluded from the concept. The lotus expresses the ubiquitous subtle expression, space, i.e., *veṭṭaveḷi*. The infinity of space and consciousness are identical. The lotus is the symbol of spiritual enfoldment, a symbol of the expanding consciousness. It symbolizes the universe in its abstract and concrete forms.

In Kambaḷi-c-caṭṭai-muṉi we come across a beautiful symbolic verse to refer to the "killing of the senses" or "absorption of the senses." He figuratively refers to the control of the five senses as the death of the mosquito (hearing), the wasp (seeing), the deer (smelling), the fish (tasting) and the ant (touching). Reference to *muppu* is found in many of the Tamil Siddha songs, especially in medicinal literature. *Muppu* stands for *vālai*, i.e., kuṇḍalinī-śakti; it also stands for, in some places, the *trikūṭa*, i.e., the sahasrāra. According to one interpretation *muppu* is of three types. They are: *vaidya-muppu*, *vāda-muppu*, and *yōga-muppu*. The first two types refer to the field of medicine and the third, *yoga-muppu*, refers to Kuṇḍalinī-Yoga. The *yōga-muppu*, may be learnt only through a guru. It consists of iḍā and piṅgalā and suṣumnā and the way to regulate them.

The two expressions *cāgā-k-kāl* and *vēgā-t-talai* as well as *vēga-k-kāl* and *cāgā-t-talai* are in frequent use in Tamil Siddha literature. By *cāgā-k-kāl* the Tamil Siddhas refer to the eternal air, that is, the principle of prāṇāyāma and by *vēgā-t-talai* they refer to the sahasrāra region. In Tamil Nadu, people who are ignorant of things are said to be "those who do not understand the head and foot of anything." We also come across two other expressions *viṭṭa-kuṟai* and *toṭṭa-kuṟai* in Tamil Siddha literature. *Viṭṭa-kuṟai* stands for "sending the prāṇa through iḍā and piṅgalā" and *toṭṭa-kuṟai* stands for "directing it through suṣumnā." (See Appendix-G).

1. 6. Two categories of sandhā terminology

According to Agehananda Bharati, *sandhā* terminology can be classified into two categories, afferent and efferent respectively. To quote him:

> A *sandhā*-term which employs object-language and 'intends' the conceptual or mystical absolute is an afferent term as when *lalana* (woman) is to mean *nirvāṇa*. Conversely, a *sandhā*-term employing the philosophical or theological language and 'intending' an objective thing or event or an action is an efferent term, as when *bodhicitta* is to mean '*semen virile.*'... . To qualify a *sandhā*-term a word must therefore be either afferent or efferent in this definition; whenever a lexeme used in *sandhābhāṣa* is neither of the two, then it is not *sandhābhāṣa* in that particular context.[22]

2. The use of language in the Tirumandiram – A curtain raiser

Before taking up for elucidation the section on *śūnya-sambhāṣaṇai*, it would be better to pass in review the different ways of the use of language in the *Tirumandiram* in general.

2. 1. The use of numerals

The first verse, which is in praise of the Absolute, is itself in a numerical language that has different meanings.

> The One is He, the Two His sweet Grace,
> In Three He stood, in all the Four witnessed,
> The Five He Conquered, the Six He Filled,
> The Seven He pervades, manifests the Eight
> And so remains.[23]

As we have already noted the use of the numerals to denote facts or ideas or allusions is a favorite device of the Siddhas and an authentic pattern of Tirumūlar. The first verse of the *Tirumandiram* is a standing example of this pattern.

"The One" stands for the Absolute, called Śiva. The Two refers to the dynamic, graceful aspect of Śiva i.e., Śakti. "In Three He stood" may have different interpretations. "Three" may mean any one or all of the following: (i) The soul (the third entity as distinct from Śiva and Śakti) (ii) The three aspects of the Absolute namely, that of creation (Brahma), that of preservation (Viṣṇu) and that of dissolution (Rudra), (iii) The three genders of creation, he, she and it; (iv) The three propensities, guṇas— *sattva* (illumination), *rajas* (activity); and *tamas* (indifference) (v) The three categories, Pati (the Lord), paśu (the soul) and pāśa (fetters). (vi) *icchā* (desire); kriyā (action) and jñāna (knowledge).

The term "Four" may mean (i) the four *puruṣārthas* (the four goals of human life)— *dharma* (righteousness), *artha* (wealth), *kāma* (desire) and *mokṣa* (liberation); (ii) the four Vedas— *Ṛg, Yajur, Sāma* and *Atharvaṇa;* (iii) the four steps to realization— *caryā* (external acts of worship), *kriyā* (service to God), *yoga* (contemplation) and *jñāna* (liberation).

The term "Five" may mean (i) the five senses; (ii) the five actions— creation, preservation, dissolution, obscuration and liberation.

The term "Six" may stand for: (i) the letter *(vaṇṇam)*; the word *(padam)*; the formula *(mandiram)*; the treatise *(kalai)*; the world *(puvaṇam)* and the truth or the principles *(tattuvam).* (ii) The six schools of philosophy or the six internal religions *(aga-c-camayam)*; (iii) the six ādhāras (mūlādhāra, svādhiṣṭhāna, maṇipūra, anāhata, viśudha, and ājñā).

The term "Seven" may mean: (i) the seventh cakra called sahasrāra; (ii) the seven worlds that is either the celestial sevens or the subterranean seven. The last phrase of the poem *uṇarndu eṭṭē* is usually translated as "manifesting the eight," the eight standing for earth, water, fire, air, space (sky), sun, moon and jīva (the individual soul). This phrase *uṇarndu eṭṭē* (in Tamil) may also be translated as "attain Him through experience." The term *eṭṭē* may be interpreted as "eight" or as "to attain," "to achieve." Much depends on how one interprets the terms in the *Tirumandiram*. This is an example to show how one and the same verse may be interpreted differently. The difference in interpreting a verse/a term exhibits the richness in the connotation/denotation of the meaning of the words used. But in the twilight verse, the words are used by the author to "conceal" the meaning. This "concealed meaning" can be understood only through experience and not through mere interpretation of the different meanings of the word or term. To understand the concealed meaning one requires a total hermeneutic of reading, an awareness that is infused in the language of the mystic.

2. 2. The use of ambiguous terms

The second line of verse 68 runs as follows: "By Nandi's grace I entered into Mūlaṉ." The term "Mūlaṉ" is used in an ambiguous sense; it may either mean "entering into the body of Mūlaṉ, the shepherd" or "entering into the *mūlādhāra*." Whereas in the previous example the terms "one" "two" "three" etc., convey one clear, unambiguous idea, (that is "three" means "three") which may be interpreted differently, in this example the term "Mūlaṉ" is used in an ambiguous, equivocal, debatable sense, which can be interpreted in either way.

2. 3. The use of allegory

In verse 521, the third line states, "the ignorant say that Śiva swallowed poison, but they know not the truth." This line is an allegorical statement. Tirumūlar says that the symbolic meaning of the phrase "Śiva swallowed poison" is not known to the ignorant.

The significance of Śiva swallowing the poison is as follows. Instead of wasting the sexual energy downwards leading to darkness (ignorance), one should direct it upwards leading to light (wisdom). The region below the throat is depicted as darkness (ignorance) and above the throat, that is the forehead, is depicted as light (wisdom). "Taking poison" stands for sublimating the sexual energy and directing it to the forehead or ājñā-cakra. By stating that the ignorant do not know the truth of Śiva swallowing the poison, Tirumūlar has suggested the significance of the allegory.

2. 4. Use of alphabet symbolism

Alphabet symbolism is a common technique that one finds in the Tantras and especially in Siddha poetry. According to Tirumūlar the mantra *na-ma-ci-va-ya* is the goad by which the five elephants, which roam in the body-forest, can be controlled.[24] The verse runs as follows:

> Five the elephants (senses)
> In the body forest roam,
> The Five Letters become the goads
> For the five elephants,
> Only they who can contain
> The five (senses) together,
> Can, unafraid, reach Primal Lord.

The five elephants are the five senses. Each letter in the mantra, *na-ma-ci-va-ya* is a goad that controls the elephant. But more is meant in this verse. Symbolically it stands for the controlling of the following sense-organs.

Alphabet	Tanmātra (subtle elements)	Sense-organ
ya	sound	ear
va	smell	nose
ci	sight	eye
ma	taste	tongue
na	touch	skin

The verse suggests that by controlling the five senses and the *tanmātras* together, with the help of the mantra *na-ma-ci-va-ya*, without fear, one can attain liberation or *Śivānubhava*.

2. 5. The use of religious symbols

Tirumūlar also makes use of religious symbols involving philosophical interpretations. In verse 1392 explaining the rapturous divine dance form of Śakti, Tirumūlar says that Śakti appeared to him having eight hands holding flower (lotus), parrot, noose, battle-axe, sword, shield, bow and the arrow.[25] The verse runs as follows:

> The Sakti that was in my mind seated thus
> Appeared with hands eight;
> Holding flower, parrot, noose, battle-axe and sword;
> The shield, bow and the arrow too
> She danced in rapture divine.

Each object she holds has a philosophical significance. The lotus stands for discriminating knowledge. The parrot is the symbolic expression of the divine sound-form of Śivam. Noose (pāśa) represents one-pointed concentration. The battle-axe stands for light, while the sword represents the destruction of bad thoughts. The shield stands for the protection against evil influences. The bow stands for the goal of the atman and the arrow stands for the oneness of jīva with Śiva. Thus the symbolic dance of Śakti stands for the philosophical support the yogin acquires in his endeavour to attain liberation from mundane existence.

2. 6. The symbolism of snake

The symbolism of snake is a common refrain that one finds in the Siddha poetry, and the *Tirumandiram* is not an exception to this type of symbolism. We may quote the following verse as a standing example of this type of symbolism of snake.

One the serpent, Five its hoods
The Four fill the thorny hole of enjoyment;
In its twain body,
It stopped raising its hoods and;
Then into a single hood it merged
Into the very body within.[26]

In Tamil language this kind of symbolism is called *pici* type of poetry, which is a kind of enigma in which an object is indicated by the description of something resembling it. The gist of this verse is: The snake is one; it has five hoods; it takes four kinds of food. It has lived its life in the snake-hole. At that stage, it stopped raising its two hoods, and merged into a single hood of the body within.

The explanation: The snake stands for the jīva, its five hoods are the five senses. Its four kinds of food (enjoyment) are, *manas* (mind), *buddhi* (intellect), *cit* (will) and *ahamkāra* (ego). The snake-hole is the body; its twain aspects are the physical or the gross body (the *sthūla-śarīra*) and the subtle body *sūkṣma* or the *liṅga-śarīra.* Leaving its two bodies (the physical and the subtle), jīva (the soul, the snake) enters into another body (hood), which is the *kāraṇa-śarīra,* i.e., the causal body.

In Indian thought one finds reference to three kinds of bodies. They are:

(i) the *sthūla-śarīra* or the gross body composed of the gross elements, i.e., *annamaya-kośa;*

(ii) the *sūkṣma* or *liṅga-śarīra* or the subtle body consisting of the subtle elements, *tanmātras* and the *prāṇamaya kośa,* the *manomaya-kośa* and the *vijñānamaya-kośa,* and

(iii) the *kāraṇa-śarīra* or the causal body which corresponds to the *ānandamaya-kośa.*

By leaving its two hoods (of *sthūla-śarīra* and *sūkṣma-śarīra*) the snake (jīva) enters into another hood (of *kāraṇa-śarīra,* that is *ānandamaya,* the state of bliss).

2. 7. Agricultural symbolism

Influenced by the environment in which he lived, Tirumūlar uses the agricultural symbolism to explain how the Siddhas harvest the body-field.

In the body-field is the seed;
The field has a fence;
In the crown of the head
The crop ripened;
If without fear they harvest not,
And feed themselves not,

They are but those
Who beg for hunger's sake.[27]

The meaning of the verse is: The seed (the *bindu*, of liberation) lies in the fenceless field of mūlādhāra. The fenced-field is the *sahasrāra* where the seed (of liberation) ripens. In between, the ploughing (meditation) has occurred in the ājñā-cakra. One can reap in this field and save the food for days to come. People who cannot perform this harvesting of the crop are but begging for hunger's sake.

2. 8. The symbolism of swan

Another type of symbolism is expressed in the following verse.

Two the swans on the river bank (of life)
The two swans separation know not,
If one says he is by himself
Then that foolish swan, grace receiveth not.[28]

In the riverbank of the life of the jīva (soul), there are two swans, i.e., the jīvātman and the Paramātman. They are distinct, but not different. Hence there is no separation between the two. If the jīvātman thinks that it is independent and existing by itself, it cannot attain liberation. Such a jivātman is called the foolish swan. "The river bank" is a significant expression. it may mean that just as a river bank is not permanent, the life of the jīva also is not permanent. The expression may also stand for (the river bank of) knowledge. The term "swan" is also a significant one in that it stands for *hamsa*, the process of breathing. By the process of breathing, every jīva is doing a *japa*, that is, the utterance of a mantra. The breath of every person in entering makes the sound of *sah* and in coming out that of *ham*. These sounds make *hamsah so'ham* (I am He). If the jīva (the ignorant swan) thinks that it is not He, then it has no chance of attaining liberation. But every jīva performs this *japa* of *so'ham* constantly, but unconsciously. This is called *ajapā-japa.* The symbolism of the two swans expressed in this verse powerfully reminds one of the Ṛg Vedic symbolism of two birds sitting on a tree, one (jīva) enjoying the fruits of the tree and the other (the Absolute) watching, but not eating.

2. 9. The symbolism of the musical drum

Music and dance find a lot of references in the *Tirumandiram.* In verse 189 the human body has been symbolized as a musical drum. The verse runs as follows:

> One this body-drum, two the rhythms keeping time,
> Five the masters who, inside, make display;
> But when the great king, indwelling departed,
> The drum lay shattered, a heap of inert clay.[29]

Here in this verse the body is symbolized as a musical drum. The drum which is made of clay has two rhythms (two time-measures in music), the two rhythms being the right and the left breaths, i.e., iḍā and piṅgalā. The drum is being played by a team of five players, that is, the five senses. The king of the drum-party is the jīva. When the jīva leaves the musical arena of the body, that is the drum, the body is as dead as clay. This symbolism is resonant of the English expression, "Dust thou art, and to dust thou returnest." In musical parlance the two rhythms (the two time measures in music) are also called *ādi-tāḷam* in Tamil, which has two connotations, one referring to "two rhythms" and another referring to the "ancient rhythms." The two ancient rhythms of the body are iḍā and piṅgalā.

2. 10. The symbolism of rice-cooking

This is an interesting symbolism suggested by Tirumūlar of cooking rice in a kitchen-hearth. The following is the translation of the verse.

The ladle in the cooking-pot of body contains the rice of nectar,
The three fires are the sun, moon and agni and the
Five fire-woods are the prāṇas,
Without wasting time get the rice of nectar cooked,
The days are passing away fast.[30]

The meaning of the verse is: The ladle in the cooking-pot of body contains, the rice of nectar – the cooking pot of the body using the ladle of suṣumnā has the rice of *bindu* (sex energy); the three fires are the sun, moon and the *agni* – the tripod of the oven contains the sun, the moon, and the fire regions; (the *agni* region, that is the abdomen region; the sun region, that is the heart region, and the moon region that is the fore-head region); the fire woods are the prāṇas – the five *prāṇas (prāṇa, apāna, samāna, udāna* and *vyāna)* are the fire woods; without wasting time get the rice of nectar cooked – without wasting the *bindu* (the sex-energy and diverting it to the sahasrāra) get at the nectar; the days are passing away fast – the days of life are numbered, so without wasting time try to get at the nectar, through Kuṇḍalinī-Yoga as early as possible.

2. 11. The symbolism of forest animals

Verse 2214 is a classical example of this type of symbolism as given by Tirumūlar. The verse is:

In the bewildered thoughts are the lions three;
In the sneering thoughts are the jackals four;

In the divided thoughts are the elephants five;
These are the foes of the contending mind.[31]

The meaning of the verse is: The internal and external foes of the contending mind are: The three lions – lust, anger and ignorance; The four jackals – mind, intellect, will and ego; The five elephants – the senses of taste, sight, sound, touch and smell. The sādhaka should know how to control these animals inside the body by cultivating detachment towards them, by developing the yogic cessation of the fluctuations of the mind.

2. 12. The symbolism of the sweet-scented fruit

In this symbolism Tirumūlar speaks of enjoying the mystical experience of *Śivā-anubhava* at the sahasrāra region. Let us see the translation of the verse.

There is a Fruit Delicious,
From fragrant flower within it ripens;
The birds within the Self
Hinder you from reaching it,
Shoot your arrow;
And drive them away;
Then you can reach Siva state
Lustrous as Pure Red Gold.[32]

The intended meaning of the verse is: There is a fruit delicious from fragrant flower within it ripens – in the sweet-scented flower called sahasrāra there is a fruit named Śiva; the birds within the self hinder you from reaching it – since the sense-oriented birds themselves cannot reach it, they prevent the sādhaka from reaching the fruit; shoot your arrow and drive them away – drive away the preventing sense-birds by directing the arrow of your spiritual, kuṇḍalinī energy upwards; then you can reach Śiva state – by sublimating the energy in the sense-organs, you can reach the sahasrāra state; lustrous as pure red gold – this sahasrāra state is the immortal (gold) state of excellence (pure red).

2. 13. The use of similes

The *Tirumandiram* is abound with verses where language is used indicating an inside meaning. In this use of language (called *aga-p-poruḷ-kuṟippu* in Tamil) a simile is given and it indicates an inner meaning. Verse 2220 contains such a simile.

The birds shrilled
Unaware of the shimmering dawn;
Bewildered were they,
Their mother unrecognizing;
Beyond Vedas stood He my Lord;
They who knew the Mystic Way
Reached to Him inside their very head.[33]

The simile contains an internal secret understanding between the beloved and the lover. They have a secret understanding to meet at a particular time in the night. But the birds, not knowing the time at night, woke up (well before the dawn) and made chirping noise. Thinking that the time to meet the lover has come, the beloved woke up and went to the pre-determined spot to meet him; not finding him at that time of night, the beloved was perplexed and sent messengers to him. But the lover came to the spot at the exact pre-determined time and the beloved was happy to meet him.

The internal meaning indicated by the simile is as follows: The five cognitive sense organs of knowledge, i.e., the *jñānendriyas* (birds) were bewildered in not knowing their source of light. In other words the *jīva-tattvas* functioned without knowing the source of truth. Due to this the soul also was bewildered without attaining God-realisation. Śiva, the ultimate reality, also did not help to remove the bewilderment of the jīva. Later on jīva, by exhibiting its genuine love towards Him (and understanding the mystic way), attained Him and enjoyed *Śivānubhava* (experience of Śiva). That is the jīva by knowing the mystic way of Yoga attained Him at the head, i.e., sahasrāra.

2. 14. The numeral "five"

The interpretation of numeral "five" should have come properly under the heading *the use of numerals.* Since the "number five" has acquired a special significance in Siddha poetry, it is discussed under a separate heading. (Refer, also Śiva-vākkiyar's verse dealing with "five" under section 1.5. of this chapter). At the hands of Tirumūlar the "number five" has acquired a significant importance, which a reader of the *Tirumandiram* will not fail to note. Though several examples can be given, we have taken only two verses for consideration, that is, verses 2025 and 2027. These two verses contain a figure of speech in which the idea of the subject matter is sought to be conveyed suggestively by the description of that which resembles it. That is, it is a figure of speech in which by using a simile, the subject of comparison is suggested or indicated.

The translation of verse 2025 runs as follows:

Five the Sense organs,
Five the Sense-birds,
Five the Fields,
The Sense-birds seek to feed,
Five the Waters,
Five their functions,
Yet are they of one lineage;

And one the hunter
That herds them together;
Nine the exits of the body
Where he in sorrow wanders.[34]

The significant meaning of this verse is: Five are the sense-organs called the *jñānendriyas* (sense-birds); five are the fields in which they seek to feed, that is, the five *tanmātras*; five are the waters, that is the five *karmendriyas*; and five are their functions. Yet they are all of one lineage. The hunter that herds them together is also one, i.e., the jīva. But the harassing senses bring sorrow to the jīva through the nine gates or openings (two eyes, two ears, two nostrils, one mouth, one urinary passage and anus). The gist of the verse is that if the sense organs go out seeking pleasure in the outside world, it is very difficult to control them.

The translation of verse 2027 is as follows:

Five are the ministers,
Ninety-six are they within,
The Five and their brood of sons within
Seek you to rule;
If the Five in their fiery passion stand,
Endless indeed is the tribute
That to the Five we are to pay.[35]

The five ministers are the five sense organs that rule the land of the jīva. The five sense-organs are like the conspiring ministers that usurp the jīva. The servants of the ministers are the ninety-six tattvas. Both the sense organs and the ninety-six tattvas reign supreme over the jīva. If the five ministers (sense-organs) stand fiery in their anger, the jīva cannot help but pay tribute (as paid by an inferior prince to his suzerain) to them. The gist of the verse is that if the sense organs start working vigorously, it is very difficult to control or appease them.

2. 15. The twilight language of the fig-fruit

Before concluding this section, let us have a curtain raiser for a discussion of *śūnya-sambhāṣaṇai* by taking into consideration two verses of the *Tirumandiram*, which contain the twilight element in them. Twilight language is to be distinguished from all the other types of language like simile, symbolism, allusion, allegory, etc. It is a specifically intended language in which the message is concealed purposely. In this sense twilight language is an intentional language, which can be understood only by a person who comes under the same mystic wave length. In twilight language the expression is ordinary, plain language but the intention is completely different from the words used.

Verse 160 runs as follows:

Fruit of fig and seeds of green to pieces chopper,
In a pot they placed, mixed and ground to paste;
Seeds of green the fruit of fig consumed,
Loud they wailed, and bore the body in haste.[36]

The intended meaning is: Fruit of fig – the egg in the womb of a woman *(curōṇitam)*; seeds of green – semen virile *(cukkilam)*; the pot – the womb; mixed and ground to paste – they became a fertilized ovum;

The gist of the poem is: The semen virile and the egg in the womb of a woman get mixed, they become a fertilized ovum, and a child is born crying and weeping, to be taken finally to the jaws of death.

This poem is in twilight language because the birth of a child is concealed by using terms of plant life.

2. 16. The twilight language of the old woman in the corner of the dark chamber

The translation of the verse is:

In the corner dark of the Chamber ...
There she was...
Intent on consorting with Blind Old Man...
She sent his veil of night,
Showered full many a favour,
Wooed with temptation diverse,
...to Her bosom took him
In wedlock holy. [37]

The intended meaning is: The (maiden) in the corner dark of the chamber– the kuṇḍalini-sakti in the mūlādhāra; intent on consorting with the blind old man – intending to remove the ignorance and reveal the wisdom in the (immortal) soul; she sent his veil of night – removed the ignorance of the soul; showered full many a favor – revealing and making him recognize the nature of paśu (jīva), pāśa (fetters) and Pati (the Lord); wooed with temptations diverse – bringing out the good sense in him, creating a shock in the worldly things, and developing a desire to seek liberation; took him to her bosom in holy wedlock – married him; became one with him.

The gist of the verse is: The kuṇḍalinī-śakti kindled the jñāna, wisdom, already existing in the jīva and absorbed him at the level of sahasrāra with Śiva-Śakti.

3. Śūnya-sambhāṣaṇai of Tirumūlar

The *śūnya-sambhāṣaṇai* of Tirumūlar fits very well into the Tāntric pattern of *sandhyā-bhāṣa* or twilight language. There is a basic difficulty in deciphering and discovering the meaning of the twilight language of Tirumūlar. One may attempt three different approaches to the problem of deciphering the meaning. First there is the meditative-descriptive approach, based on experience in practical meditation. Second there is the historical-scholarly approach based on an examination and understanding of the corpus of Siddha texts. Third there is the mystical approach, which would assign meanings to terms and symbols on the basis of intuition (mystic experience) alone. The second method, i.e., the historical-scholarly approach is adopted throughout this section in deciphering Tirumūlar's *śūnya-sambhāṣaṇai* based on the historical, textual and other evidence. The other two approaches—the meditative and the intuitive— are not specifically adopted, since the author of this chapter is not trained in meditation nor had the benefit of mystical experience. Yet these two methods may occasionally come into focus as the author firmly believes in the influence and guidance of the Siddhas in deciphering the meaning.

The verses that we discuss under this section form part of the typical Siddha poetry of esoteric meaning. Out of the seventy verses under this heading in the *Tirumandiram* only a sample of ten verses are taken up for explanation and elucidation though all the other verses are equally important and significant.

Verse 2866

Body the ...board;
Five the dice;
Three the channels
Fifty one the squares

Thus the jivas play the game;
He who thus leads them to it;
The mystery of His play
I know not.[37]

The intended meaning is: Body the board – The human body is the gambling board: five the dice – the five senses are the dice; the five senses include the five organs of knowledge *(jñānendriyas)*, the five organs of actions *(karmendriyas)*; three the channels – the three internal (sense) organs that, is mind *(manas)*, intellect *(buddhi)* and ego *(ahamkāra)*; the three channels are sometimes spoken of as the soul's power of desire *(icchā-śakti)* power of action *(kriyā-śakti)* and the power of knowledge *(jñāna-śakti)*; fifty-one the squares – the fifty-one letters which are contained in the six adharas of the body; thus the jivas play the game – the game of life is thus being played by the jivas; he who thus leads them to it – one who directs this game of the dice; the mystery of His play I know not – I do not understand or have knowledge of the secrecy or mystery of this play.

The gist of the poem is: The game of dice is being played by two persons, i.e., the jīva and Śiva. But both the players are concealed in the act of the game. The jīva who plays the game thinks that he is the sole player and does not know that there is another player in this game, i.e., Śiva; nor does he know whether the other player is actually playing with him or against him. The entire play is a mystery in that the player (the jīva) does not know that he is the soul, nor does he know the purpose of the game.

The aim of the verse is to show that *tirodhāna-śakti*, or the power of obscuration is one of the five acts of Śiva.

Verse 2869

I sowed the seed of brinjal
And the shoot of balsam pear arose;
I dug up the dust;
And the pumpkin blossomed;
The gardener-gang prayed and ran;
Full well-ripened the fruit of plantain.[39]

This is an oft-quoted verse of Tirumūlar. The implied meaning is: I sowed the seed of brinjal – I undertook the practice of Kuṇḍalinī-Yoga; the shoot of balsam-pear arose – (because of it) I got the *vairāgya* (bitter-gourd), i.e., balsam-pear; I dug up the dust – I examined the tattvas of the self (or I had philosophical speculation); the pumpkin blossomed – (because of it) I found the Śiva-tattva in me (Śiva manifesting itself); the gardener-gang prayed and ran – once Śiva-tattva was discovered in me, all my *indriyas*, sense-organs, kept quiet. Full well ripened the fruit of plantain – then I enjoyed the fruit of *Śivānubhava.*

The gist is: Due to jñāna, detachment *(vairāgya)* appeared in the sādhaka. By controlling the senses and understanding the jīva-tattvas and realizing the Śiva-tattvas, the sādhaka attained the *Śivānubhava.*

B. Natarajan gives the following implied meaning for the twilight terms occurring in this verse. Brinjal – renunciation (*vazu* plus *thalai* means shaven-head); Balsam-pear – bitterness or world negation; The dust – the tattvas or the universals that constitute the body; Pumpkin – Śiva (suggesting a liṅga covered with holy ashes); Gardener-gang – the *indriyas* or sense-organs; may also refer to malas; The fruit of plantain – *mukti* or liberation from birth. The plantain is thought of as being seedless (*vazai* comes from *vaz* and *i* – creating a pun on the word to mean 'life-giving fruit').[40]

The gist of the verse as given by Suba. Annamalai runs as follows: Instead of going astray and spending the semen virile in sensual pleasure, if one turns it into a spiritual energy or fire, and then directs it to the ājñā-cakra, there Śiva-Śakti appeared. Then the binding of the thirty-six tattvas of the soul got removed. One's awareness becomes pure and one attains *sahasrāra*. One's *karaṇas* (instruments of the jīva) were turned into instruments of Śiva *(Śiva-karaṇas)*. And then one attained *Śivānubhava*. Suba. Annamalai translates pumpkin to mean the brahmarandra or the sahasrāra. He also interprets that just as the plantain tree dies after it yields fruits, the moment the wisdom or experience of Śiva *(Śiva-bodham)* is attained, the self-conceited knowledge of the jīva *(tat-bodha)* is removed.[41]

Verse 2873

Two the piccottahs, seven the wells;
The elder draws out, the younger waters;
If into the field the water flows not,
And into waste flows,
Verily is it like the fowl
That the harlot rears.[42]

The implied meaning is: Two the piccottahs – the iḍā-nāḍi and the piṅgalā-nāḍi; seven the wells – the seven cakras; the elder draws out – exhalation occurs in the iḍā-nāḍi *(candra-kalai)*; the younger waters – inhalation occurs in the piṅgalā-nāḍi *(sūrya-kalai)*; if the water flows not into the field and waste it flows – if it does not flow through the channel of suṣumnā *(agni-kalai)* and does not reach the field of sahasrāra, it is a waste; verily is it like the fowl – it is like the male child (cock); that the harlot rears – that the harlot brings up.

The gist of the poem is: If the prāṇa which passes through the iḍā (left channel) and the piṅgalā (right channel) is not directed through the suṣumnā (middle channel) so that it may reach its field of destination, i.e., sahasrāra, the effort of the breathing technique is a waste. It is as wasteful as a harlot who brings up a male child in her house, who will not be useful to her profession in future.

"Verily is it like the fowl that the harlot rears" has been interpreted by G. Varadarajan as follows: Just as (virgin) the girl being brought up by a harlot is enjoyed and spoiled by a man to satisfy his sexual urge or desire, in the same way the kuṇḍalinī-śakti is being wasted without being directed in the proper way.[43]

Suba. Annamalai's interpretation of the verse is as follows: The prāṇa functions in the body through the iḍā-nāḍi and the piṅgalā-nāḍi. If prāṇa which starts functioning at the mūlādhāra, passes through the iḍā-nāḍi *(candra-kalai)*, the sexual energy at the sexual gland situated near the maṇipūra-cakra, will be directed upwards. If prāṇa passes through the piṅgalā-nāḍi *(sūrya-kalai)* the sexual energy will start rushing upwards. If the prāṇa passes through the two nāḍis, iḍā and piṅgalā, in equal proportion, the sexual energy will be burnt and converted into the fiery kuṇḍalinī-energy which will ascend through them and function into suṣumnā as a spiritual force. If the prāṇa does not act in this coordinated fashion and functions alternately in the iḍā and piṅgalā nāḍis, without directing upwards the sexual-energy then it becomes a wasted energy.[44]

Verse 2874

Twenty and four the cows that stray uncontrolled,
Other cows gentler are seven and five;

Well may the gentler ones a whole pot of milk give;
But jīva has the straying uncontrolled ones alone.[45]

The implied meaning is: Twenty and four the cows that stray uncontrolled – The tattvas (principles) that pertain to the jīva's body are twenty-four which are not under control; (that is their milk is of no use); Other cows gentler are seven and five – There are the other seven vidyā-tattvas (principles of knowledge) and Śiva-tattvas (principles of Śiva); Well may the gentler ones a whole pot of milk give – these seven vidyā and five Śiva tattvas give pots of milk, i.e., they pave the way for enlightenment of the soul; But jīva has the straying uncontrolled ones alone – but the jīva is interested in its twenty four jīva-tattvas (principles of jīva).

The gist of the verse is: The jīva due to its ignorance is attracted towards the enjoyment of the senses at the cost of enjoying the bliss. The twenty-four jīva-tattvas do not elevate the jīva, whereas the vidyā and Śiva tattvas elevate the jīva to a higher state of wisdom.

Verse 2882

On the mountain it rained,
The young deer leapt;
The rich ripe fruit from bunch above dropped
Like the metal on the smith's furnace,
It melted;
And over the Heart, He made it flow.[46]

The implied meaning is: On the mountain it rained – on the top of the head (sahasrāra) the illumination occurred; that is, the nectar flowed; the young deer leapt – the jīva hit at the centre of the head, i.e., the sahasrāra; the rich ripe fruit from bunch above dropped – the fruit of bliss at the sahasrāra dropped; like the metal on the smith's furnace it melted – like the metal in the furnace it melted; and over the head He made it flow – the sweet ambrosia, nectar, *Śivānubhava*, flowed from the sahasrāra.

The gist of the poem is: The nectar flowed from the sahasrāra and the jīva, the sādhaka leapt with joy. From the sahasrāra (the bunch) dropped the bliss of Śiva (the rich fruit).

Suba. Annamalai gives the gist of the poem as follows: The yogin (the sādhaka), at the sahasrāra *(citākāśa)* enjoyed the Śiva-Śakti experience. The jīva that has been nurtured by the *prakṛti*, the world, has left its jīva (limited) nature, and realized its true self. The Śivam, which is beyond the beyond, which is *mahākāśa*, has been felt by him. The yogin has become *sat-cit-ānanda*. Just as the iron-piece, which has been placed in the iron smith's furnace, becomes one with the fire, the jīva has become Śiva.[47]

Verse 2887

From the Bamboo shoot arose a Margosa tree
Close on Margosa was a Palmyrah,
In that palm is a snake
Knowing not to drive that Snake and eat it,
The Margosa tree withered away.[48]

The intended meaning is: From the bamboo-shoot arose a Margosa tree – from the bamboo-shoot of mind *manas* rose up the margosa tree of *vairāgya*; close on margosa, was a palmyrah – depending on the *vairāgya*, is the suṣumnā; in that palm is a snake – in the suṣumnā, there is the snake called kuṇḍalinī-śakti; knowing not to drive that snake and eat it – knowing not to kindle the snake called kuṇḍalinī and rising it upwards and enjoying (eat) the nectar; the margosa tree withered away – the *vairāgya* has been wasted.

The gist of the verse is: Just as the bamboo-shoot is not strong enough, the *vairāgya* born out of the sense-dependent mind will not be firm. Yet in such a mind, *vairāgya*, the bitterness towards sensual pleasure, may arise. But *vairāgya* is not enough to attain ātma-jñāna. (knowledge of ātman); one should direct and ascend the kuṇḍalinī-śakti, through jñāna, to the top of the head; if kuṇḍalinī-śakti is not directed like this, *vairāgya* is of no use.

A slightly different interpretation is given by B. Natarajan: From the bamboo-shoot (karma) arose a margosa tree (body) and very close to that was a palmyrah (suṣumnā). Knowing not how to drive the snake (kuṇḍalinī) that was in the palm, the margosa withered away (the body perishes if Yoga is not practiced).[48]

The interpretation given by Suba. Annamalai is as follows: The act of breathing starts from mūlādhāra (the bamboo-shoot). Breathing (margosa) happens through iḍā and piṅgalā. In between the nāḍis (iḍā and piṅgalā) there is the suṣumnā-nāḍi (Palmyra). At the bottom of the suṣumnā, the iḍā and piṅgalā nāḍis are intertwined like snake, where resides the kuṇḍalinī-śakti. With the help of kuṇḍalinī-śakti, after worshipping her, kindling the flame there, burning the sex-energy into a life-giving the energy, with prāṇa and kuṇḍalinī-śakti passing through suṣumnā-nāḍi and going upward by the help of the prāṇa, one should strengthen the life-giving energy and inhale that prāṇa. But this is not done by people and the entire effort is a waste.[50]

Verse 2898

Leaves none, bees none, Flower there is;
Top none, sheath none, root there is;
Bunch none, Flower to pluck there is;

Head none to wear;
The branch that bent withers not.[51]

The implied meaning is: Leaves none – In the Śivam, there are no tender leaves of the *tanmātras* (the subtle essence of the five elements– sound, touch, sight, taste and smell); bees none – there are no objects of sense-organs; flower there is – there is brilliance; top none – no one can visualize the knowledge of (the head) the Śivam; root there is – the Śivam is diffused throughout the universe *(prapañca)*; sheath none – but its existence does not depend on the universe; bunch none – it is one, not many; flower to pluck there is – there is a flower of sahasrāra to be enjoyed; head none to wear–but ordinary men are not qualified to wear it on their heads; (none but the head of the yogin can wear it); the branch that bent withers not – the sahasrāra lotus will bestow *amṛta* (it will bend), but it will not wither away at any time; it is eternity itself.

The gist of the verse is: This verse gives the *svarūpa-lakṣaṇa*, the essential nature of Śivam, i.e., Sat-cit-ānanda (existence-knowledge-bliss). All the things in the universe are the *taṭastha-lakṣaṇa*, the accidental attributes of Śivam. (This verse resembles a verse from *Kaṭhopaniṣad*).

Verse 2916

In the river of leagues Three
Are plantain trees Three;
Ruddy fruits of triple Malas they love;
They who are with the Lord exceeding;
Hoisted their Flag;
And seeking the Virgin through central suṣumnā
Inhaled the Flower's fragrance, divine sweet.[52]

The implied meaning is: In the river of leagues three – in the river of the three guṇas *(sattva, rajas* and *tamas)*; are plantain trees three – are the three plantains of (*avasthās*, states of consciousness of) waking *(jāgrat)*, dreaming *(svapna)* and deep sleep *(suṣupti)*; ruddy fruits of triple malas they bore – they brought forth the three malas (the impurities), the āṇava (ego-bondage), karma (action) and māyā (delusion); they who are with the Lord exceeding hoisted their flag – but those who enjoy the fruit of *Śivānubhava* (that is, those who have hoisted their flag in Kuṇḍalinī-Yoga) are free from these, (the three guṇas, the three *avasthās* and the three malas); and seeking the virgin – seeking the kuṇḍalinī-śakti; through the central suṣumnā inhaled the flower, fragrance, divine sweet–enjoyed the divine, sweet flower's fragrance, i.e., sahasrāra, through the central suṣumnā-nāḍi.

Another implied meaning has been suggested by G.Varadarajan for the last two lines.[53] It is as follows: Seeking the virgin inhaled the flower's fragrance, divine sweet – even though they enjoy a virgin woman; through central susumna – they had their mind-set only in the Yoga process. Though this interpretation seems to be a long-stretched one, this interpretation powerfully reminds one of Śiva-vākkiyar. According to Śiva-vākkiyar, even when a Siddha is enjoying the breasts of a woman, because of his disinterested attitude, he cuts asunder the knots of karma and does not suffer rebirth.[54] According to him the gist of the verse is that those who live in the blissful state of *Śivānubhava*, even though they enjoy a woman, will always stand in the middle, that is in a state of equanimity.[55]

The gist of the verse as provided by Suba. Annamalai is a little bit different. It is as follows: There are three zones or *maṇḍalas* in the passage of the kuṇḍalinī-śakti from mūlādhāra to sahasrāra, viz., the *agni* (fire), *sūrya* (sun) and *candra* (moon) *maṇḍalas.* (The region extending from mūlādhāra to anāhata is called *agni-maṇḍala,* the region from anāhata to ājñā is called *sūrya-maṇḍala;* the region extending from ājñā to the end of suṣumnā is called the *candra-maṇḍala*); and each region is characterized by certain powers (called *kalai* in Tamil) called *agni-kalai, sūrya-kalai* and *candra-kalai.* Of these, though the other two are useful, the important and useful one is the *candra-kalai.* The yogin who has crossed the first two *maṇḍalas* and reached the third *candra-maṇḍala* is said to have attained the highest experience. Those who have not reached the *candra-maṇḍala,* even though the kuṇḍalinī-śakti seems to help them, it will only give them trouble. Only a man who has reached the *candra-maṇḍala* through the suṣumnā-nāḍi will enjoy *Śivānubhava.*[56]

Verse 2918

Pig and snake, Cow and Monkey
Together were in the lowly Jackal herd;
Joining them not and debasing himself not,
When, in balance, deeds good and bad are equal weighed
The *Jiva,* tinier than crab's-eye berry, its ego's diminution saw.[57]

The implied meaning is: Pig – desire for excrement; standing for *tamas;* snake – anger towards enemy; standing for *rajas;* cow – calmness; over endurance towards fault; standing for *sattva;* monkey – mind, *manas,* uncontrollable nature; together were in the lowly jackal herd – together were in the lowly thirty-six tattvas; joining them not and debasing himself not – the yogin is not disturbed by these: when in balance, deeds good and bad are equally weighed – treating good and bad as equal and jīva counterpoising with Śiva; the jīva, tinier than crab's eye-berry – jīva, little by little; its ego's diminution saw – defects were reduced gradually.

The gist of the verse is: To merge with Śivam, jīva has to do away with its bad nature gradually, little by little.

According to Suba. Annamalai the gist of the poem is: The mind is dazzled by the three guṇas, *tamas, rajas* and *sattva*. The yogin should free his mind without being affected by the three guṇas, should awaken his consciousness gradually and free it from the ātma-tattvas and their impressions and become empty space.[58]

Verse 2933

When in the Garden,
The Fruit of Mango, ripened, dropped,
What matters if Jackals outside howl?
When the Primal One was by Kundalini Fire reached,
The Fleshy body that led to it,
Forever left.[59]

The intended meaning is: When in the garden the fruit of mango ripened, dropped – when the ripened mango fruit of *Śivānubhava* has been attained in the garden of sahasrāra; What matters if jackals outside howl – The disturbance by the senses (the howling of jackals) outside matters little; when the primal one was by Kuṇḍalini Fire reached – when Śiva has been reached by the process of Kuṇḍalinī-Yoga; the fleshy body that lead to it forever left – the body counts for little.

The gist of the verse is: When one has attained the sahasrāra through the Kuṇḍalinī-Yoga, the external world will have no effect on the sādhaka.

Notes on Chapter Six

1. *Tirumandiram*, 293.
2. Hariprasad Shastri, *Buddha Gan O Doha.*
3. Vidhushekara Bhattacharya (Sastri), "Sandhabhasa," *Indian Historical Quarterly*, Vol. IV, 2, pp. 287-296.
4. Buddhadasa, *Two Kinds of Language*, pp. 20-24.
5. Refer also Per Kvaerne, *An Anthology of Buddhist Tantric Songs*, pp. 5-7 for a brief account of the range of opinions on *sandhya-bhasa.* Refer also the "unacceptable view" of P.K. Banerjee. Banerjee says that the term *sandhya* is the proper name of a dialect spoken in a region of this name called the Sandhya country. (Quoted by V.Bhattacharya, *op. cit.*, p. 288).
6. Hariprasad Shastri's view.
7. Lama Govinda's view in *The Foundations of Tibetan Mysticism*, p. 46
8. D.N. Bose's view in *Tantras – Their Philosophical and Occult Secrets*, p. 137.
9. Agehananda Bharati's view in *The Tantric Tradition*, p. 170.
10. Ibid., p. 171. To quote A. Bharati:

    The oft quoted Tāntric passage, repeated in various modifications in many tantric commentaries as well as by orthodox Hindus as a deterrant and an invective against Tāntric practice, is a case in point; it says: 'inserting his organ into the mother's womb, pressing his sister's breasts, placing his foot upon his *guru*'s head, he will be reborn no more'.... In the Hindu Tāntric parlance, the 'organ' is the contemplating mind, 'the mother's womb' is the mūlādhāra....the 'sister's breasts' are the.....*anāhata* and *ājñā* respectively and the '*guru*'s head' is the.....*sahasrāra-cakra* and the implied instruction is thus translatable: He practices mental penetration through the successive centres, and when he reaches the upper-most centre, he will not be reborn, and he has thereby attained *nirvikalpa samādhi.* (p. 171).

11. Mircea Eliade, *Yoga: Immortality and Freedom*, p. 250.
12. *Tirumandiram*, 748; "there is no other reason for concealing the teachings." i.e., people should get at the great teachings only through the proper method of *upadeśa.*
13. Bucknell and Stuart Fox, *The Twilight Language*, pp. 34-35.
14. *Ibid.*, p. 35
15. T. N. Ganapathy, *The Philosophy of the Tamil Siddhas*, pp. 24-26.
16. That there are eighteen siddhis is referred to in the *Bhāgavata* where Lord Kṛṣṇa says: "Those who are experts in concentra tion and Yoga call the powers eighteen in number. Eight of these are pertaining to Me and the remaining ten are due to a perfection of *sattva.*" Swami Madhavananda (Ed.), *Uddhava Gīta*, pp. 141-42.
17. In this connection it would be of interest to note that in comparing Swami Vivekananda with other spiritual luminaries of his time, Sri Rāmakṛṣṇa said of him: "If Keshub Chandra Sen had one power which made him famous, Vivekananda had eighteen such powers in the fullest measure..." Refer: E.R. Marrozzi, "The making of Swami Vivekananda," p. 11.
18. Aru. Ramanathan, *Cittar Pāḍalgaḷ*, Vol. 2, Kāka-pucuṇḍar, 4.
19. T.N. Ganapathy, *The Yoga of Siddha Bōganāthar*, Vol. II, pp. 435-438.
20. Śiva-vākkiyar, 10.
21. The equivalents of the letters of A, U, M:

	A	U	M
Meters	Gāyatri (24 syllables)	Triṣṭubh (44 syllables)	Jagati (48 syllables)
States	Waking conscious-ness *(jāgrata)*	Dream *(svapna)*	Deep-sleep *(suṣupti)*
Periods *(savanna)* Cycles	Morning 24 years	Midday 44 years	Evening 48 years
Gods	of the elements	of the sky *(Ādityas)*	of the sphere of space *(Rudras)*
Seasons	Spring	Summer	Winter
Offering	the offered butter *(ajya)*	the fuel *(idhma)*	the act of offering *(havis)*
Ritual utterance	"Earth" *(bhūr)*	"Sky" *(svar)*	"space" *(bhuvar)*
Spheres	Earthly	Heavenly	Intermediary
Veda	Knowledge of meters *(Ṛg)*	Knowledge of contents *(Yajus)*	Knowledge of extension *(Sāman)*
Elemental deity	Fire *(Agni)*	Sun *(Āditya)*	Wind *(Vāyu)*
Manifestation of speech	Voice *(vāc)*	Mind *(manas)*	Breath *(prāṇa)*
Priestly function	The *Hotṛ* (making offering	The *Adhvaryu* (per forming rituals)	The *Udgātṛ* (singing)
Quality	Extension *(rajas)*	Cohesion *(sattva)*	Disintegration *(tamas)*
Ritual fire	of the home *(gārhapatya-agni)*	of the ancestors *(dakṣiṇa-agni)*	of invocation *(ābhavana-agni)*
Goddess	Amba	Ambika	Ambālika
Deity	Brahma (the creator)	Viṣṇu (the preserver	Śiva (the destroyer
Power	of action *(kriya)*	of knowledge *(jñāna)*	of will *(iccha)*

- Refer *Hindu Polytheism*, p. 340.

22. Agehananda Bharati, *The Tāntric Tradition*, p.173.
23. *Tirumandiram*, 1. Translation of B. Natarajan with one change of word, that is, instead of "worlds," the term "He" has been used in line four.
24. *Ibid.*, 977. Translation of B. Natarajan.
25. *Ibid.*, 1392. Translation of B. Natarajan.
26. *Ibid.*, Adaptation of the translation of B. Natarajan with certain omissions.
27. *Ibid.*, 1886. Translation of B. Natarajan.
28. *Ibid.*, 2006. Translation of B. Natarajan.
29. *Ibid.*, 189. Translation of B.Natarajan.
30. *Ibid.*, 193. Translation of B.Natarajan with certain changes.
31. *Ibid.*, 2214. Translation of B.Natarajan, slightly modified.
32. *Ibid.*, 2607. Translation of B.Natarajan.
33. *Ibid.*, 2220. Translation of B. Natarajan.
34. *Ibid.*, 2025. Translation of B. Natarajan.
35. *Ibid.*, 2027. Translation of B. Natarajan.
36. *Ibid.*, 160. Translation of B. Natarajan.
37. *Ibid.*, 1514. Translation of B. Natarajan. Certain words in the translation are omitted.
38. *Ibid.*, 2866. Translation of B.Natarajan.
39. *Ibid.*, 2869. Translation of B.Natarajan.
40. B. Natarajan (Tr.), *Tirumandiram*, p. 441.
41. Suba. Annamalai (Ed.), *Tirumandiram*, Vol. 3, pp. 530-531.
42. *Tirumandiram*, 2873. Translation of B. Natarajan.
43. G. Varadarajan (Comm.), *Tirumandiram*, Vol. 3, p. 583.
44. Suba. Annamalai (Ed.), *Tirumandiram*, Vol. 3, p. 534.
45. *Tirumandiram*, 2874. Translation of B. Natarajan.

46. *Ibid.*, 2882. Translation of B. Natarajan.
47. Suba. Annamalai (Ed.), *Tirumandiram,* Vol. 3, p. 542.
48. *Tirumandiram*, 2887. Translation of B. Natarajan.
49. B. Natarajan (Tr.), *Tirumandiram,* p. 444.
50. Suba. Annamalai (Ed.), *Tirumandiram*, p. 547.
51. *Tirumandiram*, 2898. Translation of B. Natarajan.
52. *Ibid.*, 2916. Translation of B. Natarajan.
53. G. Varadarajan (Comm.), *Tirumandiram*, Vol. 3, p. 605.
54. Śiva-vākkiyar, 182; refer also Bhadragiriyār, 53.
55. G. Varadarajan (Comm.), *Tirumandiram*, Vol. 3, p. 606.
56. Suba. Annamalai (Ed.), *Tirumandiram*, Vol. 3, pp. 567-568.
57. *Tirumandiram*, 2918. Translation of B. Natarajan.
58. Suba. Annamalai (Comm.), *Tirumandiram*, Vol. 3, pp. 569-570.
59. *Tirumandiram*, 2933. Translation of B. Natarajan.

CHAPTER 7

THE CONCEPT OF THE HUMAN BODY IN THE TIRUMANDIRAM

T.N. Ganapathy

uḍambār aḻiyil uyirār aḻivar
tiḍampaḍa meyjñāṉam cēravum māṭṭār
uḍambai vaḷarkkum ubāyam aṟindē
uḍambai vaḷarttēṉ uyir vaḷarttēṉē.

If the body perishes, Prāṇa departs
Nor will the light of Truth be reached;
I learned the way of preserving my body
And so doing, my Prāṇa too.

–Tirumandiram, 724.

7. The Concept of the Human Body in the Tirumandiram

T.N. Ganapathy

At the hands of the Siddhas the human body has acquired a special significance, which is conspicuous by its absence in the other systems of Indian spiritual thought. According to the Siddhas the human body contains in itself an immortal essence. It can be and should be transformed into a divine body *(divya-deha)* and must be made an aid to liberation and not a hindrance. The human body as such is the instrument *(mokṣa-sādhana)* and an elevator of man's liberation. Immortality is within the body; it is not the body itself; but it is in the body. As Śrī Aurobindo has said, "It is not immortality of the body, but the consciousness of immortality *in* the body."[1] According to him divinisation is not destruction of the human elements.[2] The Siddha view of the body as a *mokṣa-sādhana,* is known as *kāya-sādhana* or wisdom of the body *(deha-jñāna).* Mircea Eliade refers to *kāya-sādhana* as "*mystical physiology.*"[3]

1. Negative attitude towards the body

Though the Siddhas, on the whole, give an intrinsic value to the human body, a few of the Tamil Siddhas emphasize a negative attitude towards the body. Paṭṭiṉattār has developed the most obnoxious attitude towards the body.[4] A vivid description of the filthy nature of the human body can be found in the verses of Pāmbāṭṭi-c-cittar[5] and Kaḍuveḷi-c-cittar.[6] Tirumūlar uses the expression *vēm-kaḍam*[7] to refer to the human body. *Vēm* means destructible and *kaḍam* means the (human) body; that is, this human body is a destructible one. About the transitoriness of life in the body[8] and also about the transitoriness of youth,[9] Tirumūlar has spoken of in beautiful Tamil poetry. He advises people to give charity here and now before death's stern and relentless summon arrives.[10] People do not realize the ephemeral nature of youth (meaning the human body) even though they witness death daily.[11]

2. Tirumūlar's conception of death

In discussing the concept of the human body, it may be worthwhile to state Tirumūlar's conception of death, as it is closely related to the negative concept of body. He devotes one section for bringing out the transitoriness of the body.[12]

Speaking about the dead he says that they are forgotten very soon by the kith and kin.

The neighbours gathered together wailing loud and long,
Denied him now a name, called him corpse,
And bore him to the burning ghat and the body burnt,
Then did a ceremonial dip— and memory of him fades away.[13]

Tirumūlar further laments:

If the molded pot breaks, men keep the pieces still,
But if the body cracks, who even a whit cares to keep?[14]

By putting the dead body in the leaping flames, the relatives and friends, have also burnt and have done away with the passionate bond between them and the dead.[15] Having burnt the dead body, Tirumūlar, explains vividly how all these people hurried home.

Death strikes from life's enchanted cup
Honeyed delights of wife, cherished treasures of heart;
Kinsmen bore him on bier to the common burning ghat,
And the burden discharged, hurried home,
Having done their part.[16]

In this verse Tirumūlar uses a significant expression for the bier. He calls it as *idanam* which in Tamil means "the walking rack or loft." He also pines over the fact that once death takes place, it is immaterial to what happens to the human body.

When the energizing soul leaves this leather bag of the body,
What does it matter if the ravens feed on it, or the bystanders scorn,
Or drops of milk are poured on it and praise.[17]

Tirumūlar believes in life after death. Those who say that after death nothing remains may even say that the heavenly Gaṅgā Mandākiṉi ends, as an empty pot. He says:

They who say: "After death nothing is left;
The Jiva the five states experienced forever fled;"
They are verily unenlightened surpassing;
They might as well say:
The heavenly Ganga Mandakini
That from clouds aloft streams forth
Ends as an empty pot."[18]

In a section on Destruction, Tirumūlar speaks of four forms of death. They are: the daily death (sleep), fated death (when the soul leaves the body), pure death, (the soul is in primal quiescence), and redeemed death (the ultimate mergence of the soul in Śiva- Śakti).[19]

Patañjaliyār, a Tamil Siddha, in one of his verses assures that there is no death for a yogin. The verse asserts that even though the world is reduced to smithereens and the universe is broken to pieces, even at the time of the universal deluge there is no death for the yogin.[20] In a significant verse Tirumūlar says that the devotees of Śiva are not subject to the process of death. He likens the yogin to a king whose quarters are in the "west" and who spurns Yamā, the Lord of death. The term "west" (in Tamil *mēṟku*) is a significant one. In Siddha parlance "west" stands for the nape of the neck of the yogin where there is an invisible eye. One who has got such an eye in the nape of the neck, there is no death for him; he is an immortal being who has kicked the Lord of Death.[21] That there is an invisible eye or power of light at the nape of the neck of the yogin is vouchsafed by an incident narrated in Śrī Rāmakṛṣṇa's life. It is said that one night when Śrī Rāmakṛṣṇa Paramahamsa was going to Dakṣiṇeśwar along with another person it was pitch dark. He could not see the way. The companion, an adept in the Tantra-sādhana, thereupon walked in front and from his back emanated a light, which lit up the path for Śrī Rāmakṛṣṇa.

In this connection it would be interesting to note the view of a western mystic by name Jefferies who says that man's body is by nature immortal, and man was created immortal in body and soul. Death, according to him appears an earth not as a natural phenomenon, but as a hereditary flaw, which we inherit from defective parents; and it is with man's power to remove this flaw and thereby to become immortal in body as well as in soul.

3. The implication of the negative attitude of the body

The negative attitude of some of the Tamil Siddhas towards the human body is explainable in the background of the positive attitude developed in the doctrine of *kāya-sādhana* (culture of the body) with a view to attaining *kāya-siddhi* (perfection of the body), which is also known as *svarūpa-siddhi, yoga-siddhi* and *svarūpa-mukti* in Tamil Siddha literature. Śiva-vākkiyar calls *kāya-sādhana* as *mey-t-tavam* meaning thereby that it is the true *tapas* as well as a bodily *tapas.*[22] If the physical body is allowed to remain as a physical body with all its five limitations of *narai* (grey hair), *tirai* (wrinkles on the skin), *mūppu* (old age), *nōy* (disease) and *maraṇam* (death), then that body is unfit for the sādhaka. The spiritual aspirant must develop ways and means of transforming this physical body into an immortal essence. The Tamil Siddhas, only some of them, have highlighted the defects of the physical body in their songs in stronger terms so that the aspirant will not remain at the level of the physical body but go beyond it to achieve an immortal body. Śiva-vākkiyar calls the physical body as a deceptive threshold, and one has to 'open' it, that is, go beyond it to achieve *kāya-siddhi.*[23] Tirumūlar has devoted one section in his *Tirumandiram* dealing with "the way to *kāya-siddhi" (kāya-siddhi upāyam).*[24] The Tamil Siddhas believe that the phenomenal conditions of the body, called *uru-viḷaṅgu-mēṉi* in Tamil, do undergo change and suffer the process of destruction, but the noumenal elements of the body, called *tiru-viḷaṅgu-mēṉi* in Tamil, can be preserved for ages to come.[25] This is the reason why Koṅgaṇa Nāyaṉār warns us seriously not to treat the human body as a mere filthy one.[26]

In this connection our special attention may be drawn to one verse of Śiva-vākkiyar, the import of which may be rendered as follows: The human body can be transmuted into a divine body, but people not knowing the method of doing it simply treat the body as a dirty trap and hand it over finally to the Lord of Death and to the servants at the burning ghat so that it is burnt and destroyed. Śiva-vākkiyar asks a rhetorical question: Will the same people allow others to kidnap a beautiful lady from their house?[27] No; people should protect and immortalize and preserve the body through the method of Yoga just as they would protect a beautiful lady of their house. People who have understood the method of Kuṇḍalinī-Yoga will not allow the human body to be treated as a mere filthy thing but try to transmute it into a divine abode. In Tamil Nadu, if a person dies, it is a customary expression to say that he has "missed," or that he has "lost" (in Tamil *tavaṟi viṭṭār*). It is a significant expression in that it implies that the dead man has missed or lost an opportunity to know the secret of preserving the body without handing it over to death.

4. The human body as the temple (kṣetra)

Tamil Siddha poetry, on the whole, gives an intrinsic value to the human body. As said in the *Yoga-Vāsiṣṭha* the great city known as a body should be the source of joy, not misery; to a wise man it is like a garden that gives him pleasure, as it sets him free (4:23.2). The human body is likened to a temple. In the *Tirumandiram* we come across a number of verses praising the importance of the human body. Tirumūlar says that he had mistakenly believed the body to be imperfect but later on realized that within it resides the Ultimate Reality.[28] He speaks of *kāya-siddhi-upāyam*,[29] by means of which one can know God, the *Aṇṇal* (the father) residing in the body.[30] If one were to look carefully into this mortal physical body, one can 'see' the 'immortal thing' in it.[31] As the immortal thing resides in the body there is no demerit *(ūṉam)* to it. This is what has been revealed to us by that Reality itself.[32]

Tirumūlar uses an expression *cimiḻ* in Tamil, which means a small round box. This term is used to suggest that the knowledge of knowing the ultimate reality residing in our body is kept as a secret.[33] Tirumūlar gives a valid reason for rejecting the six religions in that they do not 'realize' or 'see' the God residing in the human body.[34] He also regrets that people do not have the proper sense to 'see' the 'diamond' embedded in the 'house of the human body.'[35] Just as heat resides in fire, God resides in the body.[36] Therefore, one has to use this body with its thirty-six tattvas, as a 'ladder' to *mukti*.[37] This aspect of the body as a way to liberation is not understood by many and hence not knowing its significance people do not take much care of it. There is one verse attributed to Tirumūlar, but not included in the official editions of the *Tiru- mandiram* which runs as follows:

> You ignorant men who search for God in heavens,
> Can the sweetness of honey be described as black or red?
> Just as the sweetness of honey is in the honey itself
> God is 'hiding' in the human body.

Tirumūlar calls the human body as the abode of God. In one of the verses he says that the Supreme Lord having transformed his body of flesh into a conscious body has entered into him and abides with him forever.[38] In Tāntric literature the temple is an image of both the macrocosm and the microcosm, the cosmic man as well as the inner being of man. The various parts of the structure of the temple are designated as features of the human body. The *pāda*, foot, stands for the base or the plinth. *Jaṅgha* represents the legs. *Bandhana* is the belt running round the entire structure of the temple. The *vimāna*, trunk, stands for the tower with its front and back, the two sides represent shoulders and neck. The *sikhara* stands for the top of the head. Tirumūlar has suggested this notion of the Tantra in one celebrated verse.

> For the Bounteous Lord
> This heart is the sanctum holy,
> The fleshy body is temple vast
> The mouth is the tower gate;
> To them that discern,

Jiva is Sivalinga;
The deceptive senses but the lights that illume.[39]

As Ganapati Sthapati has suggested: "In Tamil the Temple complex is called *Alayam* and the inner sanctum is termed as 'Perunkoil'... Tirumūlar has depicted the harmonious existence of these two aspects of a Temple as *ullam perunkoyil unudambu alayam.*"[40]

The observation of Ganapati Sthapati regarding the human form and the temple is worth noting here:

> ... the Garbagruha of a temple is indeed a living material form. In the same sense, we human beings are also material forms housing the atman or subtle energy inside. The energy space inside both the material embodying forms i.e the building and human form, vibrates and emanates waves of different wavelengths. In the case of a garbagruham, which is built by the shilpi in accordance with proportional measurement, the vibrations of the inner space will be in a particular order or rhythm. When a devotee or even a non-believer, stands before the inner sanctum of the temple and thinks of the divine energy enclosed inside, his inner space will start vibrating and at a particular time period, the waves emanating from his inner space and that coming from the garbagruham will merge and resonate with each other. At this stage, we say that the devotee has become one with the God... This is called spiritual harmony and can be compared to two veenas (wind instruments) set in the same pitch and on plucking the strings, both will vibrate and the resultant sound will resonate since both are set to the same frequency of vibration.[41] *(Garbagruha* is the *sanctum sanctorum).*

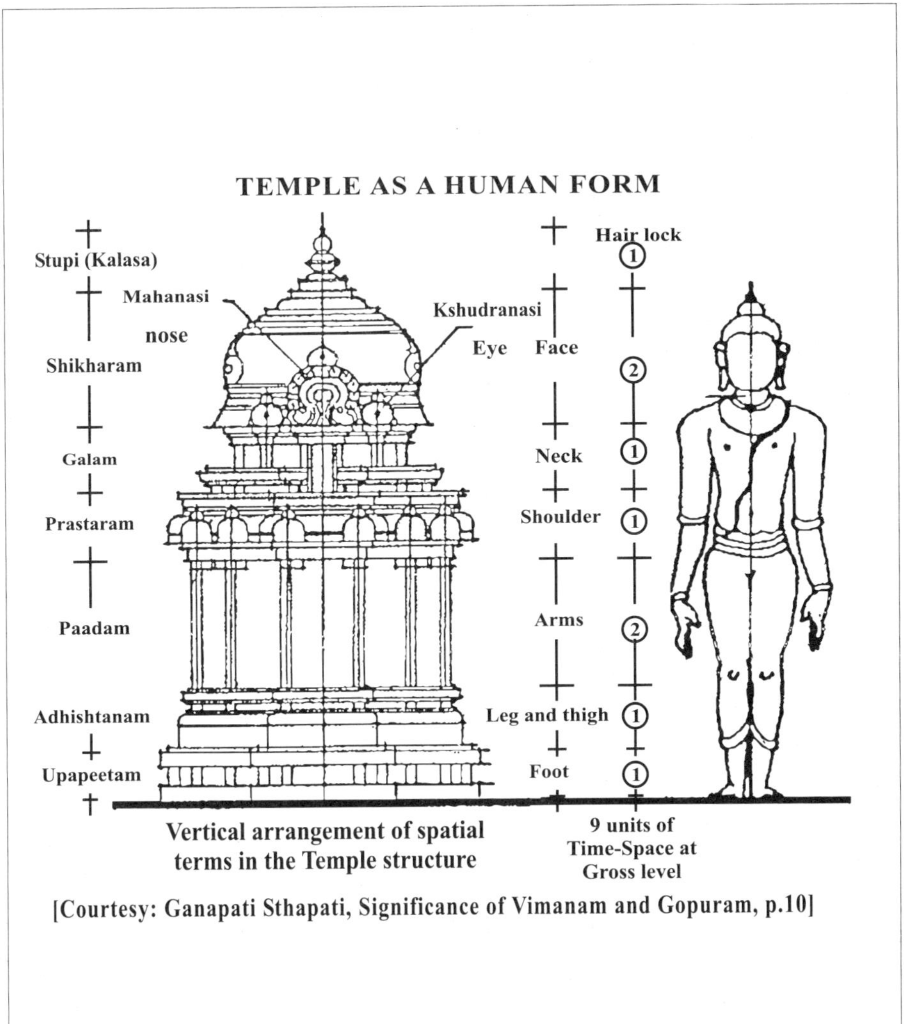

TEMPLE AS A HUMAN FORM

(Courtesy: Ganapati Sthapati, *Significance of Vimanam and Gopuram*, p.10)

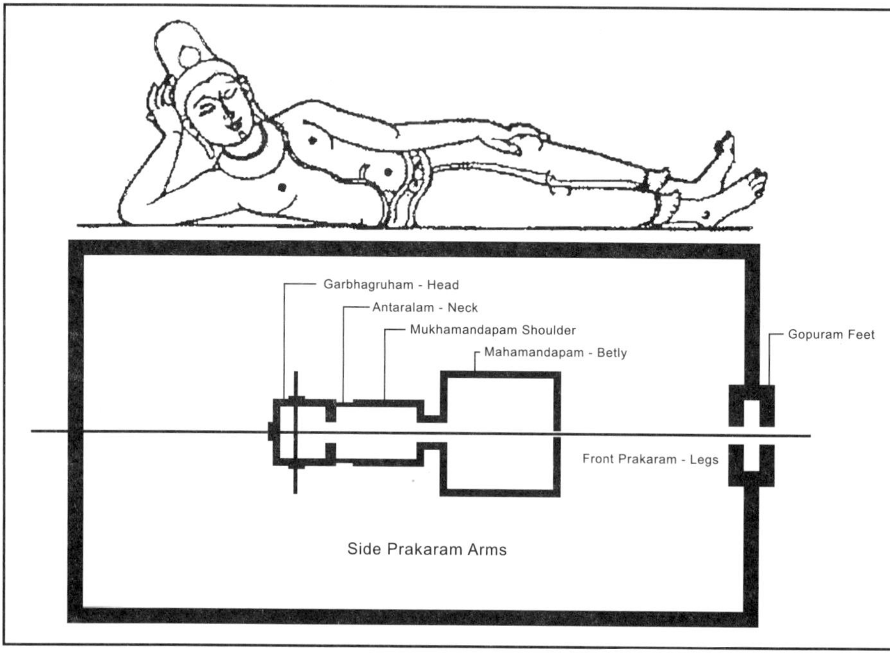

TEMPLE LAYOUT ILLUSTRATING HUMAN FORM IN LYING POSTURE
(Courtesy: Ganapati Sthapati, *Significance of Vimanam and Gopuram,* p.14)

In this connection it will be informative to note the two diagrams of Ganapati Sthapati regarding temple as a human form.

Tirumūlar appeals to people to treat the body as a place where God resides.[42] He reiterates again and again that God lives in this human body.

Mounting the Chariot of Mind
They seek the Divine Juggler;
Knowing not whither He went,
They bewail;

Wandering in lands and kingdoms far and near,
I saw Him in this fleeting Body-Land.[43]

He identifies the human body with Śivaliṅga, Chidambaram, Sadāśivaṉ and *tiru-k-kūttu.* (Divine Dance).[44]

In one of the verses he says that the God of the Yoga is in the form of the human body.[45] He also speaks of the body as a lamp.[46] From these references we can say that for Tirumūlar the body becomes the source of unimaginable bliss and is intended for one's spiritual enjoyment and emancipation. It resembles the yogin's grove. One of the Baul songs says that the yogin's material self, *rūpa,* has become divine, *svarūpa,* and that there is no difference between them. The Tamil Siddhas understood the human body as a threshold,[47] a sacred passage to the Ultimate Reality just as sacred rivers, temples, mountains, etc., are. They ask pertinently: Why should you go to these places of pilgrimage when the threshold is in you? Tirumūlar asks us to look inward. The verse is:

He who made this body-mix,
He who this body land holds,
He who within this body shines,
He is Nandi;
Him they seek and search in lands all;
They know not
He within the body stands.[48]

This is also one of the reasons for the Tamil Siddhas for not worshipping or singing in praise of any local deity or local temple.

5. The micro-macro symmetry

In Siddha literature the human body is conceived as a microcosm of the universe. One of the main tenets of the Siddhas is that whatever is in the macrocosm, *aṇḍa*, is in the microcosm, *piṇḍa*. To quote Tirumūlar:

> Dumb fools are they
> Who as Mala (Impurity) despise the body;
> Other places as holy
> They go about seeking;
> They who consider "Good this is"
> And in it seek the Lord,
> Shall experience macrocosm entire,
> In their body tenacious
> (That microcosm is).[49]

Siddhas believe that the one reality has two aspects— the absolutely great, *parama-mahat*, and the absolutely small, *parama-aṇu*. *Parama-mahat* is the diffused and undifferentiated aspect of consciousness or *veṭṭaveḷi* of the Tamil Siddhas. The *Parama-aṇu* is the condensed, potentized aspect, which is *bindu* of which the self, the living germ and material atom are lower forms. The perfect continuum remains immanent in the lower continuum. The Tamil Siddhas speak of *ucciveḷi (cidākāśa)*, experienced in one's head at the time of the kuṇḍalinī reaching the sahasrāra region and also of *veṭṭaveḷi* which is called *mahākāśa*, an all-embracing unity. They use the term *ciṟṟambalam* for jīva (the microcosm) and *pērambalam* for Śiva (the macrocosm). Tirumūlar says that the Ultimate reality (He) is in the atom *(aṇu)* and the atom is in Him and both are integrated into One without any distinction whatsoever.[50] In other words, an atom is a miniature universe. A true seer can see, folded up, in every object the whole cosmos. And he who is competent, can evolve all things out of everything. As the Tantra says: What is here is elsewhere; what is not here is nowhere. Tirumūlar expresses the same idea beautifully by saying that if you see deeply into a tender leaf, you can see the entire universe.[51] This verse has a pointed reference to Tennyson who said that if one were to understand the meaning and the significance of "a small flower in the crannied wall," one must understand what the universe and God is. That is any particular thing in the world is and represents the cosmic order in a particular way. The mahā-vākya 'Thou art that' *(tat tvam asi)* is also a similar expression of micro-macro unity.

The *Māṇḍukya Upaniṣad* speaks of the cosmic person having the generalized states of man's consciousness, that is, waking, dream, dreamless sleep and *turiya*. *Nyāsa* is a process of interiorization of the cosmos in the individual being. Different forms of *nyāsa* are described in most of the Tāntric texts and digests, especially in the *Prapañca-sāra, the Kulārṇava Tantra and Śāradā-tilaka*, such as *hamsa, praṇava, matṛkā, mantra, kara, aṅga, pīṭha*, etc. According to Tantra final liberation cannot be obtained without the experience of a preliminary stage of 'cosmicization,' that is, *nyāsa*. The human body is centered around the spinal axis, called Mount Meru. Working out from Mount Meru, the islands of the world, the oceans, mountains, stars, clouds, wind, fire and water are all located in the body. A major portion of Indian 'mystical physiology' is based on the identification of 'suns' and 'moons' in the human body. There is a brief treatise called *Hasta-pujā-vidhi*, which recommends a meditation in which the fingers of the left hand are identified with the cosmic elements. According to *Hastakāra-Yantra*, another treatise, the auspicious signs on the palms indicate the integral relation between interplanetary rhythm and the human organism. As Micera Eliade has observed, cosmicization is a process of recasting a man in new, gigantic dimensions and a process of guaranteeing him macranthropic experiences.[52] The yogin does this *nyāsa* in order to awaken the sacred forces asleep in the flesh itself. The entire Kuṇḍalinī-Yoga is an expression of the micro-macro unity. The implication of this unity seems to be that the human form is the abode of truth of which the universe is a manifestation in infinite space and eternal time, and that the sādhaka should concentrate his attention on himself and realize the truth within. Further, the human body is not only the abode of truth, but also the best medium for realizing the truth. That is, the human body is the *yantra-tattva* of the Tantras. It is the vehicle through which the dormant psychic energy kuṇḍalinī can be awakened to finally unite with the cosmic consciousness. The macrocosmic liberation from *samsāra,* the world of births and deaths, is effected through a microscopic, meditative yogic attainment. One of our major limitations in discovering and realizing the underlying unity between man and the universe is that we are used to analyzing and understanding the universe into its separate parts with the result we lose sight of the interrelationship of parts and their underlying unity.

In Siddha literature the human body is conceived as a microcosm of the universe. This feature predominates in all the Tantras in general wherever the yogic element prevails. Tirumūlar speaks of man as *piṇḍa-liṅga,* the microcosmic-liṅga, and the cosmos as *aṇḍa-liṅga,* the macrocosmic-liṅga.[53] The basic premise of Tantra is that this body is a *maṇḍala,* a representation of the cosmos. The idea of the body as the microcosm of the universe received a spiritual denotation as against the purely physical denotation of the other traditions. Tirumūlar also refers to the body as *ciṟṟambalam,* microcosm.[54] In short, the macrocosm is in the microcosm, that is, the transcendent must also be immanent, or in the words of William Blake, one can hold infinity in the palm of one's hand and eternity in an hour.

6. The concept of kāya as understood in some schools of Indian thought

The term *kāya* used by the Siddhas is translated as 'body,' but not in the sense of the purely physical abstraction but a body with a consciousness. There is no such thing as a body without consciousness. A body without consciousness is not a body, but a corpse. The terms *kāya* and *deha* have been used interchangeably. Let us pass in review, very briefly, the concept of *deha* as understood by some schools of Indian thought. In Mahāyāna Buddhism there is a development of the docetic conception of the three *kāyas* of the Buddha. They are the *nirmāṇa-kāya*, the *sambhoga-kāya*, and the *dharma-kāya*, the normal physical body, the subtle refulgent body of bliss and the body of perfect wisdom or law or truth respectively. In early Pali Buddhism a belief grew that the Lord Buddha had a double existence— the *rūpa-kāya* and the *dharma-kāya*. The *rūpa-kāya* in later Pali Buddhism was sub-divided into *nirmāṇa-kāya* and *sambhoga-kāya*. The *nirmāṇa-kāya* is the physical body, the gross physical existence, the gross body of transformation or the historical personage of the Buddha. The *sambhoga-kāya* is a beatific body, the body of bliss and light, or the refulgent body in the form of Bodhisattva. It is neither a state of formless existence nor a state of material existence. It is a body with all the implications of it, but it is a body of bliss and light. It is a very subtle body, which manifests itself in the various conditions of bliss in super human beings for preaching noble truths. In this body the impurities of physical existence are removed by light and bliss. A man with such a body of light and bliss is a Bodhisattva. He lives with his blissful body in the world of phenomenal existence, yet is never touched by the principles of defilement, and works for the upliftment of all beings.

The *dharma-kāya* of the Buddha is the quintessence of the Buddha as pure enlightenment and wisdom; it is the primordial element or the 'thatness' underlying all that exists. It is the ultimate principle as the totality of things in a state of all-existence; something like undifferentiated and unqualified Brahman of the Upaniṣads. In Tāntric Buddhism, to this well-known theory of the *tri-kāya*, the idea of the *vajra-kāya*, diamond body, or indestructible being or the *sahaja-kāya* as the fourth *kāya* of the Buddha has been added. The discovery of the *vajra-kāya* within one's own being is the ultimate experience.

In the Upaniṣads we come across the doctrine of the five *kośas* or sheaths. They are:

1. the *annamaya-kośa*, the sheath of matter,
2. the *prāṇamaya-kośa*, the sheath of vital energy,
3. the *manomaya-kośa*, the sheath of mental activity,
4. the *vijñānamaya-kośa*, the sheath of intellect, and
5. the *ānandamaya-kośa*, the sheath of bliss.

Following this, some of the Tamil Siddhas speak of the *paru-uḍal, vaḷi-uḍal, maṉa-uḍal, aṟivu-uḍal*, and *iṉba-uḍal* respectively. The theory of *kośa* is applicable to both the individual and the Cosmic Person. For the individual, *annamaya-kośa* is his physical body. *Prāṇamaya-kośa* consists of the five organs of action and the five *prāṇas*. *Manomaya-kośa* consists of *manas* and the five organs of sense. *Vijñānamaya-kośa* consists of *buddhi* and the five organs of knowledge and *ānandamaya-kośa* consists of bliss, dissociated from bodily and mental functions; it is the Self. According to the Advaita school, the individual has three kinds of bodies— the *sthūla-śarīra* or the gross body, the *sūkṣma-śarīra* or the *liṅga-śarīra* or the subtle body and the *kāraṇa-śarīra* or the causal body. The *sthūla-śarīra* (in Tamil *paru-uḍal*) is composed of the gross elements, i.e., *annamaya-kośa*. The *liṅga-śarīra* (in Tamil *nuṇ-uḍal*) consists of the subtle elements, *tanmātras* and the subtle body, i.e., *prāṇamaya-kośa, manomaya-kośa* and *vijñānamaya-kośa*. That is, the *liṅga-śarīra* or the subtle body is composed of nineteen elements: five organs of action, five organs of knowledge, the four inner instruments *(antahkaraṇa)*, i.e., the *manas* (mind), *buddhi* (intellect), *citta* (mind-stuff) and *ahamkāra* (ego) and the five *prāṇas*. The *kāraṇa-śarīra* corresponds to the *ānandamaya-kośa*.[55] According to Tirumūlar the gross body contains the following:

Lymph, blood, flesh, skin, and tendons,
Bones, marrow, fat, brain, and semen,
— Of these into one shape made
Is the body gross,
By sorrow harassed.[56]

Tirumūlar calls the subtle body as *puriyaṭṭa-kāyam*. The subtle-body contains:

Of the body thus God shaped,
In parts two,
Sukshma (Subtle) is One;
That a body of constituents eight is;
— Sound, touch, shape, taste and smell
Buddhi (Intellect), Manas (Mind) and Ahankara (Egoity)
That the Puriashta body is (subtle).[57]

The *Tirumandiram* has a full section dealing with the various divisions of the body— the *annamaya*, the *prāṇamaya*, the *mano-maya*, the *vijñānamaya* and the *ānandamaya kośas*.[58]

Swami Ramalinga Adigalar speaks of the *śuddha-deha*, the divinised material physical body, the *praṇava-deha*, the transformed subtle body and the *jñāna-deha*, the causal body of knowledge. Swami has attained this triple deathless body. Swami in one of his prose works writes:

> The glory of those who have realized the integral and perfect Bliss of the Divine is as follows: They shall have transformed the impure gross physical substances of their effectual body (asuddha bhuta karyadi) such as skin, nerves, bones, muscles, blood, semen, etc., and their corresponding causal cells of impure nature (asuddha prakriti anu) to become (1) a golden effectual body of purity (Suddha bhuta karya deha), its fineness being immeasurable; they shall also have (2) a pure causal physical body (Suddha bhuta karana deha), which will appear to sight as a golden form of body but will be unseizable like the ether of space and (3) a body of knowledge (Jnana deha), which will be both unseen and unseizable like the ether of space...[59]

About the transformation of his body into the *jñāna-deha* Swami writes:

> The skin has become supple; the influx of the nerves (i.e., nervous current) all over the body is vibrating with pauses in between (Note:- according to medical science if the nervous influx stops even for a second, man will die); the bones have become pliable and plastic in its nature; the soft muscles have become truly loosened; the blood has become condensed within; the semen has become concentrated into one drop and confined in the chest; the petals of brain have blossomed or expanded; amrita is welling up into springs all over the body and filling it up; luminous forehead perspires; luminous

face brightens up; breath full of peace becomes cool and refreshing; inner smile beams up and hairs stand on their ends; tears (of joy) flow down towards the feet; mouth vibrates into the passionate calling (of the Divine); ear-tubes ring with the sense of musically humming sound; body has become cool; soft chest moves; hands join (as in prayer): legs revolve or spin round...; mind melts sweetly; the intelligence becomes full of light; the will becomes full of joy and harmony; the individuality has enlarged itself everywhere universally...; the heart has blossomed into the universality of feeling so as to be felt by the world outwardly; the form of knowledge-body... has become blissful; even the spiritual egoism of senses has gone away; the tatvas (of body, life and mind in their lower levels) have dissolved away and are replaced wholly by Satva, the truth-principle or truth-substance which alone prevails now uniquely; attachment to objects of the senses and to the things of the world has dissolved away and only the aspiration and will towards the illimitable Grace grows and intensifies...[60]

To quote Tulasiram further,

From the reported or recorded incidents of his life it is seen that the Swami could multiply his physical form at several places or points so as to be seen by the people in crowded gatherings, as near to themselves; he had the power to make his speech clearly audible equally alike to the distant and the near of his large audience (i.e., irrespective of the distance from him) without changing his tone or loudness. His body had become so luminous and surcharged with Light that all attempts to photograph him failed; nothing of his face and figure and limbs came out in the photo negative except the white cloth he wore. He cast no shadow of his body on the ground. He left no footprints on the ground as he walked. Is it due to the mystically revolving or spinning legs he had by transformation? He writes in "Jeevakarunyam" that the transformed physical body of knowledge can move in adhara or supporting medium as well as in niradhara or the supportless (i.e. without medium) and it will be free from perspiration and impurities, aging, graying of hair, shrinking of skin and death; and it will not cast its shadow and it will be the manifestation of knowledge-body.[61]

Śri Kumāradeva, a Vīra Śaivaite, who hailed from Karnataka, but long settled in Tamil Nadu at Vriddhachalam, belonged to the eighteenth century. He also speaks about the transformation of the body and its types. In one of his works called *Śuddha-sādhakam* he speaks of the four types of body called

(i) the dark body (inconscient body called *iruḷ-vaḍivu* in Tamil);

(ii) the body of ignorance or maya (called *maruḷ-vaḍivu* or *māyai-vaḍivu* in Tamil);

(iii) the body of praṇava (called the *Aum-vaḍivu* or the *praṇava-vaḍivu* in Tamil) and

(iv) the body of grace (called the *aruḷ-vaḍivu* in Tamil).[62]

Jainism also speaks of five types of bodies: (i) the physical human body, (ii) the transformation-body "which is the natural vehicle of the higher beings and which can be acquired by the ascetic who then is able to increase its size at will," (iii) the procurement body which can be temporarily created and detached from the physical body to be projected anywhere; (iv) the fiery body which is indestructible and survives death and without whose energy the lower three bodies (i), (ii) and (iii) could not operate. (v) the instrumental body which acts as a receptacle of karma is the innermost of the five bodies of the human being.[63] In some of the Tāntric texts, knowledge about the human body is presented under the following categories: the process by which the body is formed, location of nerves, etc., within the body, quality of matter of which the body is formed, identification of the element of air in the body and descriptions of the muscles of the body.

Ayurveda, which is a science of healing, speaks of eight main divisions. These are: the healing of wounds and diseases of the lower limbs through surgery, ointments and drugs; healing of the wounds and diseases of the upper limbs; healing of all external and internal diseases of general types: healing of mental diseases; healing of the diseases of children; science of toxicology; prescription for enhancing sexual vigor and science of chemical preparations needed for medicinal and other purposes. Needless to say that this science of healing presupposes a thorough knowledge of the physical body.

In Siddha literature we come across the following types of bodies— the *sthūla-deha*, the *yoga-deha*, the *siddha-deha*, the *praṇava* or the *mantra-deha* and the *jñāna* or the *divya-deha*. Turning the *sthūla-deha*, the ordinary physical body, into *divya-deha* is what is termed as *kāya-sādhana*. The *Tirumandiram* is specific in saying that the jīva moves from one to the other bodies.[64] Tirumūlar likens the movement of the jīva from one body to another as the snake sloughs of its skin and assumes another, as the bird leaves its shell and pursues life in another form.[65] Śiva-vākkiyar explains the transformation of the physical body into a divine body on the analogy of a worm turning itself into a butterfly.[66] *Kāya-sādhana* is to be distinguished from physical culture. Physical culture aims at developing the athlete's powers; but *kāya-sādhana* aims at developing spiritual power, a power which electrifies the body and its consciousness. It is an attempt to bring about the trans-substantiation of the body, the attainment of what is called *siddha-deha*. This attainment is not an end in itself but a means to achieve the *divya-deha*, an immutable spiritual body or Śivahood. *Kāya-sādhana* implies a change of perspective where the physical existence is not denied but replaced by a permanent spiritual existence, where the gulf between the physical and the ontological (non-physical) is bridged over in a blissful existence.

7. Tirumūlar's conception of the human body

According to Tirumūlar there are ninety-six tattvas within the fortress called the human body.[67] (See Appendix-F). Tattvas are the fundamental principles of existence. Of these ninety-six tattvas, thirty-six are the internal tattvas, and sixty are the external tattvas. Of these thirty-six internal tattvas, five are the Śiva-tattvas, seven are the vidyā-tattvas and the twenty-four are the prakṛti-tattvas also known as the ātma-tattvas. The sixty external tattvas consist of:

a. the twenty-five manifestations of the five elements are: skin, bone, tendon, flesh, hair, water, blood, fat, brain, semen, food, sleep, fear, coition, sloth, running, walking, standing, sitting, lying, anger, miserliness, avarice, obstinacy and malice;

b. The ten nāḍis in the body: *iḍā, piṅgalā, suṣumnā, gāndhāri, hastijihvā, pūsa, yaśasvini, ālambusa, kuhu* and *sankhini;*

c. the ten *vāyus* in the body: *prāṇa, apāna, vyāna, udhāna, samāna, nāga, kūrma, kṛkara, devadatta* and *dhanañjaya.*

d. the three desires: wealth, children, world;
e. the five modes of speech: talking, memorizing, singing, weeping, and exulting;
f. the three guṇas: *sattva, rajas* and *tamas;*
g. the four sound forms: *sūkṣma* (subtle), *paśyanti* (incoherent speech), *madhyamā* (emanating from throat) and *vaikhari* (articulate).

From another perspective the physical body is said to consist of the five gross elements (earth, water, fire, air and ether), the five *tanmātras* (sound-potential, touch-potential, sight-potential, taste-potential and smell-potential), the five *karmendriyas* (hands, feet, organ of speech, excretory organs and generative organs), the five *jñānendriyas* (organs of hearing, touch, sight, taste and smell) and the four *antahkaraṇas (manas, buddhi, citta* and *ahamkāra).* These are called the twenty-four principles, tattvas, of the human body. Since the yogin has to transcend all these ninety-six principles to attain liberation, one must have knowledge of the *sthūla-śarīra* (the physical body), which is called *kāya-viveka.* In Tamil, *sthūla-śarīra* is called *iruḷ* or *maruḷ-deha.* This physical body is subject to five limitations (already referred to) and it is *ahamkāra* or egoism that localizes, individuates and identifies consciousness with the physical body. This is the "unripe" body. According to the Indian system of Siddha medicine the physical body is made up of seven constituent elements *(dhātus)* and three humors *(doṣas).* The seven elements are: chyle, blood, flesh, fat, bones, marrow and semen. Three humors are: wind *(vāta),* bile *(pitta)* and phlegm *(sleṣma* or *kapham).* This body of the *sapta-dhātu* has to be conquered through the heat radiated by Yoga.

According to the Chinese tradition the control faculties of the mind are effectively possible only by uniting it with the body-consciousness. They call the idea of body-consciousness as *kāya-jīva.* The body-consciousness can be understood as the perfect functioning of the seven *dhātus,* the harmonious balance of the five *prāṇas,* etc. Once the body attains the natural suppleness and agility, one receives the required maturity for the body to permeate body consciousness *(kāya-jīva).* The idea of body-consciousness *(kāya-jīva)* and its importance for maintaining harmonious life is the prime concern of the martial art practice, dealing with *marma* points. The *kāya-jīva* conception enunciated in the earlier Buddhist sources in China serves both the purposes of maintaining bodily stability and the practice of martial art.

In a small Sanskrit text, the *Yoga-Bīja,* two kinds of body are distinguished— that which is 'ripe,' *pakva* or matured, and that which is 'unripe,' *apakva.*[68] The unripe body is the one not disciplined by Yoga; it is mere *sthūla-śarīra.* When it is disciplined by Yoga, it becomes ripe or *pakva.* Tirumūlar speaks of making the body fit by roasting it.[69] In Tamil Siddha poems we come across the term *kāya-kaṟpam,* which means the process of making the body immutable and stone-like. This process consists of three methods known as *maṇi, mandiram,* and *aviḻdam. Maṇi* is *rasāyana,* chemical process, *mandiram* is the process of Kuṇḍalinī-Yoga and *aviḻdam* is the process of medicine, i.e., *auṣadha.* This unripe body is to be made ripe through the process of Haṭha-Yoga. Tirumūlar assures us that by practicing Yoga there will be no graying of hair or wrinkling of the skin.

Tirumūlar speaks of "re-directing" the senses so that they will be useful for Yoga purposes. He uses the term "changing the course" of the senses[70] and gives the examples of "the eyes that do not see and the ears that do not hear" and says that this is the way to life eternal.[71] By sublimating the senses he assures that they will become golden.[72] The senses which were like a dark dense forest, become illumined when they gain the experience of redirection or sublimation.[73] By subduing the five senses the Lord opens the sense-gates and shows the way of redemption.[74] In this connection it will be worthwhile to note a description given in *Taittirīya Āraṇyaka* of a yogin who sees, tastes, hears, smells and touches without the use of sensory organs. It is as follows:

> The blind man pierced the pearl;
> The fingerless put a thread into it;
> The neckless wore it;
> And the tongueless praised it.

In the *Tirumandiram* one finds a detailed description of the Aṣṭāṅga-Yoga[75] consisting of the following stages: *yama* – abstention or restraint,[76] *niyama* – observance of self-discipline,[77] *āsana* – posture,[78] *prāṇāyama* – breath control,[79] *pratyāhāra* – sensory control or withdrawl,[80] *dhāraṇa* – concentration,[81] *dhyāna* – deep concentration[82] and *samādhi* – super concentration/ecstasy.[83] In addition to these, there is a section on the fruits of the eight-limbed Yoga[84] giving the benefits of performing Aṣṭāṅga-Yoga. But this section does not fit well with the previous sections of Aṣṭāṅga-Yoga and one has to agree with Suba. Annamalai who feels that these eight verses are interpolations.[85]

When a body is hardened by yogic techniques, one gets what is called the *yoga-deha*. That is, the ordinary physical body has to be "burnt out" through the continual application of the fire of Yoga. Tirumūlar is happy to state that the body, which gave trouble before *yoga-sādhana* has become a good one after the

Yoga process.[86] Yoga, according to tradition, is the *yāga, yajña,* sacrificial fire, that is performed inside one's body. The Aṣṭāṅga-Yoga as discussed by Tirumūlar tells us the methods by which one can prepare the body for attaining the *yoga-deha.* He also says that by practicing Yoga at dawn, noon, dusk one will be purified from the poison of the three humors.

As body wax-like suppleness attains,
Practising yoga at dusk
The phlegm leaves;
At noon leaves the wind that is treacherous;
At dawn practised, the bile leaves;
Thus all poison from body is expelled
And you shall know no graying, nor wrinkling.[87]

The same assurance is given by Tirumūlar in the following verses:

They who effect the mystic union
With the azure-hued Sakti within
Will shed greying and wrinkling
And regain youth for all to see;
This I say is true, by Nandi the Great.[88]

Three the coils of serpent Kundalini
Ten the Vayus that agitate the body;
Twelve finger-length the Prana breath;
When the two bags of aspiration
Are tight controlled,
And you sit in meditation unwavering
The body perishes not ever.[89]

The *Tirumandiram* is emphatic that for one who does prāṇāyāma, there is no death.[90] Tirumular says that by performing prāṇāyāma the body becomes impervious even to fire.[91] The two sections— a section on the measurement of life span and another section on the breath rhythm in days of the week (called *vāra-cāram* in Tamil) speak of the importance of performing prāṇāyāma regularly and in a systematic fashion.[92]

To achieve longevity a technique of urine-therapy called *amuri-dāraṇai* is also suggested by Tirumūlar.[93] To Quote B. Natarajan:

> The fact that this practice is advocated after pariyanga yoga (or vajroli mudra) shows that this requires advanced preliminary yoga preparation. In fact, *Hatha Yoga Pradipika* couples this practice along with vajroli, and so calls it 'amaroli.' "The drinking of human urine once formed part of ancient fertility rites, and the significance of yellow-coloured water used in certain Hindu festivals, such as Holi is believed to be a relic of this scatalogical practice. The claim that drinking human urine enhances sexual powers has been substantiated, according to a recent writer, by Dr. Butenandt's discovery in 1931 that the male sex hormone could be extracted from human urine," (Benjamin Walker under the caption 'Scatalogy' in his "Hinduism").[94]
>
> This practice is referred to in *Hatha Yoga Pradipika*, pp. 82-96, as quoted in Theos Bernard's "Hatha Yoga," pp. 71-72; "In the doctrine of the sect of Kapalikas, the 'amaroli' is the drinking of the cool mid-stream leaving the first, as it is a mixture of too much bile, and the last which is useless. He who drinks amari, snuffs it daily, practices 'vajroli,' is called

practicing amaroli." Amuri (Tamil) is synonymous with *amari* (Sanskrit), meaning deathlessness.[95]

According to Suba. Annamalai this section on *amuri-dāraṇai* seems to be an interpolation. First the term "urine" (the Tamil term *ci̱ru-nīr*) has been mistakenly interpreted for another term "waters of the heaven" (the Tamil term *vā̱nīr*), which stands for the secretion of the *amṛta*, amborial juice, from the sahasrāra, which is diffused throughout the body. *Ci̱ru-nīr* is used mistakenly for *vā̱nīr*. Second, the four verses in this section, i.e., verses 846 to 848 deal with medicine and that they seem to have been interpolated by some later medicine men.[96]

The attainment of *yoga-deha*, through Yoga exercises and techniques of control, is termed as bodily siddhi in Tamil Siddha literature. *Avvai-k-ku̱raḷ* refers to the *yoga-deha* as an artistic *deha, ōviya-uḍambu* in Tamil.[97] *Yoga-deha* is a supra-material body, which is above all sorrows and sufferings, while the *sthūla-deha*, unripe material body, is the storehouse of all sorrows and sufferings. *Yoga-deha* acquires a consciousness, which is no longer troubled by the presence of a physical body, just as an insect which moves on the surface of the mud is not tarnished by the mud. That is, genuine Siddhas are "unconscious" of their physical bodies. As a Chinese saying goes: "to be unconscious of one's feet implies that the shoes are easy."

Once the *deha* is hardened by Yoga, the internal forces help the individual to arouse the kuṇḍalinī in him. When the kuṇḍalini is aroused and passes through the six ādhāras it is a process of the spiritualization of the body of the sādhaka. It is the process of the acquirement of yogic powers, siddhis, leading to a *siddha-deha* 'perfect body.' It is a 'perfect body' because the 'body' can do and be anything at the will of the sādhaka. The *siddha-deha* can have free movement in the universe and it does not have to adhere to the spatio-temporal laws of it.

It is said in Tāntric works that the power acquired in the mūlādhāra develops natural health and strength of the body, intellectual power and prolonged life. The power acquired in the svādiṣṭhāna develops a diseaseless and vital body. The power in the maṇipūra develops the natural immunity of the body, the attainment of long life and the release of certain uncommon powers. The power in the anāhata develops inner beauty and makes the body highly attractive. There is also an acquisition of uncommon sensory powers. The power in the viśuddha develops a body adamantine in hardness and strength. All these powers are called siddhis. Because of these powers it is said that the Siddhas obtain 'the rainbow body' which vanishes at will like a rainbow, leaving no trace behind. Acquisition of such a subtle body called *siddha-deha* is a fact, which cannot be set aside by a mere arbitrary denial. Due to the attainment of siddhi, the sādhaka destroys perceptibility of color *(rūpa)*, which is the cause of the perception of the body. When the possibility of perception is suspended we say that the yogin has become invisible. The light engendered in the eye of another person no longer comes into contact with the body that has 'disappeared.' That is, the yogic body is no longer an object of perception for any other man. In this way all the siddhis acquired by a sādhaka can be adequately explained.

A sādhaka who has acquired a *siddha-deha* becomes a master of his 'body.' It is a 'body' bereft of all limitations and bondage of the spatio-temporal world and is not governed by the physical laws; it is a supra-normal body. To a man who has attained the *siddha-deha* the world of sense impression does not operate. There is also the disappearance of the ego, the 'I-consciousness.'

Since the 'I' is lost, he can be everywhere at any time in any form. The *Yoga-śikhā Upaniṣad* speaks of the *siddha-deha* as a powerful yogic body, which is exempt from modification and bondage and possesses various supreme powers. That body is like the ether, even purer than the ether, and is seen to be subtler than the subtle, coarse and yet not coarse, insentient, and yet sentient.

In the next stage the *siddha-deha* is transformed into a *praṇava-deha* or *mantra-tanu.* It is the body of *nāda* or sound. This body will achieve the glow of youth.[98] It is called the *praṇava-deha* because it is achieved through an equilibrium of the sounds of the letters *a, u, m,* which stand respectively for the sun, the moon, and the fire or for piṅgalā, iḍā and suṣumnā. Tirumūlar refers to this *deha* when he regrets that there are people who do not recognize this sacred letter or mantra in the *deha.*[99] We also find a description of this body, *mandira-mēṉi (mantra-tanu)* in the *Tirumandiram.*

His Feet are Letter "Na"
His navel is Letter "Ma"
His shoulders are Letter "Si"
His mouth is Letter "Va"
His cranial center aloft is Letter "Ya"
Thus Five-Letter Form of Siva is.[100]

In the *mandira-mēṉi* the letter *na* stands for the two legs, the letter *ma* stands for the stomach, the letter *ci* stands for the shoulders, the letter *va* stands for the mouth and the letter *ya* stands for the top of the head.

[Courtesy: Mi. Pa. Somu, *Cittar Ilakkiyam*, Vol. 1, p. 344]

This 'human figure' representing the *praṇava-deha* is called the *mandira-mēṉi-c-cakkaram* in the Siddha literature. Tirumūlar refers to this *mantra-tanu* as sūkṣma-pañcākṣaram, and calls the 'body' as one which has been turned into the golden body with the alchemic pill of Śivāyanama.[101] The praṇava is compared to the boat of life, by which one crosses the ocean of *samsāra*.[102]

According to the Tamil Siddhas, the man with a *praṇava-tanu* or *deha* is a *jīvan-mukta*, "the man liberated while living" or "living liberation." Tirumūlar speaks of a *jīvan-mukta*, "the yogic adept of immortality."[103] A *jīvan-mukta* is a yogin who continues to live in his body and in the world after attaining an incorruptible pure body consisting of Aum. Tirumūlar calls him 'a saint of wisdom with a body.[104] He is also described as a man 'dead' so far as the 'physical body' is concerned.[105] To quote Tirumūlar:

The sweet speech, love intones
The loud sound, airy prana articulates

The mind within fleshy body dwells
All these you upward course (in Yogic way)
No more the thoughts of body be.[106]

The *Tirumandiram* gives a description of the *jīvan-mukta.* Tirumūlar writes:

Jiva-Mukti is the Atita (Beyond Consciousness State);
Para-Mukti is Upasanta (Divine Peace);
Siva-Mukti is Ananda (Divine Bliss);
All three are Svarupa Muktis
That from Nadanta branch
Where Pranava (Aum) as letters three (A, U, M) are.[107]

A *jīvan-mukta* is also called a *praṇava-dēśikaṉ*. In a *jīvan-mukta* the senses continue to function, maintaining contact with the external world, but the inner consciousness does not take note of it and persists in the exclusive enjoyment of the bliss of its own light. He is a 'nirvaṇised' being; his consciousness remains really centered in the higher planes of existence. He no longer possesses a 'personal' consciousness but a 'witnessing consciousness.' Even though he acts in this world, he is not conscious of an 'I-act.' As Chuang-tzu (Laotzu's great successor and Taoist thinker) has put it: The perfect man employs his mind as a mirror. It grasps nothing; it refuses nothing. It receives, but does not keep.[108]

In a bilingual manuscript (Sanskrit and Tibetan) called *Amṛta-siddhi,* authored by one Avadhuta Candra, there is a vivid description of a *jīvan-mukta.*[109]

According to Tirumūlar a *jīvan-mukta* is like the tamarind fruit where the outer cover of the fruit is detached from the inner tamarind fruit. The outer cover is like a loose jacket.[110] A *jīvan-mukta* does not 'die physically,' but is transformed into a *para-*

mukta with *divya-deha*, a body of light and bliss which is none other than the state of being and becoming one with the eternal consciousness. A *jīvan-mukta* does not 'die' to attain liberation, but is transformed into the very mode of liberation, viz., the *divya-deha*. When a *jīvan-mukta* gets into *divya-deha* he is 'oned' with Eternity, becomes one with the witness of the universe, a *para-mukta*, a permanent Enlightenment-Consciousness, a *kālātīta*, one who has transcended the ravages of space, time and death and has attained Śivahood. The standing examples for *divya-deha* are Śrī Caitanya, who had entered the Puri temple and had become a 'blaze of light,' and Ramalinga Swamigal who has entered Śivahood transforming himself into 'light.' In Tamil Nadu there is a very strong belief that genuine Siddhas 'still live' as there is no 'death' for them.

The *divya-deha* is called *cinmaya*, known as the 'body of light.' According to Rōmarṣi the mark of *sorūba-siddhi* (the attainment of *divya-deha*) is that the body will look like lustrous light.[111] Swami Ramalingam also affirms that his body has become a golden deathless body filled with light.[112] It is a 'body' of infinite space, *para-veḷi*, where one 'identifies' himself with the universal life. Tirumūlar vouchsafes the fact that he remained in this body for ages beyond count.[113] At this stage the body glows with the fire of immortality. It is called the *oḷi-uḍambu* in Tamil. As Tirumūlar says figuratively even the 'hairs' of this transmuted body will shine. When a Siddha attains *divya-deha* he attains Śivahood. Tirumūlar describes *divya-deha* as follows:

> Siva is the ground of Jnani's body,
> Jnani's body is Siva's body,
> Yogi's body is Nada and Bindu,

Mauni's body is Mukti
Beyond Voids three.[114]

Regarding the body being turned into Śivahood, Tirumūlar says that legally, morally and spiritually his body has been willed away to Śiva. He says that his body is a document, a will, which has been written by Brahma, and the witness to the will is Viṣṇu. The verse runs as follows:

He is my mother and father in one
My births seven fold seven are to Siva willed;
This the document drawn up even in days of yore;
Brahma who this world created wrote it thus;
And Vishnu the cloud-hued witnessed it.[115]

Hence *divya-deha* is referred to as *kailāya-deha* for it is a body of enlightened awareness and equal to that of Śiva. Tirumūlar refers to this stage as one where the 'five bodies' have become one with Śiva.[116] He calls *divya-deha* as *vīyā-p-para-kāyam* in Tamil, which means an immortal body, a body of jñāna or wisdom.[117]

The entire process of the passage from the attainment of *yoga-deha* till one gets *divya-deha* is called *laya*. *Laya* is a process of absorption of the cosmic principles, stage by stage, into the spiritual aspect of the Supreme Consciousness, i.e., Śivahood. The process of absorption has been technically called *apañcīkaraṇa*, disquintuplication. It may be likened to a process of untying the knots of our being through which we have fettered ourselves. The uncoiled animated kuṇḍalinī, by piercing each of the lotuses, absorbs into itself the regnant tattvas (the five elements) contained in each of them. When the ascent is made each of these tattvas enters the state of dissolution called *laya* state. In her upward process kuṇḍalinī absorbs in herself all the twenty-four tattvas. When the process of disquintuplication reaches the stage of ājñā-cakra, one gets the *siddha-deha*, which is not troubled by any of these tattvas. The *siddha-deha* is a body consisting of Śiva-Śakti principles. A further process of absorption brings into effect the final merging of Śiva and Śakti within the yogin's body where all kinds of duality are abolished forever. This state of the yogin's body is called *mantra-tanu* or *praṇava-tanu.* Leaving the ājñā-cakra when the kuṇḍalinī reaches the sahasrāra, the yogin becomes conscious of Consciousness, and obtains the *divya-deha,* an illuminated body of knowledge and wisdom. At the sahasrāra the yogin is said to 'drink' the 'ambrosial juice,' or *amṛta* oozing from the moon of the sahasrāra and gets a body with a golden hue, called *poṉṉār-mēṉi* in Tamil. Tirumūlar says that drinking deep the ambrosia, the body becomes Śiva's temple.[118] *Kechari-mudrā* is the yogic process of drinking the nectar from the sahasrāra. One who drinks the nectar obtains 'bodily immortality' and has entered a stage where his 'body' has been transformed into supreme bliss. The immortal does not require 'human' sustenance; and immortality must be understood as an act of identification with one's 'genuine roots.'

Tirumūlar calls Kuṇḍalinī-Yoga as *mey-yagam*[119] and guarantees that the *deha* will not be destroyed if one performs Yoga and also vouchsafes that one can be ever young, not affected by age.[120] He also says that if one has undergone Kuṇḍalinī-Yoga one need not be 'afraid of' or worried about his body.[121] If the body is trained, hardened and transformed by Yoga it can be and is a *mokṣa-sādhana.*

Notes on Chapter Seven

1. Sri Auribindo, *Letters on Yoga*, Part, 1. p. 20.
2. *Ibid.*, p. 125.
3. Mircea Eliade, *Yoga: Immortality and Freedom*, p. 71.
4. Refer Paṭṭiṉattār's following works: *Kōyil Tiru Agaval – 1*, lines 5-35; *Kōyil Tiru Agaval – 2*, lines 6-35; *Kōyil Tiru Agaval – 3*, lines 16-40. Especially for the terms used by him for the filthy nature of the human body refer the following works: *Tiru Ēkamba Mālai*, verse 27; *Podu*, 26 and 55; *Iṟanda Kālattu Iraṅgal*, 8 and 16-20.
5. Pāmbāṭṭi-c-citar, 60 to 69.
6. Kaḍuveḷi-c-cittar, 3.
7. *Tirumandiram*, 190.
8. *Ibid.*, 187 to 196.
9. *Ibid.*, 177 to 186.
10. *Ibid.*, 255.
11. *Ibid.*, 177.
12. *Ibid.*, Section 2, *tantra* One, 143 to 167.
13. *Ibid.*, 145. Translation of B. Natarajan.
14. *Ibid.*, verse 158. Translation of B. Natarajan. Refer Kaḍuveḷi-c-cittar's lament that ignorant people have "broken" the pot treating it as an earthern vessel, 4.
15. *Ibid.*, 150.
16. *Ibid.*, 155. Translation of B. Natarajan.
17. *Ibid.*, 167, Translation of B. Natarajan. This verse of *Tirumandiram* repeats some of the expressions used in another Tamil work by name *Nālaḍiyār* (26), which is an earlier work.
18. *Ibid.*, 2164. Translation of B.Natarajan.
19. *Ibid.*, 425 to 428.

20. S.P.Ramachandran (Ed.), *Yōga-Jñāṉa-Śāstra-t-Tiraṭṭu*, Vol.5, *Patañjaliyār-Jñāṉam-54*, 14.
21. *Tirumandiram*, 2.
22. Śiva-vākkiyar, 289.
23. *Ibid.*, 253. He calls the physical body as *kaḷḷa-vācal* in Tamil.
24. Section 13, *tantra* Three, 724-739.
25. Śiva-vākkiyar, 62.
26. Koṅgaṇa Nāyaṉār, 24.
27. Śiva-vākkiyar, 5.
28. *Tirumandiram*, 725. Paṭṭiṉattār in his *Pūraṇa-mālai* also regrets that he has failed to realize the "thou" residing in his body (verses 11, 24, 30, 47 and 68).
29. *Ibid.*, 724.
30. *Ibid.*, 733.
31. *Ibid.*, 762.
32. *Ibid.*, 791.
33. *Ibid.*, 173.
34. *Ibid.*, 1530.
35. *Ibid.*, 1843.
36. *Ibid.*, 116.
37. *Ibid.*, 126.
38. *Ibid.*, 1529.
39. *Ibid.*, 1823. Translation of B. Natarajan.
40. Ganapati Sthapati, *Significance of Vimanam and Gopuram*, p.13.
41. *Ibid.*, pp. 12-13.
42. *Tirumandiram*, 2137.
43. *Ibid.*, 2982. Translation of B. Natarajan. See also 2942.
44. *Ibid.*, 1726.
45. *Ibid.*, 2671.

46. *Ibid.*, 2367.

47. Śiva-vākkiyar is fond of using the expression *vācal,* i.e., 'threshold,' and he calls the human body as a threshold where God exists (17). Karuvūrār also uses the expression *vācal* (6 and 26). The concept of 'threshold' is a mystical one and the body is one such mystical threshold, the other threshold being the guru. In Tantra the threshold is a mystical thing. It is a boundary between two worlds, the ordinary profane world and the sacred world beyond. It is a point where we pass from one mode of being to another, from one level of consciousness to another. The term *vācal,* used by the Tamil Siddha poets, stands for the moment when we ourselves open up to new depths of our being.

48. *Tirumandiram*, 2071, Translation of B. Natarajan. Refer also 2550.

49. *Ibid.*, 2137. Translation of B. Natarajan.

50. *Ibid.*, 2010 and 2008.

51. *Ibid.*, 1769; refer also 1794.

52. Mircea Eliade, *Yoga: Immortality and Freedom*, p. 98.

53. *Tirumandiram* sections 2 and 3 of *tantra* Seven.

54. *Ibid.*, 2770.

55. *Ibid.*, 2130.

56. *Ibid.*, 2125. Translation of B. Natarajan.

57. *Ibid.*, 2123, Translation of B. Natarajan.

58. *Ibid.*, Section 1 of *tantra* Eight.

59. Quoted by T.R. Thulasiram, *Arut Perum Jothi and Deathless Body*, Vol. 1, p. 9.

60. *Ibid.*, pp. 11 and 12.

61. *Ibid.*, p. 15.

62. *Śuddha-sādhakam*, 32.

63. Georg Feuerstein, *The Yoga Tradition*, p. 194.
64. *Tirumandiram*, 2131.
65. *Ibid.*, 2132.
66. Śiva-vākkiyar, 103.
67. *Tirumandiram*, 154.
68. *Yoga-bīja*, 34, 35 and 48-53.
69. *Tirumandiram*, 2432.
70. *Ibid.*, 140.
71. *Ibid.*, 588.
72. *Ibid.*, 689.
73. *Ibid.*, 1385. This is the interpretation given by Suba. Annamalai for this verse. See his *Tirumandiram*, Vol. 2, p. 199.
74. *Tirumandiram*, 1728 and 1729.
75. *Ibid.*, 549-631.
76. *Ibid.*, 553 and 554.
77. *Ibid.*, 555-557.
78. *Ibid.*, 558-563.
79. *Ibid.*, 564-577.
80. *Ibid.*, 578-587.
81. *Ibid.*, 588-597.
82. *Ibid.*, 598-617.
83. *Ibid.*, 618-631.
84. *Ibid.*, 632-639.
85. Suba. Annamalai (Ed.), *Tirumandiram*, Vol. 1, p. 341.
86. *Tirumandiram*, 394.
87. *Ibid.*, 727. Translation of B. Natarajan.
88. *Ibid.*, 734. Translation of B. Natarajan.
89. *Ibid.*, 728. Translation of B. Natarajan.
90. *Ibid.*, 571.

91. *Ibid.*, 726.
92. *Ibid.*, sections 15 and 16 of *tantra* Three.
93. *Ibid.*, section 20 of *tantra* Three.
94. B.Natarajan (Tr.), *Tirumandiram*, pp.134-135.
95. *Ibid.*, p.135.
96. Suba. Annamalai (Ed.), *Tirumandiram*, Vol. 1 p. 456.
97. *Avvai-k-kuṟaḷ*, p. 88.
98. *Tirumandiram*, 293.
99. *Ibid.*, 954.
100. *Ibid.*, 941. Translation of B. Natarajan.
101. *Ibid.*, section 6 of *tantra* Nine; refer also 2709.
102. *Ibid.*, 1554 first line. Quoting from *Tiru-vācagam*, G.Varadarajan interprets the term "boat" *(tōṇi)* in this verse as praṇava. Refer his *Tirumandiram*, Vol. II, p. 279.
103. *Ibid.*, 2394.
104. *Ibid.*, 2694.
105. *Ibid.*, 121 and 1671.
106. *Ibid.*, 2139. Translation of B. Natarajan.
107. *Ibid.*, 2474. Translation of B. Natarajan.
108. Quoted in Alan A. Watts, *The Way of Zen*, p. 39.
109. Kurtis R.Schaeffer, "The Attainment of Immortality: From Nathas in India to Buddhists in Tibet," *The Journal of Indian Philosophy* (USA), 30, 2002, pp. 515-533.
110. *Tirumandiram*, 1064.
111. *Rōmarṣi Jñāṉam*, 12.
112. *Tiru-v-aruṭ-pā*, 12-21-6.
113. *Tirumandiram*, 80.
114. *Ibid.*, 2135. Translation of B. Natarajan.
115. *Ibid.*, 1876.

116. *Ibid.*, 2218.

117. *Ibid.*, 643.

118. *Ibid.*, 719.

119. *Ibid.*, 1032.

120. *Ibid.*, 1134.

121. *Ibid.*, 605.

Chapter 8

The Concept of Guru in the Tirumandiram

T.N. Ganapathy

teḷivu guruvin̲ tirumēn̲i kāṇḍal
teḷivu guruvin̲ tirunāmam ceppal
teḷivu guruvin̲ tiruvārttai kēṭṭal
teḷivu guru uru cindittal tān̲ē.

It is but to see the Guru 's Holy Form,
It is but to chant the Guru 's Holy Name,
It is but to hear the Guru 's Holy Word,
It is but to muse on Guru 's Holy Being,
Thus it is the soul its illumination receives.

—*Tirumandiram, 139*

8. The Concept of Guru in the Tirumandiram

T.N. Ganapathy

1. The concept of guru in Indian tradition

1. 1. Guru

The place of the guru is an important aspect in the method of the Siddhas. To understand better and to appreciate the role of the guru in the Siddha tradition, with special reference to the *Tirumandiram*, let us pass in review the concept of guru, *dīkṣā*, etc., as understood in Indian tradition.

The whole field of Indian philosophy and religion is characterized by an unanimous emphasis on the doctrine of the preceptor. The guru is the primary threshold or the first step in the ascent of the staircase to liberation. The Sanskrit term guru is derived from two words: *gu*, meaning darkness and *ru*, light. The Sanskrit root *gur* means to raise, to uplift. The guru is a principle of nature *(prakṛti)*, which leads one from the darkness of ignorance to the light of consciousness and wisdom. It may manifest through events or circumstances, but when it manifests consistently through a person, that person is known as a guru. A guru removes the darkness of ignorance or non-truth and leads his pupil towards enlightenment and truth. In the Tantras it is said that *gu* means which gives success and *ra* is that which burns impurities and *u* is Śiva. It is also stated that the guru's power is called *uṇmaṇi*. *Uṇmaṇi* is the power by which consciousness becomes free from all objects and is established in Śiva-form. A guru is the spiritual eye-opener. The guru helps the pupil to look and examine, to think and meditate, and to practice and realize. Guru means wisdom. The greatest of gurus impart the best of their knowledge in silence. The silence is not a total silence; the information is there, but expressed very cryptically. Silence means coordination of one's body, one's mind, one's all-faculties, to such an extent that every particle moves in one rhythm. In such a state there is no friction of the mind or the senses. It is said in Hindu tradition that the greatest guru is Dakṣiṇāmūrti who teaches through silence. With His grace all difficulties can disappear in a flash even as age-long darkness does the moment one strikes a match. The guru might teach also by example. What is imparted by silence or example is not intellectual knowledge only, but a kind of direct experience, the realization of a truth through living it.

1. 2. Types of gurus

Hinduism distinguishes different types of teachers. Some of them are:

1. The *ācārya*— one who performs the ceremony of *upanayana* and guides the student with appropriate rules of conduct *(ācāra)*;
2. The *upādhyāya* – tutor, who teaches the sacred lore;
3. The *rāja-guru* – the royal teacher; and
4. The *loka-guru* – the world teacher.

The *upādhyāya* generally charges fees for his teaching, whereas the guru and the *ācārya* do not.

In this connection it will be interesting to note the classification given by the *Kulāgama*, according to which there are six kinds of gurus.[1] They are (The elaborate meaning by Georg Feuerstein is given in brackets):[2]

1. *Preraka* (initiator) or he who instigates initiation by explaining its utility and that of sādhana; (the "impeller," who stimulates interest in the would-be devotee, leading

to his or her initiation (also called *codaka* in the *Brahma-Vidyā-Upaniṣad* 51).

2. *Sucaka* (inagurator) or he who inaugurates sādhana and its aims (the "indicator," who points out the form of spiri tual discipline (sādhana) for which the initiate is quali fied).
3. *Vācaka* (explainer) or he who explains sādhana and its object (the "explainer," who expounds the spiritual pro cess and its objective).
4. *Darśaka* (director) or he who definitely and clearly reveals the details of sādhana (the "revealer", who shows the details of the process).
5. *Śikṣaka* (teacher) or he who teaches sādhana and its discipline; and (the "teacher," who instructs in the actual spiritual discipline).
6. *Bodhaka* (illuminator) or he who imparts knowledge of sādhana and its object and lights up in the disciple the lamp of spiritual knowledge. (the "illuminator," who, as the texts has it, "lights up in the disciple the lamp of mental and spiritual knowledge").

A thorough knowledge of the spiritual, philosophical and religious works, practical experience, a pure life, a loving concern for the welfare of the disciple is the basic qualifications expected of a guru. That is, a guru is expected to be learned in the scriptures of the tradition to which he belongs *(śrotriya)* and well established in the Absolute or Brahman *(brahmaniṣṭha)*, that is, he should be an expert both in theory and practice.

By means of initiation knowledge is handed over without break and this perpetual movement, continuous flow, of guidance is given a name in Tantra, i.e., *ogha,* flood, current, stream, seamless, gapless flow. The *oghas* are of three types, *divya-ogha*, divine guide such as Śiva, *Siddha-ogha*, the Siddha guide, and the *mānava-ogha* ordinary human guides. According to the Bauls, the guru is the past, the disciple the future and the initiation the present. Past, present and future are thus synthesized in the communion of the guru and the disciple.

1. 3. Dīkṣā

A guru gives *dīkṣā* or initiation to the disciple. *Dīkṣā* is the giving of mantra by a guru (i.e. *upadeśa*). There is a difference between *dīkṣā and upadeśa.* Dīkṣā means complete consecretion; but *upadeśa* means communication of a mantra only. A better translation of *dīkṣā* is "empowerment," because in it the teacher carries the pupil in himself, as it were, as the mother bears the embryo in her body and "empowers" the disciple with all his jñāna-energy. The process of empowerment is like an impregnation; it is an impregnation of knowledge. In ancient times the initiate was required to stay in the guru 's asram for at least three days and three nights as though he was in the guru 's womb for those days and nights.

The *Atharva Veda* says:

The guru bringing the god-wandering celibate
Unto himself, takes him into his womb
He bears him in his womb for three nights;
All the gods gather around to look at him.[3]

In the empowerment the disciple is actually in connection with the guru; he is also in connection with the guru 's lineage, with those who have preceded him in the direct transmission of the teaching.

The term *dīkṣā* is a compound of two ideas— *dīyate* and *kṣīyate* — giving and weakening, that is, giving or endowing knowledge and weakening or destroying (removing) lower impulses and desires that stand as obstructions, thereby freeing the individual from phenomenal fetters. The term *abhiṣeka*, another term for *dīkṣā*, means confirmation and stands for an opening into a new dimension. Empowerment effects a spiritual rebirth: it means, for the individual, a total transformation. It is no wonder that Socrates claims that his mission is that of a midwife: for, he "delivers" a "new" man and "aids" in the birth of him who "knows." After initiation the individual is uprooted from his normal moorings. During initiation the individual is given a new name and the initiate is no longer the biological son of his human parents. He has given up all former associations and is "dead" for all practical purposes. To quote Mircea Eliade:

> It is just like a man who should draw a reed from its sheath— or a snake from its slough— or a sword from its scabbard,— recognizing that the reed, the snake, or the sword was one thing and the sheath, slough, or scabbard was another, etc. The initiatory symbolism is obvious; the image of the snake and its cast skin is one of the oldest symbols of mystical death and resurrection, and occurs in the literature of Brahmanism.[4]

The individual is "reborn" to grow up in a new setting. He has become a *dvija*, "twice born," that is, one who is born anew, namely, as clothed in a spiritual body or body of light and knowledge. In the words of Eliade:

> In philosophical terms initiation is equivalent to a basic change in existential condition; the novice emerges from his ordeal endowed with a totally different being from that which he possessed before his initiation; he has become another.[5]

In short, *dīkṣā* means rebirth. In Sanskrit, the bird has been called twice-born. So too is the man who has gone through the ceremony of the discipline of *dīkṣā*. He is considered to have had his rebirth from the blind development of self to the freedom of soul.

> The rebirth of the initiate is often represented dramatically by a magical representation of the act of dying and being born from the womb. Here is an example from the *Aitareya Brāhmaṇa:*
>
> "Him whom they consecrate the priests make into an embryo again." He should be bathed in water (equated with *retas*), anointed with *navanīta* or clarified butter (symbol of embryo according to the text), and purified with *darbhā* or *kuśa* grass. Then collyrium to be put in his eyes, just as it is in the eyes of the new-born. After this, the candidate will have to enter and stay in a hut, shaped like a female organ *(yoni)*. He should not come out of the hut and must not see the sun. He is to be covered at first with a cloth (symbol of the *ulva* or the placenta) and then with the skin of a black antelope (*kṛṣṇājina*, symbol of the uterus). So long as he stays in the hut, he will have to keep his hands clasped *(muṣṭi)*, just as a child remains in the womb. When all this is done, he will have to come out of the hut still covering the body with that piece of cloth symbolizing the *ulva* because the body comes out of the mother's womb under the coating of the placenta (I.3).[6]

In India, the human guru is called the *kalyāṇa-mitra* meaning spiritual friend, one who gives knowledge, which the student needs.

1. 4. Types of dīkṣās

In Indian tradition one speaks of different types of *dīkṣā* or initiation or empowerment.

1. *kriyā-dīkṣā* – initiation through ritual.
2. *varṇa-dīkṣā* – initiation through the alphabet.
3. *vāg-dīkṣā* – initiation through mantric utterance.
4. *sparśa-dīkṣā* – based upon the touch, which tends the disciple in the manner of a bird nourishing its young ones within the warm folds if its wings.
5. *dṛk-dīkṣā* – based upon sight, acts like the fish which bring up their offspring by means of sight alone.
6. *mānasa-dīkṣā* – mental, which builds like the tortoise feeding its infant, by only thinking of it.

In Tāntric literature the first three processes of initiation are called *madhura-pāka.* It is the usual ritualistic, outer process of initiation; it is a process of elimination of irrelevant elements from one 's inner being by a gradual and slow course of regular practices on the basis of the teachings of the guru. The last three processes are called *hatha-pāka.* Tāyumāṉavar goes a step forward and suggests that the mere presence of the guru or a sage is enough to initiate a man for liberation. He compares the guru to a ripe plantain fruit in the midst of the cluster of plantain fruits. The very contiguity of the ripe plantain fruit changes the unripe ones into ripe fruits.[7] This mode of initiation, as mentioned by Tāyumāṉavar closely resembles the type of initiation mentioned in Kashmir Śaivism. It is *anupāya-dīkṣā,* or initiation without external means, which is possible in the case of highly evolved practitioners who can attain enlightenment simply by proximity to an enlightened adept. In Tamil Nadu, one speaks of *Śiva-dīkṣā.* It is initiation to worship Śiva in accordance with the rules laid down by the Śaiva Āgama texts. The tenth chapter of *Mahānirvāṇa-Tantra* contains two hundred and twelve verses, which deal exclusively with *dīkṣā*.

1. 5. Gurukulas

Usually the teachers kept their students in their own houses. Serving the teacher, participating in their household duties was part of the life of the student as is learning the Vedas. Begging for food, keeping away from the pleasures of life and abstaining from the affairs of the world were part of their training. This stage of student life is called the *brahmacarya*, which is a kind of silence. It is a silencing of one's senses.

When the number of students would increase, these houses would grow into institutions called *gurukulas*; (guru means enormous, *kula* means institutions), that is educational academies, usually forest academies. In addition, ancient India had famous universities called *ghaṭikāsthānas*, centers which measured the scholarship of the scholars. Some of the famous Indian universities of ancient times are: The universities of Kāśi, Takṣaśīla, Vikramaśīla, Nalanda, Pāṭalīputra and Kāñchipuram.

The benefits from a *gurukula* and a teacher who is regarded as an embodiment of the Almighty Itself are many. The atmosphere in the *gurukula* and the guru's teachings will free the mind from ego-involvement, will dispel the darkness of ignorance, weaken attachments and passions, remove greed and awaken trust in dharma, will encourage concentration, facilitate self-understanding, support the resolve to practise earnestly and lead the disciple along the path of freedom to the highest objective, viz., enlightenment.

1. 6. Characteristics of a guru

The inclination to teach and impart the wisdom of the tradition becomes the natural part of a guru's life. Initiating a disciple is a call from within. The guru should have two motivations: (i) indebtedness and gratitude and (ii) compassion. A guru is indebted and feels deep gratitude for his lineage of gurus, i.e., *guru-paramparā.* He is released from his indebtedness by giving to others what he has received. The other motivation is compassion. A guru's relationship with his students must be free from all expectations. As the Buddha said, the guru must be a noble friend, a *kalyāṇa-mitra.*

The disciple must have *śraddha* for his guru. *Śraddha* implies two things: (i) self-confidence and (ii) implicit faith in the words of the guru. According to Bhagavad Gita one who has *śraddha* attains knowledge.[8]

The *Encyclopedia of Yoga* gives the characteristics of a good guru and a reprehensible guru:

> One who is adept in all the scriptures, who is clever, knows the essence of all the Śāstras, is soft-spoken, has all the parts of his body intact and beautiful, is born in good family, is beautiful in appearance, has control over all his senses, and always speaks the truth, is of fair complexion, whose mind is fully composed, who is benefactor like the father and mother, who observes all the sacred performances, belongs to one of the four orders of religious life (viz., is a celibate, householder, anchorite, or an ascetic), and is resident of Bhāratavarṣa such a great person endowed with all the good qualities can become a Guru. Although Ācārya and Guru are synonymous terms, yet according to the difference of characteristics of work, there is also a difference in an Ācārya and a Guru. Being

well-versed in all the Vedas and Śāstras, those who impart their theoretical knowledge to the disciples are called Ācāryas. Those all-seeing saints, who for the benefit of aspirants of emancipation, explain to the Śiṣya the successful actions and the kind of worship of the Supreme Lord as described in the religious scriptures, are called Guru. The superior Ācāryas who know all the distinctions of the Vedas and Śāstras in accordance with the seven planes of the philosophies, fully understand the three pains (Ādhyātmika, Ādhidaivika, and Ādhibhautika), and understand the three-fold language (samādhi-language, wordly-language, and the strange-language) of the Mantras and the Purāṇas, are adept in educating the mankind. The great man, who understands all the secrets of the five Saguṇa Worship (Viṣṇu-worship, Sūrya-worship, Śakti-worship, Gaṇeśa-worship, and Śiva-worship) in accordance with the five elements, and those great Yogis who know the fourfold worship (according to Mantra-yoga, Haṭha-yoga, Laya-yoga, and Rāja-yoga) such scholars, clear-hearted, adept in all actions, free of three pains, doing good to all creatures, and liberated great souls are called Guru.

Characteristics of a Reprehensible Guru— Patient of leprosy either in an early or advance stage, diseased in eye, dwarf, who has diseased nails and black teeth, who is henpecked, who has some extra organ or is deprived of some organ, who is a cheat, or a diseased person, who eats too much, or is garrulous— is a person not fit to become a Guru. One who is free from all these defects is the one who can be competent Guru for a Śiṣya.[9]

1. 7. Śiṣyas

To quote Swami Veda Bharati:

The most important qualification that the gurus look for in a disciple is that he should be rich. He should be rich in what are known in the Vedanta tradition as six treasures. These six treasures are listed below.

Shama: a quiescence, peacefulness of personality, a normally gentle temperament.

Dama: self-control over one's senses of cognition so that the eyes and ears do not keep darting about helter-skelter without control and direction, and the hand and feet do not retain a nervous discharge of energy. One should be in control of one's thoughts, desires and emotions.

Uparati: a feeling of withdrawl from the objects of desire and possessions of the world. This does not mean giving up all your involvement but simply realizing that there are immediate duties to be performed *perfectly* and *lovingly*, without seeking the fruits thereof. One constantly prays and aspires for the time when one can renounce, even if it is into the seventh incarnation from now.

Titiksha: fortitude, forbearance. One should not constantly complain – it is too hot; it is too cold; someone has insulted me; I cannot stand this; I cannot bear that. The word *titiksha* simply means the ability to bear and absorb an insult and to accept discomfort without feeling that one is repressing one's natural urges.

Shraddha: a humble faith that one is indeed on the right path and that he has found a guide and a guru who will lead him to the core aspired for.

> *Samadhana*: harmony and freedom from conflict. One should bring to resolution all one's conflicts within one's self through the practice of introspection, self-examination and the pursuit of right attitudes. Then one should bring resolution and harmony wherever conflicts appear in one's external surroundings and relationships.[10]

1. 8. Farewell Address by teacher

The following quotation from Swami Bhaskarananda aptly describes what happens to the student after his completion of education.

On completion of his education the student was called a *snātaka*, which means a "bather." The word implies that the student had successfully bathed in the water of knowledge. In today's language, becoming a *snātaka* would be like graduating from college. After graduation the students gave gifts to the teacher as a token of their respect and gratitude. There was a farewell meeting, and the teacher gave a final address to the students. The *Taittirīya Upaniṣad*, has the following farewell address given by a teacher to his departing students. This address will convey some idea about the duties and ideals of the students of the Vedic period:

> Let your conduct be marked by right action, including study and teaching of the scriptures; by truthfulness in word, deed, and thought; by self-denial and the practice of austerity; by poise and self-control; by performance of the everyday duties of life with a cheerful heart and an unattached mind. Speak the truth. Do your duty. Do not neglect the study of the scriptures. Do not cut the thread of progeny. Swerve not from truth. Deviate not from the path of the good. Revere greatness.

Let your mother be a god to you; let your father be a god to you; let your teacher be a god to you; let your guest also be a god to you. Do only such actions as are blameless. Always show reverence to the great. Whatever you give to others, give with love and reverence. Gifts must be given in abundance, with joy, humility, and compassion. If at any time there is doubt with regard to right conduct, follow the practice of great souls, who are guileless, of good judgment, and devoted to truth. Thus conduct yourself always. This is the injunction, this is the teaching and this is the command of the scriptures.[11]

This address is like the convocation address of the present day universities.

2. The Concept of guru according to the Tirumandiram

2. 1. Who is a guru?

The following two verses from the *Tirumandiram* explain who a guru is.

As declared by the Vedas and the Āgamas a guru is
Entranced in bliss, conceiving on Śiva-Yogi,
Cutting asunder the growing attachments with concentration,
Leads to the Great Guru.[12]

The summary of the verse is: A guru is a self-realized being as declared by the Vedas and the Āgamas and conceiving oneself as a Śiva-yogin, cuts asunder the growing attachments with concentration, leading one to the Great Guru.

One who reveals the real, the unreal and the real-unreal;
Merging the real and the unreal in Śiva;
Speaks the blissful words beyond the pure and the impure;
Is called the blessed guru, the leader.[13]

The summary of the verse is: The blessed guru is the leader who reveals the real, the unreal, and the real-unreal and shows how the real and the unreal merge in Śivam and reveals of that which is beyond the pure and the impure.

The conception of guru as understood by Tirumūlar in these two verses is of the highest order. The guru, according to this conception, is not a mere *ācārya*, nor an *upādhyāya* as viewed in the ordinary sense of the term. A guru is a *bodhaka* or illuminator who imparts knowledge of sādhana and lights up in the disciple the lamp of spiritual knowledge. He is not a mere guru, but a *loka-guru*, the world-teacher, Śiva Himself.

2. 1. 1. A guru is a self-realized being

A guru is entranced in bliss, a self-realized being as understood in the Vedas and the Āgamas. Realization of one's original identity or oneness with Śivam is self-realization. Self-realization is a state of spiritual impersonality. According to Tirumūlar, once self-realization is attained, the jīva (in the guru) and Śiva become one and the same.[14]

2. 1. 2. A guru is a Śiva-yogin

Self-realization is a stage of the guru becoming the auspicious Śiva.[15] The guru becomes a Śiva-yogin. It is a state of unitive experience where there is no distinction between the guru and Śivam. Śiva-Yogam consists in making a mystical equation between the guru and Śivam. The oneness between the guru and Śivam is of an extra-ordinary character. For want of a better expression, the oneness between the guru and Śivam is termed as super union or Yoga and this is what is termed as Śiva-Yogam. Yogam here means the progressive reduction of the 'I'-consciousness to the point of its complete break down and its merging one with Śivam, the

Absolute. Śiva-Yogam is infinite awareness. Tirumūlar says that the guru is Śivam, and he is the ineffable one.

To quote:

Guru is none but Siva – thus spoke Nandi;
Guru is Siva Himself – this they realize not;
Guru will to you Siva be;
And your guide too;
Guru in truth is Lord,
That surpasses speech and thought, all.[16]

2. 1. 3. A guru is a destroyer of attachments

By teaching the method of concentration the guru helps the disciple to cut asunder the ever-growing attachments. Attachments cause misery. Misery makes one wallow in *samsāra*, the world of relations, and kills one's initiative to self-realization. The real guru teaches the disciple to cut asunder the desires and passions, so that the Lord's place will be easy to reach.[17] The *Tirumandiram* says that Śivam lives in the thoughts of those who have abnegated their desires.[18] Tirumūlar as the great guru, advises the disciples to sunder even the desire to be one with God.[19]

2. 1. 4. A guru is one who reveals the distinction between the real (sat) the unreal (asat) and the real-unreal (satasat)

A guru reveals to the student what the real *(sat)* is. The real is always one. Nay to all it even as one is to set a definition to it. Therefore Tirumūlar uses the expression to refer to the Real as "the Great Aloneness."[20]

The Real is *kaivalya*, Aloneness; It is Beyond the Beyond. That is reality is beyond relations; it is the Absolute. Tirumūlar uses a significant expression *kaḷimbu-aṟuttāṉ* to refer to the irrelative nature of the Absolute.[21] *Kaḷimbu-aṟuttāṉ* is usually interpreted as one who has dispelled the impurities of the soul. (*Kaḷimbu* in Tamil means sub-acetate of copper). But its philosophical interpretation is one who is beyond all relations, one who has cut all relations. The real is an a-logical whole, as it does not fall within the bounds of logic. A true guru is one who reveals to the student what the real is without reducing the real to any particular religious concept. Only the thoughtless, the ignorant contend "That" is God and "This" is God.[22] Only the true, the spotless, the impeccable guru *(tūcu piḍittavar)* knows the root *(tūr aridal)*, that is the irrelative Absolute.[23] Tirumūlar uses the popular term "Śivam" to refer to the Irrelative, The Absolute; Śivam is not a religious concept, but a supreme abstraction; and it refers to a perfect, indescribable reality which is being defined differently by many religions; but it is never being fully or finally defined or grasped by those religions.

A guru reveals to the student what the unreal *(asat)* is. While the real is indestructible, and eternal, the unreal is that which is destructible, impermanent and which contradicts itself. *Asat* is delusion; it is māyā. A guru is one who illuminates the disciple by revealing the distinction between the *sat* – the real, and the *asat*— the unreal, the delusion.

A guru reveals to the student the real-unreal *(sat-asat)*. The real-unreal stands for the ātman. Ātman is real *(sat)* because it is of the nature of the ultimate reality, i.e. Śivam. It is unreal *(asat)* because its real nature is covered or concealed by āṇava. The ātman is deluded into thinking that it is different from the ultimate reality *(sat)*. That is, its true nature is real *(sat)*; but due to delusion it thinks that it is the unreal jīva *(asat)*. Therefore what is referred by *sat-asat* or real-unreal, is the eternal atman, deluded into thinking that it is a non-eternal jīva. In another sense, the *sat* (real) does not have/know the *asat* (the unreal, the māyā—world); the *asat*, on its part does not have/know the *sat* (the real). That which knows the real *(sat)* and the unreal *(asat)* is the ātman or jīva. Hence it is called the *sat-asat*. Ātman partakes in *sat*, its true nature being eternal and partakes in *asat*, due to āṇava. Hence it is *sat-asat*.

A guru, in short, reveals to the disciple that which is *sat*, that which is *asat* and that which is *sat-asat*.

A guru is one who shows that the real *(cit)* and the unreal *(acit)* merge in Śivam. Here the real *(cit)* stands for the ātman and the unreal *(acit)* stands for the thirty-six principles or tattvas. A guru shows the path as to how to merge the ātman with Śivam and the technique of the assimilation of the thirty-six tattvas in Śivam.

A guru is one who initiates the disciple into the blissful state by removing the māyā (delusion), i.e., both śuddha and aśuddha-māyā. A guru empowers the disciple by freeing him from delusion and initiating him into the blissful state by the mantra (*cugamāṉa col*, blissful word).

To sum up: To empower the student with his jñāna-energy, the guru must be a realized being, a Śiva-yogin, a destroyer of attachments, capable of revealing the nature of the real, the unreal and the real-unreal, with the methodology of showing how all— the real, and the unreal— merge finally in the state of Śiva, and one who initiates the disciple with the mantra which will lead the student into the blissful state. Tirumūlar also says that unless the guru reveals himself as guru, He is beyond the reach of the disciple. The verse is:

From He has none,
Yet Form He assures;
Birth He has none;
Yet is He the seed of all birth;
Beyond formlessness, too, He is,
The elusive Lord;
Unless Himself as Holy Guru reveals
None, Him reach.[24]

2. 2. The guru-paramparā (the lineage of the gurus)

According to Tirumūlar, Śivam is the real guru, whom he often refers to as Nandi. Nandi literally means the bull of Śiva, but Tirumūlar uses the name Nandi as a synonym for Śivam. Śivam with form is called Nandi; and the formless aspect of Nandi is called Śivam. In the Siddha and Śaiva traditions Nandi stands as the head of the guru-lineage. Speaking about the guru-lineage Tirumūlar says:

Seekest thou the Masters who Nandi's grace received
First the Nandi's four, Siva-yoga the Holy next;
Patanjali and Vyagrapada, who in Sabha's holy precincts worshipt
And including me to complete the number eight.[25]

Based on this verse one can say that there are eight disciples for Nandi. They are Sanaka, Sanantana, Sanātana and Sanatkumāra — all these four are also called the "four nandis" —Śivayōga-mā-muṉi, Patañjali, Vyāgrapāda, and Tirumūlar himself. These eight disciples are also called nāthas. Of these, the first four nāthas, called the "four nandis," were commanded by Nandi (Śivam) to go in four directions and spread the message of the Āgamas. At their appointed destinations they practiced Yoga and attained the status of guru in their turn and became one with the celestials. To quote the *Tirumandiram*:

> The four, each in his corner, as Master ruled,
> The four, each his diverse spiritual treasure held
> Each gave to the world whatever they have attained,
> And thus, the four Immortals and Masters became.[26]

The Great Guru, Śivam, gave *upadeśa,* spiritual initiation, to the three and the four Sanakāti-munis i.e., to Śivayōga-mā-muṉi, Patañjali, and Vyāgrapāda and to the four that is, to Sanaka, Sanantana, Sanātana and Sanatkumāra. He taught them the method (in Tamil *neṟi*) of transcending birth and death. In the words of Tirumūlar,

> The Lord (Isa) imparted (the method of) ending death and birth
> To the three and the four... [27]

This is a very significant verse since more is meant in it. In this verse Tirumūlar has omitted his name as a disciple, but in another verse he says that he ventured to compose the Āgamas and calls the Āgama composed by him as Śivāgama, which is due to the grace of Nandi's holy feet. The verses are:

> High on my bowed head Nandi's sacred Pair of Feet I lore,
> Intoning loud his Name in my heart's deepest core,
> Daily musing on Hara wearing high the crescent moon,
> Thus I ventured the Agamas to compose. [28]

> Flashed in my mind the mystic name of Sivagama;
> Straight I rose to Arul Nandi's Holy feet;
> These eyes witnessed, enthralled,
> The surprising dance in Holy Sabha;
> Thus I lived and enjoyed for seven crore Yugas.[29]

It is significant that Tirumūlar has included his name as a disciple of Nandi in separate verses, because there is a distinction between the *neṟi* (the methodology) followed by him and the *neṟi* followed by the Four and the *neṟi* followed by the Three. The initiation bestowed on the Four, i.e., Sanaka, etc., consisted in the ascetic path of renunciation of the world and its pleasures. It is the method of the *samnyāsa* (in Tamil *tuṟavu-neṟi*). But the instruction given to the three, i.e., Śivayōga-mā-muṉi, Patañjali and Vyāgra-pāda, is to be *in* the world— and take the wallowing souls out of the quagmire of *samsāra,* i.e., birth and death, by the method of devotion (in Tamil *aruḷ-neṟi*)— but not *of* the world. The aim of both the methods— the method of the *samnyāsa* and the method of devotion— is to be liberated from birth and death. Tirumūlar's significant contribution is to merge the two methods— *tuṟavu-neṟi* and *aruḷ-neṟi* and calls his method, *Tiru-neṟi* (the Supreme path). He calls *tiru-neṟi* as the great path *(peru-neṟi),* the path of Śivam *(Śiva-mā-neṟi)* and the only path *(oru-neṟi).*[30] The difference among the three methods is not a difference in kind, but a difference in degree. There is a distinction among the three methods without a difference.

Tirumūlar calls himself as Sadāśiva[31] and his work as *Tamil Śāstra,*[32] *cīlāṅga-vēdam*[33] (meaning the Yoga of discipline, i.e., the Mūlādhāra-Yoga), *Tamil Āgama*[34] (where he says that the Lord gave good birth to him so that he may bring out a good Tamil Āgama work. However Suba. Annamalai calls the *Tirumandiram* as *Sadāśiva Āgamam*).[35] Tirumūlar also says that in his work he has brought out the rich treasures of the Tamil and the Sanskrit Āgamas,[36] which were taught by Śiva to Śakti. Śiva is one whose greatness and mystery have been revealed in both the Tamil and Sanskrit Āgamas.[37] It is significant to note that Tirumūlar uses the term "Āryaṉ" to mean the guru, Śiva.[38] Tirumūlar says that Śiva, as guru, has given us the Tamil Śāstras to prevent the eruption of egoism in us.[39] He also vouchsafes the fact that he belongs to the Kailāya tradition[40] and received *dīkṣā* through Nandi (Śiva).[41] Due to the *dīkṣā* he became enlightened, lived in a "space" where there is neither day nor darkness (a place which is beyond the space-time matrix), lived with a body of wisdom (in Tamil *jñāṉa-uḍambu*, i.e., *divya-deha*) and sat under the holy feet of his guru Nandi[42] under the *bodhi* tree.[43] Thus one of the best *guru-śiṣya*, (guru-disciple) combination is that of Nandi and Tirumūlar, Nandi being the greatest guru and Tirumūlar being the greatest disciple. Yet Tirumūlar bemoans, due to his extreme modesty, that he does not know the method/the way the singers sing praising the Lord, (in Tamil *pāḍal-neṟi*); does not know the method/the way the dancer's dance (in Tamil *āḍal-neṟi*); does not know the method/ the way the seekers seek (in Tamil *nāḍal-neṟi*); and does not know the method/the way the searchers search in Tamil *tēḍal-neṟi*).[44] As a disciple, since he does not know these four methods, Tirumūlar is afraid whether there is any scope for his liberation. This is just an expression of Tirumūlar's modesty.

A little explanation is necessary for each of the four methods/ ways referred to above. Tirumūlar enumerates here the four different methods by which one may "enjoy" the presence of the Lord. The method of singing the praise of the Lord *(pāḍal-neṟi)*, the method of dancing due to the emotion of *bhakti (āḍal-neṟi)*, the method of jñāna *(nāḍal-neṟi)*, and the method of Yoga *(tēḍal-neṟi)*. The first two methods, *pāḍal-neṟi* and *āḍal-neṟi* are the methods which belong to the method of *bhakti* or devotion. The *nāḍal-neṟi*, is the method of jñāna by means of which one tries to understand the nature of reality. But the method of search, *tēḍal-neṟi* is one, which makes a search for reality inside one's body. The first two methods belong to the *bhakti-mārga* and the last two belong to the *jñāna-mārga*; and especially the search for reality inside the body, *tēḍal-neṟi*, is the method of the Kuṇḍalinī-Yoga the method of the Siddhas. For an ardent student, who is in search of liberation, all these four methods are necessary.

2. 3. The seven disciples

Tirumūlar, in his turn, becomes a guru himself. The seven disciples of Tirumūlar are: Mālāṅgaṉ, Indiraṉ, Sōmaṉ, Brahmaṉ, Rudraṉ, Kālāṅgi and Kañca-malayaṉ.

Through instruction imparting
Malangan, Indiran, Soman and Brahman,
Rudran, Kalangi and Kancha Malayan,
Come as my disciples in succession.[45]

2. 4. The spiritual hierarchy of Tirumūlar

Tirumūlar refers to seven mutts or monasteries including his own known as the monastery of Tirumūlar. Apart from this he speaks of six other monasteries following his tradition. They are the monasteries of Kālāṅgar, Agōrar, Tirumāḷikai-t-tēvar, Nādāndar, Paramānandar and Bōgar. All these mutts are breathing the eternal message of Tirumūlar.[46]

2. 5. Guru's message and his adoration

Speaking about the nature of the message of the guru, Tirumūlar says that it is subtly latent like the ghee in the milk, and the disciple who grasps the entire inner meaning of the message will merge as pure spirit in divine light.[47] Tirumūlar also says that a proper understanding of the guru's message/teaching will be achieved by the disciple by looking at the guru, by chanting the guru's name, by following the guru's message and by meditating on the guru's figure.[48]

In this connection it would interesting to note the following episode in the life of Gorakhnāth. Matsyendranāth was the guru of Gorakhnāth. Lord Śiva was the guru of Matsyendranāth. While Śiva was expounding the theory to his consort Gauri on the seashore, Gauri had fallen asleep and Matsyendranāth in the form of a fish in the sea overheard Śiva. When discovered by Śiva he was initiated and named "Matsyendranāth," i.e., the king of fishes. But at the same time he was cursed by Śiva's consort that he would for a time being, forget the knowledge thus obtained by deception. In the Bengali story of *Gorakṣa Vijaya* or *Minachetan* it is related how the guru Matsyendranāth has temporarily forgotten this knowledge and has fallen in love of the queens of Kadali in Assam, who are proficient in magic. There are only women in this state, sixteen hundred of them, all able to bewitch men who happened to come their way. Gorakhnāth, however, on receipt of this sad news of his guru's downfall goes forth in the disguise of a woman, delivers his guru and changes the sixteen hundred women of Kadali to bats, where to this day they can be found in a cave. Gorakhnāth delivers his guru by uttering "Jai Matsyendra." Kalyani Mallik, the author of *Siddha-Siddhānta-Paddhati and other Works of Nāth Yogis*, observes:

> The rescue of Matsyendranath from evil company by Gorakhnath while uttering the guru's name is another example where a guru, though fallen, is yet a guru to his disciple. Such is the high esteem in which a 'guru' was held by his *sishyas* or disciples.[49]

This episode shows the significance of chanting the name of the guru in particular and the importance of guru in general, as suggested by Tirumūlar.

Tirumūlar further says that one should learn the nature of truth by listening to the guru then one should understand the meaning of the teaching in one's own expression and after grasping the message then begin to spread it. Tirumūlar advises his disciples to weigh their thoughts and learning and then having weighed never waver about them.[50]

To achieve the best result of education, he advises people:

To walk with those who go after the Lord:
To live with those who sing His praise;
To search with those who search for Him;
And to merge with those who have attained Him.[51]

Tirumūlar says that those who adore the guru walk on the path of knowledge *(sanmārga)*. The verse is:

To see him, to adore him, to meditate on him,
To touch him, to sing of him,
To bear his holy feet on humbled head,
They that render devotion to guru
In diverse ways thus,
They indeed walk the sanmarga path
That to liberation leads.[52]

2. 6. What did the Guru teach Tirumūlar?

Tirumūlar says that before instructing him as a disciple the guru tested him entirely and after a holy interrogation only taught him the following:

He taught me the meekness of Spirit,
Infused in me the light of devotion,
Granted me the Grace of His feet;
And after interrogation holy, testing me entire,
Revealed to me the Real, the Unreal and the Real-Unreal;
Of a certain is Siva-Guru Lord Himself.[53]

The miraculous powers of Siddhis eight,
The immaculate purity of Sakti's eight,
The baptismal act supreme that turns Jiva into Siva,
The mystic powers of occult Yoga;
Of mantra, of Bhakti, and of Jnana
All these shall thou attain
If the Guru but his grace confers.[54]

To dissolve the false in the true,
To derive the omnipotent might of Truth,
To posses the bounty of splendorous Siva's grace,
To realize the fantasy of the famed Siddhis eight;
Who learns all these
But with guru's blessing?[55]

The Siddhis that are a veritable treasure-trove,
The Mukti that is salvation finite,
The heavenly Grace that vanquishes doubts and fears
And the Jnana that is essence of Vedas
All these,
When the Guru himself imparts not,
Never never shalt thou learn.[56]

He cleansed me of my blemishes,
Transformed me into Sivam Supreme,
And immersed me into His bliss infinite

Bliss that is beyond, beyond words!
The fire of His grace scorches not
Yet drank dry the three seas of my impurities;
And annihilating my primal ego to its traces
He grants me His feet of Grace;
And there does he abide, forever, in me.[57]

(Three seas of impurities are the āṇava, māyā, and karma).

2. 7. Distinction between the real and the pseudo-gurus

In order to bring out the true nature of the genuine guru, Tirumūlar has spoken of false/pseudo-gurus. Contrasting the false gurus from the genuine gurus Tirumūlar says:

They (false gurus) howl about like dogs at foot of gallows;
They peck about like vultures at carrion;
They frisk about like monkeys in merriment
They of false jnana;
But quiescent are the Siva Jnanis true,
Dead to the world, though living in body and senses.[58]

The false gurus live in the midst of worldly things, and being enamored of them fall a prey to the senses. Just as dogs wait for bones at the slaughter houses and vultures fly above concentrating their attention only on the dead bodies on the ground, the pseduo-gurus keep an appearance of gurus, waiting to entice innocent people in their fold, to cheat them and to deprive them of their money and other possessions. Their minds are without concentration and they jump like monkeys hither and tither.

On the contrary, even though they have the five senses of enjoyment and a body fit to enjoy the objects of the sense-organs, the real gurus are not even aware of them; they are disinterested in these things and live like a dead body. This concept of a real guru who is "dead to the world"/ "walking like a dead corpse" is an oft-repeated concept in later Siddha writings. But probably the first to use this concept in Tamil literature and language is Tirumūlar. This concept "dead to the world" (in Tamil *cettu-t-tiridal*), is the exact equivalent for a *jīvan-mukta,* in whom the senses continue to function, maintaining contact with the external world, but the inner consciousness is "dead" to the senses and sense-world. Even though one acts in the world one is not conscious of an "I-act." The basic characteristic feature of a genuine guru (who is a Siddha) is that he moves around the world in a disinterested and dispassionate fashion like "a walking dead corpse;" though dead in body, he is alive in awareness.

The *Tirumandiram* speaks of the ways of the pseudo-guru[59] and the ways of the genuine guru.[60]

2. 7. 1 The pseudo/false gurus

The *Tirumandiram* speaks of the "unholy guru" in very harsh terms. To quote:

A fool he is,
Wisdom none he has;
Truth he has realized not;
Versed is he not in the way,
Of Vedas and Agamas;
Humility he has none;
Of God he speaks ill;
Worldly life is his sole concern;
He verily, is the guru unholy.[61]

This verse does not need any explanation. Tirumūlar further says that "the gurus unholy seek not and they clear not the doubts regarding mantra, tantra, mahā-yoga, jñāna, bondage and mukti."[62] An unholy guru is like the blind leading the blind. Tirumūlar Says:

> The blind (the unholy gurus), who lead the blind (foolish disciples),
> Will enter into the eternal pit first fall;
> Then the foolish disciples too fall;
> And in the end in disorder together they fall,
> — The blind that lead and the blind that are led—
> Indistinguishably, jumbled together.[63]

The last line is significant. Since the unholy guru is also a foolish person like the disciple, when they are grouped together (in a class) it will be very difficult to find out who the guru is and who the student is. Such a classroom will be a place of confusion worst confounded, a helter-skelter collection of persons.

2. 7. 2 The genuine guru

Contrasting the genuine guru from the pseudo-gurus Tirumūlar says that a genuine-guru,

a. works for the self realization of the disciple, and takes him to the state beyond the tattvas;[64]

b. extricates the disciples from their karmas and puts a full stop to the miseries of unending birth;[65]

c. liberates the disciple from the pasas (attachments) and the malas (āṇava, karma, māyā);[66] and

d. imparts the peerless light of knowledge.[67]

The genuine guru is compared to an alchemist by Tirumūlar; and once the disciple is enlightened in wisdom, there is no turning back to disillusionment for the disciple. The verse in the *Tiruman- diram* is:

The black iron, transmuted into gold,
To black iron returns not;
Even so,
He who once the Guru's grace received
Does not to birth return.[68]

2. 8. Distinction between the real and the pseudo-student

Tirumūlar also speaks of the distinction between a fit disciple (*pakva* or a mature student),[69] and an unfit disciple (*apakva* or an immature student).[70]

2. 8. 1. The unfit disciple

The following is an oft-quoted verse from the *Tirumandiram*, which speaks about the acts of the unfit disciple.

They seek not the Guru that blindness cures
They seek the Guru that cures not blindness;
The blind and the blind in a blind dance shuffled
And the blind and the blind in a deep pit together fell.[71]

The unfit disciples, according to Tirumūlar,

(i) do not think of the fruits of karma, but rather the temptations of the backyard drain;[72]
(ii) do not understand the mystery of the body;[73]
(iii) are those whose lips utter one thing, the mind thinks another and the deed does a third;[74]
(iv) who stand in tangle of births to endless sorrow condemned;[75]
(v) do not snap the bonds of the soul, nor free themselves from incessant lust;[76] and
(vi) are mean liars, and strangers to grace.[77]

To quote Tirumūlar regarding the unfit disciples,

They unite in Him not,
The way Guru showed;
They seek him not,
In aimless talk indulging;
They sing Him not,
His benevolent deeds realizing;
What will they get,
They who dance and waste away?[78]

2. 8. 2. The fit disciple

The *Tirumandiram* speaks of the true disciple as follows:

O! disciple true!
In virtue, truth, compassion, discrimination and love
You pursue the Holy Feet of guru true
Constant as unto shadow;
You then gain the nectar of Finite Jñāna its crystal clarity,
And witness the many miracles it brings in train.[79]

A good disciple is one,

(i) Who finds his way with the guidance that scriptures and the blemishless guru give;[80]
(ii) Who gives his all— his body, life and wealth— to the guru;[81]
(iii) Who is sāttvic; who treads the path of dharma, with his thoughts centered on the final truth and who seeks to escape from the cycle of recurring births;[82]
(iv) Who distinguishes the real from the unreal;[83]
(v) Whose jñāna soars higher;[84] and
(vi) Who follows the Vedānta way of renouncing desires.[85]

2. 9. Abuse of guru

Tirumūlar condemns the disciple who talks ill of his guru. To quote:

... He who speaks derisive of him
Will be born a lowly cur;
And having led a dog's life for a Yuga entire,
He will be a worm born;
And then to dust shall be consigned.[86]

If a guru is maltreated,

... the country, the people and their greatness
will all as one destroyed be;[87]

"the land will fall a prey to famine"[88]

According to Indian tradition, if Śiva is angered, the guru can save the disciple from Him, but if the guru is angered no one can save the disciple.

A true guru should be kept on a par with one's mother, father and God. Only the guru can reveal the truth to the disciple. Without a guru there is no use in studying books. Unless the guru guides you, the sastras are like the excrescence growth on sheep's neck.[89]

To conclude let us recall an oft-quoted saying:

He who knows not and knows not that he knows not is a fool; shun him;
He who knows not and knows that he knows not is teachable, teach him;
He who knows and knows not that he knows is asleep, awake him;
He who knows and knows that he knows is a guru, follow him.

Notes on Chapter Eight

1. Arthur Avalon's Preface to *Kulārṇava Tantra*, p. 99.
2. Georg Feuerstein, *The Yoga Tradition*, p. 15.
3. The *Atharva Veda*, XI. 3.
4. Mircea Eliade, *Yoga: Immortality and Freedom*, p. 165.
5. Mircea Eliade, *Birth and Rebirth: The Religious Meanings of Initiation in Human Culture*, p.x.
6. Quoted in N.N.Bhattacharyya, *History of Tāntric Religion*, pp.146-147.
7. "Cuga-vari," 6, lines 5 and 6 *(tāṉē kaṉinda kaṉi kaṉivikka vanda kaṉi pōl)*
8. *The Bhagavad Gīta*, 4. 39.
9. *The Encyclopedia of Yoga*, pp. 96-98.
10. Swami Veda Bharati, *Mantra and Mediation*, pp. 185-186.
11. Swami Bhaskarananda, *The Essentials of Hinduism*, pp. 30-31.
12. *Tirumandiram*, 2057. Author's Translation
13. *Ibid.*, 2058. Author's Translation
14. *Ibid.*, 1823.
15. *Ibid.*, 2958.
16. *Ibid.*, 1581. Translation of B. Natarajan.
17. *Ibid.*, 2613.
18. *Ibid.*, 2614.
19. *Ibid.*, 2615.
20. *Ibid.*, 2450.
21. *Ibid.*, 113 and 114.
22. *Ibid.*, 1154.
23. *Ibid.*, 105.
24. *Ibid.*, 2840. Translation of B. Natarajan.

25. *Ibid.*, 67. Translation of B. Natarajan.
26. *Ibid.*, 70. Translation of B. Natarajan.
27. *Ibid.*, 71.
28. *Ibid.*, 73. Translation of B. Natarajan.
29. *Ibid.*, 74. Translation of B. Natarajan.
30. *Ibid.*, 54.
31. *Ibid.*, 92.
32. *Ibid.*, 87.
33. *Ibid.*, 77.
34. *Ibid.*, 81.
35. Suba. Annamalai (Ed.), *Tirumandiram*, Vol. I, p. 37.
36. *Tirumandiram*, 65.
37. *Ibid.*, 68.
38. *Ibid.*, 117.
39. *Ibid.*, 87.
40. *Ibid.*, 91.
41. *Ibid.*, 92.
42. *Ibid.*, 80.
43. *Ibid.*, 82.
44. *Ibid.*, 96.
45. *Ibid.*, 69. Translation of B. Natarajan.
46. *Ibid.*, 102.
47. *Ibid.*, 134.
48. *Ibid.*, 139.
49. Kalyani Mallik, *Siddha-Siddhānta-Paddhati and other Works of Nāth Yogis*, pp. 4-5 & 25.
50. *Tirumandiram*, 172.
51. *Ibid.*, 543. Author's translation.
52. *Ibid.*, 1480. Translation of B. Natarajan.

53. *Ibid.*, 1573. Translation of B. Natarajan.
54. *Ibid.*, 1575. Translation of B. Natarajan.
55. *Ibid.*, 1579. Translation of B. Natarajan.
56. *Ibid.*, 1584. Translation of B. Natarajan.
57. *Ibid.*, 1595. Translation of B. Natarajan.
58. *Ibid.*, 1671. Translation of B. Natarajan.
59. *Ibid.*, Section 34 of *tantra* Seven, 2044 to 2048.
60. *Ibid.*, Section 35 of *tantra* Seven, 2049 to 2066.
61. *Ibid.*, 2044. Translation of B. Natarajan.
62. *Ibid.*, 2045.
63. *Ibid.*, 2048. Translation of B. Natarajan.
64. *Ibid.*, 2049.
65. *Ibid.*, 2050.
66. *Ibid.*, 2052.
67. *Ibid.*, 2066.
68. *Ibid.*, 2051. Translation of B. Natarajan.
69. *Ibid.*, 1690 – 1703.
70. *Ibid.*, 1680 –1689.
71. *Ibid.*, 1680. Translation of B. Natarajan.
72. *Ibid.*, 1681.
73. *Ibid.*, 1682.
74. *Ibid.*, 1683.
75. *Ibid.*, 1685.
76. *Ibid.*, 1688.
77. *Ibid.*, 1689.
78. *Ibid.*, 2093. Translation of B. Natarajan.
79. *Ibid.*, 1703. Translation of B. Natarajan.
80. *Ibid.*, 1690.
81. *Ibid.*, 1693.

82. *Ibid.*, 1696.
83. *Ibid.*, 1697.
84. *Ibid.*, 1699.
85. *Ibid.*, 1702.
86. *Ibid.*, 531. Translation of B. Natarajan.
87. *Ibid.*, 535.
88. *Ibid.*, 536.
89. *Ibid.*, 2937.

Chapter 9

The Social Concern of the Tirumandiram

KR. Arumugam

yān̲ per̲r̲a in̲bam per̲uga iv vaiyagam
vān̲ par̲r̲i nin̲r̲a mar̲ai-p poruḷ colliḍin̲
ūn̲ par̲r̲i nin̲r̲a uṇarvur̲u mandiram
tān par̲r̲a-p par̲r̲a-t talai-p-paḍum tān̲ē.

Let the entire world attain the bliss I have attained
If the name of the Lord chanted by the great ones is repeated,
Within the heart will arise a thrilling unstruck sound
Which, when practised will lead to realization.

–Tirumandiram, 85

9. The Social Concern of the Tirumandiram

KR. Arumugam

1. Introduction

It is the general opinion of the westerners and even many Indians that the Indian mystics are neither concerned nor interested in the well being of the society. If this is so, how can the social concern of Tirumūlar be justified?

The Hindu dharma classifies life into four ideal stages. They are: *brahmacarya* (student-life), *gṛhastha* (household-life), *vānaprastha* (the life of a philosophic recluse) and *saṁnyāsa* (the life of a wandering renunciant). They were arranged in the order of increasing spirituality. The first stage is entirely devoted to study and self-discipline including celebacy. The student should have no distractions and no responsibilities other than studies and development of the skills. He should not indulge in any sexual pleasure. This is a preparatory period for the heavy responsibilities of the householder with family and carrier. After completing this stage successfully, the student has to marry and settle down as a householder. He should discharge his duties to his family and to society faithfully as a devoted citizen. After the period of active life is over and after all duties are discharged, the householder should retire, and begin to meditate in solitude on the higher things. Just as *brahmacarya* is a preparation for the life of a *gṛhastha*, *vānaprastha* is a preparation for the final stage of *saṁnyāsa*. When a man becomes a *saṁnyāsin*, he renounces all passions, all distinctions of caste, all rites and ceremonies and all attachments.

If *saṁnyāsa* is interpreted as renouncing everything to secure one's spiritual aspirations, then in what way is a *saṁnyāsin* concerned with the society? If it is true that he has renounced the world why should he be concerned about the society? It is true that society is not a disposable cup to use and throw away. It is equally true that people are duty-bound to return something to the society from which they have received basic advantages and certain basic rights. But these duties towards the society are not expected of a *saṁnyāsin* and it is generally held that a *saṁnyāsin* is neither bound by nor has any interest in the society.

These observations are only apparent and not true understanding of the concept *saṁnyāsa*. To set them right, the concept called *saṁnyāsa* must be understood properly. In the *Tiru-k-kuṟaḷ*, the Tamils' early contribution to the world of wisdom, it is hinted that *saṁnyāsa* is renouncing the attitude of "I' and "mine' and not renouncing the world.[1] The *Tirumandiram* also hints at the same understanding.[2]

To be precise *saṁnyāsa* is renouncing all of one's personal holdings. With nothing to hold on to how can one be? Tiruvaḷḷuvar, the author of the *Tiru-k-kuṟaḷ* comes out with a fitting answer "hold on to the One who holds on to nothing."[3] Tirumūlar says "If desire you must, the Lord in desire seize... "[4] It becomes clear that *saṁnyāsa* does not mean self-imposed excommunication but it means renouncement of desires.

This definition fits well for the Siddhas, who live in the society, share their attainments with the people for the benefit of the people, but remain detached from desires.

To a *saṁnyāsin* the Lord is *sarva-bhūta-stitha-ātman,* i.e., the *saṁnyāsin* sees the Lord in all beings. Each and every living being is considered to be a living temple of divinity. So the life of a mystic is very much concerned with the society in which he lives.

Swāmi Vivekānanda recalls the teaching of his guru, Śri Rāmakṛṣṇa as follows:

> It is thought that 'if one wants to attain the Vedāntic knowledge the society should be forsaken; feelings like love, piety, grace should be uprooted.' The spiritual practitioner develops hatred towards the society, thinking that the world and the beings of the world as hindrances to his spiritual practice. But... the final goal of Vedānta can be achieved even while living in the society. ... if the practitioner understands that all forms in this world are appearances of the Lord, that is all.[5]

About Jesus Christ, the Bible says: "Even as the Son of man came not to be ministered unto, but to minister, and give his life a ransom for many."[6]

One of the incidents in the life of Rāmānuja, the systematizer of Viśiṣṭādvaita philosophy, reminds one of the ideals of a spiritual aspirant. It is customary in Indian tradition that one should not speak out the mantra into which he was initiated; it is expected of the aspirant that he should keep it a secret. But after initiation Rāmānuja went to the temple, climbed on top of the tower, summoned the people around and revealed the mantra. For this act Rāmānuja was threatened with an eternity in hell. Rāmānuja said coolly "if so many people can go to heaven by uttering the mantra, I will not mind going to hell."

The *Saṁnyāsa-Upaniṣad* says: a *saṁnyāsin* should strive for the well being of the mortals around him— even though he has renounced everything.[7]

If it is held that renouncement is renouncing everything including one's concern for the other, a true renounciant will renounce the renouncement itself. Cēkkiḻār defines a true spiritual seeker as one who worships the Lord only for the sake of love and not to attain liberation.[8]

This chapter analyses the social concern of Tirumūlar, who is a *saṁnyāsin* and a mystic. In this attempt it traces the roots of Tirumūlar's social concern, his attempts at reforming the society, his ethics and his medicinal advice. This chapter also portrays the *Tirumandiram* in the contemporary context.

2. The root of Tirumūlar's social concern

In the philosophical perspective of Tirumūlar, the world is neither an illusion nor a non-existent entity as held in the Advaita philosophy. He has no reason to shrug off the world. Loving other beings as oneself is an important facet of Tirumūlar's spiritual wisdom.

The mantra that Tirumūlar speaks of in so many verses— Śivāyanama— is not merely a philosophico-mystical one, but a social one too. According to T.N. Ganapathy, *Nama* means *tyāga* or sacrifice; *Śiva* means *ānanda* or bliss; and *Aya* means outcome or result. The term *Śivāyanama* means "the result of sacrifice is bliss."[9] Tirumūlar felt bliss in sacrifice and he construed it as an opportunity to serve.

Tirumūlar who finds bliss in sacrifice sees everything as Lord Śiva.[10] Whatever is done to the jīvas is done to Śiva; because they are identical.[11] By "jīvas" he means all living creatures. He did not try to differentiate between the humans and non-humans.

This idea of Tirumūlar was elaborated by Vaḷḷalār Rāmaliṅga Aḍigaḷār:

> All souls are alike, because they are all brought to their physical body by the Lord. So they are all equal and related to each other. When one sees, hears, knows that one of his brothers is suffering from some trouble, he too suffers. This is because of the bodily relationship existing between the two.

> Likewise when one soul reflects the suffering of another soul, knowing the spiritual relationship existing between them, we should understand this is a right exercised by the souls.[12]

Vaḷḷalār calls this, *jīva-kāruṇya* (compassion to all souls). He further explains: "Where *jīva-kāruṇya* is, there knowledge and love are together. When this is so, the divine śakti will also be there. This divine śakti brings all good."[13]

This view of Tirumūlar and Vaḷḷalār has been reflected in the *Tiru-k-kuṟaḷ* also. It says:

> Of what avail is intelligence to a man if he doth not feel as his very own the pain suffered by other beings, and so feeling doth not abstain from injuring any?[14]

Tirumūlar lifts love equal to the place of God. According to him Śiva is love and love is Śiva and knowing this is knowledge.[15] To bring out this philosophy into action Tirumūlar suggests the following:

> It is for all to offer in worship a green leaf to the Lord,
> It is for all to give a mouthful to the cow,
> It is for all to give a handful of food to others before sitting down to eat,
> It is for all, good, kind words on other to bestow.[16]

In this verse Tirumūlar develops four steps. The first one instructs us to love and worship God. The second one advises us to love the other creatures. The third one teaches us to feed the other human beings. If one is unable to do any of the above, Tirumūlar suggests as a last resort the offering of good, kind words to others. Of these four steps the third one had a tremendous influence on Vaḷḷalār. This was expressed in the establishment of the *Cattiya-daruma-c-cālai*, which is meant for feeding the poor all the days through out the year. The stove that Vaḷḷalār had ignited is still burning there continuously, cooking meals for the hungry. Vaḷḷalār reasons out this charity: "When the jīvas are hungry, they become dull. Their knowledge becomes dormant. Because of this, the process of knowing God is hindered."[17] So feeding the hungry is considered both by Tirumūlar and Vaḷḷalār to be an important thing.

Tirumūlar places serving humans ahead of serving God, because God is omnipresent. One need not offer anything to the Lord because offerings made to the Lord do not reach the devotees; but the offerings made to the devotees (who are hungry), surely also reach the Lord.[18] Even the thought of feeding the true devotees is most efficacious,[19] because they are the gods on earth;[20] they are the walking temples.[21]

This should not be taken that Tirumūlar is for feeding only the devotees of Lord Śiva. The following verse of the *Tirumandiram* brings out the outlook of Tirumūlar:

Give freely to all; discriminate not o'er much;
See food served to others ere sitting down to eat;
Do not hoard, eat not in greedy haste;
The crow calls its brood to share its food, howe'er sweet.[22]

If a simple crow can do this unto his brethren, why not the humans?

It is this *jīva-kāruṇya* (compassion towards all souls) which is the root of Tirumūlar's social concern. It is this spark from Tirumūlar that lit the candle of Vaḷḷalār.

3. Tirumūlar and social reforms

Under certain pressing circumstances, some social customs and manners come into practice in society. After the original circumstances disappear, such customs become meaningless and useless. Their continued presence without any justification will disturb the balance of society. They are like wounds in the smooth surfaced skin. Mystics may help to heal such wounds when they call for the reform of the social institutions.

Casteism, untouchability and religious fanaticism are among such social ills. Though modern governments pass laws against them and try to enforce such laws, they are met with great resistance. If the anti-social elements propagating such social customs are unwilling to reform what can the legislatures do?

The mystics do not try to reform society by laws, but by teaching how to see and honour the Lord in everyone. They do not reform by threatening but by pacifying and uplifting.

The highest goal of life is to attain the love of God. This can be attained only through showering love on the other beings without any discrimination. This is the message of all the religions of the world. Says the *Tirumandiram*:

One the caste,
One the God;
Thus intense hold
No more death will be... [23]

Periyāḻvār, one of the Vaiṣṇava saints known as the Ālvārs, calls all Vaiṣṇavites as "those who belong to the caste of servants (of God)" and asks them to forget the caste distinctions and join the crew praising Lord Viṣṇu.[24] In his view all Vaiṣṇavites belong to one single caste— the caste of servants. He allows no further caste divisions among the Vaiṣṇavites.

In the view of Basava— the systematizer of Vīra-Śaivism— those who wear the Liṅga accepting the principles of Vīra-Śaivism, transcend caste distinctions and they belong to the group called Liṅgāyats.[25]

Tiru-nāvukkaracar, fondly called Appar (father), sings: Even though one is a leper, or a *pulaiya,* who eats the meat of the sacred cow, if that one is a devotee to Lord Śiva, we are prepared to worship him as the Lord.[26]

The point to be noted from the above statements is that 'if one is prepared to accept my God, I am prepared to accept him without conceding to the caste distinctions. Even if he is the lowest of all, I do not mind.' No doubt that this is a great step forward in the reform of a caste-ridden society.

Tirumūlar goes one step further. His statement "one the caste; one the God" can be interpreted as follows: Let one accept God or deny, let one belong to any caste, let one speak any language, let one be a human or a beast, as jīvas, all beings belong to one single category. Hence the statement "one the caste" —the caste called jīvas. Let one call God by any name, let one worship God by any way, let one accept God or deny God, "one the God." Tirumūlar sounds secular and sensible.

3. 1. Condemnation of untouchability

There are references about the four *varṇas* in the *Tirumandiram.*[27] References are made in the *Tirumandiram* about various castes based on profession.[28] The *Tirumandiram* does not lend support to or fervently oppose the caste and the *varṇa* systems, and condemnation of these systems do not figure in the central theme of the *Tirumandiram.* But when these systems went to the extreme of supporting the practice of untouchability, the *Tirumandiram* condemned the practice vehemently.

"Unclean, unclean," the ignorant say
They know not the place "unclean" is,
When they know the mysteries
Of that place "unclean"

Then shall they find,
The human birth itself is unclean.[29]

Those who see the Lord everywhere will never say "unclean."[30] The slogans of the other Siddhas on caste are influenced by the statement of Tirumūlar, "One the caste; one the God."

3. 2. Condemnation of religious fanaticism

The *Tirumandiram* condemns the religions when they become mere slogan shouting religions. The *Tirumandiram* also ridicules the religious fanatics as fools,[31] asses,[32] dogs,[33] etc.

4. The ethics of Tirumūlar

The ethics of Tirumūlar is almost confined in the first *tantra* of the *Tirumandiram*. Almost all the sub-titles— for e.g., transitoriness of body, transitoriness of wealth, transitoriness of youth, transitoriness of life, non-violence, non-eating of meat, not committing adultery, poverty, glory of rains, glory of giving, the love possessed, abstaining from drink— are found in the ethical treatises like the *Tiru-k-kuṟaḷ* and the *Nālaḍiyār*. But Tirumūlar puts his spiritual stamp on these.

The ethics that Tirumūlar professes is a guiding lamp to the spiritual seeker. It helps one to attain the bliss of experiencing Lord Śiva. According to T.N. Ganapathy the ethics of the Siddhas has two aspects— one which is prior to realization and the other is a result of self-realization.[34]

4. 1. The ethics which is prior to realization

Two things are stressed by Tirumūlar to attain ātma-jñāna or self-realization. One is cutting asunder the ego sense. The following verse from the *Tirumandiram* may be considered:

Myself perishing, my wealth perishing,
Body perishing and life perishing,

Heaven perishing and mind perishing,
My ego perishing– this I knew not (is union in God).[35]

In other words, once the ego dissolves and one experiences union with God, one no longer knows any loss of life, body, wealth or mind; because at this stage there is no differentiating between the knower, the knowledge and the known. Everything is lost in the ultimate union.

This "cutting of the ego sense" is advised by Tirumūlar in so many places in the *Tirumandiram*. The verses under the sub-titles transitoriness of body, transitoriness of wealth, transitoriness of youth, transitoriness of life, poverty are all flowing from this "cutting the ego sense" only.

The first step to cut asunder the sense of ego is shedding all of one's attachments. The sense of attachment to something germinates from one's attachment to the body. So Tirumūlar speaks of the transitoriness of the body. Death spares nobody. Even the Lords of our lands are subject to death.[36] It is because of the body that one develops attachments to the world. But death strikes suddenly. Tirumūlar picturises this beautifully.

The rich repast was laid and he dined and joyed,
With damsels sweet in amorous dalliance toyed;
"A little, little pain– on the left," he moaned
And laid himself to rest to be gathered to dust.[37]

When the body cracks, the relatives would not care to keep it even a while.[38]

The biggest of all attachments that rallies around the body is wealth. Whether one is young or old, beautiful or ugly wealth adds pride to him. It is true that wealth makes one proud and happy; but what is the use of accumulating wealth? Just because one has enormous money one can not wear two undergarments, two trousers and two shirts— one on top of the other; one can not eat more than what is needed. A famous poem in the Saṅgam classic *Pura-nāṉūṟu* says:

> Two the garments (upper and under)
> One the measure of food—
> For a king who rules
> The entire world surrounded by sea
> Without sharing it with any other,
> And for a hunter, the simpleton,
> Who strives night and day sleepless.
> Likewise are the other necessities.
> Wealth is for sharing.
> One wants to consume it all alone,
> He can't.[39]

It becomes clear that the pleasure that comes from wealth is very limited. Further wealth is transitory. Tirumūlar says:

> Foolish they who claim their wealth their own,
> Seeing their own shadows to them useless though
> The life that with the body comes as surely departs;
> They see not; the light that lends lustre to the seeing eye.[40]

People believe foolishly that they will live forever enjoying their accumulated wealth. They have an example in the shadow of their body to demonstrate that their belongings will not help them in need and that people cannot live with their belongings forever: The shadow belongs to the body. When the body suffers the hot sun, the shadow of the body does not offer shelter to the body to rest beneath it. The shadow of one's body may offer shelter to others to take rest beneath it but not to the possessor of it. Moreover this shadow is no permanent belonging of the body. The shadow is there with the body only when the sun is up there hot. So is wealth. It is not useful to the possessor. In the same verse, Tirumūlar also brings in another example to prove his point: Wealth is an in-between happening in life. It will surely go at one point of time or other. One must realize that even the body, which came into this world along with soul (and which is not an in-between thing as wealth is), surely departs deserting the soul all of a sudden, without serving the purposes of the soul. So also is wealth, though it is proximate to the possessor as the shadow is to the body and enduring with the possessor as the body is to the soul, it will serve no purpose. Therefore, Tirumūlar advises: seek not the transitory wealth, instead seek the light that enlightens.

Tirumūlar further explains: not only that the possessions are useless to the possessor but they also bring harm to the possessor.[41] If one loses his possessions his supporters will depart from him.[42] It is only natural that when a pond goes dry, the birds around will flee away in search of another pond full of water. Hence Tirumūlar advises to weigh well the pros and cons and throw away the transient trappings of earthly treasures and laugh at the Lord of Death.[43]

Another thing that increases one's ego is youth. That too is transitory. As each and everyday passes by, one becomes aged with wrinkles and grey hair. There is a poem in one of the five epic works in Tamil known as the *Kuṇḍala-kēci*– a work which is not available today except for some poems– depicting the transitoriness of youth and life:

> Dead is the infanthood; dead is the childhood.
> Dead is the youth; dead are the sexual appetites;
> Dying everyday, we grow aged.
> Why do we not cry for our daily death![44]

People cry for the death of others; but they are not aware that each one is dying every day, every moment. This also reminds one of the poems of Paṭṭiṉattār:

Leaving behind so many desires—
The desire for the damsels with beautiful shoulders
The desire for gold, the desire to rule this world—
One died helplessly alone and
The corpses of tomorrow are crying
For the corpse of today.[45]
How foolish it is to cry for others!

The same expression is found in the Bible also. One of the disciples of Jesus said unto Jesus, "Lord, suffer me first to go and bury my father." But Jesus said unto him, "Follow me; and let the dead bury their dead."[46]

Tirumūlar says:

They see the sun rises in the east and sets in the west,
Yet blind of eye, the truth they ne'er apprehend,
The tender calf grows old into a bull and after some time dies;
But this wonder-pageant of the world they do not comprehend.[47]

Tirumūlar tries all the ways possible to drive home the message: Behold! Do not yield to the worldly attachments that rally around the body. Cut asunder from all of them. Less the luggage, more the comfort.

The next step is cutting off all of one's desires. Tirumūlar observes: what is the essential teaching of the Vedas? Desirelessness. Vedānta is desirelessness and a Vedāntin is a desireless person.[48]

In the *Tiru-k-kuṟaḷ* it is said: whatsoever thing a man hath renounced, from the grief arising from that he hath liberated himself.[49]

This idea is echoed in the *Tirumandiram* also.

Sunder your desires, sunder your desires,
Sunder your desires even unto Lord;
The more the desires, the more your sorrows;
The more you give up, the more your bliss shall be.[50]

4. 2. The ethics which is the result of self-realization

Morality helps one to attain wisdom and wisdom thus attained refines morality. The end product of wisdom is love and love only. Wisdom shapes the sense of morality to reach this end-product. Thus flawless love becomes the central theme here, around which grow the other details. The following verse from the *Tirumandiram* makes this clear:

Killing, thieving, drinking, lusting, lying–
These horrid sins detest and shun; to those
Who Siva's Holy Feet attain and the Bliss eternal,
They come not; such men in Wisdom's bliss ever repose.[51]

Of these five ethical codes Tirumūlar gives primary importance to non-killing. He says that it is one of the flowers one can offer the Lord while worshipping internally. This non-killing is the result of love. Only those who have a compassionate heart can see the Holy feet of the Lord; others can not.[52]

You may turn your bone to fuel, your flesh to meat,
And let them roast and sizzle to the gold-red blaze;
But unless your heart melts in the sweet ecstasy of love,
My Lord, my Treasure-trove, you ne'er can.[53]

This is the essential ethical message of Tirumūlar, which lead to God-realization.

5. Medicinal advices in the Tirumandiram

The ethical advices of the *Tirumandiram* treat the soul, whereas the medicinal advices nourish the body. One is internal and the other is external. But both go hand in hand; one supplements the other. Both are intended for helping one to harvest one's final goal — liberation.

Siddha Tirumūlar in one of the verses of the *Tirumandiram* says:

Time was when I despised the body;
But then I saw the God within
And the body, I realised, is the Lord's temple
And so I began preserving it
With care infinite.[54]

Contrary to this view of Tirumūlar, Paṭṭiṉattār disgraces the body as follows:

... Container of the dirty; result of the two deeds (good and bad);
Foul smelling stuff; four foot nine holed
Broken piece; garden of bitter bottle-gourd;
Sanctuary of diseases... [55]

Further he appeals to the Lord to rescue him from the foolish belief in the body, which is going to end up as a handful of ash.[56] Some other Siddhas also have registered their view about the body in the same vein.[57]

Is it not a contradiction among the Siddhas to hold two different views about the body? No. It is not the point of Tirumūlar to advocate that the human body is the ultimate reality. He too accepts the transitoriness of the physical body, like the other Siddhas. But according to him the body is an excellent instrument to achieve success in one's spiritual endeavor. In the absence of this instrument this becomes impossible or the achievement is delayed. So having an instrument and keeping it becomes the primary task of a seeker. That is why Tirumūlar stresses that

> If the body perishes, Prana departs
> Nor will the Light of Truth be reached;
> I learned the way of preserving my body
> And so doing, my Prana too.[58]

To this verse B. Natarajan adds a note:

> This is one of the most important contributions of Mular to Tamil life and culture, brought from North. The body, according to Kaya Siddhi (*kaya* = body), provides the best, and probably the only medium for attaining *moksha,* and therefore it has to be kept always in perfect trim through yoga.

Though Natarajan rightly highlights the importance of the body, it is a disputable opinion that Tirumūlar brought this idea from the North and introduced it to the Tamil life and culture. The *Tiru-k-kuṟaḷ,* which is prior to the *Tirumandiram,* says:

> Five are the duties of the householder, namely, the oblations to the *pitrs* (*pitrs* – the ancestors), and to God, hospitality, rendering help unto relations, and the looking after of one's own self.[59]

The life and culture of the Tamils are basically naturalistic; they accept matter as a reality and hence the concept of the preservation of the body is not new to the Tamils to be introduced from the North.

Tirumūlar gives suggestions to enhance the instrument called body by way of some medical-ethical observations.

5. 1. Diseases only on the ill-willed

Ethics and the physical well-being are dependant on each other. This is reflected in the following verse of the *Tirumandiram*:

> Consumption and anaemia, asthma and colic pain—
> Such the lot of those who nothing in charity give;
> Snake and thunder, sore throat and fleshy ills,
> Approach not them others' that needs relieve.[60]

If one wants to prevent these ailments one has to be charitable and compassionate. Pari-mēl-a<u>l</u>agar, one of the commentators of the *Tiru-k-ku<u>r</u>aḷ*, while commenting on the title of a chapter *Marundu* (Medicine) writes: "ailments like paralysis and others attack people due to old deeds and due to other reasons; of these the ailments due to old deeds can not be cured until the old deeds lose steam... "[61] Tirumūlar also stands in confirmation to this view, but according to Tirumūlar not only the old deeds cause diseases but the new ones too.

The Siddha medical system is based on the concept of the three *dhātus*, that is, the three humors of the body, which are read through the pulse in the wrist. The *dhātus* are called *vaḷi*, *a<u>l</u>al* and *aiyam* in Tamil (*vāta*, *pitta* and *sleṣma* in Sanskrit— windy, bile and phlegm). Of these *vaḷi* represents creation, *a<u>l</u>al* sustenance and *aiyam* destruction. Under normal conditions the pulse rate of the three should be 4:2:1, that is, the reading of the *vaḷi* should be four beats, *a<u>l</u>al* two beats and *aiyam* one beat. Variations from this ratio indicates the presence of disease.[62] The *Tiru-k-ku<u>r</u>aḷ* also registers the same.[63]

Here it may be asked: what is the relation between the moral conduct of a person and his physical condition? The relation between them is not physical but psychological. When one commits an immoral act it causes a mental stress on him.

It is said that even ordinary things cause a mental stress in humans. It is well known that psychic stress is an important cause for the development of headache, especially tension headache, also known as migraine. Also the sudden demise of a close relative or divorce or loss of employment or failure in examination or birth of a handicapped child or sudden loss of wealth or prestige in society usually leads to a quick succession of psychosomatic changes, leading to the development of one or the other stress disorders, like hypertension etc., within the course of the next two or three months or so. It is said that it usually takes six months to a year for the development of any symptoms and because of this, many times patients may not realize the relationship between the stressful state of his or her life and the symptom complex that follows after leading such a life.

> The basic factor in the development of stress disease appears to be mental trauma which produces overtaxing of the excitation and inhibition process of the cerebral cortex. Such a mental trauma can be very acute and severe or moderate but repetitive which cannot be tolerated by the cerebral cortex. Psychic trauma acts as a trigger mechanism, which ultimately leads to the development of stress diseases such as hypertension, ischemic heart diseases, peptic ulcer, ulcerative colitis, bronchial asthma, etc.[64]

There is no doubt that immoral commitments— like killing or causing injury to the other beings, thieving, drinking, adultery, lying— cause mental stress. Mental stress leads to the disturbance of the three humors. The disturbance in the three humors brings in diseases. Thus it becomes clear that immoral commitments cause illness to the body.

Tirumūlar warns:

The aeons pass, the unreturning ages go;
The allotted span of life daily dwindles away;
The irksome body, as if squeezed by some power unknown,
Perishes; seeing this yet, they learn not charity's way.[65]

5. 2. Curing the diseases

Consider the disease, consider its root, consider the means of curing it and then set about the cure with every precaution, observes the *Tiru-k-kuṟaḷ*.[66] As far as Tirumūlar is concerned morality is the root of disease and cure. By doing prāṇāyāma one can conquer death.[67] To do prāṇāyāma one has to observe the do's and don'ts *(yama* and *niyama)* steadfastly. Thus one can make his body invulnerable by way of Aṣṭāṅga-Yoga. Tirumūlar suggests the following:

If the seminal seed thickens by sexual abstention
It shall never be destroyed;
If the body is lightened by austere discipline
Long shall the life be;
If food is eaten sparingly
Many the good that flow;
You may verily become the Lord of Dark-Hued throat.[68]

5. 3. Diseases caused by the vāyus

There are ten types of *vāyus* (airs) in the body. They are: *prāṉaṉ, apāṉaṉ, viyāṉaṉ, camāṉaṉ, udāṉaṉ, nāgaṉ, kūrmaṉ, kirukaraṉ, dēvadattaṉ* and *daṉañcayaṉ*. Of these *prāṉaṉ* serves the area between the throat and diaphragm. It controls the functions of respiration and speech. *Apāṉaṉ* governs the area below the navel.

It controls the functions of the large intestine, kidneys, bladder, genitals and anus. *Viyāṉaṉ* pervades the entire body. It spreads vitality through the system, maintaining a balanced energy flow. *Camāṉaṉ* governs the navel area, controlling the digestive and assimilative processes. *Udāṉaṉ* pervades the area above the throat. It is said to govern the five senses and the functions of the brain. Also it controls the upward flow of vital energy in the body. Over activity of *udāṉaṉ* causes such disturbances as dizziness and overheating in the head. *Nāgaṉ* controls salivating and hiccupping. *Kūrmaṉ* opens the eyes and controls blinking. *Kirukaraṉ* causes sneezing and creates the sensation of hunger. *Dēvadattaṉ* controls yawning and sleeping. *Daṉañcayaṉ* pervades the entire body, remaining even after death.

Tirumūlar observes that if the other nine *vāyus* excluding *daṉañcayaṉ*, strike a balance with the nine *nāḍis*— *iḍa-kalai, piṅgalai, ciguvai, puruḍaṉ, kāndāri, atti, alampuḍai, caṅgiṉi* and *kuru*, life endures in the body for a long time.[69] The *daṉañcayaṉ* pervades the other nine *vāyus* and the *nāḍis*; if the *daṉañcayaṉ* does not function thus, the body will swell and burst.[70] The malfunctioning of the *daṉañcayaṉ*, i.e., if the *daṉañcayaṉ* does not pervade the other nine *vāyus* and the *nāḍis* properly, it may also lead to the following diseases: boils, itches, leprosy, anaemia, paralysis, hunchback, arthritis, eye diseases like cataract and glaucoma; if the *vāyu* called *kūrmaṉ* malfunctions the eyes will go blind.[71]

5. 4. Cara-ōṭṭam or breath rhythm

It is longevity that buys time to achieve the goal of life, viz., getting liberated from the bonds. Longevity depends on breathing pattern or rhythm. Tirumūlar gives his observations about the breath rhythm under the title *vāra-caram* in the *Tirumandiram*. At sunrise on Fridays, Mondays and Wednesdays breath will begin to operate through the left nostril; on Saturdays, Sundays and Tuesdays it will begin to operate through the right nostril. On Thursdays, if that day falls in the waxing moon's fortnight, breath flows in the left; if the day falls in the waning moon's fortnight, it flows in the right. If breath begins to operate through the left nostrils on Fridays, Mondays and Wednesdays the body will glow in health and will live long. When the breath begins to operate through the left nostril on Tuesdays, waning moon's Thursdays, Saturdays and Sundays, if the yogin forces it to the right, he will get bliss.[72]

5. 5. Way to blemishless birth

While giving tips to preserve the body, Tirumūlar also gives some tips to create a blemishless body under the title "karu-uṟpatti," "Creation of Microcosm." Here he is sharing his knowledge in this regard to create flawless microcosms.

The chromosomes are the decisive factors that decide the gender of a child. The number of chromosomes is twenty-three each in the sperm and the ovum. One of the twenty-three chromosomes in the sperm is the gender-decider. The chromosomes in the ovum are always 'x' chromosomes. It is the sperm which contain both the 'x' and 'y' chromosomes. Of the innumerable sperm ejaculated, half of them contain 'x's and half of them contain 'y's. If the sperm containing 'x' chromosome enters the ovum, which is already containing an 'x' chromosome making an 'xx' combination, the product will be a female child. If the sperm containing 'y' chromosome enters the ovum, the combination is 'xy' and the product will be a male child.

The *Tirumandiram* says,

The masculine flow dominates, the infant is male born,
The feminine dominates, the infant is female born...[73]

Can we say that Tirumūlar indicates the dominance of 'y' chromosomes as 'the dominance of masculine flow' and the dominance of 'x' chromosomes as the 'dominance of the feminine flow?' If one can conclude so, then it may be asked: can we determine the dominance of masculine or feminine flows? Tirumūlar says yes. During the intercourse, if the prāṇa of the male partner operates through the right nostril, that is, in the piṅgala-nāḍi, the product will be a male child; if the prāṇa operates through the left nostril, that is, iḍa-nāḍi, the product will be a female child. That is, when the prāṇa operates through the piṅgala-nāḍi, the sperm that contains the 'y' chromosome becomes the winning sperm that enters into the ovum to make a male child; when the prāṇa operates through the iḍa-nāḍi, the sperm that contains the 'x' chromosome enters the ovum, causing a female child. So it can be held that the chromosome contained in the sperm decides the gender of the baby; the male partner's course of prāṇa decides the winning sperm. It is the breath rhythm that holds the key to fix the gender of a child.[74]

The chromosomes carry the genes. In each chromosome thousands of genes exist in pairs. Each pair of the genes plays a role in deciding the genetic characters like physical structure, color of hair, etc. Genetic engineering is the field of research which is trying to re-structure the genes by studying their characters. Fusion, deletion, inversion, transposition are some of the attempts made in this regard. This genetic engineering is aiming at creating a blemishless human body.

Tirumūlar suggests the following:

In the act of intercourse, after emission, if the male partner's breath extends five finger length, the infant born lives a hundred years. When the breath extends four finger length, the infant lives for eighty years.[75] When after intercourse, if the man is short of breath, the infant born will be a dwarf; when the breath blows feeble, the baby born may be of defective limbs.[76] At the time of union, if the mother's bowels are heavy, a dullard will be born; if urine exceeds, a dumb child will be born; if both exceeds a blind child will be born.[77] If the breath of both the partners run rhythmic together, the infant born will be exceedingly handsome; if the rhythm falters or the breath is held there will be no conception at all.[78]

To Tirumūlar everything regarding the birth of a baby is decided by the breath rhythm. A yogin, who knows well the art of breath control, can regulate his breath accordingly to achieve the premeditated results.

Tirumūlar volunteers to tell all this to build a healthy society made up of healthy citizens.

6. A contemporary reading in the Tirumandiram

Both in the West and the East, there are searing social questions regarding marriage, divorce, abortion, the rights of the unborn, chastity, adultery, alcoholism, violence, charity, materialism, individualism and capitalism. The verses of the *Tiruman- diram* could provide the contemporary seekers with some leads to the answers of these questions.

Tirumūlar never advocated against marriage. Śaivism, the religion that Tirumūlar advocates, is a naturalistic religion which allows marriage. Tirumūlar puts forth Lord Śiva Himself as an example. By presenting the Lord in the form of Umā-maheśvara,[79] which is symbolic of *bhoga* (enjoyment), Tirumūlar endorses marriage.

Divorce was something unknown to the Tamils at that time of Tirumūlar. We find no reference to divorce in the verses of the *Tirumandiram.* Even if divorce was in vogue at the time of Tirumūlar he would not have approved it. This could be inferred from his condemnation of adultery. Marriage is a social institution that helps one to meet his sexual needs. But adultery is over-indulgence. When the sexual desire can be gratified easily in the form of a wedded wife without any risk, why should one go out unmindful of the risks involved in it? Is it not a foolish act? Tirumūlar says:

> The dear, wedded wife pines within the home,
> But the lusting youth covets the guarded neighbour's mate;
> Even as one, declining the luscious ripeness of the jack,
> Yearns for the tamer taste of the thorny date.[80]

Tirumūlar wonders: when the luscious jack fruit is ready at home, why should one then climb the thorny date tree?

There is a Hindu mythological story about the fate of the king of the heavens Indra who went after Akalya, the wife of Sage Gautama. When Gautama went out of his hut to take bath, Indra entered the hut taking the form of sage Gautama and abused Akalya. When Gautama came to know this, he cursed Akalya to become stone-like and Indra to have a thousand vaginas all over his body. Indra pleaded for an amendment and Gautama amended it that instead of a thousand vaginas Indra would have a thousand eyes all over his body. This is a famous episode quoted by all who speak of adultery in the Indian context. The *Tiru-k-kuṟaḷ* sets Indra, who cannot control his passions, as an example for those who go for gratification: "Dost thou desire to know the power of the saint who hath quenched the cravings of his five senses? Look on the king of the Gods, Indra: His one example is enough."[81] The *Tiru-k-kuṟaḷ* sets forth Indra as a negative example and by doing so it tries to establish the power of the saint who has quenched the cravings of the senses positively.

In the Indian scenario, marriage is not a license to free sensual pleasure. It is an institution meant for reproduction and it carries the responsibility of upbringing the progeny in a fitting manner. So Tirumūlar comes out with suggestions to bring up the progeny right from the stages of its conception. Tirumūlar's comments on conception which aim at making a flawless body and his high-held opinion of body as an instrument to achieve the supreme result called liberation will make one realize that how remarkable it is to take birth as a human and how immoral it is to abort a baby thus denying its chance to achieve the goal.

There is a popular verse in Tamil in which poetess Avvai says: It is rare to take a human body. Even if one has taken a human body it is rare to have a flawless body. Even if one has a flawless body, it is rare that he is knowledgeable and educated. Even if one is knowledgeable and educated, it is rare to do charity and penance. If one does charity and penance, the doors of heaven will be open to him.[82]

By aborting a baby the parents deny it a fare chance to get rid of the cycle of birth and death. If the parents do not want a child they should have avoided contact. They just cannot escape from their responsibility by aborting the baby. The male must ejaculate only to procreate and not otherwise. If one wastes his semen for sheer pleasure and becomes a slave to lust, his body deteriorates.[83] (To sublimate this energy, Tirumūlar recommended various methods, which are discussed in the chapter on Yoga).

Having said that the semen should not be wasted, Tirumūlar proceeds on to say some words on the periodicity for sexual union. Of the two phases of the moon, the first eight days of the waxing moon are not appropriate for union; the six days that remain and the first six days of the waning moon are good.[84]

For those who practice Yoga, it is better to avoid the fifth, the sixth and the eleventh days after the woman menstruates. The six days in the middle of the three weeks that follow are appropriate to seek pleasure.[85]

While embracing the damsel, one should remain detached, fixing one's thoughts on God; one should remain calm and composed and should not get excited. Directing his senses inwardly one should emit.[86]

Having emitted, one should examine the laws of conception, the time of union, the time of pregnancy and delivery, the baby's length of life, and death, the baby's character, etc.[87] Having examined these, one should abstain from the maiden and should not seek further union.[88]

One verse of the *Tirumandiram* reads that except for those who plant the seed there is no harvest.[89] One can interpret this line in vice-versa that those who do not want the harvest should refrain from planting the seed. Having planted the seed one should not abort it for he has no right to do it.

Tirumūlar says that God preserves the foetus inside the womb for three hundred days in numerous ways.[90] Māṇikka-vācagar in "Pōr̲r̲i-t-tiru-v-agaval" of his *Tiru-vācagam*, explains the critical stages of the human foetus right from the first month up to the tenth month:

I escaped from the microbes on conception;
I escaped from splitting into two in the first month;
I escaped from disfigurement in the second month;
I escaped from the water secretion of the womb in the third month;

I escaped from the darkness in the womb in the fourth month;
I escaped death in the fifth month and was kicked off with life; I escaped the pain caused by the itching feeling of the womb in the sixth month;
I escaped from being born into this world as a premature baby in the seventh month;
I escaped from the counter-pressure of the womb in the eighth month;
I escaped from being squeezed out in the ninth month;
I survived along with my mother the pain of delivery
And was safely delivered into this world in the tenth month.[91]

Māṇikka-vācagar goes on to explain from what all he escaped after taking birth as a human in this world and how God helped him to overcome all these. When God takes this much interest in preserving the life of a foetus how can a human abort it? It can be inferred from what is said by Tirumūlar that abortion is the most immoral act. By aborting a baby one denies a soul its chance of getting liberated.

It is already stated elsewhere in this chapter that Tirumūlar condemns activities such as killing, thieving, drinking, lusting and lying as immoral. These acts are done out of ignorance. Killing is an act of violence. Violence is to be denounced. It helps neither the one who acted violently nor the one who fells prey to it. By killing somebody one thinks that he has taken revenge on somebody who displeased him. This is an act out of utter ignorance. The way to get out of displeasure is to get out of pleasure as well; that is, to treat both pleasure and displeasure equally. Mental equanimity *(iru-viṉai-oppu)* is the key to open the doors of heaven. Seeking more pleasure, that too by violent means, will only result in displeasure and ultimately will lead to trouble. Not only that. By killing somebody, one curbs the chances of the one who was killed to become reformed and get liberated. Moreover the doer of the violent act has to take several births to make his account of bad deeds *(pāpa)* void and there is no guarantee that he will take birth as a human in the near future.

Tirumūlar censures drinking of alcohol, because it curtails one's intelligence. The soul's natural intelligence is covered up by the fetter called āṇava-mala (ignorance). God helps the soul with a body as an instrument of knowledge to escape from ignorance. Drinking alcohol obscures the intelligence of the soul. Alcoholism makes the soul to go in the wrong direction and hence Tiumūlar vehemently condemns it.

Tirumūlar does not support measures to accumulate wealth. He is against materialism. He says: people are going after wealth. They think that every day dawns just for the sake of filling the stomach and they try hard to fill the stomach and to put a full-stop to hunger. They think that accumulation of wealth will forever solve the problems of filling the stomach. But they do not know that the key is elsewhere. Stomach will be there as long as they have a birth. Once their birth ceases, their hunger ceases. Birth is the result of the three impurities. If these three impurities are cleaned there is no birth; if there is no birth there is no body; if there is no body there is no stomach; if there is no stomach there is no hunger. Everything ceases.[92] (Although Tirumūlar appreciates the body elsewhere in the *Tirumandiram,* and advises to offer a handful of food to one's fellow beings every day, he appreciates it only as an instrument to achieve the goal, viz. liberation. No doubt that the body is to be fed, but only to that extent to keep it alive and thriving). Therefore accumulation of wealth is a vain exercise. By this way Tirumūlar registers his opinion regarding materialism and the extremes of capitalism.

If one happens to be wealthy he should share it with others without any discrimination. The crow calls its kith and kin to share the food. That should set an example for the humans.[93] It is clear that Tirumūlar is not for materialism although he accepts matter as a reality not as an illusion.

The problems of human life, according to Tirumūlar, can be tackled with the help of education. To Tirumūlar education is not mere literacy; education is spiritual, that which transcends religious divisions but teaches how to love and realize the ultimate truth. Knowing the purpose of the union of body and soul is education.[94] Those who have mastered this are educated, even if they are illiterates; those who have not mastered it are uneducated, even if they are literates.[95] This education comes easily by listening to the words of the holy and wise.[96]

The responsibility to set right the things that are in disarray in a society rests with the ruler. It is the duty of the ruler to assure that things fall in place. The ruler should punish the pretenders who don the holy garb and practice evil ways.

> The senseless fools donning sacred thread and matted locks,
> And with chanting phrases pretend to wisdom unpossessed,
> Them, the ruler of state shall, with wise men's help, take and test,
> And, for the country's good, impart words in wisdom drest.[97]

The ruler can claim one sixth of the produce of his subjects,[98] and in turn it is the duty of the ruler to defend his people. The ruler who protects his people wins the loyalty of his subjects.[99] If one does not stand in his own ordained faith and if he deviates, the ruler should not fail to punish them according to the laws laid down in the Āgamas.[100] To do all these the ruler should be an educated one.[101] Education in the parlance of Tirumūlar is spiritual education. One can say that Tirumūlar proposes a philosopher-king.

Though the ways the society conducts itself and the modes of the government have changed, Tirumūlar's advices still hold water because man is essentially the same right from the beginning, suffering from impurities.

7. Tirumandiram – A literature which shows the way: Āṟṟu-p-paḍai

Āṟṟu-p-paḍai is a kind of Tamil poetry. The term *āṟṟu-p-paḍai* is a compound of two words, *āṟu* and *paḍai*. *Āṟu* in Tamil stands for a river, a canal, or a way. In olden days, when people migrated from one place to another in search of lands of prosperity, they went alongside the rivers. They made their habitats on the banks of the rivers. Since the rivers showed the way to wealth, people named 'way' with the word which stands for river, *āṟu*. *Paḍai* is a term, which means 'the act of putting.' The combination of these two terms, i.e., *āṟṟu-p-paḍai* would mean 'the act of putting one on the way' or 'the act of showing the way' or 'the act of canalizing (guiding).' This has become an image in Tamil heroic poetry.

The definition of the *āṟṟu-p-paḍai* kind of poetry is given in the *Tol-kāppiyam*, the oldest available Tamil grammar work. It is as follows: May he be a stage actor or a singer or a buffoon or a songstress, an artiste on his/her return after getting so much of gifts from a king for his/her performance, when met with a co-artiste on the way, guides him/her to the king, describing the philanthropic nature of the king to enable the co-artiste benefited as he/she was.[102]

This definition restricts the imagery called *āṟṟu-p-paḍai* only to the stage artistes. Later the poets were also included. In any case *āṟṟu-p-paḍai* stood for guiding one to material wealth. It was

Tiru-Murugāṟṟu-p-paḍai which guided the wayfarer to Lord Murugaṉ for material as well as spiritual wealth.

Tirumūlar, the first known Tamil Siddha, used this imagery *āṟṟu-p-paḍai* completely for spiritual purposes. Tirumūlar says:

> Let the entire world attain the bliss I have attained
> If the name of the Lord chanted by the great ones is repeated
> Within the heart will arise a thrilling unstruck sound
> Which, when practised, will lead to realization.[103]

It is rightly observed by T.N. Ganapathy that the *āṟṟu-p-paḍai* concept has acquired a socio-philosophical meaning at the hands of the Tamil Siddhas. According to T.N. Ganapathy, this concept has two aspects in the philosophy of the Siddhas– one positive and the other negative. The anti-scriptural and anti-theistic attitudes coupled with their criticism of caste, idol worship, religious observances, rituals and ceremonies and their warning against pseudo gurus etc., represent the negative side of the *āṟṟu-p-paḍai* concept, while, the method of the Kuṇḍalinī-Yoga, their ethical precepts and their system of medicine form the positive aspect of the *āṟṟu-p-paḍai* concept.[104] It is to be kept in mind that Tirumūlar is not anti-scriptural or anti-theistic for he praises the scriptures.

The *Naṉṉūl,* a Tamil work on grammar defines a book as one which accomplishes all or some or at least one of the following four: virtue *(aṟam),* wealth *(poruḷ),* pleasure *(iṉbam),* liberation *(vīḍu).*[105] These four are called *puruṣārthas* in Sanskrit. In Tamil they are called *ūdiyam* or *uṟudi-p-poruḷ*. That is, these are the final goals one is striving for. Man seeks pleasure either materially or spiritually. Wealth and pleasure are material; virtue and liberation are spiritual. Hence the *Naṉṉūl* defines that a book should help one to achieve at least one of the four.

Some books revolve around the concept of virtue; some concentrate on wealth; some on pleasure; some take all the three in their fold. The *Kauṭalīyam*, the famous work of Chāṇakya, claims that it is taking all the three— virtue, wealth and pleasure— into account.[106] The *Tiru-k-kuṟaḷ* speaks directly about the three and refers indirectly about the fourth one liberation.

The books which deal with the first three— virtue, wealth and pleasure— are called *tri-varga* and books which deal with all the four including liberation are called *catur-varga.*

The *Tirumandiram* concentrates on only one of the above— liberation. It speaks about virtue only as a supplement to liberation. In that case the *Tirumandiram* may be called as *dvi-varga.* The *Tirumandiram* speaks very less about material wealth and material pleasure. Concentrating on them is not necessary for a book, which is directing people to liberation. Further in the conception of Tirumūlar, liberation is the final axis; without that the other three will become meaningless.

The social concern of the *Tirumandiram* is to direct each and everybody to liberation. The philosophical, religious and the other conceptions of the *Tirumandiram* are stemming from this concern for the other beings. Blessed are those who study it and take its advice to heart.

Notes on Chapter Nine

1. *Tiru-k-kuṟaḷ*, 346.
2. *Tirumandiram*, 2615.
3. *Tiru-k-kuṟaḷ*, 350.
4. *Tirumandiram*, 298. Translation of B. Natarajan.
5. Ra. Ganapathy, *Swāmi Vivēkāṉandar*, pp. 112-113.
6. *Holy Bible*, Matthew, 21:28.
7. N.S. Subramaniaṉ, *Encyclopaedia of the Upanisads*, p. 494. Also refer: Radhakrishnan, *The Hindu View of Life*, p. 65.
8. *Periya-purāṇam*, "Tiru-k-kūṭṭa-c-ciṟappu," 8.
9. T.N. Ganapathy, *The Philosophy of the Tamil Siddhas*, p. 190.
10. *Tirumandiram*, 2977.
11. *Ibid.*, 2017.
12. Vaḷḷalār Rāmaliṅga Swāmigaḷ, *Tiru-v-aruṭpā*, Sixth Tirumuṟai, "Jīva-kāruṇya-oḻukkam," third section, 1, p. 39.
13. *Ibid.*, "Jīva-kāruṇya-oḻukkam," 1:4, p. 3.
14. *Tiru-k-kuṟaḷ*, 315. Translation of V.V.S. Aiyar.
15. *Tirumandiram*, 270.
16. *Ibid.*, 252. Translation of B. Natarajan with a slight modification.
17. Vaḷḷalār Rāmaliṅga Swāmigaḷ, *op.cit.*, p. 20.
18. *Tirumandiram*, 1857.
19. *Ibid.*, 1861.
20. *Ibid.*, 1862.
21. *Ibid.*, 1857.
22. *Ibid.*, 250. Translation of B. Natarajan.
23. *Ibid.*, 2104. Translation of B. Natarajan with a slight modification.

24. S. Vaiyapuri Pillai (Ed.), *Divya-p-prabhandham*, "Tiru-p-pallāṇḍu," 4.
25. Edgar Thurston and K. Rangachari, *Castes and Tribes of Southern India*, Vol. IV, p. 249.
26. *Tēvāram*, 6:938.
27. *Tirumandiram*, 1721.
28. For a detailed list refer: G. Kousalya Vijayan, *Tirumandirattil Vāḻviyal Cindanaigaḷ*, p. 18.
29. *Tirumandiram*, 2551. Translation of B. Natarajan.
30. *Ibid.*, 2552.
31. *Ibid.*, 329.
32. *Ibid.*, 1538.
33. *Ibid.*, 1558; also refer 52 and 58.
34. T.N. Ganapathy, *op.cit.*, p. 197.
35. *Tirumandiram*, 2951. Translation of B. Natarajan.
36. *Ibid.*, 153.
37. *Ibid.*, 148. Translation of B. Natarajan.
38. *Ibid.*, 158.
39. *Puṟa-nāṉūṟu*, 189. Author's translation.
40. *Tirumandiram*, 170. Translation of B. Natarajan.
41. *Ibid.*, 171.
42. *Ibid.*, 209.
43. *Ibid.*, 172.
44. *Kuṇḍala-kēci*, 9. Author's translation.
45. Paṭṭiṉattār, "Tiru-t-tillai," 1. Author's translation.
46. *Holy Bible*, Matthew, 8: 21 and 22.
47. *Tirumandiram*, 177. Translation of B. Natarajan with a slight change.
48. *Ibid.*, 229.

49. *Tiru-k-kuṟaḷ*, 341. Translation of V.V.S. Aiyar.
50. *Tirumandiram*, 2615. Translation of B. Natarajan.
51. *Ibid.*, 200. Translation of B. Natarajan.
52. *Ibid.*, 273.
53. *Ibid.*, 272. Translation of B. Natarajan.
54. *Ibid.*, 725. Translation of B. Natarajan.
55. Paṭṭiṉattār, "Kōyil Tiru-agaval," 2:8-19. Author's translation.
56. *Ibid.*, "Uḍal-kūṟṟu-vaṇṇam," 24.
57. Refer: Kaḍuveḷi-c-cittar, 3 and Aḻugaṇṇi-c-cittar, 8.
58. *Tirumandiram*, 724. Translation of B. Natarajan.
59. *Tiru-k-kuṟaḷ*, 43. Translation of V.V.S. Aiyar with a slight modification.
60. *Tirumandiram*, 263. Translation of B. Natarajan.
61. Refer Pari-mēl-aḻagar's comment on "Marundu," *Tiru-k-kuṟaḷ*.
62. — , *Tamiḻ (Citta) Maruttuva-k-kōṭpāḍu*, n.p.
63. *Tiru-k-kuṟaḷ*, 941.
64. K.N. Udupa, *Stress and its Management by Yoga*, R.C. Prasad (Ed.), p. 105.
65. *Tirumandiram*, 261. Translation of B. Natarajan.
66. *Tiru-k-kuṟaḷ*, 948. Translaion of V.V.S Aiyar with a slight modification.
67. *Tirumandiram*, 571.
68. *Ibid.*, 735. Translation of B. Natarajan.
69. *Ibid.*, 653.
70. *Ibid.*, 654.
71. *Ibid.*, 655 and 656.
72. *Ibid.*, 790, 796.

73. *Ibid.*, 478. Translation of B. Natarajan.
74. *Ibid.*, 482.
75. *Ibid.*, 479.
76. *Ibid.*, 480.
77. *Ibid.*, 481.
78. *Ibid.*, 483.
79. *Tirumandiram*, 1162, 2727, 2767, 2768, 2780.
80. *Ibid.*, 201.
81. *Tiru-k-kuṟaḷ*, 25. Translation of V.V.S Aiyar.
82. Puliyur Kecigan (Comm.), *Avvaiyār Taṉi-p-pāḍalgaḷ*, p. 104.
83. *Tirumandiram*, 1938.
84. *Ibid.*, 1939.
85. *Ibid.*, 1940.
86. *Ibid.*, 1942 and 1943.
87. *Ibid.*, 1944.
88. *Ibid.*, 1945.
89. *Ibid.*, 1946.
90. *Ibid.*, 463.
91. *Tiru-vācagam*, "Pōṟṟi-t-tiru-v-agaval," lines 13-25. Author's translation.
92. *Tirumandiram*, 210 & 211.
93. *Ibid.*, 250.
94. *Ibid.*, 290.
95. *Ibid.*, 310.
96. *Ibid.*, 300, 301, 302, 305, 307.
97. *Ibid.*, 242. Translation of B. Natarajan.
98. *Ibid.*, 244.
99. *Ibid.*, 245.

100. *Ibid.*, 247.
101. *Ibid.*, 238.
102. Ka. Vellaivaranan (Comm.), *Tol-kāppiyam*, "Pura̱-t-tiṇai-iyal," aphorism 30, p. 333.
103. *Tirumandiram*, 85. Translation of B. Natarajan with a slight modification.
104. T.N. Ganapathy, *op.cit.*, pp. 190 and 191.
105. *Na̱ṉ̱ūl*, 10.
106. M. Kadireca Chettiyar and P. Sri. Ramanujachari (Trans.), *Kauḍalīyam Poruṇūl*, p. 1229.

Chapter 10

Monistic Theism of the Tirumandiram and Kashmir Śaivism

Dr. Geetha Anand and Professor T.N. Ganapathy

10. Monistic Theism of the Tirumandiram and Kashmir Śaivism

Dr. Geetha Anand and Professor T.N. Ganapathy

Introduction:

The necessity and need for writing this additional chapter in the second edition of **The Yoga of Siddha Tirumular: Essays on the Tirumandiram** arises since many readers may not know that there is a debate within the Śaiva Siddhānta, whether the **Tirumandiram** represents monistic theism or pluralistic realism. This debate has been included in full in the Tenth volume of the English translation of the *Tirumandiram,* edited by T.N. Ganapathy and published by Babaji's Kriya Yoga Order of Acharyas, Quebec, Canada (January 2010). The article under the title "Monism and Pluralism in Śaiva Siddhānta" by Subramuniya Swami of the Hawaii School maintains that the **Tirumandiram** advocates monistic theism while the article "There can be only one Final conclusion in Śaiva Siddhānta" by T.N. Arunachalam maintains that the **Tirumandiram** advocates pluralistic realism only. Now the contention of the debate is whether the **Tirumandiram** advocates monism or pluralism. A deeper study of the **Tirumandiram** will clearly show that the practice of *Śiva Yoga* as advocated in it is much closer to monistic theism, rather than pluralistic realism. This inclusion of the additional chapter is necessitated by the fact that the third chapter in the **Essays on the Tirumandiram** entitled "Saivism as conceived in the Tirumandiram" puts forth the view that the Saivism of Tirumular is pluralistic realism.

The co-authors of this essay strongly feel that the **Tirumandiram** advocates monism only. In support of the view, they take into consideration important verses from the **Tirumandiram** to show that the work stands for monism rather than pluralism. To show that it is *advaitic* (not Śankara's Advaita of *mayavāda* which is later in origin) in spirit rather than pluralistic in approach, a parallelism has been instituted between the **Tirumandiram** and Kashmir Śaivism.

This chapter contains three sections. The first section contains selected verses to show that the burden of the song of the **Tirumandiram** is monism only. The second section gives a brief account of Kashmir Śaivism representing it as a Śaivite model of monism. The third section shows the parallelism between the **Tirumandiram** and Kashmir Śaivism to emphasize the viewpoint that the **Tirumandiram** advocates monism and monism only.

This parallel study is an unexplored field hitherto. By using the term 'parallelism', it is suggested that there might have been no known historical, literary or philosophical interaction between the two systems and that there is no concrete evidence so far to say that either system has influenced the other. If this chapter induces further deeper research on the relationship between the **Tirumandiram** and Kashmir Śaivism, the authors will be very happy. Let us enter into the podium and plunge into the debate!

Section 1

Monistic view of the Tirumandiram

The refutation of the monistic view of the **Tirumandiram** by an article "There can be only one final conclusion in Śaiva Siddhanta (according to Thirumular)" which is the Dharmapuram Ādhinam's reply to the article "Monism and Pluralism in Śaiva Siddhanta" by Subramuniya Swami, a Hawaiian Śaivite, reminds one powerfully of "The Refutation of Idealism" by G.E. Moore[1]. The issue between monism and pluralism is an age-long one in philosophy, both in the East and in the West, right from the days of the Vedas and the Greeks to the modern present day. Still, the debate goes on and probably the issue is unsolvable. Hence, instead of arguing about monism and pluralism in general the present issue is confined to the *Tirumandiram,* whether it advocates monism or pluralism as "there is a great debate, nay, a battle going on between the two different groups"[2] of Śaiva Siddhanta. This present essay is an attempt in the defense of monism of the *Tirumandiram* without entering into the details, for which the two articles may be referred to.

Before discussing whether the *Tirumandiram* advocates monism or pluralistic theism let us discuss some of the features of the *Tirumandiram* that convince us that it is, at the outset, a Siddha work conveying monism. According to the Tamil Siddhas or the realized souls, the ultimate goal of life is attaining cosmic consciousness from which everything derives and to which everything returns. This ascent into the cosmic consciousness is to descend into one's own self. As Bhadragiriyar says, self-realization is "knowledge which knows knowledge through knowing knowledge" (**Bhadragiriyar Pulambal** verses 192 and 23). Tirumular says that any knowledge which does not help man to know himself is false or pseudo-knowledge.

> Knowing oneself is indeed true knowledge.
> Knowing other things is the devil's knowledge (*mandiram* 2318).

In another *mandiram,* he says that a self-realized person wins eternal life.

> To know his own self there is no decay of him
> Knowing not his own self he decays
> Having known the knowledge of his own self
> He existed to be adored by others.(*mandiram* 2355)

The Tamil Siddhas relied on the individual's effort for the attainment of liberation. The **Tirumandiram**, which is an offshoot of the pan-Indian Tantric tradition, insists on the value of Tantric Yoga as a means for the attainment of freedom and immortality. Liberation, mokṣa, or *vīdu* (in Tamil) is a mystical state referred to as *Yoga-samādhi* by Tirumular.

> Inside the Yogic samādhi is the infinite space;
> Inside the Yogic samādhi is the infinite light;
> Inside the Yogic samādhi is the omnipotent energy
> Yogic samādhi is what the siddhas are fond of.
> (*mandiram* 1490)

Though there are different views regarding the **Tirumandiram** it is to be treated without any doubt as a major work in Tamil on Tantra Śāstra.A clue to this view can be found in *mandiram* 2422.

> Means of becoming a pure soul is removal of the stains,
> And discarding the carnal desires that defile the soul
> Like a washer man removing the cloth's dirt through dirt
> The Lord applies pāśās as an antidote to the soul's dirt.

Here Tirumular says that the purity of the Jīva can be attained through *pāśās* or attachment itself. He says that just as the cloth's dirt is removed by earth-dirt (saline-earth) *pāśā* is removed by *pāśā*. This is a basic Tantra concept. Just as a washer man makes a very dirty cloth clean with more water which itself is dirty, or as some water that goes into the ear accidentally is taken out with the help of some additional water itself, Tirumular says that one can get rid of *pāśā* with *pāśā* itself. Further, Tirumular's *Pariyanga-Yoga* is an expression of this basic concept of the Tantra.

As a Tantra Śāstra, the **Tirumandiram** insists on the supreme importance of *jñāna*, wisdom, or that, which could be loosely translated as knowledge. According to Tirumular, jñāna bestows liberation.

> No ethical path excels in the world other than jñāna
> That religion is not good which rejects jñāna
> Nothing yields liberation other than jñāna

> Those endowed with jñāna outshine their fellow humans. (*mandiram* 1467)

Jñāna gives 'oneness' whereas bhakti or devotion gives fellowship.

As a Tantra work, the **Tirumandiram** began a new tradition in Tamil. Tirumular calls his yoga as *Śiva yoga*.

> Śiva yoga distinguishes cit from acit;
> Penance of Yoga-deep (*tava yoga*), Śiva's effulgence in one's own self
> Shunning wrong paths (*ava-yoga*); great bliss of love delights;
> New Yoga (*nava-yoga*) this is! Nandi gave us. (*mandiram* 122)

He calls *Śiva yoga* as a new type of yoga (*nava-yoga*). By calling it as *nava-yoga,* Tirumular indicates that this type of yoga was not in vogue before him in the Tamil country. It is only in the **Tirumandiram** that this (Śiva) yoga is being explicitly explained and discussed for the first time. Though Tirumular does not use the expression *Kundalini yoga* in any place in the **Tirumandiram**, what is discussed as *Śiva yoga* by him is actually the *Kundalini yoga,* as he speaks of *cakras, prāṇāyāma, pariyanga-yoga, sūnya sambhāṣanai* (twilight language), etc. We may, therefore, safely say that the **Tirumandiram** is the first treatise in Tamil which deals with the different aspects of *Kundalini yoga* under the name *Śiva yoga.*

One does not find any reference in the **Tirumandiram** that Tirumular worshipped any individual deity in any particular temple. His reference to Chidambaram in his work is not a reference to a place but to *ciṛṛambalam* i.e., microcosm. His reference to Nataraja stands for the manifestation of primal rhythmic energy. As Vellaivaranan says in his article on **Tiru-t-tillai in Tirumuṛais,** the word *chidambaram* occurs only in the **Tirumandiram** and nowhere in the eleven *Tirumuṛais*[3]. In this work, he does not seem to have sung in praise of gods and goddesses of local temples as done by the later Nāyanmars and Āḷwars. This is a significant feature that distinguishes Tirumular from the pluralistic saints of Śaiva Siddhānta and includes the **Tirumandiram** in the category of monistic Siddha works. Even though Tirumular speaks of the religious aspect of God, he believed in a Supreme Abstraction, a "Great Aloneness". His expression for this is *taṇi-uṛṛa- kevalam* (*mandiram* 2450). This is Śivam without any limitations or attributes. Śivam is grammatically and philosophically an impersonal conception. As Siddhas say, the ideal name for Sivam is 'It', adu, Thatness', Suchness', or ParāparamŚivam is not a personal God. It is a practice, an entryway. It is a foundational consciousness or awareness. This attainment of awareness or Śiva-consciousness is *mukti* or liberation. A deeper study of the concept of Śivam would reveal that it took two channels in Indian thought, one theistic with a personal or devotional relationship to God based on the method of bhakti and the other Tantric, i.e., absolutist, based on *Kundalini Yoga* and *jñāna*. The bhakti method is a pluralistic one as reflected in the Śaiva Siddhānta school; the absolutistic method is the monistic one as reflected in the **Tirumandiram**.

This preamble indicates that the **Tirumandiram** is a Tantra work that is monistic in spirit and content. As a Siddha work, it leans towards viewing the Absolute as a non-dual entity. In philosophy, there are two types of ontology- explicit and implicit. Explicit ontology is based on the theistic conception of God, God as a person, whereas implicit ontology is based on the notion of the Absolute, not as a person but as a principle and value, as an Absolute Freedom or as Tirumular says "A Great Aloneness". The ontology of the **Tirumandiram** is implicit in nature, that which leans towards monism rather than pluralism. Though much may be said on both sides, the **Tirumandiram** is monistic in tone and content.

In view of the above preamble, let us peruse briefly the arguments of the pluralists (stated as 'four issues') without entering into the minute details of the arguments, which are presented in the article by T. N. Arunachalam.

1. The **Tirumandiram** speaks of the three entities *Pati*, *pasu* and *pāsam* (*mandiram* 115) and that the three are eternal. Therefore, it stands for pluralism. The verse is as follows:

God, soul and bondage, the three they speak of;
Like God, soul and bondage too are beginningless;
Soul and bondage near not God
Let God approach, bondage stays not.

Interpreting this verse, the monist argues as follows and we are in full agreement with this interpretation. Let us quote the monist view as expressed by Subramuniya Swami

> While pluralistic Śaiva Siddhanta takes strength in lines one and two, monistic theism is ratified by lines three and four, where Tirumular says that ultimately there is but one Reality, not three. We find Tirumular (stating) that he has discovered that the souls and the world are beginningless, but that they end when they come into contact or proximity with Śiva. They disappear or merge in Him. Monists find that this verse coordinates perfectly with the monistic view that the essence of soul and world are as beginningless and eternal as Śiva Himself while the individual soul body has both a beginning and an end[4].

Probably the third and the fourth lines are "the saving clauses" and the first two lines are only "provisions". Let us explain what are a provision and a saving clause in the words of Sri T.N. Arunachalam himself who is an advocate and a supporter of the pluralistic view. To quote him:

> In legal enactments, we have what are known as provisions and saving clauses. A proviso is provided as part of a section or a clause. It will be generally such as to qualify or modify the contents of the very section to which it is added as a proviso. A saving clause may be such as to limit or even take away the operation of the enactment in specified cases. So for a correct understanding (underlining ours) of the sections in an enactment the provisos and saving clauses have to be carefully looked into and studied (underlining ours).
>
> Here too, in the hymns of our great saints, there may be what are apparently complete and categorical statements respecting exposition of a certain position but which may not be complete in view of certain other statements in the nature of provisos or riders that may either follow those statements or be found stated elsewhere in the same text (underlining ours)[5].

In the light of the above quotation, we may construe that the last two lines of the *mandiram* 115 as the saving clause, which supports the monistic view.

The interpretation of *mandiram* 115 in support of pluralism/ monism requires deep thinking. This *mandiram* does not indicate that there are three categories in Śaiva Siddhanta- God, soul and world. Rather it states the view that any metaphysics has to deal with three things God (*Pati*), soul (*pasu*) and world (*pāsam*) and the inter-relation between them. If interpreted thus, it is a description of the study of metaphysics or philosophy and to state that they deal with the basic tenets of Śaiva Siddhanta is a case of begging the question. In Tirumular's time, there was no system or school of Śaiva Siddhanta as such and to state that according to the **Tirumandiram** there are three entities is a clear case of *petitio principii.* Though the term Śaiva Siddhanta has been used by Tirumular, it does not refer to the system or philosophy of Śaiva Siddhanta, which is a later development out of his philosophy. The term Śaiva Siddhanta used by Tirumular just means that it is a philosophy of Śivam- an abstract idea of Godhead rather than a personal God. Tirumular may be treated as a precursor of Śaiva Siddhanta rather than a Śaiva Siddhantin himself just like saying that Buddha was not a Buddhist. The later Śaiva Siddhanta may be viewed as a pluralistic system of philosophy but to read the **Tirumandiram** with the 'spectacles' of Śaiva Siddhanta and saying that the **Tirumandiram** also advocates pluralism is not acceptable for it stultifies the issue.

Further, the second line of the verse, which says that 'like God, soul and bondage too are beginning less'- may be interpreted as the 'relationship among God, soul and world is a perennial (eternal) problem of philosophy/metaphysics' and not that the soul and bondage are eternal entities. That is, the "relationship among them" is an eternal problem of philosophy and not that they are eternal realities themselves.

2. The second argument is about the theory of creation. The pluralist says that according to the **Tirumandiram,** God is not the material cause of the universe, but only the efficient cause. Without entering into the details and intricacies of the arguments, we can safely say that an over-all reading of the **Tirumandiram** suggests a theory of emanation. The word "creation" *padaittu* in Tamil, used by Tirumular in several places especially in *mandiram* 446 and 447 refers to emanations. To say that all things are created due to His grace is to say that they emanate from Him. Further, Tirumular uses the word "play" for creation (*mandiram* 1771 and 1772) which suggests the doctrine of *'līla'*. The doctrine of *'līla'* suggests that God is not the material cause and the efficient

cause in creation. Probably, his theory is close to the theory of *cit sankoca* in Kashmir Śaivism.

3. The third argument is about the ultimate destiny of the soul. According to the **Tirumandiram** the soul ultimately merges, becomes one with God and it is not forever separate from God. It is a state of 'I am Thou' (*mandiram* 2659, 2660). That Jiva is Śiva is a constant referent in the **Tirumandiram**. The soul realizing itself becomes one with Śiva (*mandiram* 2331) *sivaṉuḍaṉ tāṉāka* is the expression. According to the pluralists, the soul and God have their individual existence and yet they are one in proximity. That is, the soul remains the soul and God remains God. However, according to Tirumular 'the proper understanding', *telivu,* regarding the ultimate destiny of the soul is that it becomes one with Śiva. The entire section 36 of Tantra 8, The Great Statement *Tat Tvam Asi* is the declaration of the identification of the individual self (*pasu/jiva*) with the Supreme Self (*Pati*). Sufis call this state of absorption of the self in the Absolute as 'ecstasy' or *Hal*. The highest form of Yoga is the merging of the Jiva with Śiva. To use the expression of **The Cloud of Unknowing** the individual souls is 'oned' with the Absolute. It is said that the Nātha Siddhas, greet each other by the mystic word *Ades*, which is a form, derived from *adis* that means 'thou art the Brahman in form'.

4. The fourth argument of the pluralists asserts that during the *pralaya,* the Great Deluge, the souls continue to exist with Śiva. When the soul becomes Śiva and when it merges with Śiva, when it is 'oned' with Śiva, as pointed out in the third issue, how can it 'exist' separately and after *pralaya*? *Pralaya* is symbolically a process of absorption of the cosmic principles, stage by stage, into the spiritual aspect of the

Supreme Consciousness i.e., Śivahood. It is a process called *apañciikaraṇa* or disquintiplication. In this process, the soul is also ultimately absorbed into Śiva. If the soul exists even after the *pralaya*, then ultimate dissolution becomes meaningless.

It is a pity that the pluralists read the **Tirumandiram** wearing the spectacles of Meykandar who lived centuries after Tirumular and thus their arguments suffer from the error of anachronism (which according to the **Advanced Oxford Dictionary** is to talk of Queen Victoria watching the television).

Section 2

Kashmir Śaivism

Monistic Śaivism became popular in Kashmir predominantly after the immigration of several important families around the 8th century A.D. King Lalithāditya of Kashmir went to Kanyakubja, the capital of King Harsha (6th century) where he met Atrigupta whom he induced to migrate to Kashmir. The famous Abhinavagupta was a descendant of Atrigupta. About the same time, Sangamāditya the great great grandfather of Somānanda, who systematized the *pratyabhijña* school of Śaivism settled down in Kashmir. Sometime after, the ancestors of Vasugupta, the author of the **Śiva Sutras** also arrived in Kashmir.

When Buddhism started its slow decline to be replaced by brahmanic thought and philosophy around 8th century, those who were following the Śaiva philosophy thought that an absolute idealism of the *advaita* school would be a good counter to the preaching of the *Śūnya vāda* of Buddhism.Buddhism was replaced by Triadism that substituted monism for the dualism of early *Śaiva Āgama* teachings.

The Śaivism of Kashmir is called the *Trika śāsana* or *Trika śāstra* or simply the *Trika* School of philosophy. The *Trika* is also known as *svātantrya vāda, svātantrya* and *Spanda*- expressing the same concepts. *Ābhāsa vāda* is another name for the system. The *Trika* School also known as *Rahasya Sampradāya* or *Tryambaka Sampradāya* developed between the 8th and 10th century A.D. This system derives its name from its emphasis on various triads.

1. It holds the three monistic *Āgamas Siddha, Nāmaka* and *Mālini tantras* in high esteem compared to the other ninety two Āgamas recognized by it.
2. The triads of power in this system are *parā, aparā* and *parāparā.*
3. Three aspects of relationship exists between the transcendent and the phenomenal- *abheda, bhedābheda* and *bheda* that is non-dual, non-dual cum dual and dual.
4. It preaches three ways of realizing the Reality namely *Śāmbhavopaya, Śaktopaya* and *Ānavopaya.*
5. It speaks of the triad consisting of Śiva, Śakti and Aṇu or Śiva, Śakti and Nara.

The Four main schools of Kashmir Śaivism

The four main schools of Kashmir Śaivism are the (1) *krama,* (2) *kula,* (3) *pratyabhijña* and the (4) *Spanda*

(1) *Krama*- This school of philosophy is Śakti-oriented unlike the other schools that are Śiva-oriented. In this respect, it is similar to the *Spanda* School, which leans towards the dynamic aspect of reality. However, it differs from the *Spanda* in the fact that while the *krama* is a Tantric system, the *Spanda* is not. It highlights unity in the phenomenal duality or the *bhedhābheda* system. It interprets immanence as an essential expression of transcendence while the *pratyabhijña* and the *kula* systems are mainly concerned with the transcendental aspect of Reality. Unlike the *kula* and *pratyabhijña* schools, *krama* system opines that spiritual progress is a stepwise process.

(2) *Kula* - This system advocates seeing Śiva in everything in the world. It emphasizes Śiva's power or Śakti that pervades the universe as kundalini. One's true nature is realized during the ascent and the descent of the kundalini śakti. This system was propagated by Sumatinātha.

(3) *Pratyabhijña*- The system of *pratyabhijña* was named after the work '**Iṣvara pratyabhijña**' of Utpaladeva. This school is based on the philosophy that liberation is recognition of what one has always been. This theory was put forth by Somānanda, the teacher of Utpaladeva in his work the **Śiva dṛṣti.**

(4) *Spanda* - According to this system the spirit, mind, body and all levels of Reality are manifestations of spontaneous vibration or *spanda*. This system was introduced by Vasugupta, the author of the **Śiva Sutras**. His disciple, Kallata, wrote the treatise the **Spanda kārika**. In this system, the seeker directs his concentration on every movement in this world. *Spanda* is awareness (Śiva) as well as the creative aspect of awareness (Śakti).

Kashmir Śaiva Literature:

The Tantras of the Kashmir Śaivism were said to have come out of the five faces of Śiva namely *Iṣāna, Tatpurusha, Sadyojata, Vāmadeva* and *Aghora*. These five mouths represent the five energies namely *cit śakti* (consciousness), *ānanda śakti* (bliss), *icchā śakti* (will), *jñāna śakti* (knowledge) and *kriya śakti* (omnipotence). The monistic Tantras of Kashmir Śaivism are the **Bhairava Tantras**, the mono-dualistic Tantras are the **Rudra Tantras** and the dualistic Tantras are the **Śiva Tantras**. There are sixty-four **Bhairava Tantras**, eighteen **Rudra Tantras** and ten **Śiva Tantras**.

The literary works can also be classified as (1) *Āgama śāstras*, (2) *Śpanda śāstras* and (3) *Pratyabhijña śāstras.* The former consists of the **Śaiva Āgamas** chief among them being **Malini vijaya, Ānanda bhairava, Vijñāna bhairava, Mrugendra, Matanga and Rudra yāmala**. The commentaries on these *Āgamas* attempt to show that they taught a monistic doctrine. The *Spanda śāstras* and the *Pratyabhijña śāstra* developed later as offshoots of the Āgama śāstra. Kallata founded the *Spanda śāstra* and Somānanda founded the *Pratyabhijña śāstras*. Among these *śāstras*, the *Pratyabhijña* is the only philosophy proper of the *Trika*.

Some of the famous works of Kashmir Śaivism are

1. **Śiva Sutras** of Vasugupta (865-925 CE)
2. **Spanda Kārika** by Kallata
3. **Śiva dṛṣti** by Somānanda (9th century)
4. **Pratyabhijña Sutra** by Utpaladeva (900-950 CE), a disciple of Somānanda
5. **Paramārtha Sāra, Pratyabhijña Vimarṣani** and **Tantraloka** by Abhinavagupta (950-1020 CE) who was also the author of around forty-five other works.
6. **Śivasutra vimarṣini** and **Spanda Sandoha** by Kshemaraja (10th- 11th century)

Philosophy of Kashmir Śaivism:

Kashmir Śaivism is essentially not a single philosophical system but a compendium of the philosophies of all the four schools of Śaivism. Abhinavagupta integrated the philosophies of these schools in his **Tantraloka** thus giving a common philosophy that is now called Kashmir Śaivism.

Kashmir Śaivism is also called *prakāṣa vimarśa svātantriya vāda* or the philosophy where the Absolute is self-luminous, self-conscious and free. This omnipotent, omnipresent Absolute Reality is everything and yet beyond everything; it is both immanent (*viśvāmaya*) and transcendent (*viśvottirna*). Time, form and space do not limit it; it is beyond any change. Its nature is bliss or *ānanda* and sovereignty, *svatantra* or absolute freedom. This self-luminous, self-aware consciousness is called *Parama Śiva* while its self-awareness is the *Śakti*, Parāśakti, or *Parāvāk*. Thus, this pure consciousness is not static; it is also aware of its own nature. *Parama Śiva* and *Parāśakti* are not two independent entities. They are, in reality, one entity that performs different functions and exists in two different states. *Śakti* is an attribute of *Śiva.* The relation between the two is one of *tādātmya* (identity) sometimes referred to as *samarasya* (perfect equilibrium). Due to the *svātantriya śakti* of the Absolute, it brings into being the cosmic drama. It brings into play its *mahamāya śakti* by means of which it veils or obscures its essential nature and assumes limited knowledge and limited forms. This power of obscuration or self-limitation is called *tirodhāna* and the limitation takes the form of *aṇutva* or atomicity. It is also called *sankoca* (or *cit sankoca*) or self-contraction. Because of this contraction, there is creation. Creation, thus, is self-imposition of limitation by the Absolute upon itself. Creation is contraction. In this state, the Absolute is called *Puruṣa* or *aṇu*. It is because of this *sankocita jñāna* or limited knowledge that the sentient and the insentient worlds come into existence.

The *svātantryia śakti* expresses itself as the *icchā śakti* (free will), *jñāna śakti* (power of knowledge) and *kriya śakti* (power to act). Self-awareness is an action, which produces a pulsation or *spanda*. The *spanda* produces polarity of 'I' and 'this'. This dynamic aspect shifts the pure consciousness to the objective consciousness, one that is the result of obstruction by thought-constructs. Through the *vimarśa* aspect, the Absolute turns either inwards or outwards. In the inwards or dispassion (*virāga*) mode, it identifies itself to be pure consciousness or supreme void. In the outwards mode or passion (*rāga*), it identifies itself as the manifested universe. This oscillation occurs due to divine play or *līla*. Both these states are real and absolute. Thus, the Absolute exists, as Abhinavagupta says, 'where duality, unity and both unity and duality are equally manifest and said to be unity'. Thus, the absolute monism of Kashmir Śaivism is that which neither refutes nor establishes diversity. Here *kriya* does not mean *karma;* it means *Spanda* or spontaneity. It is called *Pratyabhijña jñāna,* which means learning or becoming aware of the real identity of a thing. Liberation is the moment of recognition (*pratyabhijña).*

Kashmir Śaivism is non-dualistic or monistic as it unites all differences in a single entity, Śiva. It differs significantly from Sānkhya philosophy, according to which the Absolute and the Universe are two independent entities. Kashmir Śaivism explains that there is complete unity in pure consciousness, its subjective consciousness and objective perception are like a mirror and the objects that are reflected on it.

The monistic Kashmir Śaivism is also different from the monistic philosophy of Śankara. According to Śankara's Advaita, only the Absolute is real; everything else is *mitya* or illusion. The world as seen is perceived only in the *vyavahārika* or secondary state and not in the absolute *paramārthika* state. On the other hand, according to Kashmir Śaivism, both the Absolute and the manifested are real. The Absolute, the pure consciousness in its dynamic state, generates the universe and 'reabsorbs' it into itself at the end of each cycle of creation. The manifested universe that is generated thus from a real entity, the Absolute, should also be real according to the logic that the qualities in the cause should be in the effect also. However, as all the manifested exist in the Absolute like the objects reflected in a mirror, they do not have an independent existence. Abhinavagupta in his **Bodhapanchadaśi** refers to this by saying that all the light and darkness reside in the supreme light of God-Consciousness.

Advaita Vedanta says that Reality is *nirguna*, one without any qualities. However, in the secondary or *vyavahārika* state, it can be conceived as *Satchidananda* (being-consciousness-bliss). Kashmir Śaivism differs in this, in that it considers *caitanya* or consciousness as both the Absolute Being and Its nature. However, both the schools agree that consciousness is autonomous and does not need the mind or the body for its existence. In this connection we may state the Siddha viewpoint (as also reflected in the **Tirumandiram**). According to this viewpoint, the world is not lost or treated as illusory but given a new significance in its totality. The 'oneness' or *advaitam* that is expressed is not the negation of all manifestations but the fullness of manifestations. To the Siddha the world is real and not *māya.* The impermanence of each individual entity does not mean the negation of unity or oneness of the Reality. Siddha philosophy may be called spiritual monism or 'Siddha Advaita' to coin a new phrase, where the world is also one of the aspects of the fullness of the reality. The Absolute reveals itself as the world, the atman and what not. The Absolute, in terms of the Siddhas, is the 'supreme station' of the Sūfis.

The thirty-six tattvas:

According to Kashmir Śaivism, the *tattvas* or the principles are thirty-six in number. They begin with the Absolute Reality in its transcendental state, as pure consciousness or *Parama Śiva*. It is fully complete or *pūrna* in all respects. This is *Bhairava*. According to etymology, *Bhairava* means 'he whose light of consciousness joined with his power of activity (*kriya*) comprehends the entire universe in His Self'. In **Tantraloka** Abhinavagupta gives many interpretations for the term *Bhairava.*

This is followed by the *Śakti tattva* or the Energy of *Śiva*. In this state, the *ānanda* or the bliss of the Supreme is predominant. The *Śakti tattva* begins the polarity of 'I' and 'this'.

The *Śakti tattva* expresses itself as the power of will or *icchā śakti*. The Absolute at this state is called *Sadāśiva*. At this state the experience is 'I am this'. The 'I' is more prominent than 'this'. The *Sadāśiva* is the first manifestation or *ābhāsa*. Consciousness is perceptible to itself thus creating the existence of a subject and object.

The *jñāna śakti* or the power of knowledge becomes predominant next. The *tattva* here is *Iśvara* or *Aiśvarya tattva*. Here the 'this' becomes more predominant than that at the *Sadāśiva* state.

The *kriya śakti* or the power of action comes to the front next and this is represented by the *Sadvidya* or *suddha vidya tattva*. At this stage the 'I' and 'this' are of equal prominence. The experience at this state is called *parāpara* or the monistic duality an intermediate state between *para* or the supreme monistic state and the *apara* or the inferior 'dualistic state'.

Following the *sadvidya* state, the five cloaks or *kañcuka* come into play. The play of *māya* begins and the impure order of principles starts their manifestation. The word *māya* has as its root *mā* or 'to measure'. Due to *māya*, the experience of the Absolute becomes limited by time, space and form. The ideal nature of the Absolute is veiled by *māya* through its five products namely *kalā, vidya, rāga, kāla* and *niyati*.

Kalā reduces the omnipotence of the Absolute and brings about limitation of authorship. It produces division in the unlimited. *Vidya* reduces the omniscience of the Absolute and brings about limitation of knowledge. *Rāga* reduces the fully complete nature of the Absolute. Desire for things other than itself is brought about by *rāga*. *Kāla* or the time principle reduces the *nityatva* or experience of eternal existence of the Absolute and brings about limitations such as past, present and future. *Niyati* reduces the freedom and pervasiveness of the Absolute. Due to *niyati*, limitations with respect to space, cause and form occur.

Parama Śiva through the effect of *māya* manifests itself as *Puruṣa* or the limited consciousness. The word *aṇu* is used to represent its limitation in space, form and knowledge. *Puruṣa* is the subjective manifestation of the Absolute.

The objective manifestation of the Absolute is *prakriti*. Kashmir Śaivism differs from Sānkhya about the nature of *prakriti*. Unlike the Sānkhya system where the *prakriti* is universal, Kashmir Śaivism says that each *Puruṣa* has a different *prakriti*. *Prakriti* has the three *guṇas* or qualities, *sattva, rajas* and *tamas*. According to *Pratyabhijña* School, *prakriti* represents the *Śanta śakti* of *Śiva* or the sense of peace where there is equipoise of all the three *guṇas*. Thus, unlike Sānkhya where *prakriti* and *Puruṣa* are two entities, Kashmir Śaivism holds a monistic view about *prakriti* and *Puruṣa*. *Puruṣa* is the one who experiences and *prakriti* is the object of his experience.

Prakriti starts differentiating from this stage onwards and manifests as *antahakaraṇa, indriyas* and *bhūtas*. *Antahakaraṇa* or the inner instrument includes *buddhi, ahamkāra* and *manas*. *Buddhi* is the substratum on which objects are reflected. The objects may be either external- perceived through the senses, or internal- impressions, feelings etc.

Ahamkāra is the product of *buddhi*. It is the power of self-appropriation.

Manas is the product of *ahamkāra*. Along with the senses, *manas* produces perceptions and by itself it causes thoughts, concepts and images. The remaining twenty *tattvas* include the *jñānendriyas, karmendriyas, five bhūtas* and five *tanmātras* similar to the system of *Vedanta*.

***Puruṣa or Aṇu*:**

The limited Self or *aṇu* has a physical body made of the five gross elements. Its psychic apparatus is made up of the *antahakaraṇa* and the five *tanmātras* that together form the eight principles or *puri aṣtaka*.

Each individual experiences four states of consciousness- wakeful state, dreamlike state, deep sleep and the state of pure consciousness. In the wakeful state and the dream like state, the soul experiences the inferior energy of *Śiva* namely *apara śakti*. In the deep sleep state the soul experiences *parāpara śakti* and in the fourth state of consciousness or *turiya* he experiences the *parāśakti* of *Śiva*. The Absolute remains in the *turiyātīta* state, a state that is beyond even the fourth state of consciousness.

In each individual, there is *kundalini śakti* that remains coiled at the base of the spine. An individual self through yogic practices raises this force to reach one's crown when one experiences ultimate bliss. Abhinavagupta has written about *kechari mudra* and drinking of the ambrosia.

Bondage:

The limited self is subjected to bondage due to its innate ignorance, impurities or *mala*.

Āṇava mala is the limiting condition that moves the universal consciousness to a limited consciousness when the Jiva feels as a separate entity limited by space and form. This occurs due to the *icchā śakti* of the Absolute. The *māyīya mala* is the limitation brought about by the *jñāna śakti* of the Absolute. Due to this power, the perception of the limited self is deluded due to limitation in knowledge and it begins to perform acts that are either meritorious or otherwise. *Māyīya mala* brings about the third impurity or the *karma mala*. This impurity is due to the *kriya śakti* of the Absolute. *Vāsanās* or residual impressions are a result of *karma mala* that follows the individual through multiple births.

Liberation:

Liberation in Kashmir Śaivism is recognition of one's true nature. According to Abhinavagupta *mokṣa* is nothing but being aware of one's true nature. Highest achievement for a limited self is attainment of Śiva-consciousness. In this state, the entire universe appears as *Śiva* or pure consciousness. This is possible only due to descent of Divine grace. *Śiva* is very grace itself. The descent of grace occurs due to the *Śaktipāta*. The paths or means for the grace to descend or the means of attaining the supreme goal are four namely *Anupāya, Śāmbhavopaya, Śaktopāya*, and *Āṇavopāya*.

Anupāya is the method of effortless effort. It does not involve any process (*anupāya*= no-means). In this means, one resides in the state of transcendental bliss. Hence, it is also called as *ānandopāya*. This path is meant only for those who already have their individual consciousness united with the universal consciousness.

Śāmbhavopāya,also called as *icchopāya*, is the path of will where will plays a great part. In this method, knowledge of the Absolute comes through the practice of making one's mind completely free of any thoughts. The seeker gives up all personal and egoistic efforts and places himself at the feet of *Śiva* or his guru, who is the embodiment of *Śiva,* and waits for his grace to awaken the latent energies that confer supreme consciousness. To achieve liberation through this way, three methods are prescribed. They are *viśvacitpratibimbatvam, parāmarśodayakrama* and *mantrādyabhinnarupatvam*. The seeker lives in the awareness that the whole universe is reflected in one's own consciousness. This is *vishva citra pratibimbatvam* or the reflection of the image of the universe. In the *parāmarśodya kramam*, it is understood that the whole field of sounds, words and sentences are nothing but the Supreme Self. Through the grace of the Master, the seeker realizes that all sounds merge in the Supreme transcendental soundless sound. The third method or *mantrādya bhinna rupatvam* is the practice of complete subject hood. The aspirant experiences complete identity between the self and the universe or the 'I' consciousness.

Śaktyopāya, the next lower means, is yogic practice without any recitation of mantras or breathing techniques. Here the liberation occurs due to *śakti*. The seeker concentrates on any thought like 'I am everything', or 'I am bliss'. This thought is held in the mind without any break. *Śaktyopāya* is also called *madhyam datva* or centering. It is practiced by focusing one's attention on the space or junction or the silence between the end of one thought and the beginning of another or at the end of one's mental activity such as perception. Through practice of being aware of the gap in the mental activity, our true state is revealed. Kundalini yoga belongs to *Śaktyopāya*. For *Śaktyopāya,* pure intuition (*sattarka*) knowledge of the right scriptures (*sadāgama*) and a genuine guru (*sadguru*) are essential.

Ānavopāya is seeking liberation through self-effort. This method is considered to be inferior and the most tedious of all the means. It involves the five ways: *uccāra, karaṇa, dhyāna, varaṇopāsana* and *sthānakalpana*. *Uccāra* is breathing practice where the seeker develops his awareness through focusing on the incoming and outgoing breaths. *Karaṇa upāsana* is the practice of being aware of one's daily activities. *Dhyāna* is meditation. *Varaṇopāsana* is the practice of focusing on sounds heard during meditation. The focus on *anāhata* leads one to realization. *Sthāna kalpana* is the yogic practice of directing one's consciousness towards various centers in the body. The practice of *Cakrodaya* is *Ānavopāya*.

To sum up, *Ānavopāya* consists of physical and external means. For example external forms of worship in temples, observance of rituals, practices of *hatha yoga* etc. *Śaktyopāya* consists of mental practices like meditation, contemplation, concentration, visualization etc. *Śāmbhavopāya* is the means at the spiritual level where one realizes one's unity with the whole world. *Ānavopāya, Śaktyopāya* and *Śāmbhavopāya* are not numerically three *upāyas*. They present a holistic and synthetic picture of all possible means of yoga-physical, mental and spiritual forms respectively since yoga is a technique of bringing change in consciousness. *Pratyabhijña,* though is not one of the *upāyas,* is 'the' one that underlies all the *upāyas*. The efficacy of an *upāya* lies in its capacity of effecting self-recognition or self-realization or *pratyabhijña.*

Integral monism:

Mark Dyczkowski in his book **The Doctrine of Vibration: an Analysis of Doctrines and Practices of Kashmir Shaivism** (1989) explains the concept of monism according to Kashmir Śaivism. He quotes Abhinavagupta and says that duality, unity, both unity and duality are equally manifest, and there is no unity unless the diverse elements are united in the wholeness of the Totality. Dualism is not an incorrect view of reality although it corresponds to only one of the levels within the absolute. He quotes **Bhagavatotpala** on the *Spanda* concept as "In none of Your states (O Lord) is consciousness absent. Therefore You are worshipped as the yogi's dense mass of consciousness alone".

According to Dyczkowski, Kashmir Śaivism believes in an Absolute who is the one and only reality. The hierarchy of deities corresponds to the planes within the Absolute. They are empowered to do their actions by the Supreme Deity, the Consciousness. The Supreme Deity, the pure consciousness, is attained by the ascent through different levels of consciousness that ultimately result in the complete expansion or evolution of objectivity to become pure consciousness.

This supreme state is *Bhairava* or *Śiva*. Thus, everything lies within the Absolute consciousness.

The universe is an attribute (*dharma*) of consciousness, which is the bearer or the *dharmin*. An object exists only in relation to a subject who perceives them. Consciousness, in its active state when perceiving an object, manifests itself externally as the object. When the act of perception is over, then consciousness returns to its undifferentiated original state. In other words, if there are no subjects then there could be no objects. However, the subject is self-luminous and is apparent to oneself.

No object is completely insentient. Everything contains consciousness. However, it is not apparent, as the objects are not associated with the life-breath and components of an organism. Cognition is the essence (*rasa*) or own nature (*svabhāva*) of everything. To put it in a nutshell, according to Kashmir Śaivism, *mokṣa* does not mean freedom from something; it is the recognition of one's essential nature as *Śiva* or freedom. It is only that the recognition is clouded by self-imposed forgetfulness.

While Kashmir Śaivism does not recommend any ritualistic worship to a personal God, some of the latter day saints belonging to the sect such as Lalleswari, Devi Roop Bhawani and Paramananda brought in the concept of *bhakti* or devotion into the system. Similar to the Tamil Siddhas, the saints of Kashmir Śaivism revolted against ostentatious idol worshipping, empty ritualistic practices and false show of religiosity. Lalleswari's verse "those without discernment dear, read religious books as parrots recite 'Rama" in a cage" shows her contempt for performing rituals without any thought behind them. Practice of breath control and focusing inwards was recommended as a means to achieve higher states of awareness. It will be interesting to compare the songs of the saints of Kashmir Śaivism and that of the

Tamil Siddhas especially to the **Tirumandiram** to explore similarities in their philosophy and practices.

Section 3

Parallelism between Tirumular's Tirumandiram and Kashmir Śaivism

Śaivism or worship of Śiva claims its origin from the time of Mohan jo daro and Harappa civilizations that existed in the Indus Valley. Śaivism is not a single school of philosophy but a conglomerate of many small traditions brought together by their common beliefs. Some of the popular Śaiva traditions are Pāṣupata Śaivism, Kashmir Śaivism, Vīra Śaivism, Śaiva Siddhānta and Śiva Advaita. While these schools differ in some of their traditions, they share the following common beliefs: (1) the Āgamas are divine utterances similar to the Vedas; (2) Śiva is the Supreme Lord, who is immanent and transcendent. (3) Siva's powers are fivefold namely creation, preservation, destruction, obscuration and bestowing grace, (4) *Pati, paśu* and *pāsa* or God, soul and bonds are three entities that should be considered, (5) the *malas* or impurities are *āṇava, karma* and *māya,* (6) the *tattva* or principles are thirty-six in number. In the current section, we shall explore the parallelism between the philosophies of Kashmir Śaivism and the philosophy expounded by Tirumular in his **Tirumandiram**.

Some of the main principles of Kashmir Śaivism have been already described in the previous section. In this section, we will focus on some of the common philosophies between Kashmir Śaivism and the Siddhānta of Tirumular. To begin with, both Tirumular and the proponents of Kashmir Śaivism emphasize that their philosophy is not mere logical concept but an experienced one. One of the famous spiritual masters of the Kashmir Śaiva tradition describes the commentary by Kṣemarāja on the **Śiva Sutras** as a communication of the actually lived experience of a great author and that some of the sections on human spiritual experiences could not have been written about unless experienced personally. He says 'those who have not actually experienced the ultimate universal reality central to the philosophy will not have acquired a point of reference with which to understand it as the concepts are complex and hard to understand. Tirumular also says that his philosophy is based on his personal experience. In *mandiram* 2953 towards the end of the **Tirumandiram** he says:

> By merging I felt the presence of *parāpara*
> By merging I attained *Śiva-gati*;
> By merging I became consciousness of consciousness;
> By merging I witnessed many eons.

Now let us see some details on the history of Tirumular and his **Tirumandiram**.

Satguru Sivaya Subramuniya Swami, a Hawaiian Śaivite, mentions in his book **Dancing with Siva: Hinduism's Contemporary Catechism** that the first known guru of the Tamil Siddha tradition was Maharishi Nandinātha of Kashmir. Nandinātha's work, **Nandikeśvara Kāśika,** is monistic in its view about the Absolute Reality. Legend says that Nandinātha had eight disciples who were sent to different parts of the world, even as far as China to teach the world their guru's philosophy. Tirumular, one of his disciples is the prominent *guru* of Tamil Siddha tradition, who came from the Valley of Kashmir to South India (page 494). Sri K.A. Nilakanta Śastri in his article *An Historical sketch of Śaivism* in **The cultural Heritage of India** (vol.IV) mentions that according to the **Periya Purāṇam,** Tirumular came to the South from Kailāsa, the home of the *Pratyabhijña* school, animated the dead body of a cowherd and took three thousand years to compose his **Tirumandiram** (page 74). Tirumular was the first to bring the Tantra aspect of Śaivism from Kashmir to the Tamil world. Hence, it is appropriate to compare

Tirumular's philosophy collected in the **Tirumandiram** with Kashmir Śaiva philosophy to identify parallelism. Upon examination of the **Tirumandiram** verses, it becomes clear that many of its concepts are comparable to the concepts of Kashmir Śaivism. A complete comparison of individual verses will be a research project in itself, which is beyond the scope of this article. Hence, we will restrict our examination of parallelism only in some of the general concepts of the Śaiva tradition.

According to Kashmir Śaivism, Lord Śiva set forth sixty-four systems of philosophy of which some are monistic, some dualistic and some monistic-dualistic in nature. Eventually these systems were lost over time. Lord Śiva commanded Sage Durvasa to revive the knowledge and the three *mānasa putras* or 'mental sons' of Sage Durvasa namely Tryambaka, Amardaka and Srinātha revived the monistic, dualistic and monistic-dualistic philosophies respectively. Thus, Tryambaka is considered as the father of the monistic philosophy of Kashmir Śaivism. Over time, these philosophies were misinterpreted and so Lord Śiva came in the dream of Vasugupta and directed him to go to the rock-carved scriptures in the Mahadevapura mountains that later became famous as the **Śiva Sutras**. Thus, the monistic theism of Kashmir Śaivism claims divine origin to its primary work, the **Śiva Sutras**.Examination of the **Śiva Sutras** and some of the later works of Kashmir Śaivism reveals a lot of similarity in concept between these works and Tirumular's **Tirumandiram**.

The Absolute Reality:

(1) Śiva

According to Kashmir Śaivism the Absolute Reality, Śiva, is pure consciousness that is beyond the limitations of time, space and form. It is the only entity that exists. All the manifested are emanations from this Absolute Reality. Such an Absolute Reality is not a static entity but one that is also self-aware. This is the concept of *prakāṣa-vimarśa'* where *prakāṣa,* the pure consciousness, effulgence, has self-awareness or *vimarśa.* The *vimarśa* is the Supreme Power of Śiva, the Parāśakti. Due to its self-awareness, the Absolute realizes its true nature as *caitanyam* or awareness. The first sutra in the **Śiva Sutras** is *caitanyam ātma* 'the Supreme Being in consciousness'. Further, the Absolute has *svātantrya* or complete and absolute freedom. Hence, the philosophy of Kashmir Śaivism is called *prakāṣa-vimarśa- svātantrya vāda.*

We find an echo of this idea in *mandiram* 381, Tandiram 2 of the **Tirumandiram**.

Ādiyōtu andam ilāda parāparam
Pōdam adāga-p puṇarum parāparai

The beginning and endless Supreme Being (*parāparam*) which is pure consciousness (*pōdam*) realizes itself (*adāga puṇarum*) as the Supreme Power (*parāparai*).

jyoti adaṉil param tōnra-t tōnrumām
Tīdil parai adanpāl tigaḷ nādame

When the sense of awareness appears in this Absolute, which is effulgence, brilliance, flame (*prakāśa*) *parai* or Parāśakti appears. In that *parai* remains the *nāda*. This order of creation mentioned by Tirumular is in complete agreement with the monistic view of Kashmir Saivism. Tirumular calls the Absolute as *kōn* or King, one who has absolute freedom of action. This represents the *svātantrya* of the Absolute.

(2) Parāśakti

Kashmir Saivism says that Parāśakti represents the *iccha śakti* or the power of will of the Absolute. This power manifests as the *jñāna śakti*, the power of knowledge and *kriya śakti* or the power of action. The objective and subjective creations begin from this step onwards.

Creation occurs due to the divine will or *iccha śakti*. **Tirumandiram** describes this concept in *mandiram* 382 as follows:

civan sakti ennave pétitu jñānam kiriyai pirattalāl vāditta icchaiyil pandu eḻum vinduve

"The Absolute that became *Śiva* and *Śakti* further differentiated and became *jñāna* and *kriya*. The *bindu* emerged from the *iccha*."

Kashmir Śaivism describes the relationship between Śiva and Śakti as *aham* and *ahanta* or 'I' and the 'I-ness'. Śiva is the *Śaktimān,* the possessor of power while His power is Śakti. These two are inseparable yet distinct states. Tirumular describes the relationship between Śiva and Śakti as that between a gemstone and its luster (*mandiram* 383). Both do not have independent existence; the luster of a stone cannot exist without the presence of the gemstone. Similarly, the gemstone is defined by its luster. However, the luster and the gemstone are two distinct concepts. He also uses the same terms *catti* and *cāttumān* to refer to ParāŚakti and *Parama Śiva* (*mandiram* 384).

In the *mandiram* 384 Tirumular says the pure effulgence manifests as Śakti, which, by its *icchā,* embraces *nāda* and becomes *bindu* thus becoming the basis for the five pure emanations that include *Sadāśiva.* Kashmir Śaivism names the five pure emanations as *Śiva tattva, Śakti tattva, Sadāśiva, Iśvara tattva* and *sadvidya.*

According to Kashmir Śaivism, everything arises from pure consciousness because they are already existing in it. The **Tirumandiram** echoes this in *mandiram* 1932

Except from the seed there is no shoot
Except from the seed there is no way of germination
The seed and shoot are the same
That is the nature of Hara- way, realize.

This is called *satkārya- vāda* or the theory of causation, which states that the effect exists prior to its manifestation in a latent state in the cause.

(3) Impure order of creation

Following the five pure emanations, manifestation of the impure order or *aśuddha tattva* begins thus making the total principles as thirty-six in number. The thirty-six principles are the five cloaks of *māya* or *kañcuka*, the *Puruṣa, prakriti, manas, buddhi, ahamkāra,* five elements, their subtle factors, the organs of action and knowledge. Tirumular describes the creation of the subjective and the objective universes along the same lines as Kashmir Śaivism and summarizes them as follows: "the creators of the world are He and She, they have five sons. The creator also becomes the one who creates the world remaining as a resident on the flower" in *mandiram* 386. The creators are Śiva- the He and Śakti-the She. Their five sons are Sadāśiva, Maheśvara, Rudra, Viṣnu and Brahma. They may also be the five *kañcukas,* the reason for the objective universe namely *kalā, vidya, rāga, kāla* and *niyati*. The effects of these cloaks are the five hindrances: ignorance, egoism, attachment, aversion and clinging to life. These five factors turn the cosmic consciousness into limited consciousness. The subjective limited consciousness is Jiva, who is the enjoyer of the objective world, which is also an emanation of Śiva. Brahma is considered as the creator of the worlds. In this mandiram Tirumular says that Brahma is none other than the Absolute who is engaged in the act of creation.

(4) Nature of creation

Kashmir Śaivism opines that creation is a divine play or *līla*. This shows that the Absolute is not the material cause of creation. Tirumular in his *mandiram* 492 says "Śakti and Śiva due to their play created the soul, sent it through the crowd of the two māyas, revealing the *turiya* which is the process of it becoming pure, enter its *cittam* (or awareness) and make it embodiment of Śiva". This is the sequence of creation and dissolution in a nutshell. The two māyas are *śuddha māya* and *aśuddha māya*. Creation is initiated by Śiva and His power Śakti. Puruṣa is created, which is Śiva with limited consciousness that happens due to the two *māyas*. It is only Śiva or pure consciousness that raises the *Puruṣa* to the state of *turiya* when the awareness becomes pure or *śuddha* and reaches it to the final state of Śiva-hood.

Another verse of Tirumular that supports his monistic view is *mandiram* 412, which states

> That verily remains as the directions and celestials
> That verily remains as the tattva of body and soul
> That verily remains as the ocean, mountains and other objects
> That verily is the Lord of the world.

Thus, the Absolute is the subjective as well as the objective world. Tirumular mentions that the world and the body are impermanent but nowhere has he mentioned that they are unreal. Just like the philosophy of Kashmir Śaivism, the manifested world according to Tirumular is as real as the Absolute as they are nothing but the Absolute.

(5) Five great acts of Śiva:

Śiva Sutras mentions the five great acts of Śiva while explaining the *panchakriya vidhi*. Śiva performs creation, sustenance, dissolution, obscurance and bestowing of grace. We will not go into detailed comparison of Tirumular's ideas and Kashmir Śaivism's concepts on these acts. Suffice to say that Tirumular has dedicated five individual sections in his **Tirumandiram** for these five acts of Śiva (sections 9,10,11,12 and 13 in Tandiram 2). In *mandiram* 1809 he says

> Himself will create; Himself will protect,
> Himself will annihilate; Himself will obscure

Himself having done all these, He will bestow liberation
Himself will pervade and be the chief too.

(6) Five faces of Śiva

According to Śaivism, *Sadāśiva* has the five faces *sadyojāta, Vāmadeva, Agora, Tatpuruṣa, Īsāna*. The **Tirumandiram** describes these five faces of *Sadāśiva* in *mandiram* 1735. *Mandiram* 1734 mentions that the ten states of consciousness (five in ascending order and descending order), the twelve zodiac houses and the ninety-six principles of human nature all arose from *Sadāśiva*.

Kashmir Śaivism also mentions that the five faces of *Sadāśiva* represent the five states of consciousness. Further, it states that the Āgamas arose from the five faces. The *sadyojāta* face looking towards west represents the earth element and the act of creation. *Vāmadeva* faces north. It represents the water element and the act of preservation. *Aghora* faces south. It represents the fire element and the act of dissolution/rejuvenation. *Tatpuruṣa* faces east. It represents the air element and represents the act of obscuration. The fifth face *Iśāna* faces northeast. It represents the space element and the act of bestowing grace.

(7) Ritualistic worship:

Kashmir Śaivism does not deny the presence of a personal God but it does not stipulate an elaborate worship ritual for a specific deity. Similarly, Tirumular mentions Śiva with matted locks in several of his verses; he mentions the holy trinity, Brahma, Viṣnu and Rudra in many places. However, just as Kashmir Śaivism, he does not recommend an elaborate showy worship ritual. He says that the mind is the temple, the body is the shrine, the mouth is the tower-gate, the soul is the linga and the deceitful senses are the eternally burning lamp (*mandiram* 1823).

Puruṣa and bondage

(1) Bondage:

Kashmir Śaivism and the **Tirumandiram** have several common concepts about Jiva or Puruṣa. Both of them classify souls into three types based on the impurities or *mala* they possess. The three *malas* or impurities are *āṇava mala, māyīya mala* and *karma mala*. They impose limitation on the universal consciousness in form, space and time thus resulting in Puruṣa. According to Tirumular, the *malas* are five in number (*mandiram* 118). In addition to the afore said *āṇava, karma* and *māya malas*, the soul bound by *āṇava mala* impelled by *karma* and aided by body is under the influence of the concealing power of the divine. This is called *tirodhāna śakti* of the Lord. This power is also called a *mala* as it conceals the true nature of the Puruṣa. The fifth *mala* is *mayīya mala*, that which is born from *māya*. This *mala* makes the Puruṣa believe that it is existing by its own will. This mala is removed only by the grace of the Lord. The three *malas āṇava, karma* and *māya* function in both, the causal mode as well as the effective mode.

(2) Types of souls:

Jaideva Singh in his book the **Śiva Sutras The Yoga of Supreme Identity** describes classification of souls according to Kashmir Śaivism based on the *mala* they possess. *Vijñānakala* are the souls that represent the *Mahāmāya tattva* and the field of experience is pure consciousness. *Pralayākala* are those who represent the māya tattva and their field of experience is mere void. *Sakala* are those who represent all the *tattvas* up to the earth. They are full of three *malas*. They experience cause-effect relation and everything as different from them. This category includes everything from Devas up to plants and minerals. Swami Lakshmanjoo in his book the **Śiva Sūtras: The Supreme Awakening** describes that souls remain in *pralayākala* and *sakala* states because they have defined their ego in relationship to the body, vital breath, the self in the dream state and the self in deep sleep and not in relation to their own real nature of pure consciousness. When this ignorance is "driven away" by them then they enter successively the world of *mantra pramāta* (the experiencer of the mantra), *mantreśvara pramāta* and *mantramaheśvara pramāta*, which are the states of *śuddha vidya*, *īśvara* and *sadāśiva* respectively where he recognizes himself as God consciousness.

Tirumular explains the types of souls in Tandiram 2 section 15. In *mandiram* 493 he defines the souls as *Vijñānakala* or those have only the *āṇava mala*, the *pralayākala* or those who have *āṇava mala* and *karma mala* and the *Sakala* or those who are bound by all the three impurities. The *vijñānakalas* are the leaders of mantras. The eight *vidyeśvaras* belong to this category. These souls are bound by *vāsanas* or impressions, which keep them in a position of enjoyment. They are classified into three group the *vidyeśvaras*, the *mahāmantras* (seven crore in number) and the *mantreśvaras* (innumerable). The Rudras belong to the category of *pralayākala*s. They shed their bodies at the time of the great deluge. The *Sakala* are *sādhakas* who, through their own effort, strive towards liberation. This category includes Devas, Suras, Naras and Brahma (*mandiram* 2244). *Jivan muktas* are considered as *sakala* as long as they are in their body. Those who have reached the state of realization are called *śuddha*. In *mandiram* 2233 Tirumular says that they transcend the *nāda* and *bindu* states, get *praṇava* body and are absorbed in Śiva. Tirumular calls them as those in *śuddha avastha*. He further classifies them as those in *śuddha śuddha* – in the state of Siva, *śuddha kevalam* – those in the state of *upaśāntam* and those in *śuddha sakalam*- those in the state of *turiya*. Those who have completely lost the *āṇava mala* are said to exist in the *śuddhātīta* or *turiyātīta* state (*mandiram* 2255).

3. Subtle body:

The concept of *'puryaṣṭaka'* or the nature of the subtle body of a Jiva is a common theme between the two systems. *Puryaṣṭaka* are the eight components consisting of *manas, buddhi, ahamkaram* along with the five subtle elements, the tanmatras that constitute the subtle body. This is the body that the soul assumes upon leaving the materialistic body at the time of death. According to Kashmir Śaivism, this corresponds to the dreaming state. The soul enters a womb in this state before birth.

Tirumular talks about *'purriaṭṭa kāyam'* in *mandiram* 2123 while talking about the *sūkṣma sarīra*. He says 'of the two parts of the body that the Lord assigned, while describing the subtle body, the eight *sabdha, sparṣa, rūpa, rasa, gandha, buddhi, mahat, ahamkāra* are the *puriaṭṭakāyam*. He also mentions in *mandiram* 2124 that these eight constitute the *pāsam*. They bind the *Puruṣa* in ignorance. When this *pāsam* becomes realization (*uṇarvatu*) then they remove their bind over the Puruṣa. The eye in the forehead, true awareness, will be seen'.

Liberation:

Liberation according to Kashmir Śaivism is realizing/recognizing the true nature of everything as nothing but the Absolute. This is the primary philosophy of the *pratyabhijña* school. This concept is similar to the *'rājaputra nyāya'* that the school of logic invokes. This concept is explained below. Tirumular says in his *mandiram* 316 that only those who know the divine scheme are able to witness the real scene, the true nature of everything and they, after realizing it, will stand detached from the world. Only those who have learned this divine scheme are truly learned. Such learned souls will know the right goal, which is becoming Him.

In *mandiram* 1483 Tirumular says *"caṉmārkkam tān avan āgum caṉmārkkamé'* – the right path is that which to leads the soul to become

Śiva. We have already seen in *mandiram* 115 how the *Puruṣa* approaches this state.

Means for liberation:

The means or the '*upāya*' for liberation, according to Kashmir Śaivism, are *Śāmbhavopāya, Śāktopāya* and *Āṇavopāya*. The *āṇavopāya* leads to *Śāktopāya*, which ultimately leads to *Śāmbhava samāveṣa* or spontaneous flash of realization.

(1) *Śāmbavopāya*:

Abhinavagupta defines *Śambhavopāya* as the method wherein the aspirant enters the supreme consciousness through the grace of his preceptor or the Divine. This means has been explained in detail in section two of this essay. As mentioned above this is similar to the concept of 'rājaputra nyāya'. This concept is explained as follows: A child prince gets separated from the royal entourage during a hunting trip. A hunters' tribe brings him up in the forest. One day the chief minister from the king's court discovers him in the forest and tells him his true status that he is the prince of the country. Immediately the knowledge that he is the crown prince, dawns on the young man. Here, the soul is clouded by the impurities that makes it think that it is limited consciousness. Through divine grace or the grace of a guru, the true nature of the soul is revealed as supreme consciousness. Immediately the awareness dawns on the soul.

Tirumular supports this means in his Tandiram 6 where he describes the various *sādhanās* or practices for attaining the state of Supreme consciousness. Like the **Śiva Sutras** that begin with describing the *Śāmbavopāya,* Tirumular also begins his section of practices with a description of the greatness of guru. He says that guru is Śiva himself and that the guru confers supreme consciousness to the disciple. In the first Tandiram, Tirumular mentions that his guru is Nandideva.

In *mandiram* 68 he says that due to the grace of Nandi he got the name 'nātha', he sought Mulan and remained established in the right state (*nāṭṭnil yān irrundéne*). In *mandiram* 1581 he says 'Nandi said that guru is Śivam, the guru stands as Śivam, guru is the Lord beyond speech and consciousness'. In *mandiram* 1597 he says, "The great Nandi of the mighty form Placed his sacred feet on my head with his benign look, My King, Lord, One who appeared in the form of Guru, I sought him as one who dries up the path of birth". He describes how the Lord is the supreme means by saying that 'the pair of feet of my Lord are the mantras, the tantras, the great disciplines and the most beautiful abode" in *mandiram* 1604. These verses refer to *Śāmbhavopāya* where there is a sudden descent of grace resulting in universal consciousness. This occurs due to the grace of a *guru* or the Absolute.

(2) Śāktopāya:

Śāktopāya is the means where the guiding principle for realization is Śakti or power. Its three aspects are realizing *mantra śakti, sat-tarka* and *śuddha vidya*. The **Śiva Sutras** begin the section on *Śāktopāya* with the sutra *'cittam mantrah'*. The mind referred to here as *cittam* is that which reflects on and realizes the Absolute, through the use of mantra. The divine is approached through mantras, which occur from the creative pulsation of the divine. The aspirant ponders over the divinity invoked through a *mantra* and realizes that the entire universe is only the proliferation of divine consciousness. This realization is brought about by the *unmaṇi śakti* of the *mantra*. Kṣemaraja calls this śakti śuddha *vidya*. This true realization results in the knower, known and the knowledge becoming one, the pure consciousness.

Tirumular describes the technique of *Śāktopāya* while describing the Bhairavi mantra in Tandiram 4. The pure consciousness is called Bhairava in Kashmir Śaivism. His consort, the Śakti, is Bhairavi. The Bhairavi mantra results in Bhairava or pure consciousness. The

Bhairavi mantra is described by Tirumular as follows: the fourteen syllables of the mantra when recited with awareness results in the rise of the great power, Śakti, from its locus the *cinta* or *cittam*. This Bhairavi is omnipotent, omniscient and omnipresent. She is the one with no beginning or end. From her springs many gods. She is the supreme cause.

(3) Āṇavopāya:

Āṇavopāya is the path of self- effort where the aspirant engages in ritualistic worship, yogic efforts and breath-control. In this method, the Divine is approached through *buddhi, prāna* and the body. The mind fixes itself on something other than Śiva. Hence, this method is also called as *bhedopāya*. Unlike the *Śāktopāya* where *jñāna* is most predominant, *kriya* or action is predominant in this method. Hence, this method is also known as *kriya yoga*. Tirumular has dealt with this method through his description of breath control and other steps of Śiva yoga. Even though Tirumular does not refer to *kundalini* yoga by that name, his Śiva yoga is nothing but kundalini yoga. The four steps of *carya, kriya, yoga* and *jñāna* that are described in the fifth Tandiram correspond to the three means as follows: *carya, kriya* to *Āṇavopāya, yoga* to *Śāktopāya* and *jñāna* to *Śāmbhavopāya*. Both Abhinavagupta and Tirumular talk about the *kechari mudra* and drinking the ambrosia or nectar that flows down. Tirumular explains it as "when the nectar descends from the sahasrara that confers immortality to the *sādhaka*".

Pariyanga- yoga has been given an important place in both Kashmir Śaivism and in the **Tirumandiram**. The practice of ritualistic sex is the central theme of Kula system of Kashmir Śaivism. Abhinavagupta who was initiated into all the four schools brought some of the *kula* philosophies into Kashmir Śaivism. He interprets *purṇāhuti* in a different way in the **Tantraloka**. According to him, the *arani* of the supreme energy is stirred up by the libation, the semen, and the sacrifice is performed as a supreme offering of one's self to Brahman. The *purnahuti* is the offering of the seminal fluid that is sent upwards. Soma or the ambrosia is the union of Siva (Sa) and Uma (So+ma).This is *kula yāga*.

Pariyanga yoga forms an important theme in the *nātha* tradition. Tirumular, who, is also a descendent of the *nātha* tradition has described elaborately the *Pariyanga-yoga*. In this practice, the flow of seminal fluid is arrested and directed upwards. This is called *vindu-marittal* in Tamil. In Kashmir Śaivism, this is called *bindu sādhana* or *bindu dharana*. Tirumular claims that this practice confers immortality to the practitioner. Tandiram 7 has many verses on this practice. While *bindu* means the semen, it also means the highest knower or the consciousness, which is called *vindu* or *bindu*. The term *Baindavikalā* is used to indicate the power of knowership of the Highest Self.

(4) Śaktipāta:

Even though both Kashmir Śaivism and the **Tirumandiram** recommend various means for liberation, both the systems emphasize that ultimately it is not the means that grants release but divine grace. This is called *Śaktipāta*. This divine grace comes mysteriously and voluntarily to destroy all the impurities thereby revealing the true nature of the soul. There is no special qualification that the soul could possess that warrants the descent of grace. While the effect of the *māyīya* and *karma mala* can be overcome through personal effort the effect of the *āṇava mala* is destroyed only by *Śaktipāta*. An awakening comes through the agency of the Guru, his word or mantra. While the grace that is showered by God is the same, its intensity varies depending on the nature of the recipient. For the individual who has prepared himself to receive the grace in its most intense form the descent grants instant release from his physical body. Recipients of low intensity of grace are endowed with strong desire to go to the guru and seek guidance on spiritual path.

States of consciousness:

Through following various means for liberation, the *Puruṣa* experiences different states of consciousness. According to Kashmir Śaivism there are four states of consciousness namely wakeful state (*jāgrat*), dreaming state (*svapna*), dreamless state (*suṣupti*) and the state of complete awareness (*turiya*). In the wakeful state the *prāna, manas,* senses and the body are active. In the *svapna* state the function of the senses stop. Their functions are taken up by the mind and imagination. Only the *prāna, manas* and *Puruṣa* are active. In the profound sleep state, even the function of the *manas* stops only the *prāna* and *Puruṣa* function. In the fourth state, only the *Puruṣa* functions. There is also the fifth state beyond these four states, that is the *turiyatīta* state or the state of 'beyond the beyond'. Ksemaraja was the first one to describe it in his explanation of the **Śiva Sutras**. While explaining the tenth sutra in section one, he elaborates upon the different classifications of the wakeful, dreaming, deep sleep state and the state of *turiya* that are further classified based on the their phases. For example, in the *turiya* state there are three phases *turiya-jāgrat, turiya svapna* and *turiya suṣupti*. In the *turiya jāgrat* state the mind retires completely and the super mind becomes active. This state is also called *manonmana*. The function of the normal mind stops and is taken over by *unmana*. In the *turiya svapna* state the yogi enters the region of unlimited knowledge. This is called *ananta*. The yogi calls the *turiya* state *rupātīta,* as it transcends both the subjective and objective manifestations. *Turiya- suṣupti* is a state where every thing appears as a form of divine Śakti. The *turyatīta* is a state that is beyond even this fourth state. This state is full of uninterrupted I-consciousness. Here even the difference between transcendence and immanence disappears. The *jñānis* call this state *mahāpracaya*. This state is *caitanya*.

Tirumular explains the different states of consciousness in the eighth Tandiram. In *mandiram* 2142 he says that the twenty-five principles along with the soul remains in the center of the eyebrow in the wakeful state. In the *svapna* state, the organs of senses stop functioning. The soul with the ten-fold airs and the four-fold *antahakarana* or *manas* and its ramifications function in this state and remains in the throat. The third state or the dreamless state is characterized by the presence of the *Puruṣa, citta* and *prāna*. The soul in this state remains in the heart center. In the *turiya* state, only two *tattva*, the *prāna* and *Puruṣa* operate. The soul remains in the navel when it is in this state. In the *turiyatīta* only the awareness or *Puruṣa* functions.

Tirumular describes different principles or *tattva* that govern these various states. In the *jāgrath* state, the five Śiva *tattvas* are experienced. The *svapna* state is motivated by the four Śiva tattva. In the *suṣupti* state the three principles, *Sadāśiva*, Śakti and Śiva are the driving forces. The two principles Śiva and Śakti animate the *turiya* state. In the fifth state, the *turiyātīta* state, only Śiva *tattva* is experienced. This is the state, which is speechless, action-less. Tirumular calls this *mōna samādhi* (*mandiram* 2936).

Role of scriptures:

Kashmir Śaivism holds Āgamas in high esteem. The Āgamas are considered as primary sources of knowledge and as divine utterances similar to the Vedas. The various types of Āgamas of Kashmir Śaivism have already been elaborated upon in the previous section. Tirumular's view about Vedas and Āgamas concur with the viewpoint of Kashmir Śaivism. In the first Tandiram, sections two and three, he describes the greatness of the Vedas and Āgamas and mentions in several places the concurrence between these two systems. In *mandiram* 2397 he says

> Vedas and Āgamas are really revelations of God
> The former are general, the latter are specific

They are Lord's utterance with two ends
Which are different to some, non-different to the great.

Tirumular was the first one to coin the term *'vedanta siddhāntha samarasa sanmārgam'* that was used heavily by later Siddhas such as Pattinattar and Tayumānavar. In *mandiram* 2404 he says

Primal is the Veda, perfect is Āgama
These two are uttered by the Lord
Step by step the ancient Veda evolved
Into the exalted Vedānta and Siddhānta

Tirumandiram and Integral monism:

Monism, by definition, is the doctrine that defines Reality as an organic whole without independent parts. In contrast, pluralism is the doctrine according to which the Reality is composed of independent principles. The definition of the Absolute according to both Kashmir Śaivism and the **Tirumandiram** corresponds to the definition of monism and not to pluralism. The Absolute is defined not as the only entity but as the only entity that appears as plurality. The Absolute, the pure consciousness, emanates as the subjective and objective worlds that are distinct yet real states of only the Absolute. Both Kashmir Śaivism and the **Tirumandiram** differ from Śankara's Advaita, which preaches that the Absolute is the only Reality and the manifested universe is *mitya* or unreal. According to Kashmir Śaivism and the **Tirumandiram**,both the Absolute and the manifested universe are real as the manifested emerged from the Absolute. However, both these systems do not preach that the Absolute and the manifested are different entities. Only the Absolute exists in reality but it exists in different states of consciousness. Due to its *svāntantriya* or complete freedom of action and knowledge, the Absolute manifests as diversity or *bheda* through its infinite power. This *bheda* together with its existence as *abheda* or undivided, constitute its totality or *purṇatva*. Kashmir Śaivism states that the Absolute oscillates between the desire to create and the withdrawal of that desire which is the eternal pulsation or *Spanda*. Hence, the Absolute is called the Great Oneness or the composite of manifested and the unmanifested or *mahādvaya*. This viewpoint is seen in the **Tirumandiram** where it is said that when the diversity of *paśu* and *pāsa* approach the *Pati* through realization, the state of diversity or *bheda* does not exist anymore and a state of nondiversity or *abheda* is achieved. This state is not coexistence of the three different entities, the philosophy of some of the *bheda* and *bhedhābheda* schools of Vedanta. Hence, we can say with certainty that the viewpoint of the **Tirumandiram** about the Absolute is monistic and monistic only. This standpoint is not in conflict with the pluralistic view of the Absolute. This is a more inclusive and complete view about the Absolute and as Mark Dyczkowkshi puts it "dualism is not an incorrect view of reality although it corresponds to only one of the levels within the absolute".

NOTES ON CHAPTER TEN

1. Moore, G.E. *The Refutation of Idealism' Mind* 12: 433-53 (1903). Reprinted in *Philosophical Studies* and in *G. E. *Moore: Selected Writings* 23-44.

2. Refer Appendix I of The English Translation of the Tirumandiram, vol.10, p 3451.

3. Refer his article published in *the Centenary volume of the Saiva Siddhanta-p-peru-marmam*, Chennai, 2005.

4. See volume 10 of The English Translation of the Tirumandiram edited by T.N. Ganapathy, p 3435, 3435.

5. Ibid. p 3495-96.

The authors' response to the reviewer's observations on the chapter on "Monistic Theism of the Tirumandiram and Kashmir Saivism

1. About Parallelism

   The statement (section3) is about the parallelism between the Tirumandiram and Kashmir Saivism and nowhere the authors have said that there is no interaction between the Saivism of the South and Kashmir Saivism. The statement is about the relationship between the Tirumandiram and Kashmir Saivism only.

   The commentator has missed this point and he himself assumes that the authors have spoken about the relationship between Kashmir Saivism and Saiva Agama. Far from that. His assumption is precisely wrong.

   May be we are using the term "parallelism" because we do not want to assume a concrete influence between Tirumular and the philosophers of Kashmir Saivism who came after Tirumular.

2. Mrugendra and Matanga Agama belong to Kashmir Saivism. Do they consider so?

   Yes. There are some Tantras common between different Saiva schools. Refer to Arthur Avalon's article Shakti and Shakta Essays and Addresses on the shakta tantrasastra- London, Luzac & Co (1918).

3. "Tirumular was the first to bring the Tantra aspect of Saivism from Kashmir to the Tamil world". section three of the article. Commentator's remark: It is totally incorrect.

The above statement by the authors are supported by K.A. Nilakanta Sastri's article "An Historical Sketch of Saivism in The Cultural Heritage of India" (vol. IV) where he says that according to the *Peria Puranam* Tirumular came to the South from Kailasa, the home of the Pratyabhijna school.

The statement from S.S. Suryanarayana Sastri in "The Cultural Heritage of India" vol. III (1956) p387- 398. Ramakrishna Mission Institute of Culture, Calcutta.

"Tradition has that Tirumular perhaps the earliest Tamil Saiva, brought Saivism to the South from North, possibly from Kashmir"

Probaby the reviewer has "misunderstood" that the authors mean that Tirumular brought Kashmir Saivism to the South as he has mentioned that Tirumular precedes the evolution of Kashmir Saivism.

What the authors mean is that Tirumular was the first to bring the concept of Tantra and Yoga to the Tamil Nadu, not Kashmir Saivism.

By calling his yoga as nava yoga and saying that Nandi bestowed this new type of yoga (mandiram 122), Tirumular indicates that this new types of Tantra and Yoga (called Siva Yoga) were not in vogue before him in the Tamil country. Being the first reatise in Tamil on Siva Yoga or Tantra Yoga, the Tirumandiram struck a new tradition in Tamil. His is the first to bring the Tantra aspect of Saivism from the North to the Tamil Land. Before him there was no reference to Tantra Yoga in the *Agananuru* and the *Purananuru* or in the *Tolkappiyam*.

By saying that Tirumular brought the Tantra aspect of Saivism from Kashmir to Tamil land, it is suggested that both the Tirumandiram and Kashmir Saivism have the same roots in Kashmir (in Tantrism) even though Tirumandiram precedes Kashmir Saivism by several centuries and Not that Tirumular brought Kashmir Saivism to Tamil Nadu. The reviewer has bitten off more than he can chew!

4. Unmana, kodandam-

Unmana is defined as follows: Vijñānabhairava explains the upward movement of praṇava from gross utterance to subtle vibration. The movement ends in the state of unmana, the ultimate energy beyond all the mental processes. It is the state where all objectivity disappears. Svacchanda Tantra explains this state as being beyond measurement. Some say that it should be contemplated in the last part of the tuft of hair on the head and its time period is 1/512 of a mātra.

Tirumular explains in Tandiram 4 mandiram 1222 the greatness of pranava. According to him, all the mantras are included in the *pranava*. It leads to the union with Sivahood, the state where all the objectivity disappears. In mandiram 1223, he explains the pranava through the expression *'cīvan cikai angu irunda idam'*. *cīvan cikai* can be interpretted as the tuft of the Jiva or as the top of the hair on the head of a Jiva. In the first case, it has the same connotation as Kashmir Saivism. In the second case, it means sahasrāra. This state is the unmana described by Kashmir Saivism. This is also called as "the dark place", a synonym of void. Kashmir Saivism also calls this state as the ultimate void.

Anyway, to avoid confusion the authors have revised the article and deleted the sections on unmana and Kodandam as the proposed theory, that 'Tirumandiram advocates monistic theism and not pluralistic realism', has been sufficiently proved through other evidences that show its parallelism with monistic Kashmir Saivism.

5. The five acts of Siva: Swami Lakshman Joo in his book Kashmir Saivism The Secret Supreme page 87 (Universal Shaiva Fellowship, 2007) says "The grace of Lord Siva is manifested through his five acts creation, protection, destruction, concealing and revealing." The authors feel that this order is correct as it is based on the statement of an expert and guru of Kashmir Saiva tradition.

6. Pancha kriya vidhi explain more based on Tirumandiram:

   We have said already that Thirumular has dedicated five separate sections on the five acts. There is no need to expand further on this as this is explained here only to show the parallelism between Kashmir Saivism and the Tirumandiram and not to explain the details of the five great acts of Siva which is not the focus of the article.

Chapter 11

Conclusion

T.N. Ganapathy

aiya mā-k-kaḍal āl̲nda uyirkku elām
kaiyil amalagam en̲a-k kāṭṭuvān̲
maiyal tīr tirumandiram ceppiya
ceyya pon̲ tirumūlan̲ai-c cindippām.

He will reveal the truth clearly and certainly
To the souls that are lost in the ocean of doubt;
Think of that Tirumulan̲, the one with a golden hue,
Who authored the *Tirumandiram*, which clarifies!

–*Padi-pacu-pāca Viḷakkam.*

11. Conclusion

T.N. Ganapathy

One cannot write a conclusion to the ever widening and the unfathomable philosophical depth of the *Tirumandiram*. Even though Tirumular speaks of many *antas* i.e., ends such as *Vedānta*, *Nādānta*, etc., there is no real "end" or *anta* in understanding and assimilating the various ideas that glitter like diamonds in the *Tirumandiram*. The more one studies this work, the more and more one realizes its limitlessness. Such is the depth of the wisdom enshrined in the *Tirumandiram*.

Yet one may formally write a conclusion for this present work.

In any society there are two levels of interaction between itself and religion. One level of interaction is explicit, and it is between religious institutions such as churches and temples on one side and secular institutions such as government, economy, politics and so on, on the other. One may call this the level of explicit ontology, the peripheral relation between religion and society. Another level of interaction is between the views of reality and the values that characterize a culture on the one hand and the typical social institutions on the other. This one may call the level of implicit ontology, the central core of the relation between religion and society. A society maintains itself as a system because of its implicit ontology, that is, because of a fundamental consensus about value and reality among the majority of its members. The social milieu involves a common system of ultimate-value attitudes. If religion deals with ultimate Reality and society is a common system of ultimate-value attitudes, then it follows that there must be a necessary connection between the two. To reveal this necessary connection between the ultimate reality and the value-system of society is the purpose of the song of the *Tirumandiram*. As Sorokin has pointed out each society is based on some "major premise... which the civilization articulates, develops and realizes in all its main compartments, or parts, in the process of its life-career."[1] An implicit ontology, then, is the major premise on which social institutions are founded. And social action begins with man's inner attitudes and works outward to the environment, into his family, his community, etc. It works from the center to the periphery.

Explicit ontology is based on the theistic conception of God, God as a Person, whereas implicit ontology is based on the notion of an Absolute, not as a Person, but as a principle and value, as an Absolute Freedom or as a Great Aloneness *(taṉi uṟṟa kēvalam)*, as Tirumūlar says.[2] Any doctrine which purports to show the interconnection between a theistic conception of God and morality or God and society is always on the defensive and at the mercy of the opponents. A society centering round a theistic notion of a personal God, even though religious, is nonetheless an imposition on individuals and such a society fails to create a genuine community. It may be likened to a community of individuals "hounded by heaven."

Implicit ontology is concerned with God as a principle and a value and it understands religion as a state of being grasped by an "ultimate concern," to borrow a phrase from Paul Tillich. Ultimate concern is directed toward what is of final value, the supreme value that has top priority in the hierarchy of life interests. It is the one thing for which a man would renounce all his other interests. It is the standard by which he judges every other value and places each of them in the scheme of things. Such a key value is always presupposed in everything human— his attitudes and his society. In implicit ontology value becomes the objective counter part of concern, and in this sense religion as spirituality is the conservation of the highest value. The highest value may be called freedom or liberation or *mokṣa* or nirvāṇa or *veṭṭaveḷi*. When freedom becomes the objective counterpart of concern, it becomes a responsible freedom, that is, one's responsibility to the Ultimate Reality becomes also a responsibility to all men. In this way reedom is inextricably bound up with society or community at the empirical level.

What has been described so far as implicit ontology is the ontology of the *Tirumandiram*. It is a programme for the realization of values. According to it values are not extraneities grafted by man on the world; they are the ingredients of reality. Liberation or freedom is an intrinsic, universal value and is the presupposition for actualizing all the other values. It is the very basis of ethical action and social life. The *Tirumandiram* seeks to uncover and unfold this universal value embedded in each individual. It is not a theoretical and abstract belief in a Supreme Being and does not accept the religious viability of any conception of God as a separate and objective Being. According to it jīva is Śiva. Because of āṇava, one does not know it. If man is liberated from this āṇava, he knows that he is none other than Śiva. This liberation from pāśa is *mokṣa*. *Mokṣa* is not a place; it is the removal of the veil or spiritual blindness. Self-realization or knowledge of jīva as Śiva is *mokṣa*.

Some critics of Indian Sociology point out that since liberation of self has become the major concern, there is little concern for social ethics or social development in India. This criticism is untenable. According to Tirumūlar the mantra Śivāyanama is not merely a mystical concept but a social one too. It means "the result of sacrifice is bliss." That is, the social concern of the *Tirumandiram* has provided the Siddhas with one more path for the discovery of the self. The *Tirumandiram* says that the way to attain *mokṣa* is to have a kind heart.[3] Born out of this kind heart he advocates people to provide one handful of rice for the sake of the poor people.[4]

According to Tirumūlar religion is the sacred art of living, comprising dharma and *amṛta*. One who has realized this is said to be in "the living contact with the infinite." In fine the *Tirumandiram* is characterized by integration, and an "authentic transcendence" which is an experience of the whole self and not a theoretical and abstract belief in a Supreme Being. At the level of implicit ontology, love, as society's value-premise, provides the basic ground plan for the society as a whole. This is the purpose of the song of Tirumūlar's basic philosophy as enshrined in his great work, the *Tirumandiram*.

Notes on Chapter Eleven

1. P.A. Sorokin, *Social Philosophies of An Age of Crisis*, p. 277.
2. *Tirumandiram*, 2400.
3. *Ibid.*, 273.
4. *Ibid.*, 252.

Appendix-A

The Works that Unduly Claim the Authorship of Tirumūlar

1. ***Tirumūlar Tattuva-k-kaṭṭaḷai***: This work in prose form explains the Śaiva religious principles. This work also lists the ninetysix principles of Śaiva philosophy and explains them.
2. ***Tirumūlar Dyāṉa-k-kuṟippu***: This work contains twenty-eight verses. This work is all about meditation *(dyāna)*.
3. ***Tirumūlar Vālai Pañcākṣara Viḷakkam***: There are twenty verses in this work. These verses deal with the five-lettered *(pañcākṣara)* mantras concerning the *vālai*. (*Vālai* may be taken as Śakti, Kuṇḍalinī, etc.).
4. ***Tirumūlar Vaittiyam***: There are 102 verses in this work. They all speak about medicine.
5. ***Tirumūlar Vaittiya-muṟai Vacaṉam***: This work is in prose style. While suggesting remedies to diseases, this work also praises the medicinal values of *tiru-nīṟu*, the sacred ash. It also teaches how to cure diseases by uttering mantras using the sacred ash.
6. ***Tirumūlar Cocca Cūttiram***: This work contains thirty-three verses about medicine and alchemy.
7. ***Tirumūlar Taṇḍagam***: Contains ninety-eight verses regarding jñāna.
8. ***Tirumandira-c-cūttiram-200***: Contains two hundred verses concerning Yoga and alchemy.

9. ***Tirumūlar Nadi-c-cūttiram***: This work explains about various diseases and how to know them by reading the pulse; gives remedies to many diseases and explains preparation of various medicines.
10. ***Tirumūlar Vāgaḍam***: Contains twenty-five verses; speaks about medicine.
11. ***Tirumūlar Vaittiyam-600***: Contains six hundred verses about medicine.
12. ***Tirumūlar Vālai Dīṭcai***: Contains verses regarding Yoga and alchemy.
13. ***Tirumūlar Eṭṭu***: Contains only eight verses.
14. ***Tirumūlar Kuiḷigai Muṟai-50***: Speaks about medicine.
15. ***Tirumūlar Pūraṇa Mālai***: Only some verses are available. Not complete.
16. ***Tirumūlar Cūttira-t-tiraṭṭu***: Thirteen verses of Yoga.
17. ***Tirumūlar Kaṟpa Muṟai-500***: Only three hundred and sixty verses are available. Speaks about longevity.
18. ***Tirumūla Nāyaṉār Vāda Cūttiram-300***: Speaks about preparation of medicines.
19. ***Tirumūla Nāyaṉār Nigaṇḍu-300***: A sort of dictionary explaining various terms used in Siddha works.
20. ***Tirumūlar Kuru Muṟai***: About alchemy.
21. ***Tirumūlar Jñāṉam***: Included in the book, the *Siddha Jñāṉa-k-kōvai*. Contains eleven verses.
22. ***Tirumūlar Karukkiḍai Toḷḷāyiram***: Contains nine hundred verses.
23. ***Tirumūlar Āyiram***: Speaks about medicine.

24. ***Tirumūlar Karumāṉa-c-curkkam-84***: This work is published under the title *Tirumūlar Jñāṉam-84;* deals with Yoga and suggests some mantras.

25. ***Tirumandira-mālai-300***: This work containing three hundred verses speaks extensively the eight māntric rites called *aṭṭa-karumam.* This work is published by the Annamalai University with the commentary of Na. Sivapragasa Desigar.

-Courtesy: Ira. Manikkavacagam, *Tirumandira Ārāycci,* pp. 224-231 (With additions and deletions).

Appendix-B

The Categories of Souls

Souls, which are eternal, are given life and body by Śiva/ Śakti that they may rid themselves of their primordial impurities and become truly free and pure.

These souls are classified into three basic categories according to the degree of impurities they possess. In a scheme of evolution, the one class rises to the next by divesting itself of the impurities, one after another.

These three categories are called *vijñāna-kalas, praḷayā-kalas* and *sakalas,* according to the state of their evolution. Each of these three broad classifications has again sub-classifications, and in all, the hierarchy of souls is divided into ten divisions.

The *vijñāna-kalas* are the most highly evolved souls. No longer affected by karma or māyā, they are amenable to āṇava alone. They are categorized into four sub-divisions (*Tirumandiram*, 493).

1) The truly enlightened, who are totally rid of āṇava (egoity). Tirumūlar calls them as *mey-jñāṉar.* They are one with Śiva.

2) Those who are not completely rid of āṇava, but are in a calm state of inaction. They are ten in number and are called Aṇu-Sadāśivas. They are associated with the *sādākhya-tattva.*

3) Those who have realized the Self, but are still conscious of the self—the eight Vidyeśvaras. They are associated with the *īśvara-tattva.* They administer the vidyā-tattvas or aśuddha-māyā-tattvas.

4) Then are the seventy millions of Mantra-nāyakas—the lords of the mantras ending with seven end-notes (like *nama,*

svāha, etc.). They are associated with the śuddha-vidyā-tattva and are under the command of the Vidyeśvaras (*Tirumandiram*, 494).

Below the *vijñāna-kalas* are the *praḷayā-kalas*. They possess two impurities—āṇava and karma. They are categorized into three sub-divisions (*Tirumandiram*, verse 493). Among them, the first category consists of those souls which will attain liberation in the next deluge *(praḷaya)*. The second and the third categories consist of the *apakvas* (immature) and the *pakvas* (mature) bound by the two impurities. The 108 Rudras belong to the third category. In them the effect of māyā is less than that of āṇava. Taking forms from the pure māyā, they become the 108 Rudras and continue their efforts to get rid of āṇava (*Tirumandiram*, 2243). All the three categories of *praḷayā-kalas* possess the sense of egoity and experience karma in gradations of intensity (*Tirumandiram*, 495).

The *sakalas* are encumbered by all the three impurities—āṇava, karma and māyā. Among the *sakalas* are three sub-classifications (*Tirumandiram*, 493): those who have attained the miraculous powers of siddhis, but are aspiring towards eventual God-realization; those who having attained siddhis, are content with cultivating these powers; and those who are not performing yoga-sādhana, remaining powerless to conquer any of the impurities and are simply enmeshed in the world of sense experience (*Tirumandiram*, 496).

-Coutesy: B. Natarajan (Tr.), *Tirumantiram*

(With certain modifications.)

Appendix-C

The Symbolism of the Dance of Śiva

Lord Naṭarāja

The Lord of Dance has four arms. The upper right hand holds the drum, which symbolises creation. The upper left hand holds fire, which stands for destruction. The lower right hand is raised in blessing, symbolising sustenance. The lower left hand gestures toward the uplifted foot in assurance that Śiva's grace is the refuge for everyone, the way to liberation. The right leg, representing obscuring grace, footed firmly on Muyalagaṉ, the demon, who is the symbol of āṇava-mala. The uplifted left leg is revealing grace, which releases the mature soul from bondage and hence is the destination of the souls. The circle of fire represents the cosmos. Tirumūlar says: The birth of the world, its maintenance, its destruction, the soul's obscuration and liberation are the five acts of His dance.

Symbolism of Individual Parts

The matted locks of his hair stand out in many strands as he whirls around in his dancing frenzy.

The fiery ring surrounding the Lord Naṭarāja, *Tiruvāci*, represents the universe with all its illusion, suffering and pain.

In upper right hand Lord Naṭarāja holds on hour-glass shaped drum called *uḍukkai* in Tamil. The drum represents creation. Lord Naṭarāja dances to the rhythmic sound produced of this drum and ceaselessly creates the universe. This hand stands for the letter *ci* of the five-lettered mantra *ci-vā-ya-na-ma*

The lower left hand is uplifted in air across the chest with the wrist and fingers tilted downwards, palm facing down, the index finger indicating the left foot uplifted in the air to show the destination of the souls. This hand represents the letter *vā*

The lower right hand is raised in blessing in the fear-not gesture. It symbolizes the act of sustenance and represents the letter *ya.*

The upper left hand holds fire, which denotes destruction. It also represents the letter *na.*

The left foot uplifted in the air liberates the souls. This foot represents the act of grace by the Lord.

The right foot fixed firmly on the Muyalagaṉ, a demon symbolizing āṇava-mala, thereby arresting him. This foot represents obscuration, one of the five acts of the Lord and it also stands for the letter *ma*.

Courtesy:
http://www.lotussculpture.com/nataraja1.htm

Appendix-D

A Brief Discussion of the Five 'M's : Pañca-makāra

Pañca-makāra admits of literal or *mukya* reading and metaphorical or *gauna* reading. *Mukya* reading would imply *vāmācāra* or left-hand practice of Tantra and metaphorical reading would imply *dakṣiṇācāra* or right hand practice of Tantra.

Sudhakar Chattopadhyaya in his book *Reflections on the Tantra* (pp. 19-20) lists five theories of this practice of *pañca-makāra*. They are:

1. The *pañca-makāra* is nothing but a license for licentiousness. It records the age-long attempt to cover dark acts in the garb of religion.
2. The account is an allegorical one representing in disguise the various processes of prāṇāyāma, *ṣaṭ-cakra-bheda* and the ultimate bliss or happiness that the process leads to.
3. Man is drawn to the path of religion after his enjoyment is satisfied. Tantras have prescribed intense enjoyment through *pañca-makāra* that would ultimately bring a spirit of renunciation in the mind.
4. The Tantras never neglected the materialistic aspect of life and they maintain that *mokṣa* can be attained even through material enjoyment. The *pañca-makāras* are nothing but an attempt in this direction.
5. The Tantras wanted to keep their rituals and doctrines secret and therefore they have tried to confuse the ordinary people by such accounts.

We cannot deal with the five 'm's here, but we can bring out briefly a few aspects and peculiarities of them. We can safely start by saying that the five 'm's are not mere ceremony or ritual but reminders of the yogic process. In the right hand Tāntric ritual practice, *madya* (wine) becomes the symbol of intoxicating knowledge; *māmsa* (meat) implies the control of speech; *matsya* (fish) represents the two vital currents moving in the iḍā and piṅgalā; *mudrā* (parched grain) symbolizes the yogic state of concentration and *maithuna* (sexual union) symbolizes samādhi. In some cases the sādhaka used material substitutes for the five 'm's. Wine is substituted by coconut juice, meat by ginger, *mudrā* by rice, wheat or grain, *maithuna* by two types of flowers, the *liṅga-puṣpa* and *aparājita* (the first resembling the *liṅga* and the second resembling the *yoni*). In the *Kulārṇava-Tantra* it is stated that wine and meat are the symbols of Śakti and Śiva respectively, the Goddess having pierced all the *kula-pathas* (the ways of a *kaula*)—in the mūlādhāra (earth), maṇipūra (fire), svādiṣṭhana (water), anāhata (air), viśuddhi (space) and ājñā (mind)—enjoys the company of her consort in the sahasrāra. D.N.Bose and Hiralal Haldar in their book *Tantras: Their Philosophy and Occult Secrets,* say that these terms may be taken in the sense of the five chief *aśuras* of the Śrī Śrī Chaṇḍī, viz., Madhu, Kaiṭabha, Mahiṣāśura, Śumba and Niśumba (p. 186). The *Tantra-sāra* traces the practice of the five 'm's to mantras in the *Ṛg Veda.* [Mantra in Ṛg Veda I, 154.2 to be used in connection with meat; RV VII, 59.12 with fish; RV 122.20-21 with *mudrā;* RV IV, 40.5 with wine and RV X, 184-I-2 for sexual intercourse]. The *madya* though literally stands for wine, refers to the intoxicating knowledge of God attained by Yoga by which one becomes senseless of the outer world. It stands for the nectar that is said to ooze from the thousand-petalled lotus in the *brahma-randhra.* Almost all people in Tamil Nadu sing the following song from Kudambai-c-cittar:

> To those who have climbed the top of the hill
> and drunk the juice of fresh mango fruits
> O! earthern ear-ring, what is the use of coconut milk?

When a yogin has got the celestial ambrosia, why should he go in for something less than that like the coconut milk? This nectar has got several names in Tamil Siddha literature like *ucci-p-pāl, cōmacalam, madi-y-amudu, karavā-p-pāl, māṅgāy-p-pāl, kāya-p-pāl, aruḷamudu,* etc. The effort of the yogins to get at this nectar is called, by the Tamil Siddhas, as begging at the top. *Madya* also stands for the yogic process of *bhūta-śuddhi* by which the sādhaka turns inwards and unifies the kuṇḍalinī-śakti with Paramaśiva. In Tantra this 'wine' is called *kulāmṛta,* and the Nātha Siddhas called it *soma.* In primitive thought wine was regarded as a life-giving principle. Debiprasad Chattopadhaya shows that in ancient India liquor was resorted to for the purpose of overcoming death (*Lokāyata,* p. 309). One of the commonest names for wine is *mṛta-sanjīvini,* that which restores life, a name very frequently used in Siddha and Ayurvedic medical traditions.

Māmsa (flesh, meat) does not signify the physical flesh, which the aspirant should eat. It is the symbol of the flesh of the ego which must be cut with the sword of knowledge, that is, freedom from 'I' and 'mine' is *māmsa.* It stands for mastery over carnal pleasures and the destruction of the 'beast' in man. It has been enjoined that the sādhaka should kill the '*beast*' in him, constituted by merit and demerit with the help of the sword of knowledge and devour its flesh. In the *Haṭha-yoga-pradīpika* the tasting of the *amṛta* that is produced in the sahasrāra is called the flesh of the cow that the yogin eats (III, 47, 49). This expression eating of the cow's meat is used just to show that a true Siddha, as a participant in transcendence, goes beyond the Hindu prohibitions (eating cow's meat), that he is no longer conditioned by 'ethics,' that he is no longer in this world of 'mine' and 'thine.'

The *matsya* literally means 'fish,' but it symbolically signifies the inhalation and exhalation of breath. It has been said that the two nadis, iḍā and piṅgalā, have two fishes, viz., inhalation and exhalation, moving constantly up and down. It is enjoined that a sādhaka should stop their erratic movement by performing *kumbhaka* through prāṇāyāma, so that the blocked channel of the central nāḍi, viz., suṣumnā, could be opened for the ascent of the kuṇḍalinī-śakti. This is symbolically called 'the eating of fish,' *matsya-bhakṣaṇa*, and such aspirants are known as *matsya-sādhaka.*

The *mudrā* literally means positioning of fingers in prescribed posture but in the context of Tāntric sādhanā, it signifies relinquishing of association with evil. The parched grain also stands for the burning away of the kārmic particles in the sādhaka. In the left-hand practice of Tantra, *mudrā* is a term applied to the girl in the sexual rite. Even here the girl referred to is merely symbolic, whose body is compassion, and whose form is pure bliss. The sādhaka has to enjoy her in order to experience this great-bliss *mahā-sukha.*

This takes us to the last of the five 'm's that is *maithuna.* It means that the sādhaka has no more a separate existence other than the all-embracing Reality. Though *maithuna* literally means sexual intercourse, in the Siddha tradition it signifies the union of kuṇḍalinī-śakti with Śiva existing in the sahasrāra. About this *maithuna,* Śaṅkarācārya writes: The bride (the kuṇḍalinī) entering into the royal way (the central nāḍi) meets and embraces the supreme bridegroom (Śiva) and by this embrace they make floods of nectar flow. (Refer *Chintāmaṇistava*).

APPENDIX-E

Pariyaṅga Yoga

The Tamil commentators interpret "pariyanga" as "cot" and "Yoga" as that practiced on a cot (euphemistically with woman in bed). But the classical Sanskrit texts, however, use the term "vajroli" and refer to it as a mudra. The Tamil scholiasts call it Yoga, even as they call kechari mudra a Yoga.

The word "pari" means "hard" and "anga" refers to the male sexual organ. In fact, this seems to be the main import of the *vajroli-mudra* as well as Pariyanga Yoga.

In this mudra, the main object seems to be to restrain the flow of semen without loss of enjoyment through control of breath.

Verse 825: Pleasures of Sex Union Will Abide if Breath Control is Properly Practiced

Anointing her body with unguents diverse
Bedecking her tresses with flowers fragrant
Do thou enjoy the damsel in passion's union;
If thou but know how to shoot
Prana breath through the Sushumna
Their enjoyment ceaseth never.

Mantras 825 & 826

The yogi anoints the woman's body with diverse perfumes. He bedecks her tresses with fragrant flowers and then proceeds to enjoy the damsel in heightened passion. But as he does so, he draws the breath inward through the spinal cavity. The breath stands still. As the full-breasted damsel and the skilled yogi thus seek enjoyment, the liquid silver (sukhla) draws in the liquid gold *(sronita)* and the yogi, with breath stilled, masters the retention of his semen. The couple commingle in ecstatic passion the whole time.

Pariyanga Yoga, which deals with sexual acts in terms of Yoga, is a *vamacara* concept. Mular who had earlier, condemned *vamacara,* now describes this very Yoga in laudatory terms.

Verse 826: If Breath is Controlled Delicious Enjoyment Results in Sex Union

When they seek enjoyment
The Breath standeth still;
The full breasted damsel and fervent male
Stand in union exalted;
As liquid silver and gold
Their passion's emissions
In rapture commingleth.

Verse 827: Duration of Enjoyment Lengthens if Breath is Controlled

In the copulatory Yoga that is practiced
By the hero and heroine
Upward they drive the coach of breath
That hath its wheels in regions right and left;
There they collect the waters of the heaven
And never the organs tiring know.

In that conjugal Yoga thus practiced, the yogi drives the two wheeled coach of breath upward. His organ knows no weariness, and he collects the "waters of the heaven." In the Sakta Tantras the aspirant is known as hero or *veera.*

Verse 828: Restraint of Semen Flow Through Breath Control

This the meaning of that union;

When in the sex act semen flows
The yogi lets it not;
But checks it
And within retaineth
And a Master he then becometh.

Mantras 828 & 829

This then is the meaning of that mudra; in the conjugal act the yogi lets not the semen flow, but checks it and holds it within. Verily he becomes the master. He becomes master of jnana. He becomes master of enjoyment. He becomes master of himself. He becomes master of the five senses.

Verse 829: Effect of Restrain of Semen Flow

He becomes master of jnana all
He becomes master of enjoyment all
He becomes master of himself
He becomes master of senses five.

Verse 830: Sex Union Through the Pariyanga Lasts Five Ghatikas and is Bliss

This is Pariyanga-Yoga
That last five Ghatikas;
Beyond in the sixth
The damsel sleeps in the arms of lover
In union blissful
That fills the heart
And passes description.

This union lasts for five *naligas* (two and half hours). Then in the sixth *naliga* the damsel goes to sleep in the arms of the yogi lover, in blissful union that "fills" her heart in an experience that defies description.

Verse 831: Successful Practitioners Alone can Resort to Pariyanga Yoga

Unless it be,
He had on success practiced
The Pariyanga Yoga
Of five ghatika length
No yogi shall
A women embrace.

Mantras 831 & 832

Let no yogi embrace a woman unless he has successfully practiced this technique of the five *naliga* duration. If it is asked who is the yogi that had accomplished this audacious practice, the answer is "Lord Siva that wears the heavenly Ganga on his matted locks." Siva the supreme yogi, embraced Sakti of ambrosial-sweet voice thinking and not thinking of the act.

Verse 832: Lord Siva Practiced Pariyanga Yoga

Who may you ask,
Is He that achieved this audacious Yoga;
The Lord is He that wears heavenly Ganga on his matted lock;
For Ghatika five
He embraced Sakti of speech ambrosial sweetness
Thinking and thinking not of the act performed.

Verse 833: The Age of The Couple for Pariyanga Yoga

For practice of this Yoga,
Twenty the age apt for damsel
And thirty for lover;
Then does high rapture ensue;
The five senses of woman desert her,
Her mind exhausted becomes,

When she climax reaches;
But no weariness the man knows
Neither does his silvery emission flow.

For the practice of this Yoga the apt age for the woman is twenty, and for the yogi, thirty. Then high rapture ensures. The five senses of the woman desert her. She swoons and reaches the climax. But the yogi knows no weariness, nor does his silvery fluid get ejected.

Verse 834: Only Those Who Have Practiced Kechari can resort to Pariyanga

Lest the silvery liquid into the golden flow,
The artful goldsmith (practitioner) covered it up with yogic breath
The sparks (kundalini) that flew travelled up by the way of Spinal tube
There above,
He contained them with tongue's tip *(kechari).*

Only those who have practiced *kechari-mudrā* successfully can take to Pariyanga-Yoga. The yogi is an artful goldsmith. He does not allow the liquid silver semen to run into the liquid gold *(sroṇita).* As the goldsmith covers the melting metal with carbon, the yogi covers up the seminal flow with his breath control. The sparks that fly in this alchemic process by way of the spinal tube reach above; there it is contained by the tongue's tip or *kechari-mudra.*

(The following note is from K. Narayanaswamy Aiyar, *The Thirty Minor Upanisads*, pp. 207-208, which is not in B. Natarajan's translation).

In the *Dhyana Bindu Upanishad,* it is said that by performing *kechari mudra* one never loses his virility, even when embraced by a lovely woman. Where is the fear of death, so long as *bindu* (virility) stays in the body. *Bindu* does not go out of the body, so long as *kechari mudra* is practiced. Even when *bindu* comes down to the sphere of the perineum, it goes up being prevented and forced up by violent effort through *yoni mudra.* This *bindu* is two fold, white and red. The white one is called *sukla* and the red one is said to contain many *rajas.* The *rajas* which stays in yoni is like the color of the coral.

Verse 835: Pariyanga Yogi is Exalted

The yogi who is in ecstatic joy
Unexcited performs this Yoga with woman
Becomes radiant like the sun,
An acknowledged master in directions ten,
And of Ganas of groups eighteen.

If the yogi, though experiencing ecstatic joy, performs this mudra unexcited, he becomes radiant as the sun, an acknowledged master in ten directions and head of the eighteen Gana hordes (celestial hordes divided into eighteen classes).

Verse 836: Pariyanga Yoga practiced with Kechari Yoga Also

Espousing Wisdom that is denoted by Budha (Mercury)
Who stands middle of Sun and Saturn
The youthful Yogi who embraced the damsel
Knew joy infinite;
Lest the male silvery liquid flow not
Ahead of female golden one
He had his red mouth buried in the Mystic Moon.

While the yogi practices it, he does not allow the silvery liquid to flow. He should "bury his red mouth in the mystic moon" (practice Kechari Yoga).

1. A play on the word "Budha": Wednesday is in the middle of the week from Sunday to Saturday.

2. He practiced Kechari Yoga simultaneously.

There is much esoterism in these verses. The names of the planets are used in a double sense.

Verse 837: Pariyanga Yoga is Yogic Wisdom that Retains the Semen

They who perfect wisdom
And embrace woman in wisdom's beauty
Will know grief none,
Though by woman's side he be;
The liquid silver remains unspent
And flows not into the vaginal bag of woman.

He who in perfect wisdom, embraces a woman knows no grief. Although he is by the woman's side, the silvery semen does not flow into the vaginal track.

Verse 838: Freedom From Sexual Union is Attained by Pariyanga Yoga

This body that melts like wax over fire
(by sexual union)
Will no more indulge in it,
When wisdom dawns;
To those who have attained Wisdom of space
The liquid silver no exit knows.

His body, which in sexual union melts like wax on fire, will no more indulge in it when wisdom dawns. They who have attained the wisdom of space will know no exit of the liquid silver.

Verse 839: Vision of Space in Pariyanga Yoga

When you know the Void
And the light in that Void
Your mind shall be strong as a chistle of bronze;
After having tasted of the nectar
I saw the Void
With great Nandi guiding;
Beyond, I knew not.

When the yogi knows the Space and the light in the Space, then the mind shall become strong as bronze. The vision of the Space comes after tasting of the nectar through the Kechari Yoga with the guidance of Nandi.

Verse 840: Pariyanga Yoga was expounded by Sadasiva to Sakti

Who are those that rank high above?
Mal, Brahma and Nandi (Rudra) are they;
In the fourth is that Sadasiva,
Who to the slender-waisted Sakti
This expounded.

Verse 841: Immortality for Those Who Unite in Sivasakti in Cranium

If you can get to Sakti and Siva
Inside the Golden Circle within (cranium)
And then join them in union,
You may live on earth
A million, trillion years.

Verse 842: Yogis Offered Themselves Entire to God

Inhaling exhaling and retaining the breath inhaled
None knows its technique of control
And those of skill who know it
Offered themselves to Lord entire.

Verse 843: Yoga Dispels Worldly Longings

Knowing the way of self-oblation,
If they get into the Mystic circle
Of Siva and Sakti
They reach the True way;
And dark their hair turns
In youthfulness eternal,
And the One Sakti will inward abide;
In due accord
Dispelling worldly longings all.

The yogi who reaches the mystic circle of Siva and Sakti will despise all worldly longings. That Sakti is seated with Siva on the lotus above. That lotus knows neither land nor water; no stalk; no roof. Yet that lotus blossoms.

Verse 844: Lotus Cranial

There is a lotus
That neither land nor water knows;
No stalk, no root, the lotus yet blossomed yet!
City there was none; yet light there is one!
Neither above nor below is a flower, none had heard of.

There is a city above; there is a light above; but no habitation. The flower that has "neither the above nor the below" is a flower none has heard of. The lotus is in Hinduism a symbol of many things, here of the cranium.

– Courtesy : B. Natarajan (Tr.), Tirumandiram

Appendix-F

The Thirty-Six Tattvas

Parama-Śiva or Parā-samvit

Described as *atattva, niṣkala;* seventeenth *kala* = *anuttara-*, *cit-*, or *amrita-kala.*

Universal Principles

1. Śiva: means "benevolent;" masculine universal principle; *prakāśa* or "luminosity;" pure consciousness; "I-ness" *(ahamtā)*; *śaktimān; aham* contains all fifty syllables of the (esoteric) Sanskrit alphabet – from *a* to *ha; sphuratta; ullāsa;*

2. Śakti: means "power" or "energy;" feminine universal principle; *vimarśa* or "reflection, consideration, examination," i.e., self-awareness. "This-ness" *(idanta)*; has three forms: *icchā-*, *jñāna-*, and *kriyā-śakti*: intention, vision, and projection. The three *śaktis* are the essence of the three *bindus* or "seed-points," namely sun *(sūrya)*, fire *(agni)*, and moon *(soma)*; or *bindu* (belonging to Śiva), *bīja* (belonging to Śakti), and *nāda* (union of Śiva and Śakti's *bindus*); they are reflected in the three guṇas at a lower level: *sattva*, *rajas*, and *tamas*; or the Goddesses Sarasvati, Lakṣmi, and Kāli; the negating function *(niṣedha-vyāpāra)*, which in a way is also a completing function, giving consciousness the appearance of unconsciousness; *parā-vāc* or "supreme speech;"

3. *Sādākya* or "that which is named *sat* [existence, being];" also called Sadāśiva ("Ever-Benevolent"); the transcendental will *(icchā)* affirming "I am this" *(aham idam)*;

subtly emphasizing the subjective side of the One Reality; *paśyanti* stage of *vāc*.

4. *Īśvara*: means "Lord;" the creator, corresponding to the realization "this I am" *(idam aham)*; subtly emphasizing the objective side of the One Reality; transcendental knowledge (jñāna) *madhyamā* stage of *vāc*.

5. *Sad-Vidyā*: means "knowledge of being *(sat)*;" also called *śuddha-vidyā* or "pure knowledge;" I am and this is" *(aham ca idam ca)*: unity in difference; the state of balance between subjectivity and objectivity; transcendental creativity *(kriyā)*; *vaikhari* stage of *vāc*; with this universal principle the pure *(śuddha)* ontological categories end.

Limiting Principles

6. Māyā: means "she who measures;" the peculiar power by which the One Reality appears to become limited and measurable/quantifiable through the separation of subject and object. It consists in *bheda-buddhi* or the notion of differentiation. Here the universal Being becomes *paśu*, the bound consciousness/being or *aṇu* (atom/particle). This is due to the *līlā* of creation.
   This is the beginning of the impure *(aśuddha)* order of ontogenesis.
   Māyā gives rise to the 5 "coverings" or "cloaks" *(kañcuka)* as follows:

7. *Vidyā*: means "knowledge," here partial or "impure" *(aśuddha)* knowledge, a limited expression of *jñāna-śakti*.

8. *Kalā*: means "part," here partial functioning or limited activity, a limited expression of *kriyā-śakti*, which creates karma through the agency of merit and demerit.

9. *Rāga*: means "passion, attachment, clinging;" its negative expression is *dveṣa* or recoil; its remedy is *sarva-ātma-bhāva*.

10. *Niyati*: means "necessity, destiny;" the opposite of the eternal freedom characterizing Parama-Śiva; the kārmic law; law of causality; sometimes interpreted to mean space.

11. *Kāla*: means "time;" the opposite of the trans-temporal nature of Parama-Śiva who is *akāla*.

12-36. The 24 Principles of Sāmkhya

12. *Puruṣa*: means "male/man;" the principle of consciousness or subjectivity.

13. *Prakṛti*: means "procreatrix," i.e., Nature, the principle of materiality; the counter-pole to *Puruṣa*, but not radically opposed to it, as is the case in Sāmkhya metaphysics.

14. *Buddhi*: means "mind, cognition, understanding;" the transpersonal mind in which the seeds of karma reside; the basis of our ordinary consciousness; higher intelligence; the faculty that has a predominance of *sattva-guṇa*, the quality of lucidity.

15. *Ahamkāra*: means "I-maker;" the transpersonal principle of individuation by which we identify ourselves as a particular personality; the faculty that has a preponderance of *rajo-guṇa*, the quality of dynamism.

16. *Manas*: means "mind, mentation;" the "lower" mind, which is specific to a particular person and is closely connected with sensory input, the brain, and nervous system; has a predominance of *tamo-guṇa*.

17-26. *Indriya*: meaning "instrument" the 10 senses comprising:

(A) *Jñānendriya (jñāna-indriya)* or "cognitive senses:" smell *(ghrāṇa)*, taste *(rasa)*, sight *(cakṣus)*, touch *(sparśa)*, hearing *(śravaṇa)*.

(B) *Karmendriya (karma-indriya)* or "conative senses:" communication (*vāc*, lit. "vox" or "speech"), manipulation (*hasta*, lit. "hand"), locomotion (*pāda*, lit. "foot"), digestion (*pāyu*, lit. "anus"), procreation (*upastha*, lit. "genitals").

27-31. *Tanmātra*: meaning "that-only;" 5 subtle elements or energy patterns comprising: subtle element of sound *(sabda-tanmātra)*, subtle element of touch *(sparśa-tanmātra)*, subtle element of sight (*rūpa-tanmātra; rūpa* = "form"), subtle element of taste *(rasa-tanmātra)*, subtle element of smell *(gandha-tanmātra)*.

32-36. *Bhūta*: meaning "element;" 5 coarse or material elements comprising: ether *(ākāśa)*, air *(vāyu)*, fire *(agni)*, water *(jala)*, earth *(pṛthvi)*.

— Courtesy : Georg Feuerstein, Yoga Research And Education Center

APPENDIX-G

The Twilight Terms that Occur in the Tirumandiram

(It is representative and not exhaustive; the number indicates the verse in which the twilight term occurs; the Tamil term also is given).

Twilight term	Tamil term	Verse	Intended meaning
naked	*nakkaṉ*	3	Śiva
entering the village or city's gate	*ūr pugudal*	6	attaining liberation
treasure	*paṇḍāram*	152	the body; (since it treasures the soul)
tank	*kuḷam*	158	māyā; delusion
fig fruit	*atti-p-paḻam*	160	body
seeds of green	*arai-k-kīrai-vittu*	160	unbending karmas
small jewel box	*cimiḻ*	173	ignorance; secret
needle	*ūci*	183	the sense-organs
kannan	*kannaṉ*	184	iḍā-nāḍi
two rhythms	*tāḷam iraṇḍu*	189	iḍā and piṅgalā breathing
sweet mango	*tēmāṅgaṉi*	202	one's dear wife
tamarind	*puḷi*	202	other women
tank covered with moss	*pāci mūḍu kuḷam*	208	dirty womb
the false pit	*poy-k-kuḻi*	210	stomach
elephant	*kari*	285	āṇava-mala; ego-sense
lizard (varamamus)	*palli*	293/539	*vairāgya*

Twilight term	Tamil term	Verse	Intended meaning
ladder of threads	*nūl-ēṇi*	295/296	suṣumnā
nail	*āṇi*	309	the sense-organs
north	*vaḍapāl, vaḍa-ticai*	338	top of the head; sahasrāra
trident	*cūlam*	339	iḍā, pi ṅgalā and suṣumnā nāḍis
three aerial cities	*muppuram*	343	āṇava, karma and māyā
kitchen cook-house	*aṭukkaḷai*	359	mūlādhāra
nine sacrificial pits	*nava-kuṇḍam*	360	the six adharas, the two eyes & the sahasrāra
dark sea	*karuṅgaḍal*	377	maṇipūraka
foot	*pādam*	388	space, *ākāśa*
going and coming	*pōkku-varavu*	393	death and birth; destruction and creation
silver	*veḷḷi*	464	semen
gold smith	*taṭṭāṉ*	486	Brahma, the creator
garden, grove	*kollai*	541/1515/ 2912	mūlādhāra
horse	*kudirai*	564	prāṇa
elephant	*āṉai*	577	ego
mahout	*pāgaṉ*	577	jīva
public place	*podu*	589	sahasrāra
small perfume-box	*koy*	593	sahasrāra
bed-chamber	*paḷḷi-aṟai*	594	sahasrarā
mango fruit	*māmpaḻam*	624	*Śivānubhava*
mystic mountain	*aru-varai*	625	sahasrāra

Twilight term	Tamil term	Verse	Intended meaning
top branch	*kompu*	626	sahasrāra
superior gold	*cem-poṉ*	626	sahasrāra
military camp	*pāṭi*	661	mind
fawn	*māṉ-kaṉṟu*	738	the soul
mountain-spring	*cuṉai*	785	sahasrāra
square plants	*catura-p-palagai*	800	mūlādhāra
elephant's trunk	*tudikkai*	801	suṣumnā
two legs	*iru-kāl*	805	iḍā and piṅgalā nāḍis
cave temple	*uḷḷurai-kōil*	810	sahasrāra
stone	*kal*	937/1028	the head/sahasrāra
two hands	*kai-iraṇḍu*	1024	iḍā and piṅgalā nāḍis
bamboo	*vēṇu*	1092	suṣumnā
creeper	*koḍi*	1196	viśuddha
the successful place	*āḍagam (āḍu + agam)*	1207	sahasrāra
bow	*kōdaṇḍam*	1224	*bhrū-madyaka* (ājñā-cakra)
the red one	*ceyyaṉ*	1520	the destroyer (aspect of Śiva)
the dark one	*kariyaṉ*	1520	the preserver (aspect of Śiva)
the white one	*veḷiyaṉ*	1520	the creator (aspect of Śiva)
the green one	*paccaiyaṉ*	1520	the redeemer (aspect of Śiva)
the lusty-calf	*kuḻa-k-kaṉṟu*	1643	the (tiny calf of) senses

Twilight term	Tamil term	Verse	Intended meaning
escluent root	*kaṇḍaṉ*	1927	māyā; delusion
swan	*aṉṉam*	1966	the macrocosm
sound of Tamil	*tamiḻ-ōcai*	2115	the Lord
six streets	*āṟu-teru*	2868	the ādhāras
seven seas	*kaḍal-ēḻu*	2868	sahasrāra
cows	paśus	2874	tattvas, principles
house of smith	*taṭṭāṉ-agam*	2876/2924	sahasrāra
shed	*koṭṭagam*	2881	body
jackal	*nari*	2881	passions
brahmin	*pārppāṉ*	2883	ātman, self; yogin's body
bulls	*āmākkaḷ*	2884	senses
bulls	*kaḍā*	2889	breaths, iḍā and piṅgalā
owl	*kūgai*	2891/2921	lust *(kāma)*
snake	*pāmbu*	2891	hatred *(krodha)*
parrot	*kiḷi*	2891	infatuation *(moha)*
cat	*pūṉai*	2891	avarice *(lobha)*
mynah	*nāgai*	2891	arrogance *(matha)*
quail	*puḷ*	2891	malice *(mātsarya)*
mouse	*cuṇḍeli*	2891	kuṇḍalinī
white rat	*eli*	2892	pāśa
camel	*oṭṭagam*	2893	the six evils – lust etc.
robbers	*kaḷḷar*	2900	the senses
white guard	*vēḷār*	2900	Yoga
nux vomica	*eṭṭi*	2901	passions; earthly life

Twilight term	Tamil term	Verse	Intended meaning
he-bee	*āṇ-vaṇḍu*	2902	Śiva
she-bee	*peḍai-vaṇḍu*	2902	Śakti
lowly-bee	*kaḍai-vaṇḍu*	2902	jīva
lotus	*tāmarai*	2904	sahasrāra
lily	*kuvaḷai*	2904	kuṇḍalinī
fish	*kayal*	2910	woman
hare	*muyal*	2910	astral vision of the mystic moon within
reeds	*kōrai*	2911	pāśas
creepers	*ārai*	2911	desires
forest	*kāḍu*	2912	sahasrāra
hamlet	*cīr*	2912	liberation
tiger	*puli*	2914	prāṇa; breath
bauhiniaracemosa	*atti-tree*	2917	body from mūlādhāra to sahasrāra
bamboo	*mūṅgil*	2917	suṣumnā
child	*piḷḷai*	2924	jīva
temple buffalo	*kōil-erumai*	2925	jīva
lagoon	*kuḷam*	2927	body
moss	*pāci*	2927	pāśa
shy heron	*kurugirai*	2927	jīva
marching warrior	*maṟavaṉ*	2927	the guru
damsel	*mādar*	2931	kuṇḍalinī
dawn	*pulardal*	2934	jñāna
birds	*puṭkaḷ*	2934	*indriyas*; sense-organs

BIBLIOGRAPHY

Tamil

Adigal, Maraimalai. *Māṇikka-vācagar Varalāṟum Kālamum.* Madras: Saiva Siddhanta Nul Patippu-k-kalagam, 1967.

Aiyar, Ve. Saminatha. *Pattu-p-pāṭṭu* (which includes *Tiru-murugāṟṟu-p-paḍai, Paṭṭiṉa-p-pālai* and *Malaipaḍu-kaḍām*). Thanjavur: Tamil University, 1986.

Ananda Coomaraswamy. *Śivāṉanda Naḍaṉam.* C. Nataracan (Tr.). Chennai: Tamil Nadu Text Book Society, 1980.

Annamalai, Suba (Ed.). *Tirumandiram.* 3 Vols. Chennai: Indiya-p-panpadu Araychi Niruvanam, 2nd edn., 2002.

Arumugathmizhan, Karu. Thirumoolar: Kaalathin Kural. Chennai: Tamizhini, 2004

Arunachalam, Mu. *Tamiḻ Ilakkiya Varalāṟu.* 14th Century. Tiru-c-citrambalam, Mayuram: Gandhi Vidhyalayam, 1969.

Arunachalam, Pa. *Bakthi Ilakkiyam.* Chennai: Pari Puttaka-p-pannai, 1983.

Arunachalam, Pa. *Tirumandira-k-kōṭpāḍu.* Chennai: Pari Puttaka-p-pannai, 1982.

Baṭṭar, Abirāmi. *Abirāmi Andādi.* Dharmapuram: Dharumai Adheenam, 1973.

Bharathiyar, Ka. Su. Navaneedha Krishna. (Comm.). *Tiruvācagam.* Telli-p-palai, Sri Lanka: Padma Patippagam, 1954.

Bharathiyar, Yogi Suddhananda. *Tirumandira Viḷakkam.* Chennai: Manivacagar Patippagam, 2nd edn., 2001.

Chettiyar, Attavadanam Veerachamy. *Vinōda Raca Mañjari.* M. Sanmugam Pillai and N. Chandrasekaran (Eds.). Chennai: Mullai Nilayam, 1999.

Chettiyar, M. Kadireca. and P. Sri. Ramanujachari (Trs.). *Kauḍalīyam Poruṇūl*. Annamalai Nagar: Annamalai University, 1980.

Chettiyar, Muru. Pala. Rathinam. *Kaḍavuḷāl Muḍiyāda Ceyalgaḷ*. Puncey-p-puliyam-patti, Coimbatore: Maraimalai Adigal Manram, 1968.

Desigar, Dandapani. *Tirumandiram-Pañcākṣara-dīpa Urai*. Thiru-v-avadu-thurai: Thiru-v-avadu-thurai Adheenam, 1989 (I, II and III *tantras*), 1997 (V and VI *tantras*).

Desigar, Na. Sivapiragasa. (Ed.). *Tirumandira-mālai-300*. Annamalai Nagar: Annamalai University, 1976.

Ganapathy, Ra. *Deivattiṉ Kural*. Vol. I. Chennai: Vanathi Patippagam, 1982.

Ganapathy, Ra. *Swāmi Vivēkāṉandar*. Madras: Sri Ramakrishna Math, 1995.

Ganapathy, T.N. *Tamiḻ-c-cittar Marabu*. Chennai: Ravi Publications, 2004.

Ilankumaran, Ira. *Śivajñāṉa-bōdam Teḷiporuḷ Viḷakkam*. Chennai: Saiva Siddhanta Nul Patippu-k-kalagam, 1990.

Jothi, V. (Comm.). *Tiru-vilayāḍal Purāṇam*. 5 Vols. Chennai: Vardhamanan Patippagam, 2nd edn., 1998.

Kailasapathi, Ka. *Paṇḍai-t-tamiḻar Vāḻvum Vaḻipāḍum*. Chennai: Pari Nilayam, 1966.

Kecigan, Puliyur. (Comm.). *Avvaiyār: Taṉi-p-pāḍalgaḷ*. Chennai: Paari Nilayam, 3rd edn., 1973.

Kousalya Vijayan, G. *Tirumandirattil Vāḻviyal Cindaṉaigaḷ*. Vellore: Vijayan Patippagam, 1996.

Laksmanan, Ki. *India-t-tattuva Jñāṉam.* Chennai: Palaniappa Bros., 2nd edn., 1970.

Mahadevan, Kadir. *Toṉmam.* Madurai: Lakshmi Veliyeedu, 1984.

Manikkam, A. (Comm.). *Tirumandiram.* 3 Vols. Chennai: Vardhamanan Patippagam, 2001.

Manikkavacagam, Ira. *Tirumandira Ārāycci.* Chennai: Annai Abirami Arul, 1982.

Manikkavacagam, Jna. (Comm.). *Tirumandiram.* Chennai: Uma Patippagam, 2003.

Mudaliyar, Ci. Arunai Vadivel. *Śiva-jñāna-bōda Māpāḍiya-p-poruḷ-nilai Viḷakkam.* Thanjavur: Tamil University, 1991.

Mudaliyar, Ci. Arunai Vadivel. (Comm.). *Tirumandiram.* Tantras 4, 5, and 6. Dharmapuram: Dharumai Adheenam, 1984.

Mudaliyar, Palur Kannappa. *Tamiḻ Mandiram.* Chennai, 1960.

Murugesan, C.S. *Tirumandira-c-cakkaraṅgaḷ.* Chennai: Kurinji, 2003.

Nacciṉārkiṉiyar. (Comm.). *Cīvaga-cindāmaṇi.* Chennai: Sri Thiyagaraca Vilacam, 1969.

Nattar, Na.Mu. Venkatasamy and Avvai Cu. Duraisamy Pillai. (Comms.). *Maṇimēgalai.* Chennai: Saiva Siddhanta Nul Patippu-k-kalagam, 1960.

Nattar, Na.Mu. Venkatasamy. (Comm.). *Cilappadigāram.* Chennai: Saiva Siddhanta Nul Patippu-k-kalagam, 1959.

Navalar, Arumuga. (Comm.). *Naṉṉūl.* Madras: T. Racanayagam, Vidyanupalana Yandira-calai, 1958.

Navalar, Arumuga. (Comm.). *Periya-purāṇam*. Kuala Lumpur, Malaysia: Saiva Siddhanta Nilayam, 1993.

Nāyaṉār, Cundaramūrti. *Tēvāra-t-tiru-p-padigaṅgaḷ*. 7th Tirumuṟai. Dharmapuram: Dharumai Adheenam, 1964.

Nāyaṉār, Tirujñāṉa-cambandamūrti. *Tēvāra-t-tiru-p-padigaṅgaḷ*. Dharmapuram: Dharumai Adheenam, 1953 (1st Tirumuṟai). 1954 (2nd Tirumuṟai). 1955 (3rd Tirumuṟai).

Nāyaṉār, Tirunāvukkaracu. *Tēvāra-t-tiru-p-padigaṅgaḷ*. Dharmapuram: Dharumai Adheenam, 1957 (4th Tirumuṟai). 1961 (5th Tirumuṟai). 1963 (6th Tirumuṟai).

Pandarattar, T.V. Sadasiva. *Tamiḻ Ilakkiya Varalāṟu* (250-600 B.C.). Annamalai Nagar: Annamalai University, 1969.

Parimanam, A. Ma. *Tirumandirattiṟ kāṇum Kalai-c-col Viḷakkam*. Thanjavur: Tamil University, 2002.

Pari-mēl-aḻagar (Comm.). *Tiru-k-kuṟaḷ*. Chennai: Poompuhar Patippagam, 1986.

Periyakaruppan, Irama. *Pudiya Nōkkil Tamiḻ Ilakkiya Varalāṟu*. Madurai: Solai Noolagam, 1980.

Pillai, Avvai Cu. Duraisamy. (Comm). *Puṟa-nāṉūṟu*. Chennai: Saiva Siddhanta Nul Patippu-k-kalagam, 1964 (1st Vol.), 1962 (2nd Vol.).

Pillai, Avvai Cu. Duraisamy. *Śaiva Ilakkiya Varalāṟu*. Annamalai Nagar: Annamalai University, 1978.

Pillai, Ma. Rattinasabapathi. *Kāya-citti (Tirumandiram) Alladu Cāgā-k-kalai*. Chennai: Saiva Siddhanta-p-perumanram, 3rd edn., 2001.

Pillai, M.V. Viswanatha. (Ed.). *Tirumandiram*. Chennai: Rippon Press, 1912.

Pillai, Pa. Ramanatha. (Comm.). *Tirumandiram*. Chennai: Saiva Siddhanta Nul Patippu-k-kalagam, 8th edn., 1996.

Pillai, S. Vaiyapuri. (Ed.), *Divya-p-prabandam*. Madras: S. Rajam, 1955.

Pillai, Ta. Sa. Meenakshisundaram. *Tirumandiram-Kailāya-c-cittar Urai*. (selected verses only). Thiru-v-avadu-thurai: Thiru-v-avadu-thurai Adheenam, 1954.

Racamanikkanar, Ma. *Periya-Purāṇa Ārāycci*. Chennai: Palaniappa Brothers, 3rd edn., 1990.

Rajaji and Somu. *Tirumūlar Tava-moḻi*. Chennai: Vanathi Pati-ppagam, 6th edn., 2003.

Ramachandran, S.P. (Ed.). *Caturagiri-t-tala Purāṇam*. Chennai: Lotus Publishing House, 1998.

Ramachandran, S.P. (Ed.). *Vināyakar Akaval*. Chennai: Thamarai Nulagam, 2000.

Ramachandran, S.P. (Ed.). *Yōga-jñāṉa Sāstira-t-tiraṭṭu*. Vol. 5. Chennai: Thamarai Nulagam, 1997.

Ramaiah, Yogi S.A.A. (Ed.). *Bōgar Kaṇḍa Yōgam*. Vol. 3. Yuma, Arizona: International Babaji Yoga Sangam, 1982.

Ramakiruttinan, Na. *Tirumūlarum Civa-yōgamum*. Chennai: Manivacagar Patippagam, 2000.

Ramakiruttinan, Na. *Tirumūlariṉ Civāṉanda Cindaṉaigaḷ*. Chennai: Manivacagar Patippagam, 2000.

Ramanathan, Aru. (Ed.). *Cittar Pāḍalgaḷ*. Madras: Prema Pirasuram, 4th edn., 1984.

Sambandham, Tiru. *Tirumūlarin̲ Tirumandira Virundu*. Chennai: Tiru-v-aracu Puttaga Nilayam, 4th edn., 2002.

Sathiyavel Muruganar, Mu. Pe. *Tirumandiram-ōr Ar̲imugam*. Chennai: Kalaignan Patippagam, 2002.

Siddalingam, T.B. *Caiva-camaya-t-tōr̲r̲amum Vaḷarcciyum*. Chennai: Tiru-v-aracu Puttaga Nilayam, 2nd edn., 1999.

Sivalinganar, A. *Mūlan̲ Tamiḻ*. Chennai: Arul-Cudar Patippagam, 1995.

Subramanian, Na. *Tirumūlar Tiru-ner̲i*. Karaikudi: Ponmudi Patippagam, 2002.

Sundaramurthi, Ku. (Comm.). *Pōr̲r̲i-p-pahr̲oḍai*. Tiru-p-panandal: Sri Kasi Mutt, 1993.

Sundaramurthi, Ku. (Comm.). *Tiru-k-kaḷir̲r̲u-p-paḍiyār*. Tiru-p-panandal: Sri Kasi Mutt, 1991.

Sundaramurthi, Ku. (Comm.). *Uṇmai-viḷakkam*. Tiru-p-panandal: Sri Kasi Mutt, 1993.

Tagare, G.V. *Caiva-tattuvam*. Ka. Sri. Sri. (Tr.). Chennai: Alliance Co., 2nd edn., 2001.

Tamiḻ (Citta) Maruttuva-k-kōṭpāḍu. Madras: Department of Indian Medicine and Homeopathy, 1995.

Tamil Lexicon. Vol. IV, Part I. Madras: University of Madras, 1982.

Tevaneyan. *Tamiḻar Madam*. Kattuppadi Extension: Nesamani Patippagam, 1972.

Tirumūlar. *Tirumandiram*. Chennai: Saiva Siddhanta Mahasamajam, 1940.

Tiruvilangam, Mu. (Comm.), *Śiva-jñāṉa-siddhiyār Cubakkam*. Jaffna: The Jaffna Co-operative Tamil Book Publishing Society, 1925.

Uttamarayan, Ka. Cu. *Toṟṟa-k-kirama Āräcciyum Citta Maruttuva Varalāṟum*. Chennai: The Government of Tamil Nadu, 1992.

Vaḷḷalār Rāmaliṅga Swāmigaḷ. *Tiru-v-aruṭpā*. Sixth Tirumuṟai. Madras: Arutperunjothi Accagam, 1942.

Varadharajan, G. (Comm.). *Tirumandiram*. 3 Vols. Chennai: Palaniappa Bros, 6th edn., 2003.

Vellaivaranan, Ka. *Paṉṉiru Tirumuṟai Varalāṟu*. Annamalai Nagar: Annamalai University, 1969.

Vellaivaranan, Ka. (Comm.). *Tol-kāppiyam: Puṟa-t-tiṇai-iyal*. Madurai: Madurai Kamaraj University, 1983.

Vellaivaranan, Ka. (Comm.). *Tol-kāppiyam: Ceyyuḷ-iyal*. Madurai: Madurai Kamaraj University, 1989.

Vellaivarananar, Ka. *Śaiva Siddhānta Cāttira Varalāṟu*. Tanjavur: Tamil University, 2002.

Venkataraman, T.V. *Tirumandiram-Aṉubava Urai*. Chennai: Bharathi Patippagam, 1996.

Venkatramaiah, K.M. (Ed.). *Tirumandiram*. Tiru-p-panandal: Sri Kasi Mutt, 1951.

English

Aiyar, V.V.S. (Tr.). *The Kural or The Maxims of Tiruvalluvar.* Tiruvanai Koil, Tiruchirapalli: Dr. V.V.S. Krishnamurthy, 1961.

Arunachalam, M. "The Mysticism of Tirumular," *Indian Philosophical Annual.* Madras: The Dr. Radhakrishnan Institute for Advanced Study in Philosophy, University of Madras, 1976.

Aurobindo, Sri. *Letters on Yoga.* I, II and III. Pondicherry: Sri Aurobindo Ashram, 7th impression, 2000.

Awasthi, Brahmamitra. (Ed. and Tr.). *Yoga-bīja.* Delhi: Swami Keshawananda Yoga Institute, *Vikram* 2042.

Ayyar, C.V. Narayana. *Origin and Early History of Saivism in South India.* Madras: University of Madras, 1936.

Balasubramanian, R. (Ed.). *History of Science, Philosophy and Culture in Indian Civilization*, Vol. II, Part 3 - *Theistic Vedanta.* New Delhi: Centre for Studies in Civilizations, 2003.

Basu, Manoranjan. *Tantras: A General Study.* Calcutta: Shrimati Mira Basu, 1976.

Bernard, Theos. *Heaven Lies Within Us.* London: Rider & Co., Reprint, 1956.

Bharati, Agehananda. *The Tantric Tradition.* New Delhi: B.I. Publications, First Indian edn., 1976.

Bhaskarananda, Swami. *The Essentials of Hinduism.* Chennai: Sri Ramakrishna Math, 1998.

Bhattacharya, B. *Saivism and the Phallic World.* New Delhi: Oxford & IBH Publishing Co., 1975.

Bhattacharya, Vidhushekara. "Sandhabhāṣa," *Indian Historical Quarterly*, Vol. IV, 2, 1928.

Bhattacharyya, N.N. *History of the Tantric Religion*. New Delhi: Manohar Publications, 1982.

Bose, D.N. and Hiralal Haldar. *Tantras: Their Philosophical and Occult Secrets*. Calcutta: Oriental Publishing Co., 1956.

Briggs, George Weston. *Gorakhnāth and the Kānphaṭa Yogis*. Delhi: Motilal Banarsidass, 1982.

Bryant, Kenneth E. "Sant and Vaiṣṇava Poetry: Some Observations on Method" in Mark Juergensmeyer and N. Gerald Barrier (Eds.). *Sikh Studies; Comparative Perspectives of a Changing Tradition*. Berkeley: Berkeley Religious Studies Series, 1979, pp. 65-74.

Bucknell, Roderick S. and Martin Stuart Fox. *The Twilight Language: Explorations in Buddhist Meditation and Symbolism*. London: Curzon Press, 1986.

Buddhadasa. *Two Kinds of Language*. Ariyananda Bhikku (Tr.). Bangok: Sublime Life Mission, 1974.

Chattopadhyaya, Sudhakar. *Reflections on the Tantras*. Delhi: Motilal Banarsidass, 1978.

Chitkara, M.G. *Kashmir Shaivism:under seige*. New Delhi: S.B. Nangia, A.P.H. Publishing Corporation. (2002).

Datta, D.M. *The Six Ways of Knowing*. Calcutta: University of Calcutta, 1972.

Deussan, Paul. *The Philosophy of the Vedanta in its Relations to the Occidental Metaphysics*, an address delivered before the Bombay branch of the Royal Asiatic Society, Saturday, the

25th February, 1893. Published by Tookaram Tatya for the Bombay Theosophical Publications Fund, 1894.

Devasenapathy, V.A. *Śaiva Siddhānta*. Madras: University of Madras, 1974.

Dhar, Triloki Nath. *Saints and sages of Kashmir*. New Delhi: S.B. Nangia, A.P.H. Publishing Corporation. (2004).

Dictionary of Philosophy. Moscow: Progress Publishers, 2nd revised edn., 1984.

Dorai Rangaswamy, M.A. *The Religion and Philosophy of Tevaram*. Madras: University of Madras, 1990.

Drabu, Vishva Nath. *Sivagamas*. New Delhi: Indus Publishing Company, 1990.

Dupuche, John R. *Abhinavagupta: The Kula Ritual*. Delhi: Motilal Banarsidass, 2003.

Dyczkowski, Mark S.G.*The doctrine of vibration: an analysis of the doctrines and practices of Kashmir Shaivism*. New Delhi: Motilal Banarsidas, New Delhi. (1989).

Eddington, Arthur. *The Philosophy of the Physical Sciences*. Cambridge: Cambridge University Press, 1939.

Eliade, Mircea. *Birth and Rebirth: The Religious Meanings of Initiation in Human Culture*. New York: Harper & Row, 1958.

Eliade, Mircea. *Yoga: Immortality and Freedom*. W.R. Trask (Tr.). New York: Bollingen Series LVI, Panthean Books, 1958.

Feuerstein, Georg. *The Yoga Tradition*. Delhi: Bhavana Books & Prints, First Indian edn., 2002.

Ganapathy, T.N. *The Philosophy of the Tamil Siddhas*. New Delhi: Indian Council of Philosophical Research, 1993.

Ganapathy, T.N. *The Yoga of Siddha Bōganāthar*. Quebec, Canada: Babaji's Kriya Yoga and Publications, Inc., 2003 (Vol. I), 2004 (Vol. II).

Govinda, Lama Angarika. *The Foundations of Tibetan Mysticism*. London: Rider & Co., 1959.

Govindan, M. (Ed.). *Thirumandiram: A Classic of Yoga and Tantra*. 3 Volumes. Quebec, Canada: Babaji's Kriya Yoga and Publications Inc., First International Edition, 1993.

Govindan, M. *Babaji and the 18 Siddha Kriya Yoga Tradition*. Bangalore: Babaji's Kriya Yoga Order of Acharyas Trust, 7th edn., 2001.

Goudriaan, *Ted. Ritual and speculation in early tantrism: studies in honour of Andre Padoux*. New York: SUNY publications. (1992).

Govindan, M. *Kriya Yoga Sutras of Patanjali and the Siddhas*. Bangalore: Babaji's Kriya Yoga Order of Acharyas Trust, 2001.

Grimes, John. *A Concise Dictionary of Indian Philosophy*. Madras: University of Madras, 1988.

Hess, Linda and Shukdev Singh. *The Bijak of Kabir*. Delhi: Motilal Banarsidass, 1986.

Huxley, Aldous. The *Doors of Perception and Heaven and Hell*. Collected works of Aldous Huxley. London: Chatto and Windeus, 1972.

Jaideva Singh. *Z iva sutras: The yoga of supreme Identity*. New Delhi: Motilal Banarsidas. (1993).

Joshi, Kireet. *Yoga and Consciousness*. New Delhi: Consciousness Series: 2, Indian Council of Philosophical Research, 2001.

Kak, R.C. and H.B. Sastri (Eds.). *Gandharva Tantra*. Srinagar: Kashmir Sanskrit Series, Vol. XXXVI, 1934.

Kellett, E.E. *A Short History of Religions*. Middlesex: Penguin Books, 1962.

Kerenyi, G. *Essays on a Science of Mythology*. R.F.C. Hull (Tr.). Princeton: Princeton University Press, 1969.

Kingsley, David. *Tantric Visions of the Divine Feminine*. Delhi: Motilal Banarsidass, Reprint, 2003.

Kvaerne, Per. *An Anthology of Buddhist Tantric Songs*. Oslo: Norwegian Research Council, 1977.

Mahopatra, A.R. *Philosophy of Religion*. New Delhi: Sterling Publishers Pvt. Ltd., 1990.

Mallik, Kalyani. *Siddha-Siddhānta-Paddhati and other Works of Nath Yogis*. Poona: Poona Oriental Book House, 1954.

Murphy, Paul E. *Triadic Mysticism*. Delhi: Motilal Banarsidass, Reprint, 1999.

Nikhilananda, Swami (Tr.). *The Gospel of Sri Ramakrishna* (abridged edition). New York: Ramakrishna Vivekananda Centre, 1980.

Odin, Jayashree Kak. *Mystical verses of Lall : a journey of self realization*. New Delhi: Motilal Banarsidas. (2007).

Pande, G.C. *Consciousness, Neuro Science and Philosophy*. New Delhi: Consciousness Series: 3, Indian Council of Philosophical Research, n.d.

Pandey, K.C. *Abhinavagupta: A historical and Philosophical study* Varanasi: Chowkhamba Sanskrit Series office, 1963.

Patil, Narendranath and Kaul, Mrinal. *The Variegated Plumage: Encounters with Indian philosophy: A commemoration volume in Honour of Pandit Jankinath Kaul ãKamalä.* New Delhi. Sant Samagam Research Institute and Motilal Banarsidass Publishers. (2003).

Pillai, M.S. Puranalingam. *Tamil Literature.* Madras: Saiva Siddhanta Nul Patippu-k-kalagam, 1929.

Ponniah, V. *Saiva Siddhanta Theory of Knowledge.* Annamalai Nagar: Annamalai University, 1962.

Pope, G.U. (Tr.). *Tiruvachagam.* Madras: University of Madras, Reprint, 1959.

Radhakrishnan, *The Hindu Way of Life.* London: Unwin Books, 1965.

Radhakrishnan, S. *The Reign of Religion in Contemporary Philosophy.* London: Macmillan and Co. Ltd., 1920.

Rai, Ramkumar. *The Encyclopedia of Yoga.* Varanasi: Prachya Prakashan, 2nd edition, 1982.

Rajneesh, Bhagwan. *The Tantra Vision.* Poona: Rajneesh Foundation, 1978 (Vol. I). 1979 (Vol. II).

Rastogi, Navjivan. *Krama Tantricism of Kashmir,* vol.1, New Delhi: Motilal Banarsidas Publishers. (1996).

Russell, Bertrand. *Mysticism and Logic.* Penguin Books, Reprint, 1954.

Satguru Sivaya Subramuniyaswami. *Dancing with Siva: Hinduismâs Contemporary Catechism.* Kauii: Himalayan Academy Publication. (2003).

Schaeffer, Kurtis R. "The Attainment of Immortality: From Nathas in India to Buddhists in Tibet," *The Journal of Indian Philosophy* (USA), 30, 2002.

Shastri, Hariprasad. *Buddha Gan O Doha.* Calcutta: 1916.

Somasundaram, P.S. *Tirujñāṉasambandhar: Philosophy and Religion.* Chennai: Vani Pathippakam.

Stace, W.T. *Mysticism and Philosophy.* London: Macmillan, Reprint, 1980.

Sthapati, Ganapati. *Significance of Vimanam and Gopuram.* (English and Tamil versions). Chennai: Dakshina Publishing House, 2002.

Subhash Kak. *The poplar and Chinar,* Journal of Indian Studies, vol.3, 33-61 (1993).

Subramanian, N. *The Tamils: Their History, Culture and Civilization.* Madras: Institute of Asian Studies, 1996.

Subramanian, N.S. *Encyclopaedia of the Upanisads.* New Delhi: Sterling Publishers Pvt. Ltd., 1985.

Suzuki, D.T. *Zen Buddhism.* New York: Doubleday, 1956.

Swami Lakshmanjoo. *Z iva Sk tras The Supreme Awakening.* New Delhi: Munshiram Manoharlal Publishers Pvt. Ltd. (2007).

Swami Parmeshwaranand. *Encyclopaedia of the Z aivism.* New Delhi: Sarup & Sons (2004).

Thirugnanasambandhan, P. "The Bearing of Saiva Siddhanta Epistemology on its Metaphysics," *Indian Philosophical Annual*, Vol. 14. Madras: University of Madras.

Thulasiram. T.R. *Arut Perum Jothi and Deathless Body*. Madras: University of Madras, 1980.

Thurston, Edgar and K. Rangachari. *Castes and Tribes of Southern India*. Vol. IV. Chennai: Asian Educational Service, 1987.

Udupa, K.N. *Stress and its Management by Yoga*. R.C. Prasad (Ed.). Delhi: Motilal Banarsidass, 2000.

Veda Bharati, Swami. *Mantra and Mediation*. Pennsylvania: The Himalayan Institute of Yoga Science and Philosophy of the U.S.A., 1981.

Vivekananda, Swami. *The Complete Works*. Vol. II. Calcutta: Advaita Ashrama, 11th edn., 1968.

Watts, A. *The Way of Zen*. A Pelican Book, 1956.

White, David Gordon. *Tantra in Practice*. Delhi: Motilal Banarsidass, 2001.

Widgery, Albun G. *The Comparative Study of Religions*. London: Williams & Norgate, 1923.

Woodroffe, John and M.P. Pandit. *Kulārṇava Tantra*. New Delhi: Motilal Banarsidass, Reprint, 1984.

Wright, Philip Wheel. *The Burning Fountain*. Indiana: Indiana University Press, 1954.

Zunini, Girgio. *Man and His Religion: Aspects of Religious Psychology*. London: Geoffrey Chapman, 1969.

Zvelebil, Kamil V. *The Poets of the Powers*. London: Rider & Co., 1973.

Index

C

D

O

Z

About the Authors

ABOUT THE AUTHORS

Professor T.N. Ganapathy (b. 1932) retired as Post-graduate Professor and Head, Department of Philosophy, RKM Vivekananda College, Chennai. After retirement, after 39 years of service, he serves as a visiting professor at Sri Satya Sai Institute of Higher Learning, Prashanti Nilayam, Puttaparti, with a total of 53 years of distinguished service as a teacher of philosophy at his back. He was a Senior Fellow of the Indian Council of Philosophical Research (ICPR), New Delhi, from 1985 to 1988 and his project on *The Philosophy of the Tamil Siddhas* was published by the ICPR in 1993. From the year 2000, he is the Director of the Yoga Siddha Research Center at Chennai, co-sponsored by the Babaji's Kriya Yoga Order of Acharyas, Inc., Canada and the Yoga Research and Education Center, California, USA. He was the Founder-Secretary of the Tamil Nadu Philosophical Society and was also the Joint Secretary for three years and Treasurer for three years of the Indian Philosophical Congress from 1979 to 1985. He has attended several seminars in India and one at USA. He has got more than 30 research papers published in the leading journals in India and Germany and is acknowledged as a specialist in Immanuel Kant. He is the author of: *An Invitation to Logic* (1972); *Perspectives of Theism and Absolutism in Indian Philosophy* (Ed. 1978); *Mahavakyas* (1982); *Bertrand Russell's Philosophy of Sense-data* (1984); *The Philosophy of the Tamil Siddhas* (1993); *The Yoga of Siddha Bōganāthar*, Vol. I (2003); Vol. II (2004); *A Pocket Guide to Thesis Writing* (2003); *Tamiḻ-c-cittar Marabu* (Tamil) (2004); *The Yoga of the 18 Siddhas: An Anthology* (Ed. 2004); *The Yoga of Siddha Avvai* (Ed. 2004).

Dr. KR. Arumugam (b. 1970) is the Deputy Director of the Yoga Siddha Research Center, Chennai. He is a Guest Lecturer in the Department of Saiva Siddhanta, University of Madras and a Visiting Faculty in the Department of Philosophy, Sacred Heart Seminary, Poonamallee, Chennai. He was awarded a doctorate by the University of Madras for his thesis on the *Tirumandiram*. He has contributed to the book *The Yoga of the 18 Siddhas: An Anthology* and authored a book in Tamil, *Thirumoolar: Kaalathiṉ Kural* (2004).